# The Psychoanalysis of Sense

## Plateaus – New Directions in Deleuze Studies

'It's not a matter of bringing all sorts of things together under a single concept but rather of relating each concept to variables that explain its mutations.'
Gilles Deleuze, *Negotiations*

### Series Editors

Ian Buchanan, University of Wollongong
Claire Colebrook, Penn State University

### Editorial Advisory Board

Keith Ansell Pearson
Ronald Bogue
Constantin V. Boundas
Rosi Braidotti
Eugene Holland
Gregg Lambert
Dorothea Olkowski
Paul Patton
Daniel Smith
James Williams

### Titles available in the series

Christian Kerslake, *Immanence and the Vertigo of Philosophy: From Kant to Deleuze*
Jean-Clet Martin, *Variations: The Philosophy of Gilles Deleuze*, translated by Constantin V. Boundas and Susan Dyrkton
Simone Bignall, *Postcolonial Agency: Critique and Constructivism*
Miguel de Beistegui, *Immanence – Deleuze and Philosophy*
Jean-Jacques Lecercle, *Badiou and Deleuze Read Literature*
Ronald Bogue, *Deleuzian Fabulation and the Scars of History*
Sean Bowden, *The Priority of Events: Deleuze's Logic of Sense*
Craig Lundy, *History and Becoming: Deleuze's Philosophy of Creativity*
Aidan Tynan, *Deleuze's Literary Clinic: Criticism and the Politics of Symptoms*
Thomas Nail, *Returning to Revolution: Deleuze, Guattari and Zapatismo*
François Zourabichvili, *Deleuze: A Philosophy of the Event* with *The Vocabulary of Deleuze*, edited by Gregg Lambert and Daniel W. Smith, translated by Kieran Aarons
Frida Beckman, *Between Desire and Pleasure: A Deleuzian Theory of Sexuality*
Nadine Boljkovac, *Untimely Affects: Gilles Deleuze and an Ethics of Cinema*
Daniela Voss, *Conditions of Thought: Deleuze and Transcendental Ideas*
Daniel Barber, *Deleuze and the Naming of God: Post-Secularism and the Future of Immanence*
F. LeRon Shults, *Iconoclastic Theology: Gilles Deleuze and the Secretion of Atheism*
Janae Sholtz, *The Invention of a People: Heidegger and Deleuze on Art and the Political*
Marco Altamirano, *Time, Technology and Environment: An Essay on the Philosophy of Nature*
Sean McQueen, *Deleuze and Baudrillard: From Cyberpunk to Biopunk*
Ridvan Askin, *Narrative and Becoming*
Marc Rölli, *Gilles Deleuze's Transcendental Empiricism: From Tradition to Difference*, translated by Peter Hertz-Ohmes
Guillaume Collett, *The Psychoanalysis of Sense: Deleuze and the Lacanian School*

### Forthcoming volumes

Cheri Carr, *Deleuze's Kantian Ethos: Critique as a Way of Life*
Ryan Johnson, *The Deleuze-Lucretius Encounter*
Alex Tissandier, *Affirming Divergence: Deleuze's Reading of Leibniz*

Visit the Plateaus website at www.euppublishing.com/series/plat

# THE PSYCHOANALYSIS OF SENSE
## Deleuze and the Lacanian School

*Guillaume Collett*

EDINBURGH
University Press

Edinburgh University Press is one of the leading university presses in the UK. We publish academic books and journals in our selected subject areas across the humanities and social sciences, combining cutting-edge scholarship with high editorial and production values to produce academic works of lasting importance. For more information visit our website: edinburghuniversitypress.com

© Guillaume Collett, 2016, 2018

Edinburgh University Press Ltd
The Tun – Holyrood Road
12(2f) Jackson's Entry
Edinburgh EH8 8PJ

First published in hardback by Edinburgh University Press 2016

Typeset in Sabon by
Servis Filmsetting Ltd, Stockport, Cheshire,
and printed and bound in Great Britain by
CPI Group (UK) Ltd, Croydon CR0 4YY

A CIP record for this book is available from the British Library

ISBN 978 1 4744 0902 5 (hardback)
ISBN 978 1 4744 3226 9 (paperback)
ISBN 978 1 4744 0903 2 (webready PDF)
ISBN 978 1 4744 0904 9 (epub)

The right of Guillaume Collett to be identified as the author of this work has been asserted in accordance with the Copyright, Designs and Patents Act 1988, and the Copyright and Related Rights Regulations 2003 (SI No. 2498).

# Contents

| | |
|---|---|
| Acknowledgements | vi |
| Introduction | 1 |
| 1 The Body of the Letter: From Name-of-the-Father to *Re-père* | 7 |
| 2 Theatres of Terror and Cruelty: From Noise to the Voice | 50 |
| 3 The Three Syntheses of the Body: From the Voice to Speech | 64 |
| 4 Logic of the Phantasm: From Speech to the Verb | 143 |
| 5 The Speculative Univocity of Being and Language: From the Verb to Univocity | 185 |
| Bibliography | 240 |
| Index | 248 |

# Acknowledgements

This book grew out of my doctoral work conducted at the University of Kent under the supervision of Lorenzo Chiesa, and at Université Paris-Diderot under the supervision of Monique David-Ménard. I would first of all like to thank both these individuals and to acknowledge their overriding influence on the present book. I would like to thank the Centre for Critical Thought at the University of Kent, and particularly Iain MacKenzie, for providing a base since completing the PhD, as well as the Centre for Research in Modern European Philosophy at Kingston University, particularly Éric Alliez, Peter Hallward and Christian Kerslake, whose research series between 2008 and 2013 – first on the *Cahiers pour l'analyse* then on transdisciplinarity – provided much of the initial context for the writing of this book. I would like to extend thanks to Ian Buchanan and Claire Colebrook for supporting this book project and to the two readers to whom the book proposal was assigned. At Edinburgh University Press, I would like to thank Rebecca Mackenzie, Ersev Ersoy, James Dale, Peter Williams and especially Carol Macdonald, for all their help with its production and for supporting the project. Lastly, my gratitude goes out to friends and family for their presence and support when this book was being written.

# Introduction

While subtitled 'Deleuze and the Lacanian School', the primary aim of the present book is to provide a close reading of Deleuze's 1969 work *The Logic of Sense* faithful to the text. This presents an immediate difficulty in that the text is itself highly fragmentary, being comprised of thirty-four miniature chapters or 'series' whose interrelations are never fully spelled out – indeed, the form and content of the work aligned, the text's series are 'nonsense' yet collectively as a 'structure' generate sense as their superficial (yet not insignificant) by-product. The wager of the present book is that 'sense' can be made of *The Logic of Sense* by approaching this structure as a psychoanalysis of sense. Although I will be primarily focusing on the latter portion, the so-called 'dynamic genesis' which provides a psychoanalytical account of language acquisition, by reading it in parallel with a number of the book's earlier series I will show how psychoanalysis underpins the larger project.

I will argue that this psychoanalysis of sense comprises three key components, which Deleuze touches on in the preface when he writes that for him *The Logic of Sense* is 'an attempt to develop a logical and psychoanalytical novel'.[1] Firstly, insofar as 'Psychoanalysis is the psychoanalysis of sense'[2] – at least within the construction or constructivism of *The Logic of Sense* itself – Deleuze intends to map psychoanalysis directly onto the logic and ontology of sense developed in the book as a whole. This makes his psychoanalysis of sense directly ontological and not merely psychological. Secondly, this logic and ontology of sense does not pre-exist (though outstrips) its construction by language. Thirdly, the psychoanalytical clinic of logical and ontological (or better onto-logical) sense completes itself in the literary work. In short, psychoanalysis is integral to Deleuze's onto-logic of sense even if the latter outstrips the former.

More generally, by emphasising the importance of constructivism to Deleuze's early work, together with providing a novel reading of what this constructivist onto-logic amounts to in *The Logic of Sense*, I will present an interpretation of Deleuze's larger project beyond

1

*The Logic of Sense*. This reading seeks to emphasise the continuities between his 1960s and 1990s writings, particularly as found in *What Is Philosophy?* (1991), without pasting over their differences, as well as providing an interpretation of his 1960s ontology which challenges some of the conventional wisdom surrounding the Anglo-American reception of his work.

An investigation of Deleuze's engagement with the Lacanian school in *The Logic of Sense* and during the years surrounding its production, which is the secondary aim of the present monograph, supports this larger endeavour and does not supplant it. Moreover, what I will develop in the following chapters is in no way intended as either a synthesis of Deleuze and Lacan or as a Lacanian reading of *The Logic of Sense*. My approach seeks instead to remain faithful to the specificity of both Deleuze's project and of the Lacanian concepts he engages, so as to more accurately show what he does with them and why. As such my secondary aim is to show through a close reading of *The Logic of Sense* how and why Deleuze engaged with Lacan's school during the late 1960s, which centres on two main points. Firstly, the dynamic genesis, as I read it, is a psychoanalytical account of language acquisition and as such ties up closely with the concerns of Lacan's school. Secondly, what I will show to be the central pivot of Deleuze's onto-logic of sense as a whole, namely the bodies–language relation, is fleshed out within the dynamic genesis through a creative appropriation of the work of the Lacanian theorist and clinician Serge Leclaire. Leclaire argues that if, following Lacan, the unconscious is structured like a language, this structure is literally inscribed on the erogenous body, making the erogenous zones, in their linguistically mediated differential relations with one another, the privileged fulcrum of the bodies–language relation.

While examining Leclaire's work and Deleuze's appropriation of it allows us to better understand *The Logic of Sense*, it also sheds light on Deleuze's ability in this text to offer an alternative philosophical interpretation of the work of the Lacanian school to the one found either elliptically in Lacan's own output or in contemporary philosophical appropriations of it. Since I consider psychoanalysis to be closely bound up with the onto-logic Deleuze develops in *The Logic of Sense*, examining Deleuze's philosophical engagement with Lacan's school and using Leclaire's work to better understand the dynamic genesis reveal themselves, ultimately, to be reverse and obverse sides of the same project.

Through this comparative analysis I will also be able to help

*Introduction*

illuminate an under-acknowledged aspect of Deleuze's pre-Guattari output, by emphasising how Deleuze's work on psychoanalysis in *The Logic of Sense* helped advance – or at least accompanied developments in – the thought of the Lacanian school with regard to the theorisation of the Oedipus complex. As a by-product, this will help shed light on the prehistory of Deleuze and Guattari's *Anti-Oedipus* (1972), demonstrating how some of the themes and arguments of *Anti-Oedipus* – most notably the critique of the Lacanian analysis of the function of the father during the Oedipus complex – are anticipated by his solo 1960s writings on psychoanalysis. Needless to say, I will not be focusing on the latter work in the present study which is consecrated to a reading of the pre-Guattari Deleuze of the 1960s and of *The Logic of Sense* in particular.

As I have stated, the present book is rooted firmly in Deleuze studies, and my discussion of his engagement with Lacan serves primarily to better understand Deleuze's thought. In regard to this, I have chosen the dynamic genesis to investigate, in its relation to the larger ontology of *The Logic of Sense*, for a number of reasons. Firstly, it, together with *The Logic of Sense*, has tended to receive less attention than other works from the same period, and even if this has shifted in recent years the book often remains misunderstood and misrepresented. This goes hand in hand with a larger crisis regarding the interpretation of Deleuze's work.[3] Secondly, *The Logic of Sense* is often read in terms of the ontology of *Difference and Repetition* (1968), when in fact its importance lies in its having made significant advances beyond it which risk being obscured.[4] These two have in turn been exacerbated by the uneasy way in which *The Logic of Sense*'s adherence to certain core structuralist and psychoanalytic tenets sits with the books co-penned with Guattari that would come after it.

One of my claims in the present monograph is that taking seriously Deleuze's philosophical engagement in *The Logic of Sense* with structuralism and psychoanalysis (indeed structuralist psychoanalysis) allows one to fully discern the genuinely Deleuzian ontology (or onto-logic) involved, or at least that Deleuze finds a way to engage with these disciplines and projects which nourishes, rather than detracts from, his independent ontology – and moreover which does not simply subordinate these disciplines to it. Indeed, I will argue that in *The Logic of Sense* there is no ontology independent from this very engagement. I agree with those who would characterise his work more generally, from *The Logic of Sense* onwards, as an attempt to think the ontologies of contemporary modes of thought

3

and practice (and equally to aesthetically re-think or re-imagine them so as to mine their ontological potential), and structuralism would have undoubtedly been the most significant of these during the late 1960s. In short, even if the structuralist details are – for most Deleuzians[5] – anachronistic features of the 1969 work, my examination of Deleuze's larger methodological articulation of structuralist psychoanalysis, and language more generally, with ontology, which much of the present book hinges on, as well as of core features of the ontology itself, will be of relevance to Deleuze studies as a whole.

My first chapter will outline the 1950s Lacanian reading of the Oedipus complex, and the manner in which one disciple in particular, Serge Leclaire, sought to offer an alternative – I argue more immanent and singular – approach to it, and to the linguistic structure of the unconscious more generally. I suggest that Leclaire's emphasis on the body's tightly interwoven relation to language provides a reading of Lacanian theory, including Oedipus, which counters the criticism that the work of the Lacanians prioritises language over bodies and structure over experience. The point of this chapter is, firstly, to offer a reading of the Lacanian school more sympathetic to its evolution during the 1960s than one finds in some reductive and hostile overviews, and secondly to use this reading as the basis for later chapters which show how Deleuze engaged with their work. In particular, I will hone in on one aspect of Leclaire's work, his case study 'Poord'jeli', and show in later chapters how Deleuze reworks it within the terms of his own framework.

In the second chapter onwards, I will turn to the dynamic genesis – or psychoanalytic portion of *The Logic of Sense* – and provide an account of how, in Deleuze, ontologically univocal sense emerges from language's interwoven relation to bodies. The first of these will focus on the transition from 'noise to the voice' – showing how, to analyse this first developmental position or stage, Deleuze utilises Melanie Klein's psychoanalytic thought and Antonin Artaud's literary innovations.

The third chapter will provide a close reading of the three syntheses of the body as they appear in *The Logic of Sense*, demonstrating language's role in this genesis, and showing how Deleuze reads together Klein and the work of the Lacanian school, in his novel reworking of psychoanalytic theory. Here I will particularly emphasise Leclaire's work, showing how Deleuze creatively appropriates it through his own theory of 'esoteric words' as extracted from his reading of Lewis Carroll.

*Introduction*

In the fourth chapter, I will turn to the relation between speech (discussed in the third chapter) and language, arguing that Deleuze's theory of the proposition in *The Logic of Sense* can be understood in terms of structuralism's speech/language distinction, the theory of speech (or of the body) psychoanalytically informing the theory of the proposition as its reverse side. I will show that for Deleuze this hinges on a linguistic and propositional analysis of the verb's function in the sentence, which I will argue accounts for his conception of the functioning of the psychoanalytic phantasm.

In the fifth and final chapter, I will sketch out the ontology – or better onto-logic – of univocal being – or of univocal 'sense' – which I consider Deleuze to mobilise in *The Logic of Sense*, emphasising its essential relation to the psychoanalytic phantasm, but also the latter's necessary insufficiency with regard to literature as that which most fully realises the phantasm and its univocal ontology. I will show how the framework developed throughout the rest of the dynamic genesis directly informs this ontology, and how the psychoanalytic clinic nonetheless remains folded into his 'critical' literary analytical frame.

## Notes

1. Deleuze, *Logic of Sense*, p. x, translation modified.
2. Ibid., p. 105.
3. See, for instance, Mackay's editorial introduction to volume three of *Collapse*, 'Unknown Deleuze' (2007).
4. There are two in particular. The first concerns immanence: *The Logic of Sense* develops an immanent ontology (and indeed one interwoven with its univocity, as I will show in Chapter 5), in a way that is lacking from the earlier work. Deleuze makes this point fairly explicitly in the preface to the Italian edition of *The Logic of Sense*, republished in *Two Regimes of Madness*, writing 'The concepts remained the same – but reorganised according to this dimension [the "surface"]. The concepts changed then' (p. 65), noting further that *Difference and Repetition* still adhered to the 'depths' and the 'heights', without prioritising the immanent 'surface'. The second of these is the role of constructivism, and philosophy more generally; *The Logic of Sense* is arguably the first text of Deleuze's to develop a constructivist ontology, which it can be argued is something it shared with every text after *The Logic of Sense* (I explain what I mean by constructivism in Chapters 3 and 5). In this regard, *Difference and Repetition* is still too abstract in only thinking univocal being rather than accounting for its production, even if the latter is no doubt touched

on by it (indeed it is hinted at on the book's final page, suggesting such a transition to the work that would come after it). Deleuze makes this point in the preface to the Italian edition as follows: 'For me [*The Logic of Sense*] continues to represent a turning point: it was the first time I sought, however tentatively, a form that was not in keeping with traditional philosophy' (p. 63).

5. For those sympathetic to Lacan's work, the present book may show ways in which Lacan's work can be given an alternative ontological interpretation to the ones found in Badiou and Žižek. There are also some commentators highly sympathetic to Deleuze, such as Paul Livingston, who would not consider structuralism and Lacanian psychoanalysis as in any way anachronistic reference points today – see particularly Livingston, 'How do we recognize strong critique?'

# 1

# The Body of the Letter: From Name-of-the-Father to *Re-père*

## 1.1 *The Oedipus Complex from Freud to Lacan*

Freud considers the Oedipus complex – the classical narrative of the boy's desire to sleep with his mother and to kill his father – to constitute the 'peak of infantile sexuality'.[1] For Freud, in the Oedipus complex the boy develops an attachment or 'object-cathexis for his mother',[2] originally related to her breast. The boy deals with the father by 'identifying himself with him', and while for a time these two relationships (boy–mother, boy–father) 'proceed side by side', the 'intensification' of the boy's 'sexual wishes' in regard to his mother portrays the father as an obstacle and it is, for Freud, from this that the Oedipus complex originates.[3] Despite emphasising the heterosexual nature of the complex (boy–mother), Freud sees the erogenous zones as 'subordinated to the primacy of the genital zone'[4] only after puberty. Prior to puberty,

> a number of separate instincts and erotogenic zones [pursue] independently of one another [. . .] a certain source of pleasure as their sole sexual aim.[5]

For him, the Oedipus complex targets boys and girls differently – the girl undergoing a 'negative' form of the complex[6] – but he seems to contradict himself by allowing the heterosexuality of the complex to coexist with a non-genital reading of the zones prior to puberty. Pre-puberty, the zones are autonomous and independent of the genital zone for both the girl and boy, and treated much the same for both sexes.[7]

Because of what he calls 'complet[e] contradict[ions]'[8] in the Freudian conception of the relation between the genital and other zones, Lacan considers both girls and boys to undergo the same initial stages of the Oedipus complex. Lacan argues that the two sexes only fully differentiate themselves upon the initial resolution of the complex, and that the parents' sexes are also only fully distinguished from one another for the infant at this stage. For Lacan, the partial resolution of the complex refers to the infant's assuming a sexed identity – male or female – which allows the infant to differentiate itself from the mother and father. From the infant's viewpoint, just prior to the resolution of the complex, its parents cannot be identified with their sex (typically, but not necessarily, the father with masculinity, the mother with femininity) even if by now the infant will be aware of their difference and will have a premonition of their sexual difference.[9]

Following Lévi-Strauss, Lacan considers entry into the symbolic dimension of language and culture to be governed by the incest taboo. For Lévi-Strauss, the distinction between human culture and animal nature hinges on the incest taboo, which enjoins kin and social groups to circulate their women. In *The Elementary Structures of Kinship* (1949) he shows that in disparate societies, marriage laws are designed to foster an ongoing circuit of exchange and interdependence between unrelated or less closely related groups, adapting Marcel Mauss' understanding of the socioculturally productive role of gift exchange in traditional societies to the exchange of women. Lévi-Strauss maintains that

> [t]he incest prohibition is at once on the threshold of culture, in culture, and in one sense [. . .] culture itself.[10]

For Lévi-Strauss this is itself both the support and an extension of the structure of the unconscious, which he considers in terms of a network of binary oppositions – modelled on the differentiality of the phoneme – structuring cultural and social reality:

> 'Kinship systems', like 'phonemic systems', are built by the mind on the level of unconscious thought.[11]

Following the principles of phonology, Lévi-Strauss considers any sign to be inherently meaningless and essentially dependent on a corresponding opposed term or network of opposed terms: 'sense always results from the combination of elements which are not themselves signifying.'[12] Culture is composed of networks of coupled terms structured as binary oppositions. One element alone is meaningless without its corresponding half.

We can see then that the circulation of women is always also a circulation of signs, and the differentiality of the man/woman binary can be said to function as a privileged oppositional couple for the emergence of symbolic thought and culture.[13] While the cultural institutions of kinship and marriage mark an 'overflow of culture into nature', the shift from nature to culture 'can and must necessarily take place in the field of sexual life'.[14] Whereas genital organs are found in nature, it is culture alone which couples and opposes them as a binary opposition – male/female. Furthermore, culture must use nature (genital organs) to differentiate itself from nature, translating a perceived sexual difference in nature into a binary opposition in culture. Lacan is influenced by Lévi-Strauss when he approaches Freud's reading of the Oedipus complex and the early questioning of the 'phallus' evidenced by such cases as 'Little Hans':

> Let us thus concur with Marcel Mauss' clear formulations: . . . The structures of society are symbolic; individuals, in so far as they are normal, use them in real behaviours.[15]

Lacan re-conceives incest as the sexual indifference perceived in the 'imaginary' stage. The infant enters what Lacan calls the 'symbolic' when it can *symbolically* distinguish between the sexes – which means understanding sexual difference in accordance with cultural norms, namely as a binary (or symbolic) opposition.

Turning to the genital zone, Lacan targets Freud when the Frenchman writes that in infancy the genital drive 'is not at all articulated like the other drives'.[16] For Lacan

> the passage from the oral drive to the anal drive can be produced not by a process of maturation but by the intervention of something that does not belong to the field of the drive – by the intervention [. . .] of the demand of the Other [. . .] [T]he genital drive is subjected to the circulation of the Oedipus complex, to the elementary and other structures of kinship.[17]

When the infant enters the symbolic or cultural order, the genital zone comes to coordinate the other zones and drives. While drives are initially lodged in a distinct zone and pursue their own aims, for Lacan the genital zone distinguishes itself from the oral and anal zones because it is subjected to the Oedipus complex, and this allows it to integrate and reorient the other zones and drives towards the symbolic. The genital zone does this thanks to what Lacan calls the 'dialectic of desire'[18] and according to Lacan's tripartite distinction between need, demand and desire.[19] While biological need can be satisfied by the real breast of the mother, what Lacan calls demand exceeds the simple urgency of need. It points rather to the infant's demand for the desire *of* the other (namely the mother). The infant *demands* to be *desired* by the other, and this demand necessarily operates through the infant's *voiced* demands, through its speech, providing a line of access from the imaginary to the symbolic domain of language.[20] As Lacan puts it:

> Demand [...] bears on something other than the satisfactions it calls for. It is demand of a presence or of an absence – which is what is manifested in the primordial relation to the mother [...] [D]emand annuls the particularity of everything that can be granted by transmuting it into a proof of love.[21]

Everything that the infant is granted is treated as an (always inadequate) proof of the other's love, and Lacan defines desire as neither the 'appetite for satisfaction'[22] nor the 'demand for love', but their differential – the 'difference that results from the subtraction of the first from the second'.[23] This is a development of Lacan's theory of the 'mirror stage' (see section 2.3), since the infant now seeks to recognise itself in and as the object of the other's desire. Here Lacan follows Kojève for whom 'all human Desire ... is finally a function of the desire for recognition.'[24] By introducing a dimension of desire into the field of imaginary identification, Lacan provides identification and the Oedipus complex with an underlying dynamic pointing beyond the imaginary stage.

While Freud considers the mother to treat the young boy as 'a substitute for a complete sexual object', thus 'rousing [his] sexual instinct',[25] it is at least ambiguous whether the mother's desire for the penis or complete sexual object symbolised by the young boy is, for Freud, a cultural or natural condition. Conversely, Lacan considers the relations between the infant, mother and father, which set the stage for the playing out of the Oedipus complex, to be completely bound up with the shift, identified by Lévi-Strauss, from nature to culture or, for Lacan, from imaginary indifference to symbolic opposition.

Lacan first formalises this mutual interdependence of the dialectic of desire and the Oedipus complex in his Seminar IV on object relations from the mid-1950s. Firstly, while the imaginary parental imago – modelled on the real breast – offers the infant a reassuring image and model of unreflexive self-mastery, this mirror is not passive and faultless but has a life of its own. Identifying with something living, whose love for the infant may be unpredictable and wavering, introduces the infant into a world of occasional or frequent dissatisfaction, which inevitably leads to the infant's realisation that this other is a distinct being and hence that the infant is more than its shadow. Lacan calls this situation the infant is caught in

## The Body of the Letter

'imaginary frustration'.[26] The suggestion that the mother and infant are not fully self-sufficient entities, and that the mother's object of desire is not entirely coextensive with the infant, gives rise to the infant's positing of a third term, the father.[27] The father need not be entirely incarnated in a real person, it is the infant's representation of that which the mother desires *beyond* the infant, both to make sense of the patterns of dissatisfaction it experiences and to account for what the mother desires *in* the infant. Lacan refers to this second question as '*Che vuoi?*', meaning 'What does [the Other] want of me?'[28] The 'imaginary father', is the agency the infant posits as bearing the object corresponding to the mother's desire.[29] In Lacan's terms, the mother is seen as being 'deprived' of something – the 'symbolic phallus' – belonging to or overseen by the agency of the imaginary father.[30] The infant thus binarises its experience into two fields (+/−), which we can only abstractly call the 'mother' and 'father' at this stage since the infant is unaware of sexual difference. Crucially, this proto-differential structure which is lived at the level of the imaginary is not associated with sexual difference, with a clean separation between male/female, and by association neither with a distinct cut between self/mother.

During this stage, the infant unwittingly symbolises the mother as being 'deprived' of something and symmetrically the father is symbolised as having that which the mother is deprived of. This reproduces the very cultural system that motivated the mother to initially desire the infant on account of her own symbolic lack of the phallus. Lacan considers the mother's biological lack of a penis to retroactively be the cause of her desire for the symbolic phallus, which only symbolises the penis.[31] The symbolic phallus is the cultural or symbolic attribution of masculinity to the male penis and, symmetrically, the symbolic or cultural attribution of femininity to the woman insofar as she does not 'have' the symbolic phallus. Cultural biases attribute to the woman a symbolic lack insofar as sex is symbolically – in both the Lévi-Straussian and Lacanian sense – coupled with the penis and thus only makes sense at the level of language by being opposed to it, requiring the vagina to figure as a lack in order to exist symbolically or linguistically. Biological sex is only retroactively justified as the 'natural' basis for a distinction which binarises sexual difference as an inseparable couple (male/female, or +/− as now fully sexuated). But importantly for our developing argument in what follows, in the Lacanian reading of the Oedipal scenario, this symbolic rendering of biological sex organs as +/− is *always already present in latent form* at the level of the imaginary proto-sexuated +/– perceived by the infant in the mother's comings and goings.

Now, the infant, regardless of gender, is considered as a phallus by the mother, motivating her desire for her child. Lacan considers that what the mother desires 'in the infant', which 'saturates and satisfies' both her and the infant, is the 'phallic image' the mother has of the infant, unbeknownst to it.[32] For Lacan the infant 'is' the phallus the mother lacks, the object of her desire,[33] since her ability to satisfy the desire of the infant *with whom she identifies* to some extent, is simultaneously her ability to satisfy her own desire or lack. We see that the dialectic of desire is asymmetrical, since even if the mother's desire for the infant is independent of the infant's sex, she nonetheless desires the phallus in the infant *because of* her own symbolic castration. In this way, the infant is pulled into a cultural interpretation of biological sex through the mother's desire for the infant, even if he or she does not yet perceive the mother as female. The infant must learn that his or her own demand for the mother's desire for him or her is already motivated by sexual difference, since without the mother's own symbolic castration the infant would not be able to command her desire so readily, and could not use her to centre its erogenous zones. From a different but related perspective, without her symbolic castration her relation to the infant would not itself figure as a binary structure of absence/presence, which is how the infant initially relates to her at the imaginary level.

This means that while the infant knows nothing of sexual difference, which for Lacan is ultimately a symbolic and cultural construction (even if paradoxically grounded in nature), the love and absence thereof (frustration) experienced by the infant is caused by sexual difference. The mother desires the infant because s/he is the phallus, and even if the mother does not desire him or her because of his/her *sex*, she desires the infant because of *sexual difference*. Her desire is founded on her being deprived of a symbolic object (and 'lacking' an imaginary one, the 'imaginary phallus' (see Seminar IV)), which as such is an element caught in a binary relation with her privation. Frustration motivates the infant to posit a deprived mother and a symbolic phallus capable of (momentarily) overcoming her privation – beyond the imaginary phallus she desires in the infant – and the model sticks because her desire can be figured in binary or symbolic terms.

The Oedipus complex finally comes to a head when the infant realises that he or she can no longer even partially embody this symbolic phallus for the mother, at the level of the imaginary. While the infant 'is' the phallus for the mother, the father or a third (typically male) party 'has' the phallus (the cultural interpretation of their biological sex).[34] When the infant aligns the having or being of the phallus with sexual difference, namely the binary male/female, the infant realises the mother's desire is not for the infant (who 'is' the phallus) but for he who 'has' the phallus. In other words, insofar as the infant is an (imaginary) phallus, the mother can attempt to 'have' the phallus by desiring the infant; but to the extent that the father or a male third party sexually 'has' the phallus on account of their gender, it is they whom the mother desires beyond the infant qua imaginary phallus. Or, to put it another way, the mother can only desire her child so long as it remains the imaginary phallus, since as soon as the infant takes on a symbolically sexed identity (boy/girl), the mother will be perceived as desiring the infant for something that is shared by all men (if it is a boy), rather than specific to him, or for something that the girl 'is' only insofar as she herself figures 'as' the phallus for symbolically marked males.[35] Castration amounts to the loss of the imaginary phallus – the infant's imaginary identification with the mother and capacity to satisfy her desire on what are seen as non-symbolic grounds – and the alignment of 'biological' sex with symbolic gender.[36]

Furthermore, Lacan explains that through his/her demand for the mother – for her presence when she is absent – the infant establishes for himself/herself a series of oppositions – presence/absence – reunified in what he calls the 'symbol of frustration'.[37] The infant learns that desire is connected to sex by pre-symbolising the mother's desire for the phallus in terms of this couple, the 'fundamental condition' of a symbolic order.[38] The classic Freudian example of this would be the game of '*fort! da!*' played by his grandson Ernst. Freud explains that at the age of one and a half, Ernst could make use of a few words to communicate with those around him.[39] Among them was the enunciation 'o-o-o-o', representing the German word *fort* (gone), which was coupled with its opposite *da* (there). This couple 'o-o-o-o'/'*da*' was articulated by Ernst by his throwing a wooden reel with a string tied to it out of his cot (*fort*), and pulling it back in (*da*). For Freud this marked Ernst's 'great cultural achievement' of 'instinctual renunciation',[40] meaning that he had learned to no longer directly invest the presentation of his mother (imago of the breast), but instead to invest her symbol.

The advantage of this is that once she is symbolised the infant is no longer in the 'passive' situation of being 'overpowered' by any prolonged absence of the mother.[41] By symbolising her, the infant constructs the first symbolic couple (absence/presence), or rather symbolises her as the phallus itself (/). The infant can no longer relate to the mother directly, but only via the terms of the phallus (her presence/absence), and thus in terms of a binary which will later be confirmed as identical to her sex (female = absence; male = presence).[42] In other words, by pre-symbolising the mother's presence and absence as the couple presence/absence, the infant not only makes up for the mother's absence by means of an 'absence' proto-symbol,[43] but also – thanks to its coupled form – replaces her very presence with the 'presence' proto-symbol.[44] The mother's presence and absence is therefore replaced by the play of the couple absence/presence, itself now more of a stable object capable of integrating the drives than the mother herself. The infant identifies with the binarity of this couple, and as such with the phallus. The phallus – itself founded on the translation of biological sexual difference into binary terms – motivates the oscillation in the mother's own desire, not least because others, such as the father, also embody the phallus for the mother.[45]

With regard to *fort/da*, Freud notes that although throwing the reel out of the cot was unpleasurable since it was associated with the mother's absence, the more it was repeated the more 'satisfaction' and 'interest'[46] Ernst derived from it because of his capacity to actively master his own passive state of frustration.[47] Correspondingly, the '*da*' was met with 'joy'.[48] Earlier in 'Beyond the Pleasure Principle', where we find this case study, Freud explains that pleasure and unpleasure are related to 'qualitative thresholds of pleasure and unpleasure',[49] associated with intensive quantities which the pleasure principle seeks to maintain 'constant' and 'stable', by cancelling any build-up of charge that exceeds the habitual thresholds determining pleasure.[50] These thresholds are organised as a 'pleasure-unpleasure series',[51] and Freud suggests that this 'series' is capable of being regulated by the infant's construction of words like '*o-o-o-o*'. Such words allow the infant to balance out and stabilise their 'qualitative thresholds' of pleasure and unpleasure. Ernst's repetition of the act of losing and re-gaining the mother balances out his pleasure-unpleasure series, granting him a degree of self-mastery.

For Lacan, '*fort/da*' represents what he calls the 'Desire-of-the-Mother',[52] the pre-symbolisation of that which conditions her desire, namely symbolic castration. Castration occurs the moment the infant effectuates a conversion from this maternal desire to the 'Name-of-the-Father'. In the mid-1950s, Lacan views this as occurring through the infant's apprehension of the father as symbolic phallus by means of the *mother's speech*:

> The father is present only through his law, which is speech, and only in so far as his Speech is recognised by the mother does it take on the value of Law. If the position of the father is questioned, then the child remains subjected to the mother.[53]

Although this father need not be the biological father, Lacan calls him the 'real' father to the extent that the symbolic, paternal, function (Name-of-the-Father) must be (partially[54]) embodied in a concrete figure.

This name/no! (*Nom* and *Non!* are homophonous in French) both locates the infant within the symbolic as the bearer of a name (the infant's given proper name and particularly the infant's/father's surname – mark of tradition and injunction to follow suit),[55] and installs the incest prohibition at the level of the infant's repression of, or inability to return to, the imaginary phallus, capable now of only seeing there the symbolic phallus and 'name' of the father (as the symbolic condition of the mother's desire for the infant qua imaginary phallus). Castration (or 'symbolic castration') is hence defined by Lacan as the symbolic lack (for the boy and girl) of an imaginary object (the imaginary phallus). Rather than libidinally intending the imaginary phallus, the infant now intends, or identifies with, a symbolically defined identity (the name). For the Lacan of the 1950s, this therefore means the maternal function succeeds to the extent that it engenders its own repression.

## 1.2 Leclaire and the Body of the Letter: Intrication and Singularity

One of Serge Leclaire's major theoretical contributions to Lacanian thought is his innovative work on the 'letter', and more specifically his understanding of how linguistic structure is anchored to the erogenous body. In his first and most important book, *Psychoanalyzing* (1968), Leclaire defines the letter as inseparably bound to or 'intricated' with the 'object' – that is the partial object (or 'object (a)') of the drive as tied to an erogenous zone – and considers them both as immanently or internally co-generated and co-dependent.[56] In this respect he extends further, and arguably beyond Lacan,[57] a tendency within Lacan's work which accelerated during the 1960s and 1970s, namely to concede greater underlying importance to the body and the drive in the conceptualisation of linguistic structure, within which terms Lacan famously sought to re-interpret the Freudian unconscious.[58] In this sense, Leclaire helps catalyse or at least accompanies a discernible shift in Lacan's work from the universality of the phallic function and 'Name-of-the-Father', to a greater emphasis on singularity and on the 'not-all' of the phallus in relation to the corporeal processes it forms in a more unilateral manner in his early work.

First of all, it is necessary to re-familiarise ourselves with the basic tenets of Lacan's re-reading of the Freudian understanding of erogenous zones before we can tackle Leclaire's own contribution. Freud discovered the sexual role of 'erotogenic zones'[59] through his studies of hysteria and other 'psychoneuroses', as 'apparatuses subordinate to the genitals and as substitutes for them'.[60] As Leclaire puts it, in Freud the erotogenic zone

> designates an area of the body that is capable of becoming the centre of *an excitation of a sexual type* and, principally, the portals of the body through which occur the exchanges of the organism under the sign of the most intensely pleasurable or unpleasant emotion and sensations.[61]

Based on his studies of infantile sexuality, Freud considered the erogenous zones (particularly the oral and anal zones) to have a certain autonomy and independence with regard to the genital zone, insofar as they imply their own 'pregenital sexual organisation'.[62] Lacan and Leclaire after him will dispute the 'pregenital' nature of erogenous zones to the extent that they are inseparable from the phallus and the capture of the infant's genital zone by the differential (+/−) terms of the mother's castration,[63] but Freud's discovery that any part of the body is capable of taking on a sexual function is nonetheless central to the psychoanalytic theory of the body. Lastly, while Freud initially believes erogenous zones to be limited to only the outer covering – the skin, mucous membranes and orifices[64] – he later extends this to all internal organs to the extent that they too can be invested with sexual libido, and thus can become part of one and the same erogenous body or surface.[65]

Building on his Seminar X, where he first fully articulates his theory of the object (a), Lacan dedicates a number of chapters from his famous Seminar XI to the Freudian notion of drive, dispelling any claims as to its purely 'instinctual' basis and arguing that it is inseparable from its point of juncture on the surface of the body with the signifier and symbolic order, as mediated through demand by the desire of the Other.[66] First of all, whereas in his last works Freud conceived any part of the body to be potentially erogenisable, Lacan sides with the earlier Freud in conceiving of only a small number of erogenous zones, with their corresponding objects: Freud's oral and anal zones (and the breast and faeces), with the addition of the zones tied to the 'scopic' and 'invocatory' drives, namely the eyes and ears (and the Other's gaze and voice).[67]

Through close analysis of the terminology Freud adopts in 'Instincts and Their Vicissitudes', Lacan contends that the drive, as bound to a zone, is inseparable from: a *rim-like surface* (*un bord*),[68] such as the anal sphincter, the teeth and lips, the slits of the eyes, and openings of the ears (Freud's *Quelle* or 'source' of the drive); a partial *object* specific to that drive and zone which, building on though departing from Freud's *Objekt*, Lacan claims is one of his truly original contributions to Freudian thought, and which he defines as an 'object (a)' (or *objet petit a*);[69] and the 'thrust' (*Drang*) of the drive as it leaves the rim, *intends* its object (its 'aim', *Ziel*), encircles or curves around it and finally *brings it back* to the zone or rim, thus satisfying its *goal*, its goal being this *circuit* of the drive.[70]

Lacan speaks of the circuit as 'paradoxically [...] attaining its satisfaction without attaining its aim'.[71] The thrust or intentionality of the drive aims to encircle the object but can never reach it nor make it return to the rim (its goal) since the object is fundamentally lost. Nonetheless, something returns, some goal is achieved, namely the completion of the drive's circuit into which is built this failed intentionality towards the object (a) (or successful intention to fail), and through which pleasure is still produced. As Lacan puts it, 'the *aim* is not what he brings back, but the itinerary he must take [the goal]'.[72] Furthermore, if the object (a) evades the drive's aim, it is nonetheless essential to its goal. There cannot be a circuit of the drive without the object (a) as impossible aim; there can be no self-distancing of the thrust by which the drive gains a minimum of differentiality needed for the pleasure-unpleasure series of the pleasure principle (pleasure as cancelling of difference).

Lastly, the rim-like structure of the zone is bound to morphological determinants, but ones nonetheless profitably chosen for their ability to materially support a differential linguistic structure. For instance, alluding to phonetics, Milner notes the oppositional structure of 'shelves and barriers' (*plages et barrières*) making up the oral zone ('the teeth in opposition to the lips'[73]), propping up speech while also functioning erogenously as a rim.[74] Since, for Lacan, the unconscious is famously 'structured like a language', it is necessary to understand how the body itself is capable of being inserted into a structure made up of oppositions between differential terms, and even how its morphology lends itself to materially supporting such a structure, insofar as language is inextricable from the unconscious, for Lacan, which in turn is libidinal or seated in the erogenous zones.

Turning to Leclaire, he follows the late Freud and not Lacan in conceiving of any part of the body as potentially erogenisable. However, he endorses the overall structure of Lacan's conception of the drive and its zone as presented above. Focusing for now on the relation between a zone (or letter) and its object, Leclaire's theorisations are delicately attuned to their mutual engenderment, adapting and extending Lacan's notion of the object (a) so as to make it more flexible and applicable to any part of the body (thus anything can become an object, just as any part of the body can become a zone). This also has the effect of allowing Leclaire to conceive of *precisely how* the zone's ties to differentiality and language are both supported by and react back onto its corporeality, its rootedness in the body. The zone can be said to differentially and even linguistically condition the drive's access to its object – acting as a frame or hinge, or serving as what Leclaire sometimes calls the *singular lock* or linguistic code to its corresponding object's *singular key*. Indeed more generally, Leclaire aims to develop an account of the body in which its singularity is not subtracted by the universality of linguistic structure, but rather impacts on our very understanding of this structure thereby arriving at a more immanent psychoanalytic structuralism.[75]

Leclaire thus conceives of the object as a kind of fleshy mirror, the letter's embodiment as an iterable material receptacle, which I will try to unpack in what follows. I will do this by focusing on the letter's three conjoined and constitutive differences (in all three of which the object is necessarily also present). These are: *intensive* or libidinal difference, *sensible* difference, and phallic difference or *alterity*, which I will approach in this order.

To begin with, being the seat of a drive, each zone is characterised by what Leclaire calls libidinal intensities or intensive differences, which he borrows from Freud. Freud first conceived of libido in terms of intensity on the basis of a quasi-neuroscientific quantitative-qualitative model of electrochemical charge, or 'excitation', building up in neurons and triggering them once past their defining qualitative thresholds, thresholds mediated by symbolisations which serve to 'bind' and thereby release this charge.[76] While he almost immediately abandoned the neuroscientific basis of his theory, the insight that libido was marked by rises and falls in intensity remained. Leclaire writes that 'to escape from' the 'impasses' of Freud's 'energetic metaphor', it is enough to shift the emphasis away from 'tension' and onto 'difference': pleasure is now to be understood as a 'play of differences, and no longer a system of charges'.[77]

For Leclaire, a zone is initially constituted by a sudden increase or spike in intensity, which he associates with Lacan's notion of *jouissance*. *Jouissance* can be represented by an infinite line, and indeed one which is displaced in relation to itself rather than linear, since linearity implies a fixed starting and end point (Leclaire speaks of it as the 'quick of desire').[78] *Jouissance* is traumatic and radically resistant to conceptualisation because it is without form or definition. Every zone is marked and initially constituted by glimpsing this line, which it attempts to both *grasp* and *protect against* by marking it with sensible qualities as binary relata, a starting and end point as it were, establishing between these two singular points a sensible difference from now on bound to that zone. The drive seated there will aim to re-cathect or re-intend this difference – which we can see is now equally sensible and intensive – so as to re-live the cancelling of this difference, reduction in intensity being as we saw Freud's definition of pleasure.

He gives various suggestive examples to illustrate this point. He firstly likens *jouissance* to a greased rope being climbed; the aim is to attain it, to reach the top, but the real experience of it is closer to the sudden slip and fall. When this occurs, sensible differences are sought out in the immediate environment to latch onto so as to halt the fall, or rather so as to take a snapshot of it before it is lost completely, and which can be used to later relive the experience in faded form. Now the point is that *jouissance* as such, the rope extending to infinity, is *insensitive* or devoid of experiential content at the libidinal or intensive level; this is provided entirely by the markings or sensibilia used to grasp it. By marking a 'starting' and 'end' point on this line – sensible thresholds here acting as the minima and maxima of the duration of the captured experience – it is not so much that *jouissance* can be grasped within limits but rather that pleasure can be derived *from jouissance*, pleasure being the cancelling *of* difference. If *jouissance* is an uncountable quantity, sensible qualities as binary relata mark on the line a 0 and 1, or a − and a +, namely the sensible thresholds within which an associated *difference in intensity* can be defined.[79] The larger the difference in intensity, the greater the pleasure produced by cancelling that difference.

The letter can be defined as the *trait* (or sensible difference) marking the *syncope* of the drive.[80] The term 'syncope' has a number of connected meanings in Leclaire's lexicon. Medically it points to a sudden woozy loss of consciousness, a fainting spell; this is also captured by the cinematic term 'fade-out', with which Leclaire associates the term; in music, as well as in linguistics, it refers to the stress being placed on the 'weak-' or 'off-beat' of a measure, as in for instance jazz (for which we can imagine the stress would be placed on the second and fourth beat of a bar in four-four time, rather than on the first and third). Leclaire speaks of the 'syncope of pleasure' because the first sensible quality or relatum one latches onto during an intense experience is given its full import only in relation to the second, 'off-', beat which delimits and forms the experience – both the degree of pleasure attained (the intensive difference cancelled) and the sensible form of the experience (its qualitative thresholds). Consciousness fades as intensity increases, but the second, syncopated, beat forestalls the eclipse or fade-out of consciousness by retroacting on the first and thereby cancelling the 'quick' of desire,[81] the slipperiness of the greasy rope, by translating it into what Freud calls a 'mnemic image' or presentation.[82] The second beat establishes the thresholds between which the intensity can be measured and thereby cancelled, while also giving the zone the means to repeat the experience in the form of the mnemic image.

This image loses the intensive content of the experience while retaining the sensible form.[83] Since there is no pleasure derived from intensity without its sensible delimitation, the mnemic image serves to both *constitute* the pleasure of the initial experience – as the momentary halting of a fall – and to allow the drive to repeat it. The drive does this by re-cathecting or re-intending the sensible difference associated with a movement of intensity or libido seated in a particular zone. This accounts for the drive's 'fixation' on its object, the ineradicable drive to *repeat the cancelling of difference* within the singular thresholds that constitute and determine each zone and each drive seated there. Each zone is therefore marked by a letter first off because a sensible-intensive difference is opened up in and *as* the zone as such, on which the drive becomes fixated due to the urge to repeat the pleasure extracted from it. We see that this fixation is associated with a *repression* of the intensity of the experience, since by proto-symbolising it – sensibly marking it – the traumatic core of the experience (pure intensity, self-displacing movement) is lost. The letter is hence at once *symbolisation* (as a mnemic image), *fixation* (of the drive on its object),[84] and what Freud calls the 'primary repression' of instinctual need in favour of its cultural mediation by a 'psychical representative'[85] of the drive.[86] In short, following Freud, affect is *constituted* by the terms of its repression in a presentation.

The object serves in this respect to physically incarnate or embody these sensible qualities or binary relata within the thresholds demanded by the corresponding zone. It must firstly trigger the drive libidinally – prompting a spike in intensity in the zone – by functioning as a stand-in for that which the drive intends: for instance, the breast in the case of the oral zone, the gaze in the case of the scopic register, and so on; although, strictly speaking, any object can serve this function, as we see in fetishism, and anything can be an object since any part of the body can be erogenised by (what will become) that object – a piece of rubber, an item of clothing, some cotton wool.[87] Secondly, the object must carry with it the singular sensible difference which marked and constituted its corresponding zone (for instance, the voice's singular timbre or pitch).[88] Building on Freud, Leclaire shows that what is *re-encountered* in the object is not the object itself but the mnemic image – the sensible difference of the original encounter – which it brings to mind or embodies by falling under the zone's sensible thresholds. Hence *what* is being cathected in the object is its ability to bring about what Freud calls the 'hallucinated' return of that memory, which is incorporated into the object and treated as real.[89]

By coming to momentarily embody the mnemic image, the object serves to *cover over*, to cork or suture, in short to cancel the difference that marks a zone. In this respect a zone yearns for its object as that which can offer respite from the irritatingly bare, uncollapsible *openness* marked there by its founding sensible-intensive *difference*. We saw that this difference is capable of forming a *unit*, as a unity of its maximum and minimum thresholds (+/–), by relating and cancelling these thresholds as an experienced and remembered pleasure. But this unit exists only at the level of the mnemic image and not the body, since the former is generated by repressing the latter, which still nonetheless *remains open and uncancelled* at a more buried level. Being repressed, this opening is not cancelled but offset.[90] The difference marking the zone is therefore a *perpetually open* wound that no object can ever suture for more than an instant. The mnemic image – as unit/unity – serves to allow the zone as wound to re-cathect or re-intend the experience of closure or of cancelling (of relating the + to the –); but this can only be experienced in hallucinated form (as a memory of something that never happened) precisely because the cut of the zone can never heal. The mnemic image is hence *already* a (hallucinated) memory of the *object*, and not a presentation of the zone's inaugural experience (the cut), even before it is re-cathected through fixation.[91]

Here we arrive at the third, phallic, difference of the letter. The zone is literally cut open by the sensible-intensive difference, installing there a glimpse of the *jouissance* associated with radical alterity, namely the *sexual difference* which motivates – through her own symbolic cut/castration – the mother's desire for the infant (even though the infant does not yet perceive this as sexually motivated). In other words, the body is cut up into zones by sexual difference even before the infant is castrated (the global body cut off from the mother). The mother serves as what Leclaire calls the 'letter-holder', a kind of pen that inscribes the letter on the infant's body,[92] and which Leclaire associates with the phallus as 'at once the letter and the stylet that traces the letter'.[93] She embodies the lost object, but it is important to note that this object is a retrospective illusion since the perpetual *lack* installed in each zone or cut (as the desired-for return of its object) is nothing else than the *obverse side of the unconscious drive to repeat* (the cycle of loss and subsequent return) as motivated by the pleasure principle. It is therefore not the letter-holder that the drive lacks and intends but its manifestations (letters, inscriptions of difference, openings of zones).

Just as the object does, the phallus underlies all three differences of the letter, being that which stimulates *jouissance* at the level of the drive's intimation of alterity and pleasure at the level of its cancelling. The drive ultimately uses the object to *temporarily bridge* the alterity of the other or letter-holder, and to temporarily cancel the difference separating self/other. The gap *between* the –/+ (or 0/1) of any zone on the surface of the body is in a way the distance between the infant as such and the mother – the *quantitative* difference at the sensible-intensive level is strictly correlated with a difference figured as *alterity* (or rather with the cancelling of a difference figured as alterity).

This third difference is in turn associated with a fourth, *phonemic* or *graphic* difference, the minimal structural-linguistic difference – as materialised or made sensible in sound or in writing – capable of distinguishing between two distinct significations, such as the phonemes b/p in *billard/pillard* (billiards/plunderer), or the graphemes ←/→.[94] This grants Leclaire's 'letter' its properly linguistic status, hence its name. In an earlier text, echoing Lacan's own conception of the 'letter',[95] Leclaire defines it as a signifier (phoneme or grapheme) incapable of being coupled in a one-to-one relation with a signified or linguistic concept, so as to form the Saussurian unity of signifier and signified the linguist calls a 'sign'.[96] For Leclaire, although there are many signifiers which cannot be fixed to a signified, what gives a signifier the status of letter proper is its being associated with a zone's sensible-intensive-phallic difference, in short its being directly inscribed on a zone. Hence, Lacan and Leclaire after him speak of the 'materiality' of the letter – its being not only a sensible or materialised phonemic/graphic difference, but also one that is corporeal or directly libidinal and erogenous.

As such, for Leclaire the letter is radically *unconscious* and the erogenous body is to be viewed as *a set of letters*. In his work we can conflate the *erogenous body*, the *order of the letter* and, to a certain extent, the *unconscious* itself.

## 1.3 *Poord'jeli* as Re-père

'Poord'jeli' – or 'Poor(d)j'e-li' to give it its full form – is Leclaire's transcription of a, if not necessarily the, kernel of the unconscious organisation of one of his analysands, an obsessional neurotic in his thirties known to us as Philippe. Not only does Leclaire believe he has uncovered key letters in Philippe's unconscious, but moreover that this word points to something deeper still, namely the principle of their coordination, the principle which makes of them a single set (the erogenous body as such). It thus has key ties to the phallus and Oedipus complex, and to a process of self-naming or literal-objectal self-construction.

Leclaire came to it through his analysis of the famous dream with the unicorn. Quoting Philippe, Leclaire narrates the dream as follows:

> The deserted square (*place*) of a small town; it's odd, I'm looking for something. Liliane – whom I do not know – appears, barefoot, and says to me: it's been a long time since I've seen such fine sand [...] a unicorn (*licorne*) crosses our path; we walk, all three of us.[97]

Leclaire explains that what 'underlies' this dream is the unconscious desire to drink and, as we will see, more profoundly still a kind of botched *desire for castration*, which functions as the unifying centre of not only the dream but also of Philippe's unconscious.[98] Although lacking from the dream's manifest content, this desire is reconstructible at the level of the *letter*, the phonemes and phonemic relations involved, and thanks to further material provided by Philippe's own commentary on the dream and the events it alludes to.[99]

Philippe woke from the dream with a strong thirst, which he claimed was triggered by his having recently eaten salted Baltic herring.[100] Earlier in the day, he had been walking in the woods with his niece, Anne, and they had come across deer tracks (*pieds* in French hunting terminology, also meaning feet) near a stream where the animals had been drinking. These events no doubt trigger the dream, but only because they reactivate distant and buried memory traces which hold the key to Philippe's unconscious. Leclaire traces these memories back to events which took place between the ages of three and five, which is to say during the Oedipal stage, and more specifically as a reaction to events occurring earlier, probably from very early infancy.[101] For the sake of clarity, I will present these events in chronological order, and I will be heavily drawing on my account of Lacan's reading of the Oedipus complex as presented in section 1.1.

First of all, Leclaire hypothesises that Philippe was the target of a particularly unwavering maternal desire, which he claims lies at the basis of much obsessional neurosis.[102] Through his relations with his mother he was unable to intimate the symbolic phallus as the third term beyond the infant–mother imaginary dyad. She preferred Philippe to not only his siblings but also her husband, with whom she had fraught relations. This maternal fantasy structure cocooned Philippe within a protective shell closed off from the rest of the world, which while protecting him from the trauma of lack and sexual difference, also prevents him from accessing desire as that which lies beyond demand.[103] Leclaire notes that at this age Philippe used to like walking barefooted to harden his soles, giving himself calluses (*cornes*, in French),[104] and that he strongly cathected this impenetrable hide, the entire surface of his skin and particularly the *feet* and the *forehead* serving as privileged erogenous zones. On his forehead lay a scar caused by an accident when young, and this was used, Leclaire contends, to phallically mark and single him out as distinct from his siblings and father and as his mother's favourite, thanks to this insignia of maternal desire.[105]

Something striking about this is that Leclaire seems to be arguing here for a *corporeal inscription* or *bodily mediation* of the Lacanian account of the Oedipus complex.[106] The Oedipus complex, the interaction between infant, mother and father, literally takes place on the surface of the body. The imaginary phallus or image of bodily unity is *literally* inscribed on Philippe's body at the level of the sensible-intensive differences marking the skin, feet and particularly the forehead (as associated only secondarily with the phoneme *corne*). We need to distinguish ontogenetically between the sensible-intensive differences inscribed on the body, and the later overcoding and restructuring of these differences by means of a second *properly structural* phonemic layer, by which I mean a set of differential elements and relations involved in a fully integrated libidinal economy. The first layer, composed primarily of sensible-intensive differences, is tied to the imaginary phallus; but as the infant progresses through the Oedipal stage, acquiring more language and arriving (or trying to arrive) closer to the symbolic phallus latent in the imaginary one, a new layer of phonemic differences attached to the zones and *converging on the symbolic phallus* will react or fall back onto the *first layer* of differences, which nonetheless provides a support and starting point for the second layer. Using Philippe's case I will try to show how this process takes place.

We can see that the accidental cut on the forehead *opens* the erogenous zones to desire and alterity, which I showed in the previous section characterises the initial constitution-inscription of any zone. Desire and alterity are originally inscribed there as Philippe's mother tends to the wound and in its place leaves a different, erogenous, cut, that of her desire for the infant. But this desire and the alterity it communicates are soon over-saturated or expended in the mother's over-willingness to satisfy the infant's every demand, the flow of desire solidifying as a crust or scab as the infant progresses through the Oedipal stage and still has no intimation of the symbolic phallus. The cut of maternal desire inscribed on the forehead hence becomes sutured, covered over, but not by an object. Now, for a zone to have an object it must be lost; there must be a gap between the desire first inscribed there marking it as a zone, and the impotence of the infant's demands for its return. An overly keen mother will thus inhibit the proper functioning of a zone. Philippe's forehead is thus landed with not an object but an imaginary phallus – and hence an *image*, the image of a mythical bodily unity/impenetrable hide – which wraps itself around the entire surface of his skin or body.

Leclaire explains that between the ages of three and five, at the height of the Oedipal stage, Philippe would vacation with his family on an Atlantic beach. Among the individuals present was Liliane, his mother's cousin, who, Leclaire contends as one of his fundamental interpretive claims, Philippe sought out to replace or rather re-structure his primary identification with his mother, recognising or intuiting in her elements that would allow him to overcome his developmental impasse. In his spoken interactions with her, his staged demands targeted at her, he would be granted a little more access to Lacan's '*Che vuoi?*' Of chief importance was that Liliane had a healthy relationship with her husband, a desire going beyond her nephew whom she nonetheless cared for, as well as the fact that she was the cousin of Philippe's mother, and so occupied a roughly parallel position within the family's kinship structure.[107] But beyond this, as we shall see, what takes on an astonishingly overriding importance at this point is the network of *phonemic differences* she allows Philippe to form at the libidinal level, and which Philippe uses to integrate his erogenous zones into the symbolically determined kinship system of which she is a part. This requires us to dispense with thinking of Philippe's re-calibration as taking place at the level of a psychological agent simply 'seeking out' a new identificatory model. Rather, we are dealing with Oedipal intentionality at the level of an inter-subjective structure, where the zones' drives are embedded in far larger systems and where agency is to be located at the level of this embeddedness.[108]

As Leclaire reports, Philippe often used to say *choif*, a contraction of *j'ai soif* ('I'm thirsty'), which was especially targeted at Liliane and used so as to identify himself with her desire:

> he used to say 'I'm thirsty' (*j'ai soif*) (or rather, it is reported, *j'ai 'choif*'[109]), virtually flaunting that declaration – often motivated in that burning summer – as a sort of insignia of himself ('me'!), Philippe, lost as he was on the immense beach. But this representative formula was fixated most of all through the agency of Lili, to the extent that the phrase 'I'm thirsty' had become a sort of password when Lili, in order to address him or talk of him, said: 'Philippe-I'm-thirsty'.[110]

This is not a thirst for water but for desire itself or, indeed, for castration; it is a self-identifying or self-constructing *statement* rather than a demand (at one level[111] it says 'I am, or rather would like to be, thirsty', not 'I would like my thirst satiated').[112] As a letter limited to one zone – the oral zone and its drive of conservation – *choif* can be said to erect a bridge between Philippe's body and the tentative and partial access to the symbolic phallus Liliane embodies for him.[113] It is the starting point of a fuller integration of his libidinal body into the symbolic as such but, being attached to only one zone, this letter is not yet fully *differential* and likewise the oral zone is not yet fully *integrated* into the others, both of which are essential to the symbolically determined body. In short, we need far more phonemes to be in play for the body to converge with the symbolic, and they need to be determined as phonemic *differences*, rather than as free standing words, in order to have a structuring impact on the zones.

Arguably the most important phonemic difference is the articulation of 'li' and 'corne' in '*licorne*' (unicorn in French), and I would contend that Philippe's entire erogenous body will be marked and constituted by the inscription of the phoneme or letter 'li' on the zone of his forehead (or more specifically on the zone constituted by the scar). Liliane was known as 'Lili' to both Philippe and her husband, allowing Philippe to straddle the imaginary and symbolic phallus through the indistinction between himself and Liliane's marital object of desire. It also allowed him to partially merge his identity with hers through the coincidence of the 'ili' in both their names. I would go so far as to argue that the symbolic phallus – or something approaching it – becomes inscribed on Philippe's body thanks to the phoneme 'li', providing the other phonemic differences inscribed on his zones with their core orienting axis. The 'li' is inseparable particularly from its difference from 'corne'. The 'corne', which in French means both horn and callus, condenses the head and the feet, in short Philippe's skin or erogenous body from head to foot. Whereas they are held together as a single *image*, the impenetrable hide, in the earlier imaginary scenario, '*li-corne*' points to a *symbolic* articulation. The two phonemes are *distinct*, they point to zones that are fragmented because they are now capable of desiring again, and as we know the functioning drive fragments the body into its zones. But they are also both *co-articulated*.[114]

It is the symbolic phallus, through the agency of Liliane and the phoneme 'li', that re-articulates the zones it fragments. It does this by positing something the body has *lost*, by positing something *outside* the body which thus constitutes the body as a symbolic set (rather than imaginary unity).[115] The 'li' is phonemically distinct from the 'corne' rather than fused with it as a single body; furthermore, if in French *corne* covers the meaning of callus and horn, it is the double status of the 'li' as both horn or *forehead* and as something lying *outside* the body, that allows it to transform the imaginary phallus into a symbolic one. This is because 'li' can refer to the erogenous zone of the forehead, as in *'li-corne'* ('li' = unicorn's horn, *'corne'* = callus, i.e. 'li' = forehead and *'corne'* = foot, and so *'li-corne'* = the erogenous body from head to foot), but it can also refer to the phoneme 'li' itself, as *distinct from* the imaginary unity of the body (wherein *'corne'* in *'li-corne'* refers to both 'horn' and 'callus', i.e. 'forehead' and 'foot', the body from head to foot). If the imaginary phallus prevents the forehead as erogenous zone from accessing its object (the imaginary phallus as suture is its 'object'), the gap between demand and the desired object is reopened by Liliane, and I would claim that she provides the forehead with the phoneme 'li' *as both letter and object*. This is indeed Leclaire's definition of the phallus.[116]

We can say that the phallic horn 'li' *tears through and re-opens the prematurely sutured 'cut' on the forehead*, fragmenting the imaginary unity of the body but also allowing its newly re-opened zones to re-converge on the symbolic phallus, as phonemic articulation of *'li-corne'*.[117] *'Li-corne'* finally takes on a third sense as the conjunction of Liliane (the phoneme 'Li' and the access to the symbolic phallus she embodies) and Philippe (*'corne'*, the erogenous body from head (*'corne'*) to foot (*'corne'*)), which is possible only because Philippe is now *internally split* between his body (*'li-corne'*, head-foot) and the symbolic phallus (the phoneme 'li' as object and letter, i.e. phallus) located outside it yet which makes of his body as such a set. His zones (*'li-corne'*, head-foot) can only be grouped symbolically and libidinally as a set because the principle of their synthesis lies in the difference between 'li' as letter-object and 'li' as the zone of the forehead marked by this phoneme, meaning that the zone of the forehead is not only intricated with its object, as per any functioning zone, but with *all of the body's zones' objects*, to the extent that their convergence on the phallus synthesises them as an erogenous body and is founded in the zone of the forehead.[118]

Although *'li-corne'* lies at the core of Philippe's erogenous body, it is only one albeit privileged phonemic articulation located inside the larger construction 'Poord'jeli', or 'Poor(d)j'e-li' to give it its full (castrated) form.[119] The following glossary analyses some of the other articulations. Some are very obvious; others are connected to Poord'jeli by only one phoneme:

- *Corne* (horn, callus), with ties to *licorne* (unicorn), *corps* (body)[120] and *fort* (strong, fat), the latter pointing to the toughness of the imaginary hide and also to Liliane's rotund figure and large breasts.

*The Body of the Letter*

There are further connections with *port* (port), as tied to the Atlantic; with *mort* (death), pointing to the death drive or desire for castration, as well as to Philippe's deceased paternal grandfather and uncle (see below), and to the stultifying imaginary phallus; and finally *or* (gold), the golden sand, and Leclaire notes Philippe's mother would call him by *chéri tresor* ('cherished treasure').

- *Je/J'e* (I), with ties to 'J. E.', identifiable on the monogrammed luggage of 'Jérémie', Philippe's deceased paternal grandfather who, like Philippe's own premature suture-tomb, died very prematurely. This points, on the one hand, to the withdrawn and absent father (who is only abstractly present at the level of the symbolic, and whose premature death runs parallel to Philippe's premature suture due to the absence of a strong paternal function), i.e. the inadequacy of the symbolic phallus in Philippe's relations with his mother. On the other, it refers to the 'Name-of-the-Father', which imposes itself, after being modified as Poord'jeli, onto Philippe at the level of the 'I' (*je*). Since 'Jacques' is both the name of Liliane's husband and of Philippe's deceased paternal uncle (his father's older brother), it is possible that Philippe uses the former, rather than his own father, to move nearer to the paternal function, using the phonemic association between his paternal lineage and Liliane's husband. We also see that there is an eventual split between Jacques and Philippe at the level of j'e (or J. E.) upon castration. More generally, the J. E. also points to the only contribution made by the paternal function or Name-of-the-Father to Philippe – the provision of phonemic differences with which he will have to construct Poord'jeli, the latter providing him with what Leclaire calls his symbolic 'bearings' (*repère* in French, meaning bearings and repeat father, *re-père*, or new father).[121] Lastly, since Jacques is also the name of Philippe's older brother, we find a structural parallelism between the deceased uncle and the maternally disfavoured older brother of Philippe.
- *Lili* (Liliane), with ties to Philippe, and to *lit* (bed), namely the marital bed and site of both incest (Lili-Philippe) and the incest taboo or 'Name-of-the-Father' (Lili-her husband).[122] There are also fairly clear ties to *il* (he), when read backwards, which is held in differential tension with *elle* (she), in 'jeli', later split or castrated into 'j'e' and 'li', splitting male (*il*) from female (j'e-li), and partially tied to the 'je' (I). There is a further connection with *lolo* (vulgar word for breasts), which connects to the oral drive, and to Lili's large breasts as noted by Leclaire.[123]

- *Moi-Je*, (Me-I), with which Philippe would identify himself around the same time as '*choif*' (I'm thirsty), which also contains part of '(m)oi', and which when reversed as 'foich' contains part of (M)**oi-Je** ((f)**oich**), the French 'je' and 'ch' being similar in pronunciation. They both also have ties to the 'a' sound in *plage* (beach), where his new identity was first constructed, and we find '(pl)**age**' in (M)**oi-je**. Note also the narcissistic imaginary dyadic form of Moi-Je, where self-other are both 'me', which needs to be broken open, using '*choif*', to access the symbolic phallus and desire.
- *Pauvre Philippe* or *pauvre trésor* (poor Philippe/poor treasure), by which his mother would refer to him. There are connections with the injury to the forehead. This 'poverty' is, however, one of desire not of corporeal 'weakness', at the imaginary level. This connects to *peau* (skin, i.e. the erogenous body), and if we sever the 'P' (*peau, pauvre* Philippe), we have *eau* (water, the desire for castration), accessed by losing the imaginary ties associated with the 'P'.
- *Philippe Georges Elhyani* is the name given to Philippe by his parents, which when contracted covers most of 'Poord'jeli'. In this regard, Poord'jeli is a veritable self-re-naming. From his names' constituent phonemes, Philippe selects for Poord'jeli the '*or*' (gold) and '(g)**orge**' (cleavage and throat, pointing to the oral drive and Lili's breasts) of '*Georges*'. Leclaire notes that pronounced the French way, with a 'G' that's softer than in the English pronunciation, Georges is identical to *je'orge* (and (G)eorges to *oor(d)j'e*), hence containing the '*je*'. The '*je*' can also be located at the level of the syncope produced by the mute 'e' ending of Philippe when followed in French by a consonant (here *e'Georges*), whereby the 'weak beat' of the 'G' is emphasised and serves to retroact on the 'e' to produce the '*j'e*', which appears backwards in *e'G*. The 'P' of Poord'jeli comes from the syncope of (Phili)**ppe** in relation to Georges, with the 'li' of Philippe and of Elhyani fusing the first and last name, and with '(G)**eorges'El**(yani)' appearing as (P)**oor(d)j'e-l**(i). It therefore seems that to construct his new name, Poord'jeli, Philippe draws primarily on the least (symbolically-culturally) important, middle, name, and furthermore on its (phonemic) *difference* from 'Philippe' and 'Elhyani'.[124] Leclaire calls 'Poord'jeli' the 'secret replica of the proper name, cipher of the unconscious',[125] replacing the 'Name-of-the-Father' (which is both the proper name (Philippe) given to the subject and the father's surname).[126]
- *Pied* (foot). Notice the silent 'd' in the castrated form.

## The Body of the Letter

These are only in fact a small number of the phonemic differences at play, and show how almost infinitely interconnected the unconscious literal order is. In this glossary we can also note the complex interconnection between the first, imaginary, series (sensible-intensive differences, erogenously localised phonemes and contractions), and the second, symbolic, one (phonemic differences and relations, desire and castration), showing that the latter builds on rather than simply replacing or overwriting the former. We can note that the structural interrelations of phonemic differences transcends any attempt at erogenously localising or pinpointing any one phonemic difference or letter, since we are approaching the body now as a set of letters or integrated differential structure. A third point is that I have tried as much as possible to show that what is at stake are phonemic *differences*, where the relations formed with others are more fundamental than the phonemes themselves.[127]

Lastly, Leclaire claims that in presenting us with the core phonemes, there has not been the 'least interpretation' involved on his part, since he relies on the phonemes he notices *are fixated on and given a singular phonetic quality when they appear in the analysand's speech*. That is to say they are pronounced, intonated and stressed in a singular manner, and reappear uncommonly frequently in the analysand's everyday speech. They continue 'clinging to his body', they are constantly at work pulling his discourse down to the level of the body, loosening the connection between signifier and signified by manifesting aspects of their materiality.[128]

Now, it is also possible to approach the word structurally at the level of the internal relations of the *unconscious functions* present therein. It is implied by Leclaire's argument that in its full form, 'Poor(d)j'e-li' is the site of the articulation of the functions of the letter, object and subject, as formulated by Leclaire. I examined the letter-object intrication in section 1.2, but Leclaire posits the subject – the Lacanian split subject or subject of the unconscious ($) – as the third and final term around which the unconscious is structured, which he also attempts to conceive of in an equally immanent or interwoven manner, being inseparable from the other two terms (and vice versa). Turning to this immanent tripartite relation will help us more fully understand how Leclaire conceives of the letter-object intrication and the letter's phonemic basis, as well as the structural location and function of the symbolic phallus in the unconscious.

By reading it from left to right, 'Poor(d)j'e-li' can be decomposed into letter (*peau*, skin, the body made up of erogenous 'portals' or as a set of letters), subject (*j'e*, the split '*je*' or 'I'), and object (-*li*). Philippe, as split subject (*j'e*), is located and split between his erogenous body (*peau* or *corne*[129]) and the object of his drive ('li' as symbolic phallus). Leclaire theorises that the subject's function, in its immanent relation to letter and object, is precisely to act as the *economic principle* of the integrated libidinal order of the unconscious, a function he calls 'alternating commutation'.[130] The subject is needed in addition to the letter and the object because once overlaid by a layer of phonemic (and graphic) difference, it is no longer possible to repress-fixate a literal-objectal intrication without the subjective function, as tied to the symbolic phallus. While a letter qua trait or sensible difference brings together two qualities as binary relata, once overlaid by phonemes letters can no longer resolve or cancel the intensive difference they mark, because phonemes (and graphemes) are capable of opening onto every other phonemic (and graphic) difference in the unconscious. Mnemic images are relatively self-contained, and even if associated in part with a phoneme and/or grapheme, the infant does not yet have the conceptual means to coordinate them with each other. However, once the symbolic phallus does arrive, as coordinating principle of differential relations, any intensive charge affecting a zone can only be resolved at the global level, or at the level of an expression of unconscious meaning which brings into play far more presentations, all the body's zones and a much larger network of binary oppositions.[131]

The symbolic phallus, which Leclaire also calls the 'letter of the lack of the letter',[132] is defined by its conspicuous absence within the system it holds together. From a slightly different perspective, as both letter and object it is perpetually located 'outside' the body, incapable of being intricated with a zone as an object and inscribed there as a presentation or signifier. Nonetheless, the symbolic phallus is *indirectly* inscribed on *all* zones, and provides the principle of their global integration at the level of the continuum of phonemic differences spread out over all the zones' defining phonemes.[133] This way it is the ever-displaced principle of the production of pleasure in all the zones.

For Leclaire, the object 'positivises' the zone's constitutive lack, the ineradicable sensible-intensive difference inscribed in each zone, causing it to be forever open to objects that can step in to partially embody and, through phonemic/graphic symbolisation, momentarily cancel this difference. The object is a '1' to the zone's '0': the zone wishes to repress its constitutive difference to produce pleasure (0),

## The Body of the Letter

which can only be achieved by fixating the object that embodies this difference (1) and the phonemes/graphemes that resolve it by producing sense at the global level. Each zone is a literal-objectal alternating commutation between 0/1; but if the symbolic phallus' coordination of zones means that *jouissance* can only be repressed-fixated and produce pleasure at the global level of the unconscious system, this 0/1 cannot be confined to any one zone.

This is where Leclaire's third term, the subject, comes in to play, to explain how literal-objectal intrication can occur at the global level, and it is held in strict correlation with the symbolic phallus. Leclaire defines the subject as the bar (/) between the 0 of the letter(s) and the 1 of the object(s) (which we can already see regroups all the zones), or from a different perspective as the 'series of similarities in each one of the elements' or phonemes, in which this sameness amounts to a 'simple alternation without any other determination'.[134] At one level the subject is merely the 'alternation' back and forth between '(d)'j', 'e'G', 'j'e', 'li-corne' and so on, extending in fact to every single phonemic difference making up the unconscious or erogenous body due to their shared convergence on the symbolic phallus. We see here that the syncope is no longer only a syncope of pleasure, but now a fully linguistic and linguistically structured one. But from another perspective, the subject takes on the function of pivot of the unconscious, serving as the integrative principle of its libidinal economy and of its phonemic relations at the global level. Once they are overlaid by a convergent layer of phonemic/graphic difference, and thanks to the subject, syncopes of pleasure which were formerly limited to local zones (letter-object intrications) take on a global resonance. Hence, while we saw in section 1.2 that *jouissance* is repressed-fixated in a mnemic image tied to a zone, we can see here that it can be located more fully at the level of the subject as the bar separating – or conjoining-disjoining ($\lozenge$) – the linguistically or symbolically coordinated body/object (0/1).[135]

In a sense, the subject is split between the body and the symbolic phallus, as object of all the zones, because the phallus puts the subject of the unconscious in place by detaching itself from the zones' objects, symbolising the 'lost object' as such (the sum total of the lost objects marking each zone). As split or bar (/), the subject provides the erogenous zones with an integrated economic principle of *jouissance* (0/1 at the global level).[136]

In the above, to an extent we find an internally-motivated search for the symbolic, Philippe's erogenous zones intending or seeking out the greater access to the symbolic phallus provided by Liliane, giving rise to a singular unfolding of sexuality.[137] However, we have also seen, if perhaps only implicitly, that the new Name (*re-père*), Poord'jeli, serves both to further access the symbolic *and* to build an imaginary defence against it and the father's 'No!' (as embodied by Liliane).[138] In this way, Poord'jeli provides a middle ground, a kind of compromise formation, between the Name-of-the-Father and the Desire-of-the-Mother, using the latter to help symbolically shape the former rather than being unilaterally repressed by its symbolic (or 'metaphoric') function. The singularity of the letter-object intrication, and of its articulation with the symbolic phallus at the level of the differential structure of the unconscious, thus grants the bodily drive a role that appears irreducible and resistant to its unilateral subsumption under linguistic structure and the universal Law of the 'paternal metaphor' of the early Lacan.

## 1.4 Conclusion: The Names-of-the-Father

While he does not mention this problematic in his first presentation of the case of Philippe, with Laplanche in 1962, there are a number of indications that by 1968 Leclaire was mobilising Poord'jeli partly as an attempt to reformulate Lacan's Name-of-the-Father, anticipating by a number of years the intensification of Lacan's own critique of his concept from the 1950s as found in Seminars XXI (1973–4), *Les non-dupes errent* ('The Names-of-the-Father'/'The Non-duped Err') and XXIII (1975–6) ('The Sinthome').[139]

This new concept already appears at the end of Seminar X (1962–3), where Lacan writes that he intends the seminar of the following year to be devoted to the 'Names-of-the-Father' – the Name now as pluralised (and arguably singularised), and 'not for nothing', in light of the 'shortcoming of the father function'.[140] It is instructive that it is in Seminar X – in which he first develops the object (a) – that we witness this shift, since we have seen above how Leclaire uses the object (a) (the Li-) precisely as a stand-in for an inadequate Name-of-the-Father (Miller fittingly entitled the final session of the seminar 'From the *a* to the Names-of-the-Father'). Indeed, earlier in *Psychoanalyzing*, Leclaire calls this object the 'concrete element that in correlation with the literal articulation but in the place of the name', or 'as substitute for the "name of the father"', performs 'a stable function in the economy of desire', providing the drive with its symbolic object as analysed above at the level of an integrated libidinal economy made possible by the symbolic phallus.[141]

In the seminars Leclaire gave at the University of Vincennes in the autumn of 1969, published as *Oedipe à Vincennes*, he seems to have further extended his insights concerning the '*re-père*' as formulated the previous year. Indeed I would argue that, primarily building on his 1968 re-reading of the case with the unicorn, *Oedipe à Vincennes* sketches out a general theory of Oedipus, a theory of the respective roles of the paternal and maternal functions in the genesis of an unconscious literal organisation, which at least tacitly functions as a critique of the unilateral dynamic of the Lacanian Name-of-the-Father of the 1950s and anticipates Lacan's full theorisation of the Names-of-the-Father in the 1970s. For Leclaire, the 'paternal function' in general is now to be seen as structurally 'situated between the singularity of the erogenous body and the universality of the law' or of 'discourse'.[142] The 'maternal function' serves to distinguish between the organic body and the erogenous body by instilling in organs of need singular demands for the return of the literal objects (or objectal letters) inscribed there, now giving rise to 'the [erogenous] body conceived as surface'.[143] This is what I discussed above in terms of the primary, imaginary, layer of inscription. The paternal function serves to 'assure' this abstraction from the organic by 'cleaving' their relation.[144]

At the same time that it cleaves their relation, however, the paternal function 'permits a fantasy to give rise to a libidinal organisation', using fantasy to fold sexuality back onto the body's singularity and materiality by 'conjoining', in a 'concrete manner', the 'universality of certain pre-existent fantasies', such as those of 'seduction, castration, or even murder', with what is 'singular' or particular to an erogenous body.[145] This gives rise to what Leclaire calls a 'singular fantasy presiding over the libidinal organisation of the individual'.[146] In the example above, we saw how Liliane carries out the paternal function for Philippe, relaying between the erogenous body produced by Philippe's relation to his mother and the universality of discourse together with its accompanying fantasy formations (centring above all on sexual difference or the symbolic phallus). Leclaire argues in these seminars that the paternal function does this by being inclusively-excluded (extimately) from the body's zones or singularities, providing them with the differential logic of their relations and thereby counting them as a set (functioning as 'the name of one's own set', cf. Poord'jeli),[147] as we have seen above regarding the paternal function (Liliane) as letter-object (phallus), or 'letter of the absence of the letter'.[148] Thus, while the paternal function cuts the body off from itself qua organic need, it also prepares for language's fantasmatic *return* to the body; the paternal function opens the body up to the universality of discourse but in a twofold movement which partially returns to its material singularity. We will see how it does this for Leclaire in section 3.5 below, as it constitutes Leclaire's theory of fantasy (the split-subject's conjunctive-disjunctive relation to the object (a)).

In *Anti-Oedipus*, Deleuze and Guattari approvingly refer to these seminars.[149] In what follows, I will show that this is because, prior to *Anti-Oedipus* and before Guattari, *The Logic of Sense* was already creatively engaging the work of the Lacanian school and Leclaire's work in particular, in an attempt to reconceptualise the Lacanian account of the Oedipus complex.

## *Notes*

1. Freud, 'Three Essays', p. 226
2. Freud, 'The Ego and the Id', p. 371.
3. Ibid., p. 371.
4. Freud, 'Three Essays', p. 207.
5. Ibid., p. 207.
6. See Freud, 'Three Essays'.
7. Ibid., p. 219.
8. Lacan, Seminar XI, p. 189.
9. This is amply documented for instance in Freud's case study 'Little Hans'.
10. Lévi-Strauss, *Elementary Structures*, p. 12.
11. Lévi-Strauss, *Structural Anthropology, Vol. 1*, p. 34. I borrow this quotation from Bowden (2011).
12. Ibid., p. 182.
13. Lévi-Strauss examines the interdependence of nature and culture in the incest taboo in Chapters 1–2 of *Elementary Structures*.
14. Ibid., p. 11. Lévi-Strauss' reasoning is that 'the sexual is man's only instinct requiring the stimulation of another person' (p. 11) and so is inherently social. He is careful to explain that the cultural does not actually enter the domain of nature, nor vice versa, but that nature and culture cross over each other at this juncture (p. 11).
15. Lacan, Seminar XI, p. 181.
16. Lévi-Strauss, quoted in Bowden (2011), p. 182 n. 8.
17. Ibid., pp. 180–9. In Seminars V–VI, Lacan also repeatedly invokes Lévi-Strauss' *Elementary Structures* when discussing Melanie Klein's

account of infantile sexuality, which points to a far more self-sufficient process of maturation than does Lacan's, and which Lacan systematically associates in these seminars with the imaginary.
18. See Lacan's 'Subversion of the Subject', p. 317.
19. Butler, in *Subjects of Desire*, p. 192, argues that this is derived from the work of Kojève, who opposes biological or animal need to human desire, and like Lacan this distinction manifests itself for Kojève through speech.
20. See Lacan's Seminar I: 'speech [is] a function of recognition [...] Speech is that dimension through which the desire of the subject is authentically integrated on to the symbolic plane. It is only once it is formulated, named in the presence of the other, that desire, whatever it is, is recognised in the full sense of the term. It is not a question of the satisfaction of desire, nor of I know not what [...] love, but, quite precisely, of the recognition of desire' (p. 183).
21. Lacan, 'The Signification of the Phallus', p. 317.
22. Indeed, 'demand cuts off the need from [...] life', see Lacan, 'The Direction of the Treatment', pp. 292–3.
23. Lacan, 'The Signification of the Phallus', p. 318.
24. Quoted in Butler, *Subjects of Desire*, p. 76. This builds on Hegel's dialectic of recognition, as developed in the *Phenomenology of Spirit*.
25. Freud, 'Three Essays', p. 223.
26. Lacan, Seminar IV, p. 269. Translations from the still untranslated Seminar IV are mine.
27. Ibid., p. 85. Chiesa, in *Subjectivity and Otherness*, p. 64, argues that the dual infant-mother relation of early infancy is always from the beginning marked by a third term since the mother already lacks the symbolic phallus in the symbolic (her proper dimension). Hence, in Seminar IV Lacan speaks of the agency of the 'symbolic mother' (p. 269) even if the infant relates to her as an imaginary phallus during the stage of frustration (on this last point see also Chiesa, ibid., p. 64). This puts the infant in the strange position of straddling two dimensions – imaginary and symbolic – thanks to the agency of the mother's desire.
28. Lacan, 'Subversion of the Subject', p. 345. See also Lacan, Seminar IV, p. 169.
29. Lacan, Seminar IV, p. 269.
30. Ibid. pp. 54–6, p. 269.
31. Chiesa, in *Subjectivity and Otherness*, p. 75, makes this point in the following way: the mother is *really* deprived only when she lacks *symbolically*. The vagina is only a real lack from the viewpoint of the symbolic, but in the symbolic it is a real lack nonetheless. Or, put otherwise, it is a real lack of a symbolic object. It can also be noted that the protuberance of the penis offers a *Gestaltic* basis for figuring

sexual difference phallically, whereby sex is phallically defined by the absence or presence of the penis (rather than of the vagina).
32. Lacan, Seminar IV, p. 56.
33. Lacan, 'The Signification of the Phallus', p. 320.
34. Ibid., p. 320.
35. The girl internalises the Oedipus complex in a different manner because her symbolic castration relates to her real privation while the boy's relates to his loss of the imaginary phallus (namely his imaginary identification with the mother). The girl loses this imaginary identification too but continues to embody or 'be' the phallus, while the boy 'has' the phallus. On the opposition of having/being the phallus see Fink, *The Lacanian Subject*, and Chiesa, *Subjectivity and Otherness*, pp. 86–7; on the feminine Oedipus complex see Chiesa, ibid.
36. Consequently, the boy will 'have' the phallus, like the father, thanks to his male sex organ, and be desired by women because of the assignation of the symbolic phallus – namely the object of desire of the mother, on which the infant girl's erogenous zones were centred from an early age – to the male sex organ. On the contrary, the girl will continue to 'be' the phallus, but now only as the object of desire of men. Men see in the woman a real privation associated with the woman's desire for the man's own symbolic phallus, allowing the man to continue centring his erogenous zones on the (mother's, and now woman's) desire for the phallus which the male infant 'was' for the mother and which the adult male 'has' in opposition to the woman.
37. Lacan, Seminar IV, p. 67.
38. Ibid., p. 68.
39. Freud, 'Beyond the Pleasure Principle', p. 283.
40. Ibid., p. 285.
41. Ibid. p. 285.
42. For Lacan the symbol of frustration is indifferent to the mother's biological sex (see Seminar IV, p. 67), but nonetheless we see that it will come to centre on her sex thanks to this pre-symbolising of her sexual difference.
43. It is symbolic since it relies on its binary coupling with the system of relations constituting the symbolic, but it does not yet fully belong to language (hence proto-symbol).
44. This means the infant has undergone what Freud terms 'primal repression' (see 'Repression', p. 147), and the birth of the unconscious order (see 'The Unconscious').
45. See Lacan, Seminar IV, p. 85.
46. Freud, 'Beyond the Pleasure Principle', p. 284.
47. Ibid., p. 285.
48. Ibid., p. 284. Freud also notes that Ernst started associating the two with his own appearance and disappearance in a mirror, showing that

indeed the mirror stage was itself symbolised by Ernst, paving the way for his entry into the symbolic order (p. 284, n. 1).
49. Ibid., p. 277.
50. Ibid., p. 277. This derives from the fundamental principle, in Freud, that pleasure is associated with a 'diminution' in the 'quantity of excitation', and unpleasure with an 'increase' (p. 276). This comes from Freud's early 'Project for a Scientific Psychology'.
51. Freud, 'Beyond the Pleasure Principle', p. 300.
52. This term, along with the Name-of-the-Father, are discussed in terms of the relation of the signifier to the signified in 'On a Question Preliminary to any Possible Treatment of Psychosis'. The paternal 'metaphor' names the process of deriving a repressed signified (the Desire-of-the-Mother) from the paternal signifier (the Name-of-the-Father). For a helpful discussion of these points see Lemaire, *Jacques Lacan*, Chapters 7–8.
53. This is taken from a summary of Seminar V published in *Bulletin de Psychologie*, 1956–7, quoted in Lemaire (1996, p. 83).
54. As Chiesa puts it in *Subjectivity and Otherness*, quoting Lacan, 'nobody has ever fully occupied the paternal function [...] [B]eing a father [...] means being a "real person covered by a symbol"' (p. 81).
55. As Fink explains in *The Lacanian Subject*, p. 53, the proper name functions for Lacan as a 'suture', naming something that does not yet exist but which will come to exist by this very interpellation into a symbolically structured reality.
56. Furthermore he posits the letter in a relation of co-dependence with not only the object but also the subject, as discussed in section 1.3.
57. Eyers, in *Post-Rationalism*, pp. 18–23, has recently made this claim, considering Leclaire's letter-object intrication to go further towards immanentising the psychoanalytic conception of the object than one finds in Lacan's own work.
58. In *Against Adaptation*, van Haute is particularly vocal about the subordination of the body to linguistic form in Lacan's work.
59. This is the Freudian term, also used by Leclaire, but in *The Logic of Sense* the term is translated as erogenous zone and I follow the translators' usage.
60. Freud, 'Three Essays', p. 169.
61. Leclaire, *Psychoanalyzing*, p. 45.
62. Freud, 'Three Essays', p. 198.
63. See Lacan, Seminar XI, p. 180.
64. See Freud's 'Three Essays': 'the skin, which in particular parts of the body has become differentiated into sense organs or modified into mucous membrane, [...] is thus the erotogenic zone *par excellence*' (p. 169).

65. '[The] whole body [as] an erotogenic zone' (from Freud's 1938 *Outline of Psychoanalysis*, quoted in Leclaire, *Psychoanalyzing*, p. 45).
66. On this point see, for instance, Laplanche and Pontalis' 'Fantasy and the Origins of Sexuality': 'When Freud asked himself whether there was anything in man comparable to the "instinct in animals", he found the equivalent, not in the drives (*Triebe*), but in primal fantasies' (p. 14).
67. Importantly, Lacan does not consider the genitalia to themselves constitute an erogenous zone to the extent that there is for Lacan no sexual drive proper to the genitals, but as we saw in the previous section the infant's entire erogenous body from the oral stage onwards is nonetheless proto-sexually marked due to its relation to the imaginary phallus.
68. The French term also carries with it the sense of an edge or border.
69. This stands for 'little other' (*autre*, in French), as opposed to the big Other (*Autre*) of the symbolic, namely the symbolic phallus (determinant of the structure of language, +/−) and incest taboo (as well as the cultural conventions of a society more generally) that will make of the mother a barred (m)Other. See Chiesa, *Subjectivity and Otherness*, for a comprehensive overview of the symbolic in Lacan.
70. See Lacan, Seminar XI, pp. 162, 177–9.
71. Ibid., pp. 166, 179.
72. Ibid., p. 179, emphasis in the original.
73. This is the phonetic distinction between the labial and dental.
74. Quoted in Leclaire, *Écrits*, p. 88. Lacan also notes the vacillation of the rim, its differential opening/closing motion (see Seminar XI).
75. Leclaire makes this project clear in *Psychoanalyzing*. See, for instance: 'the term *structure*, in its common use, is not altogether correct to describe what surfaces of the unconscious in the singularity of the cases with which the analyst is confronted [...] [W]hat is important for him or her [the psychoanalyst], above all, is the renewal of this structure in every singular adventure [...] [A] correctly conceived structural approach intrinsically includes the study of this moment of engendering of *an* unconscious' (pp. 124–5, emphasis in the original). Correlatively, Leclaire considers psychosis as the most 'singular' 'structure' (qua 'madness') to the extent that it does not 'accomplish' the 'renewal of the structure [of neurosis/normality]', since it lacks the central phallic function (see *Psychoanalyzing*, p. 125).
76. See his 'pre-psychoanalytic' text 'Project for a Scientific Psychology'.
77. Leclaire, *Démasquer le réel*, p. 58, translation mine.
78. We see interesting parallels with Deleuze's notion of 'becoming' here, as it is defined in *The Logic of Sense*.
79. Leclaire gives as examples the fringes of acidity of a taste, the quality of a particular shade of red noticed at the height of orgasm (and pre-

sumably within differential thresholds, between two qualitative limits of that shade), or the differential tangents of the curve of a ball cupped in one hand.
80. Lacan himself also uses this term – see, for instance, Seminar XI, p. 156.
81. This entire structure of subjectivity is clearly indebted to Miller's 'The Suture (elements of the logic of the signifier)', and Leclaire was fairly explicit about his desire during these years to give the 'suture' – Miller's highly experientially abstracted theory of the Lacanian subject – a *corporeal* basis (and arguably a more singular grounding), as I will show in the following section. Along similar lines, in *Time Driven*, Johnston characterises Leclaire's project as a 'balance between phenomenological and structuralist [e.g. Millerian] approaches to psychoanalytic theory' (p. 352).
82. Freud first develops and examines this term in *Interpreting Dreams*, particularly Chapter VII.
83. In *Psychoanalyzing*, Leclaire characterises the letter as 'detachable' (p. 101) or 'abstract materiality' (p. 89), abstract because it can be detached from any particular object as fleshy instantiation or iteration *of* the letter, but material because we are dealing with sensible differences that *must* be embodied by a physical object and cannot be merely imagined.
84. In 'Instincts and their Vicissitudes', Freud defines fixation as a 'particularly close attachment of the instinct to its object' (p. 119), which he says 'frequently occurs at very early periods of the development of an instinct'. However, later in 'Repression' (1915), he claims that fixation becomes 'attached' to the 'psychical representative' of the drive (p. 147), and Leclaire is following here the Freud of 1915.
85. See Freud, 'Repression', p. 147.
86. All three are also captured in Freud's notion of a 'thing-presentation', as developed in 'The Unconscious' (1915), which can have a sensible source that is olfactory, tactile, kinaesthetic, visual, graphic, auditory and so on. Leclaire endorses the breadth of this list (for instance on p. 93 of *Psychoanalyzing*). Leclaire's letter can also be said to provide the mechanism that accounts for precisely how Freud's thing-presentation constitutes-represses affect.
87. Leclaire qualifies this by saying that in fetishism one can usually contiguously re-link the fetish, through the chain of evolutions of the object, to an organically definable organ (see *Psychoanalyzing*, p. 41).
88. This tension between the former and the latter, the object and the letter, lies at the heart of neurosis for Leclaire. Any object, in the psychoanalytic sense, mixes both, but for him obsessional neurosis is marked by overvaluing the letter, while hysteria is defined by overvaluing the object (see *Psychoanalyzing*, p. 102).

89. In Seminar XI Lacan also emphasises this aspect of pleasure (see pp. 166–7).
90. We can say that fixation on an object is the result of a return of the repressed difference it covers over, a compulsion to repeat (and then re-repress).
91. Here, and in Leclaire's theory of the syncope more generally, we see close points of proximity with the Lacan of Seminar XI, in which he writes that whereas the pleasure principle is opposed to the 'real' (what I discussed above in terms of *jouissance*), which is 'impossible' (resistant to conceptualisation), the 'real' is nonetheless 'so present in [the pleasure principle]' despite being 'never recognised in it as such', as 'illustrated' by the 'hallucinatory' nature of pleasure or of the satisfaction of the drive, being as it is 'paradoxical' or conceptually impossible (see pp. 166–7).
92. Leclaire gives the example of the mother playing with the infant's navel and locating at the differential edges of the place traced by her finger's play an 'exquisite difference' marking that area of the body as zone, as well as giving it its object, namely the finger of a (typically heterosexual) other capable of repeating the sensation. Leclaire notes that for the infant's zone to be erogenised, it must also therefore be the erogenous *object* of the mother: the infant's navel comes to define the sensible-intensive thresholds of the mother's finger as zone. Here Leclaire is drawing on Freud's seduction theory, which Laplanche and Pontalis argue, in 'Fantasy and the Origins of Sexuality', he never fully abandoned but rather transformed.
93. Leclaire, *Psychoanalyzing*, p. 123.
94. As is well known, for Saussure the founder of structural linguistics, a 'signifier' is defined *solely* by its *difference* from the other signifiers making up a linguistic system such as a natural language, signifiers essentially being devoid of positive characteristics when divorced from this structure. See de Saussure, *Course in General Linguistics*.
95. See, for instance: 'By "letter" I designate the material support that concrete discourse borrows from language' (Lacan, 'The Agency of the Letter in the Unconscious', p. 163).
96. See Leclaire, 'Les éléments en jeu'. The sign is then held, for Saussure, in another one-to-one correlation with its referent as objective term (for instance the designated billiards or plunderer).
97. Laplanche and Leclaire, 'The Unconscious', p. 136.
98. Ibid., pp. 136–7.
99. Here Leclaire is following Lacan's method of dream interpretation. See Lacan, Seminar II, pp. 146–71, for his structural-linguistic reading of Freud's analysis of the dream of Irma's injection; see also Part V of Lacan's 'The Direction of the Treatment'.
100. Laplanche and Leclaire, 'The Unconscious', p. 137.

*The Body of the Letter*

101. We will see below that '**Anne**' stands in for 'Liliane', and the deer for the '*li-corne*', or unicorn, and possibly the Baltic herring stands in for the Atlantic ocean.
102. More specifically, Leclaire writes in *Psychoanalyzing* that 'she was impatient to satisfy her passion at the level of bodily needs. Philippe was washed, fed, warmed, cared for in accordance with the excessiveness of the maternal phantasms' (p. 76).
103. Ibid., p. 76.
104. As Leclaire puts it in *Psychoanalyzing*, at this age Philippe 'loved his feet' and 'took pleasure in their play' (p. 74), 'dreaming' of 'making his feet as hard as horn', which is also *corne* in French, 'so as to be able to walk without injury', or to 'run on the beach without fear of hidden pitfalls' (p. 74).
105. Ibid., p. 76.
106. This has not to my knowledge yet been commented on in the secondary literature. This view is further supported by a parallel interpretive strategy in evidence in Leclaire's reading of Freud's 'Wolf Man' case study in *Psychoanalyzing* and 'Les éléments en jeu'. The Wolf Man's faecal column, lodged in his bowels, articulates mother, father and self – penetrated, penetrator, penetrated-penetrator (the latter as unconscious unity of faeces, baby or foetus, and penis) – the anal zone being the site of inscription of the imaginary phallus which he attempts to use as a defence against castration or the symbolic phallus. He does this by associating the zone with the letter 'V', which has the function of initially locating there a defensive wolf-phobia, and later a fundamental fantasy through which he is born and reborn from his constipation and enemas (compare with Philippe, who is born and reborn from his head – see below). Furthermore, I will show throughout my third chapter that Deleuze seems to borrow this aspect of Leclaire's theory. McNulty, in 'Desuturing Desire', develops a very good reading of Leclaire's re-opening of the Wolf Man case.
107. Her physical attributes may also have had a role to play, her rotund figure and large breasts indicating a desire/appetite and ability to satisfy Philippe's own 'thirst', as well as being short and so physically nearer Philippe's own height.
108. At this point, contingency and chance become concepts worth examining, as does the kind of probabilistic structure that would be needed to account for how such a progressive selection and structuration of phonemic differences could take place as the one Leclaire describes. The statistical model of the Markov chain, which marries chance and probabilistic dependence on only the previous $(n - 1)$ link in the chain, could be a useful tool to analyse this structuration, and Deleuze and Guattari use it in *Anti-Oedipus* precisely to understand how the unconscious structures itself according to sequences of signs it

encounters (p. 42); this page refers to Lacan's *écrit* on Daniel Lagache, in which he invokes 'ordinal series' and 'this game of lotto'.

109. It should be noted that '*choif*' itself *already* contracts '*j'ai soif*', the '*ch*' and the '*j*' being pronounced in a similar manner in French ('sh' and soft 'j'), making it unnecessary for Philippe to have said '*j'ai choif*' rather than just '*choif*'. Philippe may have remembered this fact incorrectly or repressed it. This is important because the '*choif*' condenses the 'I' (*je*) into it, being the site of the re-birth of the subject.

110. Laplanche and Leclaire, 'The Unconscious', p. 145.

111. The situation is nonetheless more complex than this; Liliane will not offer a complete way out, and *choif* is partly a statement that Philippe would *also like to hold onto his primary imaginary identification* all the while finding what I call below a compromise formation between the imaginary and symbolic phallus.

112. In 'The Unconscious', Leclaire describes this as the 'capture of drive energy' stemming from the oral drive 'in the web of signifiers' (p. 167), when need is articulated as demand. On this basis, the oral drive, and later the entire erogenous body, can separate itself from the drives of conservation and become properly sexual. Leclaire stresses that it is not enough, however, to articulate this need verbally, as it is reported Philippe did almost constantly when with his mother. One also needs the *other's recognition of the desire underlying the demand* as distinct from the need, and thus *the recognition of the other's desire* in one's own demand for water (this builds on points discussed in section 1.1, regarding Lacan's dialectic of recognition). In short Philippe's mother satisfied his thirst only at the level of need, and by not recognising his right to desire and to feel her own desire and lack, he was unable to transform this need into an Oedipally operative demand. Hence, Leclaire stresses the importance of Liliane saying the words 'Philippe-*j'ai-soif*', which inadvertently and explicitly communicates *her desire and thirst* to him – above all '*Lili's desire for her husband*' (ibid., p. 168, emphasis in the original) – allowing his '*choif*' to finally become a properly Oedipal demand and his oral drive to now be signifierised and to desire. Leclaire (ibid. pp. 140–1) locates here Freud's 'representative of desire' (*Vorstellungrepräsentanz*).

113. We can deduce from this that '*o-o-o-o*'/'*da*' would have been only the first esoteric word Ernst constructed, and would have to be conjoined with others in order to take on the function of phallus proper.

114. Leclaire offers Lacanian theories of the body a more nuanced understanding, therefore, of its imaginary basis. Whereas the body's unity is generally considered as *imaginary*, at least for the early Lacan, Leclaire (and Deleuze after him) shows that there is also a way of *really* synthesising the body by means of a *symbolic* element. In Philippe's case history, the imaginary unity of the body *artificially* unifies it by

preventing it from desiring and thus from being fragmented by the drive. Once it desires, the body's fragmented zones are, however, reunified by the symbolic phallus inscribed on it (although 'unity' takes on a different sense at this level, being an ex-centric centring centred on the displacement of the phallus). For Éric Laurent, prior to his 'Radiophonie' from 1970, in which Laurent considers Lacan to first fully incorporate the advances of Baltimorean 'post-structuralism' into his theoretical edifice (and perhaps also Deleuze's work), the symbolic qua 'external point' impacts the body via the imaginary and identification (this is the Lacan of symbolic 'dis-incarnation', which he identifies in such texts as 'Science et vérité'), whereas the Lacan of 'Radiophonie' onwards states that the symbolic takes shape (*prend corps*) through a *direct* process of incarnation. In 'Radiophonie' Lacan speaks of the *incorporeal* body of the symbolic (and here we see a possible allusion to the Stoicism of *The Logic of Sense*), the body as made incorporeal through the symbolic, as nonetheless the reverse side of the symbolic's being incarnated. See Laurent's 2014–15 seminar 'Parler lalangue du corps', particularly the first session, and Lacan, 'Radiophonie', pp. 58–9. For a useful overview of Lacan's conceptions of the body throughout his teaching, see Verhaeghe, 'Subject and Body'.

115. Leclaire notes in 'Les éléments en jeu' that a small something lost from the body is the precondition for castration, as prefigured by defecation.
116. See Leclaire, *Psychoanalyzing*, pp. 137–8. The phallus proper is both letter and stylet, as we saw, and this stylet impresses itself directly on the body thus taking on an objectal function. It is also the hinge between letter-object on account of the third, phallic, difference of the letter (see section 1.2). But, to the extent that we can conceptually distinguish the phallus as third difference (and as 'stylet') from that phallic letter which distinguishes itself from all others (which are also phallic, but only thanks to this stand-alone letter), such as the priority of the 'Li' in relation to Philippe's other letters, it is also necessary ontogenetically to conceive of the phallus qua object-letter in terms of a *privileged letter* (for the obsessional, see below) – a letter of the lack of the letter – that comes to stand in for the object of the drive *tout court*. On the phallus as both letter and object see also *Oedipe à Vincennes*, p. 80 and *Démasquer le réel*, p. 97.
117. In *Psychoanalyzing*, Leclaire develops a similar point in a different context, writing that Philippe is 'born (or reborn) from his own head' (p. 86).
118. This delicate interplay of zones, particularly the scar on the forehead and the feet, and their links to the symbolic phallus, or castration, is conveyed well in a dream Philippe had a little after the dream of

the unicorn, and in which, running on a beach, a boy slips and a leg slides into a hole in the ground. Releasing a scream, he later finds that there is no injury or blood only a scar (ibid., p. 75). The foot is both forehead (bearing a scar) and foot, as well as standing for the entire erogenous body that upon castration, with the resolution of the Oedipus complex, is lost to him.
119. In Seminar XI, Lacan agrees that the two 'syllables' of *'licorne'* are the site of the fundamental conjunction within 'Poord'jeli' (*Poord* (*corne*) – *jeli* (*Li-*)) (p. 250).
120. Principally the women's bodies, and particularly Lili's, 'finally unveiled on the beach' (*Psychoanalyzing*, p. 78) as is Philippe's in correlation with them (now as finally desiring).
121. Ibid., p. 86.
122. As Leclaire puts it, '*lit*' evokes for Philippe the '"happy couple" formed by Lili and her husband', by which we can infer fully sexuated and desiring, 'in contrast to the more difficult relationship between his own parents' ('The Unconscious', p. 146).
123. Leclaire, *Psychoanalyzing*, p. 78.
124. This ties up particularly well with Leclaire's theory of the subject as the syncope or function of alternating commutation between terms.
125. Ibid., p. 81.
126. See also Lacan's Seminar XII, lesson of 7 April 1965, in which Lacan states that Poord'jeli is 'above all something which functions as a proper name [...] insofar as it can be fragmented, be decomposed, be rediscovered, infiltrated into the proper name of someone else'.
127. This structure is formalised by Leclaire in one of his seminars given around the time of *Psychoanalyzing*, in which he opposes the *binary structure* (*binarité*) of relations between phonemes to the *bi-polarity* (*bi-polarité*) of the relation of a phoneme to a zone's libidinal movement, such that between these two axes we have the entire unconscious structure at play: differential relations between phonemes and relations between phonemes and zones, and, it is implied, as a diagonal cutting across both axes, we have in turn relations between zones as mediated by differential relations between phonemes. See Leclaire, 'Compter avec la psychanalyse (1966–7)', pp. 97–105.
128. Leclaire, *Psychoanalyzing*, p. 85. In a passage that sounds almost Deleuzian, Leclaire calls these phonemes '"sensitive" in the physical sense of the term', i.e. as singularities or turning points in physical systems (ibid., p. 85). Compare with Deleuze: 'Singularities are [...] points of tears and joy, sickness and health, hope and anxiety, "sensitive" points' (*Logic of Sense*, p. 63).
129. I discussed this above, *corne* as both horn and feet, the body from head to foot.
130. Leclaire, *Psychoanalyzing*, p. 100. This phrase alludes in part to alter-

nating currents in electronics (+/−), the idea being one of continued movement back and forth between these two polarities.

131. We can even suggest that sense, which is expressed or produced by resolving two or more phonemic/graphic differences (such as *li-corne*), is what intensive quantity or *jouissance* transmutes itself into in the unconscious. While it is not necessarily true that we need *every* phonemic/graphic relation in the unconscious to be activated to express sense, and thus cancel a zone's *jouissance* or intensive spike, enough are brought into play for it to be possible to neutralise intensity only at the global erogenous level. As such, intensity is no longer repressed-fixated in local zones but on the erogenous *body tout court*.

132. Leclaire, *Psychoanalyzing*, p. 137.

133. The symbolic phallus is more fully understandable as the *difference* between the phoneme 'li' and the semanteme or designating element 'lit' – the marital bed of Liliane and her husband (the only other person for whom Liliane is 'Lili'), which is the point of conjunction (Poord'jeli) and later disjunction between Philippe (Poor(d)j'e) and the object (-li).

134. Ibid., p. 131. Compare with Lacan, Seminar XI, where he develops a theory of the subject bound to the 'topological community' of zones and 'topological unity of the gaps in play' in the unconscious, 'gaps that the distribution of the signifying investments sets up in the subject' (p. 181).

135. Repression is therefore initially the repression of *jouissance* (0) and the fixation of traits or sensible-intensive differences as associated with objects (1) (primary repression); it then becomes the repression of the erogenous body (0), or of its letters' sensible-intensive singularity, in favour of the generality of their phonemic/graphic differential relations (as long as they can enter into meaningful propositions – see Chapters 3–4), and the fixation of the symbolic phallus (1) (secondary repression).

136. We see this, in a formulation Leclaire is very fond of, in the internal syncope of the 'd'j', occurring between the silent 'd' of Poor(d)j'e-li and the 'j' of 'j'e', which is itself also a syncope, 'j'e', between body or letter (0) and object or phallus (1). In this regard Leclaire notes another of Philippe's dreams, in which he is doing a summersault, and which Leclaire views again as a fantasmatic self-constitution or re-unification, by throwing or folding his body (*peau*, *corne*, Poord) over itself (*j'e*), landing 'jubilantly' on the object (li), re-unifying its severed halves, symbolically retroactively overdetermining the unconscious, and stopping his 'fall' into the world (slipping down the greased rope). Poord'jeli in this respect acts as not only a self-naming but also a fantasm of re-unification, as modelled on Lacan's model of masculine fantasy as the desire for symbolic-real unity ($◊a). We can see that the

'Poord'jeli' form – which we must view as not yet castrated – appears in this regard to fuse Philippe and Liliane (*j'e* and li), and pleasure – the internal syncope (') – is displaced to the relation between them and the skin (*peau*, Poord), rather than splitting the subject from the object. The symbolic phallus is not yet distinguished from the zone's object, the object is not yet castrated or lost; there is not yet any distinction between body and phallic object, between 'Poor(d)' and 'li', as disconnected by the '–'. This means, in short, the *jouissance* is not repressed, occurring on the surface of the body, whereas in its castrated form, Poor(d)j'e-li entails the repression of *jouissance* which is now banished to the unconscious.

137. We see this, for instance, when Leclaire puts the accent on the death-drive – or desire for castration – conceiving it as, quoting Freud, the '"bedrock", the foundation of the castration complex', allowing the 'development and the organisation of the sexual drives', and '*finally* [...] giv[ing] rise to the development and structuring of language' ('The Unconscious', p. 144, emphasis mine).

138. This is captured by Leclaire when he says that with Poord'jeli, Philippe 'rediscovers his primal scene as often as he impugns it' (*Psychoanalyzing*, p. 86). Poord'jeli impugns paternal desire or the desire of the other (of the imaginary mOther), and thus attempts to evade the full brunt of castration. See also Leclaire, 'The Unconscious', p. 147.

139. Grigg, in *Lacan, Language, and Philosophy*, notes that by Seminar XVII (1969–70, contemporaneous with *Oedipe à Vincennes*), Lacan was referring to the Oedipus complex as '"Freud's dream"' (p. 38), which is also around the same time that he begins fully incorporating the object (a) into his conception of structure.

140. Lacan, Seminar X, pp. 336–7. This next seminar was aborted after two sessions and seemingly postponed to the 1970s – I will return to this in section 3.6.

141. Leclaire, *Psychoanalyzing*, p. 62.

142. Leclaire, *Oedipe à Vincennes*, pp. 26, 28, all translations mine.

143. Ibid., p. 33. In *Psychoanalyzing*, p. 48, Leclaire gives anorexia and alcoholism as but two examples of how this derailment of need can be vested in the very organ in which the self-preservative drive was initially located, both functioning as a form of self-mastery of demand.

144. Leclaire, *Oedipe à Vincennes*, p. 27.

145. Ibid., pp. 26–8.

146. Ibid., p. 28. In a later text, Leclaire will refer to this as a 'knotting' of the maternal and paternal. See Leclaire, *A Child Is Being Killed*, p. 3, translation modified.

147. Leclaire, *Oedipe à Vincennes*, p. 26.

148. In *Oedipe à Vincennes*, Leclaire explains that this term is the letter (0) in obsessional neurosis but the object (1) in hysteria (p. 26), which

links up with the point made in section 1.2 that obsessional neurotics overemphasise the letter and hysterics the object, while necessarily maintaining both. As we saw above with Philippe, the letter functioning as object (the 'Li') counts the body as a set in obsessional neurotics, but the *object* functioning as object does so in hysterics (or the objectal-letter for obsessional neurotics functioning as object of the drive, and the literal-object for hysterics functioning as object of the drive).
149. Deleuze and Guattari, *Anti-Oedipus*, p. 419, n. 26.

2

# Theatres of Terror and Cruelty: From Noise to the Voice

## 2.1 Artaud and Klein

While, for many, Deleuze's philosophy is synonymous with his concept of the 'body without organs', and even though he first explicitly develops this concept in *The Logic of Sense*, a large part of the present book argues that it is rather the *organ-ised* body – here figuring specifically as *incarnated structure*, building explicitly on Leclaire – on which his onto-logic of sense hinges. Nonetheless, this body only emerges later on in the 'dynamic genesis', the psychoanalytic portion of *The Logic of Sense* which provides a psycho-sexual account of language acquisition and of the emergence of sense, and first we must turn to the dis-organ-ised body of Klein and Artaud.

In *The Logic of Sense*, Deleuze develops his conception of the body without organs based on a reading of the work of Antonin Artaud. In the radio play *To Have Done with the Judgement of God* (1947), Artaud writes:

> Man is sick because he is badly constructed [...] there is nothing more useless than an organ. When you will have made him a body without organs, then you will have delivered him from all his automatic reactions and restored him to his true freedom.

Artaud considers the 'Judgement of God' to 'construct' the body as an organism, which is to say a body composed of organs. Above all, for Artaud, this means organ-ising the body in terms of sexuality. As Susan Sontag explains, 'Artaud demonizes sexuality in everything he wrote', opposing it to a 'pure body – divested of organs and [...] lusts'.[1] Furthermore, along with sexuality Artaud denounces language itself.[2] For Sontag, writing in Artaud is experienced as 'an agony' that 'supplies the energy for the act of writing', which 'give[s] form to intelligence'.[3] This in turn defines the body for Artaud in terms of a corresponding 'capacity for intelligence and for pain', and not a 'capacity for sensuous pleasure'.[4]

In *The Logic of Sense*, Deleuze similarly considers Artaud to develop an affective theory of language, which he argues sheds light on the schizophrenic experience of language and the body.[5] Above all, he argues that there are for Artaud two types of word: the 'passion-word',[6] which he calls a 'pure language-affect',[7] and the 'action-word',[8] which is either a 'breath-wor[d]' or 'howl-wor[d]'.[9] For Deleuze, these two types of word correspond to the two poles of the schizophrenic experience of the body: 'the passion of a fragmented organism' and the 'action of a body without parts [organs]'.[10] Deleuze explains that 'phonetic elements', which are the sounds made by words considered separately from their meaning or sense, and particularly 'consonants', 'act directly on the body, penetrating and bruising it';[11] here the body is *passively* subjected to and fragmented by external forces. Howl- and breath-words, however, have *'values which are exclusively tonic* and not written',[12] 'tonic' in linguistics meaning related to *pitch*. Furthermore, by palatalising consonants, which means pronouncing a word so that the tongue is near the palate, breath-words are 'incapable of being decomposed' or 'disintegrate[ed]', 'fusing' or rendering 'indissociable' the consonants;[13] this makes them *active*. Howl-words are thus phonetic elements when considered as 'active howls' in 'one continuous breath'.[14]

An example of this can be found in the following fragment of Artaud's translation of Lewis Carroll's 'Jabberwocky':

*Jusque là lò la rourghe est à rouarghe a rangmbde et rangmbde a rouarghambde.*[15]

We see here a breath-word – *'rangmbde'* – which fuses consonants and cancels phonetic articulations or differences by palatalising them as a single breath. As Deleuze puts it, we have in 'illegible and even unpronounceable' words such as *'rangmbde'* 'many active howls in one continuous breath', howls which are 'welded together in breath, like the consonants in the sign that liquefies them'.[16] The consonants have become active because they no longer react to the original phonetic elements but deform and reform them as a single breath. While consonants are bruising, passively affecting the body and making it howl with pain as the body is fragmented and sliced by each one, Deleuze describes consonants now within 'howls-breaths' as 'active howls' which are welded in breath. *'Rangmde'* welds howls (consonants) within breath and in doing so it renders them active and no longer bruising. While the aspect of pain in Artaud's experience and theory of language is well documented, Deleuze considers action-words to correspond to a 'glorious body', namely the body without organs,[17] which 'transform[s] the painful passion of the body into a triumphant action'.[18]

The same duality presents itself in the first chapter of the dynamic genesis, 'Twenty-Seventh Series of Orality'. Deleuze opposes the activity of Artaud's 'theatre of cruelty' to the 'Passion of the nursing infant' in the 'theatre of terror', 'whose unforgettable picture Melanie Klein painted'.[19] Klein considers the infant, during the first three to four months of life, to occupy the 'paranoid-schizoid position', to which Deleuze is alluding. Klein's notion of 'position' builds on Freud's[20] distinction between an oral and anal 'stage' in infantile sexual organisation but, unlike Freud, centres on the very earliest months of the infant's development.

I would suggest that Deleuze superimposes Artaud's work onto Klein's thought so as to make the earliest stages of development, as found in Klein's account, amenable to a linguistic rendering of these processes *without* unilaterally submitting them to it, as we find to an extent in the early Lacan. The intention is to give voice to the body (without organs) in its initial irreducibility to structured (i.e. non-schizophrenic) language, and not to hold onto a pre- or non-linguistic expressivity of the body, as we find in Klein's non-linguistic psychoanalysis. This ultimately serves Deleuze's larger project of developing a univocal theory of language. As he puts it, his turn to Klein 'is intended to sketch out "orientations" only',[21] by which he means a way of accounting for the topological or 'vertical' progression from the dimension he calls the 'depths' to that of the 'heights' (we shall explore this vertical movement in this chapter), and then, 'laterally', to the 'surface' (to be explored in the next three chapters).

## 2.2 *The Paranoid-Schizoid Position*

For Klein the paranoid-schizoid position is characterised by both persecutory anxiety and by processes of 'splitting'.[22] Anxiety derives from internal and external sources, which 'persecute' the infant. These are derived on the one hand from the infant's internal needs and drives, and on the other hand from external factors such as the frustrations and gratifications experienced by the infant in regard particularly to feeding. The infant develops an 'object-relation' with the mother's breast, which is its primary source of nourishment. This builds on Freud's notion of the 'oral stage' of infantile sexuality. Freud explains that the infant's first 'pregenital' sexual organisation is oral or 'cannibalistic', since

*Theatres of Terror and Cruelty*

sexual activity has not yet been separated from the ingestion of food [...] [T]he sexual *aim* consists in the incorporation of the object.[23]

The infant is 'cannibalistic' for Freud because the infant literally incorporates the other person, who at this stage is the food itself, as associated with the mother's breast.

Klein builds on this when she considers the infant to split the mother's breast (formerly considered as good) into a 'good' and a 'bad' object, in order to help it bring some semblance of order to and thus overcome the anxiety associated with the external frustration it experiences in regard to the presence and absence of the breast, as well as with the internal pressure from the oral drive.[24] The infant simultaneously 'introjects' into its body and 'projects' onto the mother these good and bad 'partial objects', or instances of nourishment and dissatisfaction associated with the maternal breast. The infant does not at this stage have a body as such, so mechanisms of introjection and projection help constitute its sense of its own body, which is not yet sharply distinguished from that of its mother. The mechanisms of introjection and projection indeed

> generate the psychological sense of the infant's relation to these objects which, at the physical level, is primarily bound up with activity in the oral zone (e.g., swallowing or spitting out), and later with activity in the anal, urethral, genital, and other zones identified by Freud.[25]

Thus the infant *physically* spits out in order to *psychically* distinguish itself from the bad object – for instance food that makes the infant ill – and swallows in order to incorporate the good object (nourishing instances of the breast). The infant projects its internal life impulses or needs onto the good and gratifying breast which it incorporates into its psychical sense of self, and to which it attributes these internal, satiated qualities. At the same time, the infant projects its destructive impulses and attributes them to the frustrating and 'persecuting' bad object.[26] Thus for Deleuze here 'everything is communication of bodies in depth',[27] an 'infinite identity' where 'contraries communicate' but only because the 'identity of each finds itself broken and divided', making each term at once 'the subject, the copula, and the predicate'.[28] The infant (subject), its qualification as feeding (predicate), and the flow of food linking the infant to the mother's breast (copula) form an infinite identity in the depths, from the point of view of the schizoid position.

Now, for Freud, the oral stage is followed by the anal pregenital organisation, bringing into play the opposition active/passive, which 'runs through all sexual life' from then onwards.[29] The infant's capacity to actively master its own 'somatic musculature' or anal sphincter puts it in a position of activity in regard to its own passive anal zone.[30] The infant now has a second partial object at its disposal. However, for Deleuze both the oral and anal stages of development must be considered as passive in relation to the activity of the body without organs. This is because Klein's good and bad objects are, for Deleuze, to be considered as having the same function as phonetic elements or consonants in Artaud's practice of language. Deleuze explains that Klein's mechanism of splitting is ultimately self-defeating,[31] since the infant's attempt to stave off anxiety will give rise to a never ending process of splitting the good object, as oriented towards an unreachable ideal of the 'good', since frustration and anxiety can never be completely mastered.[32] As Deleuze puts it 'one can never be sure that the good object does not conceal a bad piece'.[33] As such, in the schizoid position Deleuze opposes the introjected and projected partial objects, which are ultimately all 'bad', to the body without organs.

We saw at the start of this chapter that the body without organs manifested itself in schizophrenic language as an activity responding to wounding phonetic elements. Similarly, in his discussion of Klein's schizoid position, Deleuze also associates the body without organs with noise, rather than just with the partial objects themselves. This is indeed the definition of the 'dynamic genesis' – it is above all the genesis of language from the noise of the body in the depths of the schizoid position. When Deleuze writes 'And then the first stage of the dynamic genesis appears', this is already seven pages into his dense discussion of Klein's work. The 'dynamic genesis' is above all the dynamic genesis of *sense and language*, and so the entirety of Deleuze's engagement with psychoanalysis in this book must be understood as oriented by this question.[34] He follows this sentence with:

> The depth is clamorous: clappings, crackings, gnashings, cracklings, explosions, the shattered sounds of internal objects, and also the inarticulate howls-breaths of the body without organs which respond to them [...] This schizoid system is inseparable from the terrible prediction: speaking will be fashioned out of eating and shitting, language and its univocity will be sculpted out of shit.[35]

It is clear that if the body without organs is to be opposed, in the schizoid position, to the (bad) partial objects, its function is precisely to provide the unity they lack in themselves (the 'good' object). This is why Deleuze writes that 'what the schizoid position opposes to bad' – namely 'oral and anal' and 'introjected and projected' – 'partial objects [...] is not a good object, even if it were partial', but rather:

> an organism without parts, a body without organs, with neither mouth nor anus, having given up all introjection or projection, and being complete, at this price.[36]

While the infant's organism is literally fragmented by its internal objects, because introjection and projection give rise to a runaway train of splitting, the body without organs is capable of reunifying this fragmented organism thanks to its 'howls-breaths'.[37] If we examine the earlier quotation, we see that the 'howls-breaths' of the body without organs 'respond' to the 'shattered sounds' of the partial objects. We find this point made again in a different context right at the end of the chapter when Deleuze writes that, first, 'the maternal voice must be decomposed [...] into literal phonetic sounds and recomposed into inarticulate blocks'.[38] The role of the body without organs within the first stage of the dynamic genesis thus already points to the presence of linguistic or proto-linguistic elements within the infant's development. Deleuze's point seems to be that while undergoing processes of splitting, of projection and introjection, running alongside this process is a 'theatre' of cruelty in which the body without organs responds to the associated noises. Whereas Deleuze speaks explicitly in the earlier thirteenth series, on Artaud's art, about the schizophrenic being directly 'bruised' by consonants, it is more likely that in the case of infantile development Deleuze is referring primarily to noises *associated* with processes of splitting which carry their own independent affective charge (though later for the schizophrenic, Deleuze implies this charge may be directly communicated through noises).

If noises are passive, accompanying introjected and projected partial objects and the splitting of the body that ensues, the body without organs steps in at this stage to give noise, and indirectly language, a more prominent role in the first stage of the genesis. Whereas the body is passively affected by mechanisms associated with noise, the body without organs on the other hand actively synthesises the body precisely by acting on the noises associated with the body's splitting. Noises no longer have a merely passive and accompanying role, and now it is precisely *because* they are noises that they can function generatively and actively within the formation of the body. The body without organs appears, in this light, to be the organism's *capacity for being affected* specifically by noise.[39] While it is the *body* that is fragmented by processes of splitting, it is the body without organs that is affected by the noises *associated* with these processes and, secondarily, that can thereby use these noises as the basis for a reconstruction or synthesis of the body. Though, it is not the body fragmented by processes of splitting that is re-synthesised by the body without organs; rather the body without organs synthesises itself, as a 'pulsation' or spiritual plane doubling the corporeal body within the depths and offering it an alternative image of unity lacking at the level of lived corporeality.[40]

The body without organs therefore takes on a more prominent role than do noises because of its capacity to weld together these shattered sounds as a continuum. The noises themselves are shattered insofar as they each correspond to an instance of the organism's experience, which we have seen is characterised by a fragmented existence caused by the splitting produced by its mechanisms of introjection and projection. But they nonetheless all *share* their quality of being noisy. Or, to put it another way, since the body without organs is specifically defined as a capacity for being affected by proto-linguistic phonetic elements – i.e. noise – it can reconstitute a continuity of experience at the level of noise which is otherwise lacking at the level of the partial objects' other psychical and physical qualities. The shredding of the organism thus has as its reverse side the smooth continuum of the howls-breaths of the body without organs – the howls the infant produces in response to its passions and in order to unify its bodily experiences.[41] Indeed, the infinite identity of the depths is only possible thanks to the body without organs.[42]

Thus, by introducing Artaud's body without organs into Klein's schizoid position, Deleuze introduces a fundamental aspect of noise into this position lacking in Klein's own account, which for Deleuze is essential to the passage from Klein's schizoid (populated by bad objects) to manic-depressive position (associated with the good object).

## 2.3 The Manic-Depressive Position

If the body without organs provides an alternative image, or reverse side, of the body, it is only by being opposed to it and its fragmentation, and thus cannot directly act on nor help synthesise the body fragmented by processes of splitting. However, the body without organs prepares for the emergence of the Kleinian good object, which does function, in the depressive position and after, to directly act on and help synthesise the corporeal body. While the body without organs is thus opposed to the bad partial objects, it is not itself Klein's 'good object'. Nonetheless, it allows for the good object to emerge. In Deleuze's reading, the good object is actually something called the 'Voice', which emanates from a dimension radically opposed to the corporeal depths – namely the ideality of the 'heights'. While the depths are noisy, the Voice is a sound *distinguished* from the corporeality of noise,[43] because it conveys a *meaning*, even if at this stage the meaning is lost on the infant.[44]

While, for Klein, the processes of splitting characterising the schizoid position shred the infant's body (and for Deleuze construct the continuity of the body without organs as its reverse side), and centre it on an idealised and unattainable 'good' object, the positing of such an unreachable good object is nonetheless important for the development of the infant's ego, relieving the infant's anxieties even if they eventually provoke new ones.[45] Thus for Klein the infant 'projectively identifies' with the good object, even if it is only an ideal, which also allows the infant's shredded organism and its partial objects and associated feelings to begin integrating themselves by converging on the idealised good object.[46] In the depressive position the infant seeks to constitute for itself a complete good object and to identify itself with that object. Klein calls it the manic-depressive position, first of all because the infant experiences the good object now as something lost; it returns to the object it formerly sought to continually split, attempting to recover its phantasised unity, and this position is thus marked for Klein by guilt and sorrow.

Now, for Deleuze it is the body without organs itself which allows the infant to return to the object it had formerly continually split. Splitting means that the noises associated with the 'shattered sounds of internal objects' form a single howl-breath.[47] For Deleuze this has the crucial function of immanently generating the Voice. The shattered sounds the body without organs synthesises not only share the fact of their being noisy; some among them also share the fact that they are noises corresponding to people speaking. Deleuze points out that the infant is surrounded by a 'familial hum of voices which already speaks of her [the infant]',[48] and that 'from among all the sounds of the depth',[49] the good object extracts a Voice. What Deleuze means here is that among the shattered sounds of internal objects of the schizoid position, those corresponding to sounds made by voices are synthesised as the good object or Voice.

Even if the body without organs gathers together the material basis for the good object, it, however, belongs to a different dimension to the body without organs and the (bad) partial objects, which inhabit the 'depths'. The Voice is held aloft in the 'heights', producing a 'tension' between the two dimensions.[50] Deleuze modifies Klein's work by replacing the good object with the body without organs, but this is only a support for the second departure from her work. The good object, for Deleuze, actually belongs to an entirely different ontological plane to the bad partial objects, namely the domain of ideality, as opposed to the corporeality of the depths.[51] But even if Deleuze speaks of the Voice's 'transcendence in height',[52] the idealised good object must 'extrac[t]' a Voice from the depths, as already synthesised as howls-breaths by the body without organs.[53]

Bowden has argued that Deleuze models his conception of the good object on Lacan's notion of the *Gestalt* or imago of the maternal breast, as found in his 'Les complexes familiaux' and 'The Mirror Stage'.[54] He points out that Lacan's notion of the imago of the maternal breast is an 'unconscious representation whose content is given by sensation', which would seem to correspond to the Voice.[55] However, contra Bowden, it is clear that for Deleuze it is the body without organs and not the biological *Gestalt* of the breast, nor the Voice itself, which gives the good object its form.[56] For Lacan, the infant's pre-maturity at birth, or 'motor incapacity and nursling dependence',[57] direct it to 'identify' with a 'specular image' or form which, following Freud, he calls the 'ideal-I'[58] or 'ideal ego'.[59] This specular image is a form of unity, and it is modelled on the unity the infant's body experiences when in contact with others who themselves have greater self-mastery and motor-coordination than the infant's own 'fragmented body'[60] – namely his or her primary caregivers. The infant projects this experienced unity onto the other person as an imago or image of unity, and continues to identify with the form it has projected onto them, allowing it to further model itself on that person or form.[61]

For Deleuze it is rather thanks to the body without organs' synthesis of noise, and the ensuing extraction of the Voice, that the infant's body can integrate itself; contra Lacan, it is an *oral-aural* and not a visual synthesis.[62] Nonetheless the positing of the good object in a dimension of ideality, following Lacan's work, is of key consequence for the dynamic genesis since it allows us to leave the corporeal depths of noise and accede to the ideality of the Voice,[63] crucial for the infant's acquisition of language. At this point we must now leave Artaud's schizophrenic art and move to the perverse writings of Lewis Carroll, whose work lays the foundations for the rest of Deleuze's dynamic genesis.

## Notes

1. Sontag, 'Artaud', p. xlix. On writing in Artaud, see also Chiesa, 'Lacan with Artaud', who also discusses Artaud's equal criticism of psychoanalysis.
2. 'All writing is garbage' (quoted in Sontag, 'Artaud', p. xxii; also quoted, with a modified translation, in Deleuze's *The Logic of Sense*, p. 100).
3. Sontag, 'Artaud', p. xxii.
4. Ibid., p. xlviii.
5. See 'Thirteenth Series of the Schizophrenic and the Little Girl', pp. 95–107, which develops an opposition between the language of the 'depths' and the language of the 'surface', as found in the work of Artaud and Lewis Carroll respectively. See also Sauvagnargues, *Deleuze and Art*, pp. 61–5.
6. Deleuze, *Logic of Sense*, p. 103.
7. Ibid., p. 100.
8. Ibid., p. 103.
9. Ibid., p. 101.
10. Ibid., p. 102. They correspond to the two poles of the dimension he calls the 'depths'.
11. Ibid., p. 100.
12. Ibid., p. 101, emphasis in the original.
13. Ibid., pp. 101–2. Excessive palatalisation effectively cancels the concavity of the mouth and its capacity for a range of differential relations between dental, labial and other of its morphological features.
14. Ibid., p. 102.
15. Ibid., p. 106. This is a translation of Carroll's 'in the wabe' from the second line of the poem. These are portmanteau words which fuse a number of words, including the French for road, route and rule, as well as '*Rouergue*', a former province of France near where Artaud was living at the time. Deleuze notes that if Artaud started attempting to translate Carroll's work, he soon realised that, poetically, their projects were non-communicating, belonging to heterogeneous 'dimensions', even if some of the literary methods they use (such as portmanteau words) are superficially similar (ibid., pp. 104–5).
16. Ibid., p. 102.
17. Ibid., p. 101.
18. Ibid., p. 100.

19. Ibid., pp. 103, 215.
20. Freud, 'Three Essays', p. 198.
21. Deleuze, *Logic of Sense*, p. 216.
22. See Klein's 'Notes on Some Schizoid Mechanisms'. I am also drawing here on Bowden's thorough account of the first stages of Deleuze's dynamic genesis, in *The Priority of Events*, pp. 191–205.
23. Freud, 'Three Essays', p. 198. Freud continues: '– the prototype of a process which, in the form of identification, is later to play such an important psychological part' (p. 198). The breast is the basis of the infant's series of identifications.
24. Klein, 'Notes on Some Schizoid Mechanisms', p. 297. Bowden explains that the infant does this in order to 'make the [infant's] physical satisfactions, frustrations and other feelings [...] "psychologically meaningful"' (*Priority of Events*, p. 192). This converts 'raw sensation into an experience endowed with a certain quality: good or bad'. On this topic, see also Heimann, 'Certain Functions of Introjection and Projection', p. 155.
25. Bowden, *Priority of Events*, pp. 192–3.
26. See Klein, 'Some Theoretical Conclusions Regarding the Emotional Life of the Infant', pp. 198–236.
27. Deleuze, *Logic of Sense*, p. 220.
28. Ibid., p. 200.
29. Freud, 'Three Essays', p. 198.
30. Ibid., p. 198.
31. Deleuze, *Logic of Sense*, p. 216. Here Deleuze defends Fairbairn's thesis that 'in the beginning, only the bad object is internalised', quoted and rejected by Klein in *Developments in Psycho-Analysis*, p. 295. Contra Klein, Deleuze states that 'introjection [...] does not allow what is wholesome [the good] to subsist' (p. 216).
32. In 'Some Theoretical Conclusions', Klein explains that the infant will develop an 'unconscious phantasy' relating to the ideal good breast. She writes that in these phantasies 'the good breast tends to turn into the "ideal" breast which should fulfil the greedy desire for unlimited, immediate and everlasting gratification. Thus feelings arise about a perfect and inexhaustible breast, always available, always gratifying' (p. 202; quoted in Bowden, *Priority of Events*, pp. 194–5).
33. Deleuze, *Logic of Sense*, p. 216.
34. This point has been inadequately emphasised in the secondary literature (see Hughes, *Deleuze and the Genesis of Representation*; Widder, 'From Negation to Disjunction in a World of Simulacra: Deleuze and Melanie Klein'; Bowden, *Priority of Events*). It also helps answer the question that is often put to Deleuze's engagement with psychoanalysis concerning his turn to Klein. In the following chapters I will be reading the dynamic genesis above all as an account of the emergence of language from the body (and vice versa).

35. Deleuze, *Logic of Sense*, p. 220.
36. Ibid., p. 216.
37. Indeed, earlier Deleuze states that the two poles of schizophrenic language – the words-actions and the words-passions – can be identified with the two 'poles' of the 'depths' (ibid., p. 101) – namely the partial objects and the body without organs. Partial objects are splintered sounds or are associated, for the body without organs, with splintered sounds, and the body without organs binds them as howl-words within a single breath.
38. Ibid., p. 222. This is a reference to the writings of the schizophrenic writer Louis Wolfson. In Deleuze's preface to Wolfson's *Le Schizo et les langues*, he compares the psychoanalytic partial object to a 'fragmented word' (*mot éclaté*), and the 'complete object or the indecomposable word' he likens to 'breathing knowledge into words' (*insuffler le savoir dans les mots*) (p. 23). This is therefore a very similar framework to the one adopted vis-à-vis Artaud, and explicitly shows that the fragmented word is to be understood as engaging the psychoanalytic concept of partial object. Likewise, he opposes in Wolfson's psychosis 'breath' to signification: knowledge is not signified by the word but breathed directly into it (*insufflé*), and similarly the object is not designated by the word but 'imbricated in, fitted into (*emboîtée*)' it (p. 23) – here the partial object has become woven into the texture of language. Thus, for Deleuze, Eros (the pleasure principle) is knowledge in its state of breath and the thing in its state of being fitted into the word (*emboîtée*) (p. 23). This can be compared to the howls-breaths of Artaud's body without organs. It seems Deleuze's reading of Artaud is therefore in turn influenced by, and possibly influenced, his reading of Wolfson, which he also discusses in the thirteenth series (p. 107).
39. This appears to be a linguistic and constructivist adaptation of Deleuze's conception of the will to power in Nietzsche, as plastic (undetermined but determinable) affective form. See Deleuze, *Nietzsche and Philosophy*, pp. 39, 46–51, 57–9.
40. In *Logic of Sense*, Deleuze writes 'This depth [or "pulsation"] acts in an original way, *by means of its power to organise surfaces and to envelop itself within surfaces*' (p. 141, emphasis in the original).
41. Similarly, in his *Francis Bacon* (1981), Deleuze writes of Bacon's 'scream-breath' (p. 45), taken from his superimposition of Artaud's problematic of the body without organs onto the screams of Pope Innocent X painted repeatedly by Bacon. Deleuze connects this with the question of 'how to make colours audible' (ibid., p. 57). He argues that the body without organs is defined by thresholds not organs, a threshold being defined by the 'amplitude' at which an external force meets the oscillating 'wave' of the body without organs, and by the corresponding quantity of force of the organism at that amplitude

(ibid., pp. 44–8). (Here Deleuze is drawing on his earlier reading of the differential principle of the will to power in Nietzsche, in *Nietzsche and Philosophy*, Chapter 2). Thus the body without organs expresses organs (or colours) as qualities corresponding to interacting quantities of force. Making colours audible is therefore a question of translating silent (and 'invisible', *Bacon*, p. 61) forces into colour via the scream-breath of the body without organs which reacts onto or expresses its affections by painting them.

42. Deleuze, *Logic of Sense*, p. 220.
43. As Deleuze puts it earlier in the book, the ideality of the Voice 'prevents [language] from being confused with the sound-effects of bodies, and abstracts it from their oral-anal determinations [the oral and anal stages]' (ibid., p. 189).
44. The Voice, for Deleuze, 'has at its disposal all the dimensions of organised language' (ibid., p. 221), the only problem is the infant cannot understand it – 'It is no longer a noise, but is not yet language' (ibid., p. 221). We will have to wait until the next chapter for a fuller understanding of the ideal potential of the Voice, in contradistinction to noise.
45. See Klein, 'Some Theoretical Conclusions', p. 209.
46. See Klein, 'A Contribution to the Psychogenesis of Manic-Depressive States', and 'Some Theoretical Conclusions', pp. 203–4.
47. Deleuze, *Logic of Sense*, p. 220.
48. Ibid., p. 263. Here Deleuze is drawing on Laplanche and Pontalis' observation in 'Fantasy and the Origins of Sexuality' that what the infant hears is of key importance for their psychic development.
49. Deleuze, *Logic of Sense*, p. 221.
50. Ibid., p. 217.
51. For Deleuze 'The entire system of introjection and projection is a communication of bodies in, and through, depth' (ibid., p. 215). Deleuze makes the connection between the heights and ideality explicit when he compares the heights to Plato's world of Forms (ibid., pp. 145, 219).
52. Ibid., p. 218.
53. Ibid., p. 221. See also ibid, p. 217, which states that the good object extracts its 'form, that is, its completeness and integrity', from the body without organs.
54. Bowden, *Priority of Events*, p. 200. We see this most clearly when Deleuze states 'The good object is by nature a lost object' (*Logic of Sense*, p. 218), referring to an article by Pujol (see ibid., p. 224, n. 5). The 'lost object' would seem to refer to Lacan's notion of the imago of the breast as the infant's unconscious representation of the imagined plenitude of intra-uterine life, as found in his '*Les complexes familiaux*', which is close to Klein's unconscious phantasy of the idealised good breast.

55. Bowden, *Priority of Events*, p. 201.
56. In 'The Mirror Stage', Lacan explains that the *Gestalt* or representation of the breast is bound up with the human 'species' (see p. 3).
57. Lacan, 'The Mirror Stage', p. 2.
58. Ibid., p. 2.
59. Lacan, Seminar I.
60. Lacan, 'The Mirror Stage', p. 5.
61. Ibid., pp. 2–3. Lacan notes that this is before the imago is in turn 'objectified in the dialectic of identification with the other' (ibid., p. 2), which is brought about by language (ibid., p. 2). We saw in the previous chapter how the imaginary situation of the infant during the mirror stage is dialecticised by the infant's introduction into the symbolic dimension of sexual difference and language.
62. While Lacan suggests that the 'inclination of the plane mirror is governed by the voice of the other' (Seminar I, p. 140) – whereby the 'plane mirror' is a figurative mirror of imaginary identification – this happens only 'subsequently' through the 'symbolic relation' (ibid., p. 140), meaning when the infant begins to acquire or at least engage with the level of language proper. In short, Deleuze locates the voice at an earlier stage of development than does Lacan. I depart here from Bowden (*Priority of Events*, pp. 203, 253, n. 67) who does not seem to appreciate this point and the fact that Deleuze is attempting to grant the schizoid and manic-depressive positions some autonomy vis-à-vis the symbolic.
63. We can clearly see this reliance on Lacan's mirror stage in 'How Do We Recognize Structuralism?', where Deleuze associates the imaginary with the ideal 'heights' as opposed to the real depths (p. 172) and with the notion of an imaginary 'double', a term which Lacan also uses in his article ('The Mirror Stage', p. 3).

# 3

# The Three Syntheses of the Body: From the Voice to Speech

## 3.1 Introduction: Lewis Carroll's Three Types of Esoteric Word

In the preface to *The Logic of Sense*, Deleuze spells out his aims in this book. He writes that in Lewis Carroll's work one finds a 'chaos-cosmos' or paradoxical unity of 'sense and nonsense', 'but' that

> since the marriage of language and the unconscious has already been consummated and celebrated in so many ways, it is necessary to examine the precise nature of this union in Carroll's work: what else is this marriage connected with, and what is it that, thanks to him, this marriage celebrates.[1]

Firstly, this marriage of language and the unconscious – or this paradoxical unity of sense and nonsense – appears to allude to the work of the Lacanian school, which he later adds has 'completely renewed the general problem of the relations between language and sexuality'.[2] Secondly, to contribute something original, in light of Lacan's work – but also, it is implied, because Lacan's work has not yet reached its own ground (as conceived by Deleuze) – Deleuze is saying here that we need to turn to the work of Carroll, so as to examine 'what else' language and the unconscious are connected with. This third term, it is implied, is more fundamental than either language or the unconscious taken separately, underlying them both and accounting for the importance of their relation.

It is clear, not least from the book's title, that this third term is 'sense' or more precisely 'the Univocity of sense',[3] in short *univocal* sense understood as ontologically bypassing what are termed 'sense' and 'nonsense', or language and the unconscious/sexuality/the body, respectively, when taken separately. For Deleuze, univocal sense is both the ontological ground of, as well as being *produced by*, the articulation of the unconscious/sexuality and language, bodies and language or, more fundamentally, being and thinking. Throughout his work on Bergson and Spinoza, and as a way of moving beyond the dialectical and ultimately overly anthropological terms of Hegel (even as read through Hyppolite), Deleuze speaks of a provisional dualism of powers that manages to produce an insubstantial monism in certain conditions.[4] For instance in *Foucault*, he writes that Bergson's and Spinoza's philosophies both entail a 'provisional stage that subsequently *becomes a monism*',[5] a monism-effect that for Deleuze is also 'becoming' itself.

This is later formulated in *What Is Philosophy?* (1991) as the distinction between '*Nous*' and '*Physis*', the two powers or 'facets' of the 'plane of immanence': 'image of thought' and 'matter of being'.[6] In this latter text, at the level of *materiality*, and at the level of fixed *images* tied to propositional concepts, thinking and being are distinct or held in a relation of dualism (logically, that of denotation); whereas when immanently articulated, being becomes in-corporeal and thinking loses its image, disjunctively synthesising itself with the in-corporeal being it expresses through this immanent articulation.[7] I aim to show in what follows that Deleuze adopts in fundamental regards a parallel onto-logical framework in *The Logic of Sense*, which we must understand as an onto/logy of the very *difference (/)* thinking/being.

As what I tentatively term a plane of immanence,[8] sense points to an *absolute equality* and even paradoxical *reversibility* of thinking and being – in this book figured in terms of bodies-language – all the while *maintaining* the radically unsublatable or uncollapsible difference in kind (or 'non-relation'[9]) between the two, which can be used to helpfully characterise Deleuze's entire philosophical project.[10] The plane of immanence can be described as an incorporeal monism-*effect* and not a pre-existing substance; yet the equality-reversibility of thinking and being it makes possible onto-logically undergirds and founds both thinking and being as such. Hence, as monism-effect, the plane of immanence does not precede *either* the articulation of its two powers or series, *or* the ('constructive') *mechanism* by which such an articulation will be brought about, even if it paradoxically grounds them *both* in the monism-effect they produce. Moreover, this monism-effect does not ultimately fall back onto or privilege either half of the articulation; it is only a monism-effect to the extent that it maintains their *absolute equality* as well as their radical difference in kind *throughout* the trajectory that leads from this dualism to the third term in which they will paradoxically become reversible.[11]

To recapitulate these points, thinking and being are not immanent 'to' the plane of immanence, which does not itself substantially precede the 'immanence' (= equality-reversibility) of their articulation, being nothing else than this very immanence – though as an effect grounding the cause such that, paradoxically, they are *its* two reversible facets even if the plane does not precede their articulation. This is why the plane of immanence is inseparable from becoming: thinking and being are immanent (i.e. to one another) only as mutual becoming-other (the becoming-being of thought and the becoming-thought of being). This is also why, as ground or better as (un)ground, the plane of immanence does not constitute a substantial monism but an ongoing and never fully realised monism-effect genetically glued to its underlying provisional or quasi dualism. Thinking and being never fully become-other for this would cancel their becoming and reprioritise one half of the articulation; as such, they never reach a convergent point of synthesis, only an ongoing disjunctive one attesting to the internal onto-logical difference of the plane.

In this way, we should view 'sense' as *in-corporeal* (and not ideal), as bypassing the dualism of corporeality-ideality or bodies-language which is nonetheless its cause, being precisely the bypassing *of this dualism* and maintaining a direct relation to its radical difference in kind. Sense is the plane of immanence proper to language, it is a specifically linguistic monism-effect, or the index of the immanence of the articulation of bodies and language, as well as their onto-logical ground (a ground produced by the immanence of their articulation). As Deleuze puts it:

> Things and propositions are less in a situation of radical duality and more on the two sides of a frontier represented by sense. This frontier does not mingle or reunite them (for there is no more monism here than dualism); it is rather something along the line of an articulation of their difference: body/language.[12]

Now, my claim here is that, in attempting to understand both this deeper underlying 'what else' that language and the unconscious – or language and sexuality, in short *language and the body* – are connected with *and* by using the study of language and the unconscious to frame this 'what else', Deleuze simultaneously (1) uses the structural articulation of bodies-language as the constructive means with which to produce a plane of immanence ('incorporeal sense'), and (2) resultantly, he provides an ontological interpretation as well as a reconfiguration of the work of the Lacanian school. Both these points appear to be crystallised in Deleuze's formula 'Psychoanalysis is the psychoanalysis of sense'[13] – this strategically placed claim implies

## The Three Syntheses of the Body

that Deleuze aligns himself with structuralism-influenced psychoanalysis, and that his divergent conception of sense marks his point of disjunction with it.[14] Point (2) will be primarily examined in this chapter, while point (1) will be gradually fleshed out over the course of Chapters 3–5.

Regarding (1), here I side with Éric Alliez who makes the crucial point, albeit without developing it in detail, that *The Logic of Sense*

> gives a real dynamic for the [. . . ] equation Expression = Construction – with Structuralism as the contemporary [in 1969] form of Constructivism. A Constructivism which under-stands the sphere of expression as purely *linguistic* in the sense that there is *no structure without language* – verbal or non-verbal. [. . .] *The Logic of Sense* is going to be an incredible attempt to examine the conditions under which Structuralism [. . .] may be adequate to the expression of [. . .] [bodies'] affects and mixtures.[15]

Deleuze appears to be suggesting as much when he writes that 'Structure is in fact a machine for the production of incorporeal sense' (also quoted by Alliez).[16]

Deleuze develops his theory of 'expression' throughout his first monograph on Spinoza – *Expressionism in Philosophy: Spinoza* (1968) – written at the same time as *The Logic of Sense*, and it can be characterised as this immanent derivation of an onto-logically grounding monism-effect from a provisional dualism of powers. On the book's final page we read

> what is expressed everywhere intervenes as a third term that transforms dualities [. . .] What is expressed is sense: deeper than the relation of ['real'] causality, deeper than the relation of ['ideal'] representation.[17]

Whereas 'representation' is

> located in a certain extrinsic relation of idea and object [. . .] at a deeper level idea and object express something that is at once common to them, and yet belongs to each: [. . .] the absolute in two of its powers, those of thinking [. . .] and being.[18]

The absolute, sense, has thinking and being as its two powers or halves, while being the *product* ('What is expressed is sense') of their immanent articulation.[19] If 'structure' is itself a 'machine for the production of [. . .] sense', we can see how *The Logic of Sense* could be said to provide Deleuze's theory of expression with its corresponding 'constructivism', namely a machine or mechanism that can account for it.[20] In short, something *other than expressionism* itself is needed to articulate being and thinking in an immanent manner, which can be partly understood at this stage in terms of Deleuze's lifelong opposition to all theories of emanation, the notion that being emanates from a higher transcendent source.[21] Construction is needed along with expression, though this is not to say that onto-logical being emanates from the constructive machinery either; indeed, it is precisely by *twinning* both that we can avoid an emanative conception of immanence and sense.[22]

This conjunction of projects and disciplines is ultimately made possible, for Deleuze, by means of the work of Lewis Carroll.[23] Deleuze notes that the theme of this quasi-dualism of bodies/language 'runs through all the works of Carroll'[24] at the level of the opposition eating/speaking, which Deleuze gives a psychoanalytic interpretation, tied to the oral drive's evolution into speech.[25] For the purposes of this chapter, what Deleuze also finds in Carroll's work are three types of 'esoteric word' – which he characterises as connective, conjunctive and disjunctive, and associates them with three 'series' of the same name; it is using these words, and their associated 'series' or 'syntheses', that Deleuze attempts to onto-logically re-configure aspects of Lacanian psychoanalysis. Here I will examine the three types, before moving onto their insertion into the dynamic genesis.

The first, connective, type synthesises one or more propositions as a single series by 'contracting the syllabic elements of one proposition, or of many propositions which follow one another'.[26] For example, the 'Unpronounceable Monosyllable' (Carroll's phrase quoted by Deleuze) 'y'reince' takes the place of 'your Royal highness'.[27] The aim of this is to extract 'the global sense of the entire proposition' and to 'name it' with either a single syllable, with syllabic elongation, or with an 'overload' of consonants.[28] The purpose of this type of word is to connect or synthesise by naming *pre-constituted* propositions or 'sub-series' which are not modified, only counted as one, by this name.

The second, conjunctive, type, which Deleuze says is most characteristic of Carroll, 'circulates' between propositions or series and cannot be pinned down by any single one.[29] They are denoted by a profusion of names, or by 'indeterminate' names such as 'thing' or 'it'; but 'not one' of these denoting names 'is the word which circulates', which is 'displaced' in relation to all of them.[30] For instance, in Carroll's *The Hunting of the Snark*, although the tale centres entirely on the 'hunting' of this entity, it can never be fully pinned down at the level of denotation since we never discover what it is. It compounds 'shark' and 'snake', and at the end of the story, we find out that 'the snark *was* a Boojum' after all, yet we are not told what a 'Boojum' is.[31] Despite lacking in reference as well as sense, Deleuze states that 'as such' it is nonetheless capable of conjoining the two orders of bodies and language.

For Deleuze, while language establishes itself in a duality with bodies as external states of affairs – to which it refers and the sense of which it expresses – this dualism is also *internal* to language at the level of the distinction between the propositional dimensions of 'denotation' and 'expression'.[32] A proposition can denote a body – 'A cat is sat on a mat' – but it can also express a sense which inheres only in language, even if it is attributed to the thing – for instance 'The man is forgetful'. Although this proposition refers to the forgetfulness of the man, the adjective 'forgetful' is not itself a body that one could point to, but a sense expressed by language.[33] While 'forgetful' could qualify a physical quality in the man, a neurological defect and so on, Deleuze is concerned with distinguishing the order of corporeal bodies and qualities from the order of incorporeal senses: he stresses that the proposition's dimension of expression relates only to incorporeal 'events' which cannot be confused with corporeal qualities.[34]

Returning to Carroll, these two dimensions internal to language (onto-)genetically[35] *precede* and onto-logically found the very distinction between words and things, propositions and states of affairs. The whole of the 'Fourth Series of Dualities' suggests that the duality of language is not so much that of denotation and expression but, more profoundly, that of *eating* and *speaking*. Deleuze claims this twice: a 'denoted thing is essentially something which is (or may be) eaten'[36] and '[d]enotations refer always to bodies and, in principle, to consumable objects'.[37] Deleuze takes this from the work of Carroll,[38] giving it a psychoanalytic interpretation stressing the dual function of the oral zone, and onto-logically locating this organ as the very site of the passage from quasi-dualism to monism-effect.

Deleuze shows how, even though we are never presented with either a fixed denotation of the snark or with an expression of its sense, the snark's double status as blank word (or word = x) is *productive* of both the sense and reference of the narrative. Deleuze quotes from the following extract:

'They sought it with thimbles, they sought it with care;
They pursued it with forks and hope'.[39]

While both 'thimbles' and 'forks', and 'hope' and 'care' are nouns, only the first two are denoting words (referring to 'designated instruments').[40] While thimbles and forks are instruments to be used on physical bodies,[41] hope and care express an incorporeal sense which cannot subsist independently of bodies yet which cannot be reduced to them. Yet by using the 'it' of the snark – they sought 'it' with thimbles, they sought 'it' with care – Carroll manages to offset this key distinction, allowing these two heterogeneous dimensions to be conjoined as a 'convergent series' within the esoteric word itself (the snark or 'it'), without nonetheless negating their difference in kind.

By being displaced in relation to itself at the level of *denotation* – being both shark and snake … and Boojum, and ultimately an empty 'it' (or object = x) – the conjunctive esoteric word allows both bodies, on the one hand, to be conjoined (shark + snake = snark), *and bodies and language*, on the other (they pursued 'it' with forks *and* hope). It conjoins a number of bodies and allows *that singular set* of conjoined bodies (centring on the 'it') to itself be conjoined with language or the dimension of expression (they pursued it with forks *and* hope), precisely because their conjunction as a set (at the level of *bodies*) is *expressed by* the esoteric word itself (which belongs to *language*).

The third, disjunctive, type is Carroll's famous 'portmanteau' word, which levers open the dualism conjoined within the previous type and holds these now divergent series in tension with each other within the disjunctive esoteric word itself. Although 'snark' appears to be a portmanteau word (combining shark and snake), it is only one at the level of 'content' not at the level of 'function'.[42] It does not function as one since it can only hold together heterogeneous series by being displaced in relation to them, and as shark and snake is ultimately bound to the series of denotations or of bodies. On the contrary, 'Jabberwock' – the monster from Carroll's famous poem in *Through the Looking-Glass* – both compounds words at the level of content (jabber = a verb expressing an animated or voluble discussion, *wocer* = an Anglo-Saxon word signifying offspring or fruit) *and* functions as a portmanteau word.[43] It holds together in tension – without trying to resolve this enveloped paradoxical dual-status – denotable bodies (*wocer*) and expressible senses (jabber), which snark can only do by being *displaced over* bodies rather than *suspended between* bodies and language.

For Deleuze, Carroll's work has the advantage therefore of not cancelling the difference in kind between bodies and language, speaking/eating, and even of fashioning esoteric words which can account for how these two dimensions can come together in the word itself.

Deleuze rigorously aligns these three types of esoteric word, and their associated series, with *phonemes*, *morphemes* and *semantemes*, respectively, which are the three types of minimal unit composing linguistic structure. The question that guides the second stage of the dynamic genesis – the shift from the voice to speech – is as follows: 'to what extent can we link phonemes to the erogenous zones, morphemes to the phallic stage [or "phallus of coordination"], and semantemes to the evolution of Oedipus and the castration complex [or "phallus of castration"]?'[44] I will try to answer this question by examining Deleuze's three 'series' of sexuality – the connective synthesis of partial zones, the conjunctive synthesis of the global erogenous body during the phallic stage, and the disjunctive synthesis of the unconscious and pre/conscious systems with the partial resolution of the Oedipus complex (castration) – showing how Deleuze's syntheses of the body are aimed at immanently re-configuring the work of the Lacanian school, as well as how they contribute to his account of the genesis of univocal sense.[45]

## 3.2 Connective Syntheses of Partial Zones

Deleuze bases his overall account of the earliest years of infantile development on the work of Melanie Klein. While in the previous chapter I gave an overview of the schizoid position and suggested how Deleuze conceives of the move to the following, depressive, position, here I will demonstrate how the erogenous zones of an organ-ised body appear with the advent of the depressive position, in its reaction to the schizoid 'depths' of the body without organs. I will show how, in Deleuze's reading, this tension between the two positions lays the corporeal foundations for the infant's confrontation with the Oedipus complex.

In the first, connective, synthesis, the erogenous zones are constituted as uncoordinated 'partial surfaces'. Deleuze reminds us that while the oral and anal *stages* of infantile development involve the one being prolonged into the other, one must distinguish between *stage* and *zone*, even if temporally they are roughly coincidental, all three Freudian stages of infantile sexuality – oral, anal and sexual or phallic – emerging for Klein during the first year of life.[46] While we saw the anal *stage* encroaches on the oral and subsumes the activities and objects of the latter under the former, the oral and anal *zones* each 'isolate' a 'territory' and invest it with their activities – for instance sucking for the oral zone, excreting for the anal zone.

During Klein's schizoid position, the ego, for Deleuze, is lodged in the body without organs, which provides its own kind of synthesis of experience, as well as the great reservoir of libido feeding its mechanisms of introjection and projection. However, with the arrival of the depressive-schizoid tension between height and depth – now reconfigured as a manic-depressive verticality – the body without organs gives way to local egos 'bound to the territory and experiencing satisfaction',[47] which 'perceive' the introjected and projected partial objects of the schizoid position now as 'images' projected onto these 'partial surfaces' (the breast, and later thumb-sucking, for the mouth; faeces for the anus). Likewise, the drive now becomes partial even if it entertains complex relations with the other zones, and finds in its zone a distinct libidinal source.[48]

Deleuze thereby distinguishes the deep 'simulacra' or partial objects of the schizoid position, from their projection as 'images' onto the infant's partial zones or surfaces. We cannot even say the zones are 'cut up on the surface', since the surface 'does not preexist them'.[49] The condition for this production of partial surfaces is the arrival of the depressive position, and the subsequent transformation of the destructive drives of the depth – as tied to processes of splitting – into *narcissistic* libido. For Deleuze, this gives rise to the birth of properly sexual libido – libido which detaches itself from both the destructive drives and drives of conservation, and invests images as objects of 'auto-erotic' satisfaction.[50] Satisfaction is now tied to the *image* or self-perception of satisfaction, rather than to that of need as founded on the zone's access to the real partial object or simulacrum. Hence the partial object of the breast (the physical act of '*suction*') gives way to the self-perception or 'image' of the *satisfaction derived* from '*sucking*',[51] as found for instance in thumb-sucking which is the projection of the mother's breast onto the infant's own body.[52]

In the manic-depressive position, the egos or partial surfaces are offered the alternative of identifying *either* (depressively) with the superego or 'Voice',[53] as Deleuze calls it, *or* (manically) with these local and partial egoic-idic images. This situation recalls Freud's early paper 'On Narcissism: An Introduction' (1914), in which he postulates a hydraulic model of libido, whereby 'object-cathexes', which Freud considers to be the only properly sexual energy, are distinguished from 'ego-libido', as two poles drawing on the same continuous and finite source of energy (libido).[54] As Freud states, '[t]he more of the one is employed, the more the other becomes depleted'.[55] Deleuze fundamentally disagrees with certain features of Freud's theory of libido, since he considers sexuality or libido proper to only emerge with the construction of the surface;[56] nonetheless, the depletion of libido from the partial zones as it is invested in the good object, and vice versa, would seem to correspond to the 'vortex id-ego-superego'[57] and 'vertical' tension of the manic-depressive position, with the good object figuring here as superego and in tension with the local egoic-idic zones. Indeed Deleuze mentions Freud shortly after introducing the manic-depressive position.[58]

To identify depressively means the egos are unified in their shared centring on the Voice, while through this unilateral dependence are subjected to its vagaries, no less present in the heights than in the depths of the previous, schizoid, position. But now, the Voice subsumes and unifies the variety of fragmented experiences, lived as bad partial objects in the depths of the schizoid position, projecting them onto the Voice as polar opposites: *presence-absence* – associated with the infant's varying degrees of frustration vis-à-vis the mother or primary caregiver's ability to gratify the infant's wishes – and *unharmed-wounded* – associated with a now transposed variant of the problem of bodily unity. Deleuze stresses that unharmed-wounded points to a new nascent figure, that of the mother's body in its relation to the infant's varying ability to *coordinate* its partial zones. 'Wounded' means uncoordinated, and to mend the mother's wound is tantamount to coordinating the infant's erogenous zones.[59]

Conversely, to identify manically with one's own images (primary narcissism) fails to coordinate them, since the ego at this stage is fragmented into partial zones and in need of an additional unifying element. The infant has no way out of this deadlock. Closing oneself off from the vagaries of the absence-presence oscillation of the superego or Voice, in a bid to protect the local egos from frustration and anxiety,[60] is by necessity to fall into a state of uncoordinated, wounded, primary narcissism. The unreachable ideal of unity and wholeness promised by the advent of this new, depressive, position is therefore soon met with disappointment, by the infant, which neither pole of manic-depression can forestall.

This is the importance for the depressive position of the arrival of a third, properly sexual or phallic position, by the end of the first year of life – which Deleuze refers to as the, third, 'sexual-perverse' position of the surface, for reasons that we will explore in later chapters. If, for Deleuze, zones are inseparable from the problem of their coordination, it is clear that this can be fully achieved neither by 'indirect',[61] depressive, means,[62] nor through the two direct, manic, options available to the zones: 'contiguity' (the zones' 'topological' proximity to one another),[63] and the internal projection of the image of one zone onto another. While the direct means of achieving this may attain a certain integration of two or more zones, it cannot assure a global integration of the whole erogenous body because taken as a set, erogenous zones lack a shared experiential medium since they open onto radically distinct fields.[64] Without the presence of an additional element that can stand above them, the zones' sensory-experiential fields spiral away from each other, lacking any common measure.

Although the 'indirect' means of depressive identification does offer such a solution, we have seen the barrier it butts against. Hence, while privileging the indirect method, Deleuze immediately adds that 'it is nevertheless true that the *direct* and global function of integration, or of general coordination, is normally vested in the genital zone'.[65] However, we must not read this as granting the genital zone an innate, endogenous privilege and centring function vis-à-vis other drives, as we find in Klein, since Deleuze makes it clear that it has this privilege and directly coordinates the erogenous body only thanks to the *phallus*, as the image proper to the genital zone.[66] The phallus is not projected onto the genital zone in the same way that the images of the other (primarily oral and anal) partial zones are, being defined as 'an image that the good ideal penis projects over the genital zone' of the body of 'the little girl as well as the little boy'; '[The infant] receives this gift (narcissistic overinvestment of an organ) as the condition by which he would be able to bring about the integration of all his [or her] other zones.'[67]

We can understand these quotations, firstly, on the basis of the thoroughly clinically-documented psychoanalytic observation that the parent, particularly the mother, plays an important role in shaping the infant's ideas about its genitalia, insofar as the parents occupy a castrated, genital, dimension of existence which will be indirectly or at times directly communicated to the infant.[68] We will see in the next section that this overinvestment points to a strongly *Lacanian* influence.

Secondly, these quotations are to be understood in terms of Deleuze's adoption of Klein's work. What projects this image is what Deleuze calls the 'good ideal penis' of the heights (formerly the Voice)[69] – to be understood, following Klein's innovation, as the *combined* figure of the mother and father, or as Deleuze puts it 'mother provided with a penis, father with breast'.[70] For Klein, this combined figure appears during the second quarter of the first year, with the depressive position, as a phantasy of constant parental copulation (hence mother with penis, father with breast). It is on the basis of this phantasy, and the strength of its associated envy and jealousy, that the infant will be able, or not, to distinguish *between* the parents later on in the Oedipus complex, the phantasy sometimes accompanying the infant far into adulthood.[71] Whereas Freudian and Lacanian psychoanalysis emphasises the infant's disavowal of the mother's lack of a penis during the phallic stage – at between the ages of around two and five – Klein therefore locates Oedipal questions much earlier on, during the first year of life and at the beginning of the second.[72]

This overvaluation immediately brings about 'important changes' to the depressive position, in Deleuze's reading, initiating the start of the third, Oedipal, position, which I tackle in the next section. In short, the good ideal penis is split at this point into a mother and a father *image* – as the direct development of the phallus as image of the genital zone. Before I develop this further, it is helpful to both recapitulate my argument so far and to anticipate certain points developed in the next section.

The vertical tension of the manic-depressive position resolves itself genitally or phallically, which will give way to the production of a single ('horizontal') *surface*. It remains to be seen how the genital zone can do this both *directly*, which is to say *libidinally*, and *indirectly* or through processes of symbolisation and idealisation relating to the superegoic heights. But it is clear that the genital zone does not have this privilege innately on account of some instinctual drive to copulate, otherwise the phallus as image would be furnished ready-made by the partial zone, as is the case with feeding and excretion. The figure of 'secondary narcissism' emerges here precisely because, through the genital zone, there is a way to bring together the primary narcissism of partial zones and local egos bound to their territories, on the one hand, and on the other the depressive identification with the good object.[73] Insofar as the good object leads to the good penis, as that which bestows on the infant the gift of narcissistic genital overinvestment, he or she is now able – and indeed is encouraged – to shoot for both a *present and unharmed* good object, or rather, now, phallus.

Manic primary narcissism turns away from the vagaries of parental absence/presence, in short frustration, by satisfying itself with (uncoordinated) partial zones and objects. Overinvestment of the genital zone gives the infant, however, a sense of omnipotence and power associated with this increased flow of libido into the body or ego, *without* the ensuing loss of coordination with which it is usually correlated, according to Freud's hydraulic model. The parents' oscillating absence-presence no longer concerns the infant directly, since its unifying and convergent source of libidinal self-mastery is now located in the body.[74] Likewise, the mother's wounded body – the still uncoordinated partial zones, whose coordination the phallus still needs to carry out – is something the infant can set to work on rather than finding solace in manic primary narcissism.

The inadequacy of the good object of the manic-depressive position, being absent-present and wounded-unharmed, is now something that the infant of the third, properly Oedipal, position sets himself the task of overcoming, the 'good intentions' by which Deleuze defines the Kleinian Oedipus complex. Hence, Deleuze theorises that during this third position, the mother and father images will be respectively associated with the negative poles of the disjunctions of the good object: the father will be withdrawn again into the heights, as an *absent* Voice, whereas the mother will be determined as a *wounded* body in need of repairing thanks to the infant's wielding of the phallus. As Deleuze puts it, the infant will never again feel so good, will never again have such good intentions,[75] since for a brief while – extending to the age of around five according to the Freudian chronology – the paternal absence and maternal wound will have no direct bearing on the infant's own libidinal pleasure-unpleasure series or libidinal-hydraulic pump, since the entire phallic stage (Freud) or Oedipal position (Klein) will be marked by an – at first successful – attempt at erogenous coordination ('conjunction').

The term 'connection' can now be defined, which in fact takes us outside the bounds of Klein's work and prepares for my discussion of Lacan and Leclaire below. Connection refers to: firstly, the (ultimately unsuccessful) attempt during the manic-depressive position to, either directly (manically) or indirectly (depressively), coordinate the partial erogenous zones, or partial surfaces, as a single erogenous body, or 'physical surface'. This recapitulates my argument so far. Particularly as we move from the depressive position to the beginnings of the properly Oedipal position or phallic stage, this first definition of connection becomes bound up with four further definitions, which give it a decidedly *proto-linguistic* basis: (1) the connection, or subsumption, of images under a single zone as intensive thresholds of said images; (2) the early stages of the infant's process of attaching a phoneme, or phonemic difference, to each zone or intensive threshold; (3) the ensuing privileging again of the oral zone as the zone which speaks said phonemes; (4) the construction of the first, connective, esoteric words.

Deleuze particularly develops these points in 'Thirty-Second Series on the Different Kinds of Series', his Leclairian-Lacanian series, which he intends the reader to reconnect with – so as to complete – what was said about erogenous zones within the *apparently* Kleinian 'Twenty-Eighth Series of Sexuality'. In the later series he writes that sexuality must be understood as being serial and as having its own series – connective, conjunctive and disjunctive, with their associated structural-linguistic elements.[76] Insofar as the depths are tied to the drives of conservation, rather than narcissistically investing images of self-satisfaction, the depths are not, for Deleuze, serial as they are not sexual, the first, connective, synthesis emerging with the partial surfaces or zones.[77] Deleuze also gives us a more detailed description of the physical structure of an erogenous zone in this later series than the one given in series twenty-eight, which covers definition 1 above, which he then shows must be understood in terms of definitions 2–4 above, which I will now tackle in this order.

Firstly, an erogenous zone is marked by 'the distribution of a difference of potential or intensity, having a maximum and minimum',[78] specifying later that it is an 'intensive quantity'. While zones are described as 'singularities' in the earlier Kleinian chapter, they are here explicitly connected to the notion of 'series', as tied to linguistic-structure more generally, which Deleuze tells us is 'founded in the erogenous zone of the surface'.[79] This reference to language is at an initial level to be understood in terms of the zone's *differential* structure – its incarnating a maximum/minimum pole at the level of its singular intensive thresholds, and thus its ability to establish differential relations with other zones on the same basis. While he specifies in the earlier chapter that a zone's singularity is 'constituted by the orifices [. . .] marked by the presence of mucous membranes',[80] he qualifies this in the later series as 'most often' constituted in such a way, leaving room for a Leclairian-late Freudian framework in which the entire body is potentially erogenisable.

We should specifically not understand 'connection' as pointing to the linking up of different zones, however, which is reserved for the conjunctive synthesis. Rather, what is initially connected in the first series or synthesis are a partial zone's *images* or objects of satisfaction. The zone's intensive thresholds condition – and are initially determined by – the images capable of falling under it,[81] and the thresholds of each zone are to be seen as connecting or 'contracting' its images as a single connective series or partial zone.[82]

Secondly, Deleuze writes that

> what the child extricates from the voice upon leaving the depressive position [is] an apprenticeship of formative elements before any understanding of formed linguistic units. In the continuous flow of the voice which comes from above, the child cuts out elements of different orders [phonemes, morphemes, semantemes], free to give them a function which is still prelinguistic in relation to the whole and to the different aspects of the sexual position.[83]

Explicitly building on Leclaire's 'extremely interesting thesis', he later adds that erogenous zones can be viewed as marked by a 'letter', which 'at the same time, would trace its limit and subsume under it images or objects of satisfaction'.[84] A letter, or as he later expounds 'phonemic difference in relation to the difference of intensity which characterises the erogenous zone', thereby 'traces' the 'limit' of the zone and 'subsumes' under it its corresponding images, to the extent that a letter is defined by the 'relation' of a phonemic difference to the zone's intensive difference. While the (phallic) *principle* of this phonemic inscription brings us to the second, conjunctive, synthesis or series, phonemes extracted from the Voice are initially 'prelinguistic' in relation to the 'different aspects of the sexual position' – erogenous zones, the phallus of coordination and the phallus of castration – and, we must deduce, are initially inscribed on zones independently of their phallic centring. Fixating on the Voice upon leaving the depressive position, Deleuze notes the infant's 'extreme sensitivity to phonemic distinctions of the mother tongue',[85] while being 'indifferent' to the larger signifying units in which they are packaged and which structure them (namely morphemes and semantemes).[86]

Although the infant does not have access to what the Voice *signifies* ('all the concepts and classes which structure the domain of preexistence' inhabited by the caregivers, and which structure the phonemes, morphemes and semantemes composing their speech), and although he or she can only grasp what the Voice *denotes* at the level of the good object itself, or on the other hand the introjected and projected bad partial objects, the Voice nonetheless 'manifests' – through 'intonation'[87] or 'tonality'[88] – the

> emotional variations of the whole person (the voice that loves and reassures, the voice that attacks and scolds, that itself complains about being wounded, or withdraws and keeps quiet).[89]

The infant's relation to the Voice as good object – its absence/presence and its being wounded/unharmed – at the cusp of the Oedipal stage, is therefore manifested at the level of *phonemic difference*. These differences are attached to the infant's zones even if they remain pre-linguistic at this stage, to the extent that the infant's erogenous centring on the Voice as good object is entirely mediated by the Voice's phonemic 'manifestations' in intonation. Thus the infant's oral zone regains the privilege it had during the oral stage of the schizoid position – albeit no longer as the 'howls-breaths' of the body without organs – narcissistically 'enjoying' an 'essential privilege', to the extent that he or she 'would make an active apprenticeship of phonemes', associating them with zones, 'at the same time that [he or] she would extract them from the voice'.[90] Zones are therefore initially constituted as intensive thresholds, and at the end of the depressive position (prior to the onset of the Oedipal one), these thresholds will in turn have been associated with pre-linguistic phonemes tied to the manifestations of the Voice, on the one hand, and on the other to the images or objects of satisfaction corresponding to these manifestations.

Thirdly, the genital 'overinvestment' by the Voice at the start of the Oedipal stage must be seen as going hand in hand with this 'privileging' of the oral zone at the level of (pre- or proto-linguistic) speech. The infant's capacity to speak (in his oral zone) the phonemic differences attached to *all his zones*, allows them to converge on his speech. This privilege of the oral zone at the level of pre-linguistic speech is itself in turn founded on the primacy of the genital zone at the start of the Oedipal or phallic stage, since it is through this zone that the infant will forge a connection with the Voice (which the infant attempts to 'project' onto its genital zone so as to restore the good object).[91] Though as we will also see in what follows, the genital zone needs to *rely* on this secondary privilege of the oral zone at the level of speech in order to fulfil its Oedipal duty of 'mending' the mother's wound and 'restoring' the father (which takes place entirely through speech). This secondary privilege of the oral zone is lastly bound up with its being the site of Carroll's eating/speaking, of the quasi-dualism of bodies-language, as Deleuze makes clear in the first, programmatic, series of the dynamic genesis, titled 'Of Orality'.

Fourthly, not least because the zone's intensive thresholds cause it to 'contract' its series of objects, the erogenous zone is finally associated with the notion of 'connection' at the level of the first, connective, type of esoteric word, which contracts one or a sequence of propositions, naming it with a single syllable and extracting its global sense. Since zones are soon associated with pre- or proto-linguistic phonemes, it is not hard to see how one can bridge these two senses of 'connection' (esoteric and intensive). Freud's recounting of Ernst's famous '*o-o-o-o/da*' is a clear example of this kind of esoteric word, since '*o-o-o-o*' contracts '*fort*' as an elongated syllable. We see the same in '*Choif*', the contraction of '*Philippe j'ai soif*'. In this way, and extending Deleuze's work further than he himself does, I would hypothesise that connective esoteric words *phonemically synthesise* or contract the objects of satisfaction falling under the *oral zone*. However, at this stage the body still lacks the 'phallus of coordination' (or second type of esoteric word) which it will use to link up the body's zones as a global conjunctive synthesis or series. Hence I would maintain that the oral zone, and its connective esoteric word, provides the point of conversion of the drives of conservation (vested in the oral zone) into the properly sexual drives, which detach themselves from the drives of conservation and now fixate on (esoterically synthesised) *images* or objects of satisfaction associated with nourishment.

### 3.3 Conjunctive Synthesis of the Global Body

In the previous section, I mentioned that the overinvestment of the infant's genital zone preconditions his or her entry into Klein's Oedipal phase of development or Freud's phallic stage. It is now necessary to examine precisely how this overinvestment allows the infant to move from internally connected, yet externally and globally uncoordinated, partial zones, to a single erogenous body or 'physical surface'. This process, for Deleuze, is identical to the infant's traversal of the Oedipus complex. Furthermore, I will demonstrate how for us to understand the underlying mechanisms at work, we need to move from the Kleinian framework Deleuze appears at first blush to be seated in, to a (Leclairian and Lacanian) fully structural-linguistic framework.

To approach the Kleinian Oedipus complex, Deleuze particularly stresses her notion of 'reparation'. In Klein, reparation is bound up with the depressive position's reaction to the schizoid position, and refers to the infant's attempts to repair the mother's body, as wounded in the previous stage due to processes of splitting.[92] The body is slashed or fragmented into proto-zones during the preceding schizoid position, through the introjection and projection of partial objects or internal penises. Yet, Deleuze strategically claims that

## The Three Syntheses of the Body

reparation occurs not in the depths but on the *surface*, introducing this term at the end of the twenty-eighth series devoted to erogenous zones. In the twenty-ninth series he goes on to base his entire account of the Kleinian Oedipus complex on the infant's attempt to repair or 'mend' the mother's body – by which he means to coordinate his[93] erogenous zones and their images, as narcissistic surface projections of the partial objects initially introjected into and projected onto, or rather as, the mother's fragmented body. Being now projected onto his zones as images, the infant tries to mend the mother's slashed body – which is to say the partial objects fragmented by splitting – at the level of the coordination of his own body.

Whenever Deleuze uses the term reparation he associates it with another – that of 'evocation' – which is not a Kleinian or obviously psychoanalytic concept. The *reparation* of the mother's wounded body is, we must conclude, for Deleuze the *reverse side* of the *evocation* of the absent father or Voice (as its obverse side). Deleuze goes on to associate them with two parental object-relations or mechanisms, those of restoration and summoning, respectively.[94] The infant aims to restore to the surface, so as to complete, the depressive position's ideal of a fully present and unharmed good object, just as he or she wishes to summon the absent father with his or her 'evocative' (and 'restorative') 'phallus'.[95]

While 'images' as objects of satisfaction are projected onto erogenous zones, the image of the phallus, soon decomposed into a 'mother image' and a 'father image', is what is projected onto the genital zone. But we must be careful not to interpret 'mother image' and 'father image' as two largely distinct, partially gendered, and soon to be sexed whole objects,[96] as we find in Klein, nor even as maternal and paternal poles of a differential phallus (+/–), as we find in the Lacanian account.

This is because Deleuze explicitly distinguishes between what he confusingly calls 'pre-genital' and 'Oedipal' parental images,[97] as follows: the former arise at the same time as the mother and father images, and are produced through reparation-evocation; the latter appear only at the tail-end of the Oedipal position, and are genetically founded on the former. Since Deleuze associates the latter with 'semantemes', elements of language capable of denoting external objects (such as he/she), and the former with pure phonemes lacking any reference, it is necessary to postulate, (1) a layer *between* the combined mother-father image, or good ideal penis of the depressive position, and the whole objects of the mother and father who appear later on in the Kleinian Oedipal position; (2) the mother and father images precisely as involved in the dynamic which *allows us to progress* from the one to the other.[98] I will return to this latter point in the following two sections of the chapter, but for now we can understand this in terms of Deleuze providing Klein with the *underlying linguistic mechanism* which can account for this *movement* from the good ideal penis to parental whole objects characteristic of the Kleinian Oedipal position.

Thus I claim that 'mother' and 'father' images, at this stage, are primarily *positional orientations*: surface and height, as perceived *from the viewpoint of* the phallic infant bound to the physical surface. Repairing the mother is to coordinate the partial drives and images of the *physical surface*, whereas summoning or evoking the father is to bring the Voice of the *heights* down to (and thereby coordinate) the physical surface – literally by projecting the Voice onto the genital zone.

I would also argue that while Deleuze appears to be working within a Kleinian framework, what he primarily borrows from Klein is actually the *greater independence* from symbolic overstructuring which her work grants what Lacan disparagingly calls the 'imaginary' dimension of the Oedipal stage. As a consequence of this, by reading Klein and Lacan together, I would suggest that Deleuze gives the *imaginary* a *structuring* role with regard to the symbolic – in short, a bilateral engendering of the corporeal and the linguistic, as a corrective to the tendency for a unilateral inscription of the symbolic onto bodies in the early Lacanian account of the Oedipus complex. While Lacan criticises Klein throughout his seminars of the mid-1950s for overemphasising the infant-mother dyad, at the expense of the paternal symbolic triangulation of this dyad,[99] we have seen that in fact the Kleinian Oedipus complex is marked by what we can term an *imaginary triangle* (mother-father-infant),[100] according to which, as Heimann puts it, the infant 'meets with *two* persons, mother *and* father, and this situation includes their interrelationship'.[101] It seems to be at this level that Deleuze seeks to understand the Oedipus complex in a way that is both thoroughly *linguistic* and *structural*, as well as resistant to the aforementioned leanings of the early Lacan.[102]

Secondarily, Deleuze identifies in her conception of 'position' a *confrontation of dimensions* which, using Carroll, he locates at the level of the tripartite distinction of surface/height/depth (as correlated with the 'imaginary triangle').

Both of these together are used by Deleuze, I contend, so as to establish an ontological re-configuration of the Lacanian account of the Oedipus complex and structure of the unconscious. This emerges later on in the dynamic genesis. He writes that the Voice as good object 'provides the subject matter or quality of parental Oedipal images', being 'always the source of disjunctions', namely absent-present, wounded-unharmed, mother-father image, and even *height-surface itself*, insofar as the height within which it is 'lost' and 'withdrawn' constitutes its 'proper dimension', and does not pre-exist the *perspectival* failure to grasp it from the viewpoint of the (pre-castrated) physical surface.[103]

It appears that the Voice's function, as source of disjunctions, is entirely conditioned by its linguistic and ontological characteristic of being transcendent with regard to an individual who has not yet acquired language. The dynamic genesis is above all a philosophical investigation of language acquisition, which he believes the Lacanian school has not thought through with enough care. He indicates this a few pages before the dynamic genesis starts, writing

> as we shall see [i.e. in the dynamic genesis] [...] [i]t is this new world of incorporeal effects or surface effects which makes language possible [...] which [...] prevents it from being confused with the sound-effects of bodies, and abstracts it from their oral-anal determinations [...] Pure events ground language because they wait for it [...] It is what is expressed in its independence that grounds language and expression – that is, the metaphysical property that sounds acquire in order to have sense, and secondarily, to signify, manifest, and denote, rather than to belong to bodies as physical qualities.[104]

Being a projection into the heights of the (oral-anal) schizoid processes of splitting, as well as of their associated 'noises' or 'sound-effects', as we saw in Chapter 2, the 'Voice' is at an initial level to be viewed as an effect (not yet a 'surface effect'). Although the Voice is not the 'pure event' grounding 'language and expression',[105] it has a crucial role to play at the level of *providing the initial distinction* between corporeality and ideality at the level of a proto-language, of 'meta-physically' abstracting ideal sound from physical corporeality.[106] From the depressive position onwards, the infant is capable of distinguishing between brute corporeal noise and ideal sound as that which we saw phonemically 'manifests' the emotional variations of the good object, and it seems to be that for Deleuze it is on this (equally linguistic and ontological) basis that the infant is capable of distinguishing between the mother image and father image during the Oedipal position, as well as of conceiving of a good and lost object as such and, correlatively, a wounded mother.

Furthermore, it is not simply because being as onto-logical difference is provisionally divided into a quasi-dualism of corporeality and ideality that language and Oedipal processes must adopt this dualism. Rather, Deleuze strongly implies, as can be partly deduced from the quotation, that as soon as the ideality of sound is detached from the corporeality of noise – which has a developmental or ontogenetic basis – we have the precondition for both language and this onto-logical split (of what will become the plane of immanence). In other words, the initial emergence of the Voice *expresses* a quasi-dualism of erogenous surfaces/ideal height, one latent in onto-logical being but waiting to be expressed for the infant (and as culturally conditioned by the phallus). If the earliest stages of infantile development are discussed within the framework of Klein, as I have demonstrated in Chapter 2, it seems that the primary reason for doing so, for Deleuze, is to understand *how* the Voice emerges from the corporeality of bodies during the depressive position, and most importantly to understand how this onto-logical distinction it makes possible conditions the *very terms of* the infant's Oedipal relation to the parents. In short, if the Lacanian phallus is an at least partly linguistic construction – as I showed in Chapter 1 – then it is *ontologically* problematic for it to directly structure the oral and anal stages (as Lacan believes[107]), since the shift from the schizoid to the depressive positions *onto-genetically*[108] conditions the emergence of language for the individual.

Nonetheless, such an argument is ultimately intended to support an *overarchingly Lacanian* conception of ontogenesis and the Oedipus complex, one that is re-worked on the basis of this onto-logical problematic exposed here. Moreover, Deleuze relies on the Lacanian conception of the phallus – as modified by him – to explain and understand the immanently causal logic of the articulation being-ontogenesis-language. Deleuze argues that the phallus and the Voice are mutually exclusive: the zones do not converge on the Voice because it is transcendent with regard to the surface to which they are bound,[109] and so the 'phallus of coordination' must be literally constructed by an agent occupying the physical surface. However, once constructed, the phallus (of coordination) 'itself gets involved in Oedipal dissociations',[110] producing what Deleuze calls the 'phallus of castration', the Lacanian symbolic phallus. The

## The Three Syntheses of the Body

Voice, in its tension with the physical surface, splits the phallus open (vertically) while the phallus always attempts to bring the Voice down to the surface: these two tendencies – *phallic convergence*[111] of (physical) surface-height and the *Voice's* dissociative *divergence* of (physical) surface-height – are for Deleuze the two fundamental poles driving human sexuality. In short, during the Oedipal stage the zones cannot converge on the Voice because it belongs to the heights, whereas the zones belong to the surface and need a *pre- or proto-linguistic* 'phallus' (of coordination) to be located there to carry out that function.

At one level, the Voice can be understood as the Lacanian symbolic phallus *prior to castration*. Since castration ultimately *cements* the *quasi*-dualism of bodies-language (corporeality/ideality) by *embodying* the very distinction as a now mutually exclusive or *binary* and thereby *distorted*[112] psycho-physical *dualism* – which we can understand at this stage in terms of *thought's* repression of the erogenous *body* after castration – the Lacanian symbolic and *linguistic* phallus cannot act as such on an individual who is not yet castrated. This binary distortion of being's quasi-dualism is the condition of possibility of language as such, and if castration is linguistically mediated, for Deleuze following Lacan, the infant's castration *conditions* that which *will have* acted on him, namely language in its discrete opposition to corporeality.

Lacan has a distinction between two kinds of phallus (imaginary and symbolic), but for Deleuze they do not adequately capture the ontological difference in kind between pre- and post-castration. We must thus examine in detail what the phallus of coordination is for Deleuze, and how it can condition at the *pre- or proto-linguistic* level what will retroactively have been a fully *linguistic* inscription of the symbolic phallus (the Voice).[113] The problem is not so much that the ideal heights of the Voice cannot inscribe themselves on the corporeal depths, contravening the quasi-dualism of bodies-language, corporeality/ideality, since the physical surface is itself constituted thanks to the Voice's distinction from the pure materiality of the schizoid depths. The problem is more that the physical surface-height (Voice) relation is precisely the *pre-castrated* form of the bodies-language relation, and so cannot be treated in a way that presumes the infant exists in the same ontological space as the caregivers.

Deleuze signals the ultimately Lacanian nature of his account of the Oedipus complex late on, writing that in its evolution and in the line which it traces, the phallus marks always an excess and a lack, oscillating between the one and the other and even being both at once. It is essentially an excess, as it projects itself over the genital zone of the child, duplicating its penis, and inspiring it with the Oedipal affair. But it is essentially lack and deficiency when it designates, at the heart of the affair, the absence of the penis in the case of the mother. It is in relation to itself that the phallus is both a defect and an excess, *when the phallic line merges with the trace of castration*, and the excessive image no longer designates anything other than its own lack, as it takes away the child's penis. We are not going to repeat the characteristics of the phallus that Lacan has analysed in several well-known texts ['at once excess and deficiency, never equal', etc.].[114]

The italicised part is important because it shows that it is only excess and lack when the phallic line – that of the phallus of coordination managing the Oedipal position – merges with that of castration. Pre-castration, the phallus as phallus of coordination cannot be conceived in this binary manner, not even as the proto-sexuated +/− of the Lacanian imaginary phallus. The latter implies the infant need only tap into the mother's speech to convert the Desire-of-the-Mother into the Name-of-the-Father, whereas Deleuze will claim that more is needed to effectuate this conversion. As I will show in the next section, for Deleuze the *infant's speech* is required to bridge them, and in a way that is fully attuned to their ontological and linguistic difference in kind.

Nonetheless, we now have the resources to finally unravel the mysterious terms and processes found in Deleuze's description of the Oedipal stage of development. The mother image, as 'wounded', and the father image, as 'absent', is this essentially tied correlation of maternal real privation/paternal symbolic phallus, *when viewed from the perspective of a pre-castrated infant*. Indeed he writes that there is a 'sharp distinction' between mother and father images.[115] The mother's 'wound' or 'lack' is inseparable from the father's being 'absent', his withdrawing into the ideal 'heights', just as with his power to 'mend' the mother's wound through his 'presence'.

Furthermore, this paternal power comes from what we have already seen is the 'overinvestment' of the infant's genitalia, at the start of the Oedipal stage (by the 'good ideal penis'). Even for non-male infants, as we saw in Chapter 1, the infant is phallically invested by the mother as that which the mother lacks. Hence, the phallus, the father's genitalia when perceived in relation to the mother's, is 'excessive', overvalued. The (male and female, pre-castrated) infant's

## The Three Syntheses of the Body

genital zone, as 'excessive image', attests to this cultural structural imbalance, and their castration thereby entails the image 'designating [...] its own lack', as the girl and boy realise they were only invested by the mother on account of their phallic nature for the mother.[116]

While not yet binarised/castrated, the surface-height distinction becomes intensified through this 'sharp distinction' between parental images (and through the phallus they articulate), whereas the vertical tension of the manic-depressive position belies a *continuity* of height and partial surface. In the depressive position, the disjunctions subsumed under the Voice as good object – absent/present, wounded/unharmed – are all four located in the *heights* with which the infant *projectively* identifies. As we saw, this kind of identification fails to coordinate the zones because it does not relate to a global body, only to a transcendently unified Voice in which the infant's identity is alienated. It is only with the arrival of the phallus that the state of being wounded becomes associated with the *coordination of the partial zones*, and the state of absence with their *incoordination*. With the phallus, the zones establish a new relation to the heights based therefore on ('horizontal') coordination not ('vertical') projective identification.[117]

This actually *exacerbates* the Voice's state of always having greater self-unity (even if only as a unity-through-transcendence[118]) than do the zones, even those of the coordinated physical surface. Although self-unity is now sought on the infant's body itself, rather than through alienating identification with the heights, the Voice is now by definition considered as *absent* from the viewpoint of the (thereby essentially 'wounded') surface, if partly because it cannot by definition relegate itself to this dimension, and hence remains an impossible ideal and mirage of self-unity. This does not, nonetheless, prevent the infant during the Oedipal position from attempting this 'Herculean' task.[119]

In short, it is the *cultural overvaluation* of the infant's genitals that lures him or her into attempting to establish self-unity at the level of the surface – where the genital zone is located – and which re-establishes the Voice's disjunctions at the level of the split *between* the surface and the Voice itself, *exacerbating* the tension between height and depth (being's quasi-dualism) by positioning the Oedipus complex at this inter-dimensional border: the father becomes, by definition, absent (from the surface), the mother essentially wounded. The splitting of the good ideal penis into two images (mother and father) is in this sense identical to the translation of the overvaluation of the infant's genital zone into an apprehension of the very (castrated, linguistically conditioned) structure that motivated the parents (qua initially good ideal penis) to initially overinvest this zone.[120]

We can discern here a process closely analogous to Freud's primary repression, as examined in Chapter 1 using the case of *fort/da*. If the good ideal penis (combined mother-father) combines, for Deleuze, absence/presence and wounded/unharmed as a transcendent unity, then the mother image and father image replace *both* absence and presence (and, correlatively, the states of being wounded and unharmed). In other words, not only does the later Oedipal scenario, for Deleuze, imply a prioritisation of absence and being wounded, as associated with the father and mother images respectively, but presence and being unharmed as such become *inherently barred*, reduced to being a function of, or derived from, the former. Presence is the *presence of* the absent father, rather than presence *tout court* and in an absolute or unmediated fashion; similarly, being unharmed is the momentary *mending of* the wounded body (using the presence of the absent father).

Likewise, *fort/da* replaces both presence and absence, substituting the 'symbol of frustration' for what are now its two poles, which prohibits, via primary repression, unmediated access to an absolutely present and unharmed (in Freudian-Lacanian terms, non-phallic) mother. However, in Deleuze's Kleinian terms, what is repressed is rather unmediated access to the combined mother-father figure, and what the infant relates to now is both the mother *and* father (-image), rather than just the (paternally overstructured) mother as we find in Freud and Lacan. Lastly, we must note that this state of affairs, in Deleuze's reading, comes about with the arrival of the *phallus* – which we have noted is Lacanian in conceptual provenance – and we will see in due course how this phallic overvaluation is bound up with a process of *symbolisation* (the creation of esoteric words).[121]

I would also claim that the term 'evocation', as bound to the infant's attempt at phallically repairing the mother, serves no discernible function during the Oedipal stage unless we understand it in terms of the Lacanian notion of demand. The term evocation is not a Kleinian or even apparently psychoanalytic term, and is not required for the Kleinian process of reparation, yet it accompanies the term reparation whenever Deleuze uses it, and thus they seem to be structurally interdependent. At an initial level, they clearly reduplicate the excessive/lacking structure of the (castrated) phallus, since to repair the mother is to evoke the father, to repair the physical

## The Three Syntheses of the Body

surface is to evoke and summon the heights to the surface. Moreover, in his numerous positive discussions of the Lacanian notion of demand, in *Difference and Repetition*[122] and 'How Do We Recognize Structuralism?',[123] he speaks of it as a 'question', the '"question" of the phallus'.[124]

In a passage from a text by Lacan, which Deleuze refers to when speaking of the 'question' of the phallus, we find the line

> the function of language is not to inform but to evoke. What I seek in speech is the response of the other. What constitutes me as subject is my question. In order to be recognised by the other [...] In order to find him, I call him.[125]

In *Difference and Repetition*, Deleuze particularly stresses Leclaire's contribution to the notion of the 'question', which he claims in Leclaire is the 'fundamental category of the unconscious',[126] a discovery he considers to be of 'enormous importance',[127] and which he claims requires us to move away from Freud's view that the unconscious desires rather than questions.[128] Rather than desiring, the unconscious must question, and so we must view, I think, 'evocation' as going beyond mere demand, although demand is arguably the primary way in which the infant 'evokes' the Voice during the Oedipal stage.

In *The Logic of Sense*, I would claim that Deleuze adopts this framework when he defines the esoteric word as a 'question',[129] which must be 'enveloped' in and 'developed' by the esoteric word, as singular 'problem'.[130] To demonstrate this and substantiate my claim, I will develop in what follows a close reading of the function of conjunctive esoteric words as precisely the means by which the phallus of coordination attempts to bring together and articulate mother-father during the Oedipal stage, and as the very basis for their later castration when the esoteric word transforms itself into a disjunctive type. Thus, by constructing a conjunctive esoteric word, as phallus of coordination, a word which is bound up with demand and the 'question' of the phallus more generally – in short the *spoken interactions* between the infant and primary caregivers – the infant mends the mother's wounded body by providing her with an object (the demanding infant). This mends her wound by phallically centring her erogenous zones, just as it phallically centres or coordinates the infant's erogenous zones through her desire for the infant. And it mends her wounds by embodying the symbolic phallus she lacks, bringing the withdrawn Voice of the heights down to the surface where it functions to mend or coordinate – and temporarily satisfy or suture – both the mother's erogenous zones and the infant's. The infant mends her wounds by using his or her power of speech – and ultimately the construction of an esoteric word – to embody the paternal phallus, both at the level I have described, and at the level of language itself, using the ideality of its phonemes, morphemes and semantemes, which the infant cuts out of the Voice, to fashion demanding words.

As such the infant can be said to *literally incarnate the Voice*[131] or father image in his or her own body – which this incarnation thereby coordinates and constitutes – through the act of speech. Constructing an esoteric word is the process of incarnating phonemes, morphemes and semantemes extracted from the ideality of the Voice in erogenous zones. Rather than the mother embodying the paternal function through her speech (either with or without the real father), as we find in Lacan, it is therefore the *infant's speech* which determines its *own* paternal function.

As we can see, Deleuze's Voice – and, I will show, esoteric word – tacitly critiques and offers an alternative reading of Lacan's Name-of-the-Father. In contradistinction to its formal power and capacity to structure the drive through repression of the imaginary phallus, the Voice in Deleuze's account is marked by its *withdrawn impotence and neutrality* vis-à-vis the processes occurring on the surface. Reinforcing my earlier claims, Deleuze states that the Voice 'awaits the *event* [of castration] that will make it a language',[132] and as such it is incapable of linguistically carrying out the function of the Lacanian 'No!/Name-of-the-Father'. Even if, like the Name-of-the-Father, the Voice 'conveys tradition' (the paternal surname), and requires that the infant be viewed from, and inserted into, the viewpoint of their proper name (the domain of preexistence), even before they can understand what it means[133] – in itself it *fails to carry out* the function of the Lacanian 'no!/name'. As 'no!', it 'forbids without our knowing what is forbidden, since we will learn it only through the sanction [castration]';[134] as 'name', it is surpassed by the infant's singular *self-nomination/self-castration* – which occurs when the infant constructs for itself a new name by using an esoteric word.

While both of these hold to some extent in Lacan,[135] what truly distinguishes Deleuze from the psychoanalyst (or at least the Lacan of the 1950s) is that access to the symbolic (or the 'domain of pre-existence', as Deleuze calls it, structuring the Voice) is subjectivated in an always *singular* manner for the philosopher, contra the universalising tendencies of Lacan and his symbolic register. Summarising my argument so far, regarding the Klein-Lacan dynamic at stake in Deleuze's work, we can say that: (1) we have an Oedipal triangle which – though at a level of *greater remove* than we find in Lacan's work – centres on the *symbolic phallus*; (2) nonetheless, this *triangle is imaginary* to the extent that the father *does not directly* carry the symbolic Law/language with him, which must be constructed by the infant.

As I will now demonstrate in the following sections, if the Voice fails to 'forbid' because it 'awaits the event', and as such is not yet fully linguistic; and if, as I will show, the infant's self-nomination produces a 'castration-effect' or singular 'event'; then it is the *infant* who provides that with which the Voice can be said to impose its 'sanction' (castration), namely the event which makes of the Voice a language. The infant is retroactively castrated by that with which *he or she* provides the Voice (its linguistic function and power). Thus I aim to have shown in this section that Deleuze's ontologically grounded claim that (propositionally structured) language cannot directly impact upon bodies requires him to seek an alternate model of castration in which the infant self-castrates by providing the Voice with the 'event' that renders it linguistic and hence castrating.[136]

## 3.4 Poord'jeli as Esoteric Word

Deleuze refers to Leclaire's 'Poord'jeli' in *The Logic of Sense*, using it as a prime example of an esoteric word, one which necessarily begins as a conjunctive one (phallus of coordination) and evolves into a disjunctive one (phallus of castration) with the partial resolution of the Oedipus complex. His thirty-second series, which I have claimed details the structural-linguistic mechanisms underlying reparation and the Oedipal position, culminates in a short but dense reading of this case, through which Deleuze finally explains how the phallus (of coordination then of castration) functions.

Citing 'the secret name Poord'jeli, that a child gives himself (*se donne*)', as an example of one, Deleuze writes that

> the esoteric word in its entirety plays not the role of a phoneme or of an element of articulation, but that of a morpheme or of an element of grammatical construction represented by the conjunctive character. It refers to the phallus as an agent of coordination.[137]

If I showed in section 3.2 that the infant inscribes 'pre-linguistic' phonemes on his zones as 'connective series', we have here the means to understand how these connective series are 'conjoined' as a conjunctive series within a conjunctive esoteric word like 'Poord'jeli', as well as how the connective series' erogenous zones are capable of being coordinated by the conjunctive esoteric word acting as phallus of coordination.

By conceiving of Poord'jeli as an esoteric word, I would argue that Deleuze's primary aim is to incorporate Leclaire's theory of the *re-père* into his own framework and ontology, generalising it as Leclaire himself would do in *Oedipe à Vincennes* as a model for the paternal function as such, while also modifying it. Thus for Deleuze the Oedipus complex amounts to the self-nominating construction of an esoteric word. To argue for this, even if it is only implied, he must first of all be able to show how the conjunctive esoteric word can stand in for the phallus as such, and indeed become the phallus of coordination. While Leclaire articulates his reading of Poord'jeli with the Lacanian phallus, even if he tempers its universality, Deleuze will need not so much to do away with the Lacanian phallus as to show how the esoteric word can embody the coordination phallus in its entirety, and serve as an even less universalistic alternative to it. From a different perspective, Deleuze forges his notion of an Oedipal esoteric word by articulating Leclaire's conception of the letter, not with the symbolic phallus, but with his Carrollian theory of esoteric words – which is more fully attuned to the difference in kind between bodies/language or denotation/expression.[138]

To begin with, Deleuze conceives of letters as *phonemes*, and the esoteric word acting as phallus as a *morpheme*. Leclaire, on the other hand, does not make this distinction, explicitly describing the letters 'li', '*corne*', and so on, as 'monemes', which is another term for morpheme.[139] Whereas phonemes are the smallest units of *language*, morphemes are the smallest units of *meaning*, and morphology refers to the packaging of phonemes into larger and more complex signifying units, principally at the levels of grammar and syntax. For instance, in conscious discourse the morpheme '*licorne*' articulates the phonemes 'li-' and '*corne*' and derives a signified from this articulation, within a fixed one-to-one relation of signifier and signified.[140] However, we have seen that in Poord'jeli, each phoneme is open to or contaminates the signified of almost every other phoneme (e.g. 'li' signifies even without '*corne*'), such that we cannot even speak of signifieds which implies a fixity of relation with its signifier. As such,

## The Three Syntheses of the Body

for Leclaire, in the unconscious each phoneme functions as or *is* a morpheme, to the extent that its capacity to 'signify' (produce unconscious sense) is not limited to the phonemic relations sanctioned by the morphological conventions of conscious discourse.

Instead, for Leclaire, the 'syntax' of unconscious letters derives from the coordinated relation between the phonemic differences and the sensible-intensive differences marking zones, and thus ultimately derives from the symbolic phallus as that which is equally, or absolutely, displaced in relation to and behind all letters. The syntax of Poord'jeli, what holds its letters together, is the phallus as that which is displaced behind, or not identical with, every one of these letters, while simultaneously being Poord'jeli itself as this singular set of letters held together by the phallus.[141] Hence the phallus can be said to provide the body's letters with a single axis on which they can align themselves and through which they can form differential relations with each other, relations which are always both sensible-intensive and phonemic (or graphic).[142] This is what I analysed above in terms of the 'desire to drink' or the desire for castration underlying Poord'jeli. We must therefore view the phallus, for Leclaire, as itself a self-displaced or non-self-identical *signifier* ('letter of the lack of the letter') which provides the letters' *signified*, a signified that is not unitary but fragmented or displaced over all the (non-absent) letters, being as it is the unconscious sense *these letters produce* in their (intensive-phonemic) relations with one another.[143] In short, for Leclaire the phallus lies on the same plane as the letters, and morphemes are inscribed directly on zones.

Deleuze argues that we must re-configure Leclaire's correlated phonemic-intensive letter, and re-conceive it along explicitly phonological and phonetic lines as a '*bundle of distinctive traits* or differential relations'.[144] Each zone is to be seen as 'analogous to one of these traits and determined by them [the bundle] in relation to another zone'.[145] If I wrote in section 3.2 that phonemes are cut out of the Voice through an erogenous 'active apprenticeship', it is more accurate to say that a zone is inscribed, and defined as a 'connective series', by *a distinctive trait*. Being an ideal form cut out of an equally ideal 'sonorous *continuum*' (the Voice as such),[146] we must ask how phonemes cross the threshold between ideality and corporeality and come to be inscribed on bodily zones, thereby functioning as 'letters'. This seems to happen precisely by extracting from a phoneme its constituent distinctive traits which, in phonetics, refers to the material and morphological support of phonemes. For instance, Jakobson distinguishes, as mutually exclusive or as binary oppositions, between 'voiced' and 'unvoiced' traits produced by the lips (such as the English /b/ and /p/, respectively), as well as distinguishing between the labial, the dental (/d/, /t/), the labio-dental (/v/), and so on, which are determined by the morphological limitations of the mouth and throat.[147]

Furthermore, if a letter or phoneme is a *bundle* of distinctive traits, and each zone analogous to one or more of these traits as well as being determined by the entire bundle in relation to another zone, then zones can be coordinated on the same body simply by *phonetically sharing phonemes*. We can also reverse this and say that as soon as we have *phonemes*, which spread their traits across distinct zones, we have a coordinated body. This accounts for Deleuze's claim that in his critique of Leclaire, there is 'cause for (*matière à*) a new image (*nouveau blason*) of the body founded on phonology',[148] since it provides a way of explaining the linguistic structuring and coordination of the body, in conformity with the radical difference in kind between bodies/language, and without directly requiring the Lacanian phallus to do this. We must now explain how, for Deleuze, this works, which I will show is explained through his theory of esoteric words.

I already touched on how this happens in section 3.2: the infant initially cuts phonemes out of the Voice purely on the basis of its being the 'manifestation' of an 'emotional variation' of the Voice as good object, which the infant will associate with one or more of his partial zone's libidinal movements or intensive differences, since during the depressive position the zones projectively identify with the good object and in relation to this identification transform their partial objects into images. This means phonemes do not have to be inscribed on zones to be *attached* to them. At an initial level, we can say that the *distinctive traits* supporting a phoneme which is cut out of the Voice by the infant will be inscribed on a zone by *coinciding with the libidinal movement* associated with the emotional variation the phoneme manifests.[149] The infant will associate particular distinctive traits with particular libidinal movements of the body because they coincide temporally. In fact, this association occurs, above all, because those distinctive traits are the *very means by which he or she connects to* – and thereby records and fixates on, or avoids – the *cause* of a particular libidinal movement tied to the Voice which, lying in a different dimension (that of the heights), has no direct means of being recorded on the infant's body, nor even of affecting it.

## *The Three Syntheses of the Body*

The first phonemes and distinctive traits cut out of the Voice and inscribed on the body, respectively, will have a 'function' which is 'still prelinguistic in relation to the whole [morphemes and semantemes] and to the different aspects of the sexual position',[150] namely the phallus of coordination and the phallus of castration. These first phonemes will be connected rather with the depressive position, as we saw in section 3.2. Being as they are pre-phallic or pre-Oedipal, and hence cut out and inscribed on uncoordinated *partial zones*, these phonemes will be pre-linguistic phonemes – *pre-phonemes* as stand-alone units not involved in differential relations with each other. Though to be clear, during the Oedipal stage, letters as phonemes do not become phonemes proper either, to the extent that the infant is still located outside the 'domain of preexistence' of the heights, as structured by the concepts and classes of morphology or signification, and so his phonemes do not function as the atoms of language proper or significant discourse.

However, thanks to the esoteric word, letters as phonemes do become 'elements of articulation', which means they start entering into differential relations with each other. The esoteric word itself acts as a morpheme or 'element of grammatical construction', with the proviso that this 'grammatical construction' is non-sensical or, rather, produces what Deleuze calls 'co-sense', which is *non-semantic sense* or sense that lacks a communally shared referent.[151] We can view letters as phonemes, therefore, as *co-sensical phonemes*, and the esoteric word as a *non-semantic morpheme*. Indeed, this conveys well the meaning of 'esoteric' – it fails to point outside itself but is 'meaningful' to that singular body. Furthermore, it functions by denoting said body, a denotation which is *self-referential, producing* that which it denotes. Just as the connective esoteric word '*choif*' denotes the newly created oral zone as now tied to sexuality and detached from the drives of conservation, so too must we view this as occurring at the global level of the erogenous body with the conjunctive esoteric word.[152]

The conjunctive esoteric word is therefore to be seen simply as the *set* of phonemes the infant cuts out of the Voice and attaches to its zones during the Oedipal position. These phonemes are now phonemes as elements of articulation, but only because the morpheme provides their traits with a constructive form within which they can articulate as differential elements. Since the esoteric word is nothing else than the set of phonemes tied to erogenous zones during the Oedipal stage, these phonemes take on no more sense than the 'pre-phonemes' of the depressive position, but since they are now fully differential, they function phonemically (albeit co-sensically and non-semantically).

What holds these phonemes together, provides them with a 'syntax', is the shared reparative-evocative project animating them, and we must conceive of a shift at this point, whereby the infant no longer passively depends on the Voice's 'emotional variations' to determine which phonetic traits are inscribed on his (or her) zones, but now takes more of an active role in *selecting* phonemes based on the drive to repair the mother through the 'question' of the phallus, his staged demands and enunciated interactions with those around him. This is prepared for by the parental overinvestment of the genitals, at the level of the narcissistic omnipotence and sense of self-mastery the infant feels at this point, spurring him on to mend the mother and restore the father. At the start of the Oedipal stage and thanks to secondary narcissism, the infant identifies with his own genital zone rather than with the Voice, and so with the parental enjoinment to repair-evoke, which now ultimately determines the selection of phonemes. As such, whereas the depressive position likely entails more of an emphasis on the inscription of phonemes' traits on the *ear*, the Oedipal stage entails a movement of those phonemes to the *oral zone*, since heard phonemes will increasingly be spoken or parroted by the infant who uses them in his staged demands targeted at the mother.

Returning to the phonological and phonetic framework Deleuze adopts, we can say that the conjunctive esoteric word *coordinates* the zones by *conjoining* the connective series of traits associated with each partial and then coordinated zone. Zones will fixate on the esoteric word itself because it provides the equally linguistic and libidinal principle for coordinating/conjoining the zones/connective series, thus acting as phallus of coordination. Differential relations between traits tied to zones will be determined as *phonemes* only in relation to the esoteric word, which therefore conjoins distinct 'connective' series and allows phonemes to be expressed on what is now an *erogenous body*, whereas traits are always inscribed initially on what are uncoordinated partial zones.[153] Indeed, Deleuze writes that phonemes – along with morphemes and semantemes – 'build' the body itself or physical surface, since its erogenous coordination is inseparable from the conjunction of its connective series of traits and connective syntheses of images or objects of satisfaction.[154]

Thus the drives will no longer fixate on the Voice as good object,

## The Three Syntheses of the Body

and now intend – by means of 'good intentions' – the conjunctive esoteric word itself. The zones cannot converge on the Voice,[155] which is defined by its transcendence or withdrawal from the physical surface, and so the phonemes initially cut out of it will find in the conjunctive esoteric word, to which they will become attached as its elements of articulation, an improved means of erogenous coordination and the stabilising of the pleasure-unpleasure series. This in turn is supported by – but only partly conditioned by – the parental overvaluation of the infant's genital zone, since the reparative-evocative 'good intention' – the aim of constituting an unharmed/present mother-father unity on the surface – will reinforce the pleasure gained from coordinating the zones through the esoteric word. Reparation-evocation enjoins the infant to mend the wounded mother and restore the absent father, a dualism their state of castration exacerbates and renders more severely binary and oscillating than the infant's ability to understand why, being initially presented in the depressive position with four terms: absent/present and unharmed/wounded.

As I showed in section 3.3, their castration overemphasises the absent/wounded binary relation by excessively marking the genital zone due to its phallic reference. The esoteric word hence manages to satisfy the need to work on the absent/wounded halves, since the construction of an esoteric word is tantamount to the restoration of the Voice, at the level of the phoneme cut out of it and tied to a zone, whereas the creation of the esoteric word itself and the demands it accompanies function reparatively to centre the mother's and infant's zones.[156] In short, if in the depressive position the infant passively accepts the Voice's emotional variations – unharmed/wounded, absent/present – and patterns his drives after them, in the Oedipal stage the infant is spurred on to actively bring about a transformation in the infant, mother and father. That the infant specifically chooses the negative poles of each, *and* attempts to articulate them in relation to each other, shows how the infant has by this stage been pre-conditioned by the parents to enter into a castrated interpretation of sexual difference (and ultimately of the quasi-dualism of onto-logical being), which we saw is for Deleuze a *linguistically* expressed binary opposition or discrete separation, not one that exists prior to or independently of human castration. Esoteric words may appear to the infant to be serving as solutions to this problem, but only exacerbate it by playing along with the very terms of the parents' castration (the identity of absent/wounded).

It seems that Deleuze's motivation for subtly and painstakingly re-working the Leclairian letter can be put down to the following two factors: firstly, as we have seen, he is unable to conceive of morphemes as inscribing themselves on the body on ontological grounds; secondly, and more interestingly as it concerns Leclaire, it allows him to replace the symbolic phallus with an esoteric word.[157] The esoteric word is *literally a word*, or more specifically a kind of series and synthesis (the *conjunction* of *connective series* or syntheses), even if it takes on the function of the phallus of *coordination* at the level of *zones*. If, in *Oedipe à Vincennes*, Leclaire speaks of the production of a 'singular fantasy', Deleuze implicitly asks why we need to conceive of it as a synthesis of the singular *and the universal*. By doing away with the symbolic phallus in his construction of the esoteric word, Deleuze arguably attains a more fully singular understanding of the infant's self-castration/self-nomination, as there is nothing universal about an esoteric word – it is not structured by the 'letter of the lack of the letter'. Although we have seen that the construction of this word is propped up by the parents' overvaluation of the infant's genital zone, and thus by their own (symbolic) castration, I would suggest that Deleuze manages to *preserve more distance* between singularity and castrative pre-conditioning than one finds in Leclaire's formulations from the late 1960s, and thus grants the body's singularity more autonomy and structuring power over linguistic form (as ultimately pre-conditioned by parental castration).[158]

Along similar lines, Monique David-Ménard has convincingly and comprehensively suggested that, whereas Lacan conceives of the relation between the universal and the particular in purely logical terms (and on this basis understands the phallic function as underlying the difference between the sexes and particular bodies' relation to language), Freud is 'more Deleuzian than Lacan'.[159] David-Ménard shows that by 1923, Freud no longer believed the phallus (as sign of sexual difference) to be capable of fully coordinating and subsuming under it the erogenous zones and partial drives (as first claimed in 'Three Essays'), and considers Deleuze's work to be more attuned than Lacan's to the 'subtleties' and singularity of the drive vis-à-vis universal pre-established structures.[160]

While Deleuze cannot do away with the Lacanian phallus as such, esoteric words allow him to displace it to the following, disjunctive, series post-castration, and this is Deleuze's primary difference from Leclaire in his treatment of the case, for whom we saw the symbolic phallus inscribes itself at the level of the 'Li'. The reparative-evocative drive underlies the construction of the name – the parents' castration, and the castration phallus at that level alone, pre-conditioning the infant's construction of the name; but since the castration phallus has no linguistically efficacious power prior to castration, as I maintained in the previous section, it comes down to the *infant* to translate the parents' castration into what will become linguistic terms for the infant. This accounts for the singularity with which the infant self-nominates/self-castrates.

I would also suggest that by invoking the theme of a 'conditioning-conditioned structure'[161] in his discussion of Oedipal esoteric words, Deleuze is gesturing to this relative independence from pre-established universalities. The term alludes to and is an extension of his post-Kantian, largely Maïmon-inspired, project aimed since the 1950s at immanently and genetically accounting for the conditions of thought.[162] It can also be understood at the level of his understanding of structure as a 'problem'. Drawing on differential calculus, and its contribution to post-Kantian thought, Deleuze shows in Chapter 4 of *Difference and Repetition*, in his 1967 essay 'How Do We Recognize Structuralism?', and in *The Logic of Sense* (particularly in the series on structure, the problem and on the 'Static Logical Genesis'), that we must distinguish between two kinds of equation, which in the structuralism essay he terms 'imaginary' or 'axiomatic' on the one hand, and 'symbolic' or properly 'structural' (and problematic) on the other.

In the first kind of equation – giving the example '$x^2 + y^2 - R^2 = 0$' – Deleuze writes that the 'values' are 'not specified' yet 'must have a determined value' for the equation to hold (to add up to zero).[163] We can also see that the form of the function is pre-established or pre-determined, requiring only the addition of particular inputs. The second kind, for example '$y\, dy + x\, dx = 0$', involves elements which 'have no determined value themselves', but which 'nevertheless determine each other reciprocally'.[164] Dy (change in y) is, as Deleuze puts it, 'totally undetermined in relation to y', and the same for dx and x; 'each one has neither existence, nor value, nor signification'.[165] Yet, the equation as a whole gives rise to a complete determination of the elements held in reciprocal or differential (i.e. an undetermined) relation. Hence, we must distinguish the differential elements, on the one hand, from the 'singularities' or values 'corresponding to the determination of differential relations';[166] there is a difference in kind between problem and solution which we do not find in imaginary equations.[167] Furthermore, we can see that the form of the function is involved in a fully immanent relation of *co-determination* with the inputs, progressively determining *itself* as it determines its corresponding solutions. It is undetermined but determinable at the level of its singular values.

For Deleuze:

> This process of a reciprocal determination is at the heart of a relationship that allows one to define the symbolic nature [...] [T]he determination of phonemic relations proper to a given language ascribes singularities in proximity to which the vocalisations and significations of the language are constituted. *The reciprocal determination* of symbolic elements continues henceforth into *the complete determination* of singular points.[168]

Whereas differential relations and elements within the structure cannot as such be determined, according to the structuralist principle which holds that relations are prior to the terms being related, these relations and elements nonetheless determine 'singularities' or 'values' which react back onto (without nonetheless determining) them. Hence, 'li' and '*corne*', as elements lacking any inherent signification while being caught in differential relations with each other and all other letters forming an unconscious (as well as, at a further level of remove, with all the possible phonemic relations sanctioned by a given language), will give rise to effects of signification ('singular values'). This is thanks to the morphemes or morphemic thresholds of a particular language, functioning as 'singularities in proximity to which [...] significations are constituted', such as '*licorne*'. 'Li' and '*corne*', as differential elements caught in relations with one another, are never themselves determined as such qua phonemes. Yet they do give rise to a complete determination extending away from their order and into the domain of signification (that of morphology).

Interestingly, in the structuralism essay he gives Leclaire's work on the erogenous 'letter' as an example of a 'problematic'/'symbolic' structure. Structure's 'symbolic elements [...] refer to "libidinal movements" of the body, incarnating the singularities of the structure',[169] and internally contributing to their linguistic determination as productive of effects of signification. Symbolic elements (traits and phonemes) tied to libidinal movements of the body are to be associated with the level of a reciprocal determination of differential elements, whereas what they 'incarnate' (the effects of signification or 'singularities of the structure') lies at the level of signification or morphology, which occupies a different plane.

Leclaire's work on the letter can indeed be seen as partly motivated by the overly formalistic ('axiomatic' we could say) reading of Lacan's work presented by J.-A. Miller in 'Suture (elements of the logic of the signifier)', which relies on the arithmetic logic of Frege (itself modelled on the mathematical axioms of Peano).[170] In this respect, Deleuze can be seen as doing to Leclaire what Leclaire does to Miller, which is to say further stressing the singular independence of the drive from fixed universalities, here in the form of Leclaire's tacit reliance on the symbolic phallus.[171] In *The Logic of Sense*, an esoteric word (which he defines as a 'function')[172] provides the integrative morphemic thresholds conditioning the 'resolution' (as singularities or phonemes) of the problems, or differential relations between differential elements, provided by the zones' relations of distinctive traits. But in accordance with this 'conditioning-conditioned structure', we must view the internal thresholds of the esoteric word as contributed to as much by the traits and body's libidinal movement as vice versa, with the parents' castration and overinvestment of the infant's genitals preventing this process from ever doing away with the symbolic phallus altogether.

Poord'jeli as morpheme or function is gradually built through the progressive amassing of internal thresholds – 'li', '*corne*', '*peau*', etc. – added to this agglomeration by distinctive traits derived from the Voice and attached to zones, and finally transferred to the esoteric word as morpheme. Conversely, the larger the morpheme becomes, the greater is its structuring or determining power over the continued selection of phonemes from the Voice and the attaching of these phonemes to zones. The more determined the esoteric word becomes the more it conditions and structures the zones and reparative drive. However, this word is not pre-established, rather it is built up piece by piece by being provided with what are initially traits as tied to zones' intentions. In short, Deleuze's aim is to construct a theory of the phallus understood as an immanent co-determination of morphemic thresholds and differential phonetic traits, to be used as a challenge to any universalist treatment (or universal/particular logic) of the phallic function.

Thus for Deleuze the phallus is not able to *coordinate* the *zones* without the esoteric word which *conjoins* the *connective series of traits*. But the esoteric word, likewise, is not built out of the blue, despite being singular, and depends indirectly on a pre-conditioned form of castration indirectly imposed on the infant from without and pre-determining his construction of the esoteric word at the level of his reparative-evocative drive.

Summarising what has been established so far:

1. Phonetic elements are directly *inscribed* on *partial* zones as connective *series* of traits and connective *syntheses* of images. Traits are associated with the zone's intensive differences and libidinal fixations on the Voice as good object, at the tail end of the depressive position; but this gives way to a freer principle of selecting phonemes – no longer directly tied to the Voice's manifestations of 'emotional variation' – once the infant enters the Oedipal stage. At this point, the causal principle underlying the selection of phonemes from the Voice, and their association with the zones' intensities, can only be understood at the level of an inter-subjective structure in which the following three dynamically condition one another: (a) the reparative-evocative drive preconditioned by the parents' castration; (b) the zones' intensive differences and associated traits, as pre-conditioned by the singularity of the infant's experiences during the depressive position; (c) the singularity of the phonemes available to the infant during the Oedipal stage, which react onto and partly re-shape the zone's intensive differences and associated traits.
2. Phonemes come to be *expressed* on the erogenous *body* they 'build', as conjunctive synthesis of connective series of traits, and as coordination of zones, while being located ontologically at a further level of remove from corporeality than traits. Being inseparable from their articulation with all the other phonemes making up the morpheme or esoteric word, phonemes cannot be reapportioned to discrete zones on the basis of where they were initially inscribed qua phonetic trait, just as the zones, through the esoteric word, become indistinguishable at the level of the integrated libidinal economy of a global erogenous body. It is therefore through phonemes that zones combine, just as it is through esoteric words that traits produce phonemes. Even if letters are corporeally *inscribed* as phonetic traits, letters are actually *phonemes*, since letters imply an integrated libidinal economy. It is in this sense that, for Deleuze, the traits of any phoneme are inscribed on more than one zone, since at the global erogenous level there is a phonemic continuity which we do not find at the phonetic level; phonemes transcend their *phonetic* localisation in the partial zones.
3. The morpheme as esoteric word *hovers over the surface* of this erogenous body, at the level of greatest remove from corporeality, coordinating the zones as it does so by providing the principle of the 'co-sense' the zones produce, and on which they fixate

as object and effect of reparation-evocation. It is the conditioning form of the zones, but one that is progressively constructed throughout the Oedipal stage, starting with the connective esoteric word tied to the oral zone.

4. Since phonemes retroactively depend on morphemes, the phonemes building the *body* are paradoxically a function of the phallus or esoteric word hovering *over* it, as a conduit straddling the *ideality* of the Voice (and the phonemes initially cut out of it) and the *corporeality* of the phonetic elements inscribed on the partial zones. This straddling expresses esoteric (non-semantic) phonemes as (a) *more corporeal* than the forms cut out of the Voice, which spoken by the Voice participate at their own level in a fully propositional and referential order of language from which the infant is cut off; (b) as *more ideal* than the phonetic elements first inscribed on uncoordinated partial zones, prior to the construction of the esoteric word.

To prepare the move from the second to the third stage, which again is equally sexual and linguistic, we need to turn to the issue of parental images. For Deleuze, during the sexual-perverse position the parents are 'fragmented according to the zones'.[173] *The parents literally figure as the phonemes or singularities inscribed and expressed on the body of the infant* (li-*port-mort-corps-corne*, etc.), to the extent that the infant's relation to them is conditioned by the drive to mend the mother's wound and restore the father (both as pre-conditioned by their castration at their own level), and since he or she achieves this through the construction of an esoteric word, with phonemes produced by esoteric words working to bring together both surface/height and mother-/father-images. Deleuze calls them 'pre-Oedipal' or 'pregenital' parental images, since they precede genital sexuality as targeted at a heterosexual other after puberty, and they are precisely *how* the Voice comes to be incarnated in the infant's body in his or her relations with the mother. Parental images not only accompany, they *are* the phonemes expressed on the body, to the extent that they are phallically centred. By being pre-conditioned by the parents' own castration, the infant produces phonemes which respond to this sensed need to articulate the mother's 'lack' and father's 'excess' in a binary articulation. As such, once the infant is libidinally marked by phonemes produced by this process, he or she has planted the seeds of his or her own castration.

These seeds grow into and castration arrives in the form of

'semantemes', which are the smallest units in language capable of *denotation* (and thus sense proper[174]), such as 'he/she'. They are inscribed on the genital zone once the infant acquires enough language and knowledge of the parents' relations – or the domain of preexistence more generally – to record the parents now as complete whole objects, and as sexuated individuals, which Deleuze calls 'Oedipal' parental images. Leclaire's examples are '*Joli corps de Lili*' (Lili's beautiful body), '*Le lit de Lili*' (Lili's bed), which Deleuze mentions as examples of Oedipal semantemes. Finally, this is the moment of castration because at the level of the structural distinction between esoteric phonemes and semantemes, the infant's coordination phallus (the set of phonemes) has now given way to its own 'Oedipal dissociations' – the Voice has returned as the source of all disjunctions and of all disassociations (namely of surface/height). In other words, the Voice as the *pre-castrated phallus of castration* (how the infant perceives the castrated parents' comings and goings) merges with the *phallus of coordination* – thereby producing the phallus of castration as lived by the infant – when the infant's phallus of coordination (set of phonemes) disassociates itself from the semantemes inscribed on the genital zone.[175]

We will explore this in detail in the next section, but the main point here is that castration is the structural clash between two kinds of image – pregenital and esoteric-phonemic, Oedipal and semantic – which reproduce as a self-fulfilling prophecy the very tension that the infant had aimed to overcome with the construction of an esoteric word: the bringing together of surface and height. Surface and height are now re-disassociated at the level of the disjunction of esoteric phonemes and semantemes (semantemes are closer to the ideality of the concept than esoteric phonemes are), castrating the infant by having pre-conditioned him to attempt to merge mother/father at the level of surface/height via phonemes, with semantemes as the trigger to the bomb of the infant's own making.

## 3.5 Disjunctive Synthesis of the Unconscious and Pre/conscious Systems: The Castration-Effect

At the end of the Oedipal position, reparation reveals itself, for Klein, to be impossible, because while Oedipus in Deleuze's narrative had 'good intentions' – bringing together the mother and father, mending the mother's wound and restoring the banished father – he instead brings about their disjunction. Mother and father are now disjoined not merely as distinct images – which we saw were associated with distinct registers of thought as viewed by the *same* dimension, the Voice/body as construction of the physical surface – but as fully *distinct surfaces* or divergent series. Instead of a physical surface (the erogenous body), we now have two series or surfaces: the physical surface as erogenous body or the Freudian 'unconscious system' *tout court* (*Ucs.*), and the 'metaphysical surface' or Freudian 'preconscious-conscious system' (*Pcs.-Cs.*). According to Freud's landmark 1915 article 'The Unconscious', while the unconscious is radically barred, the preconscious is *potentially* but not actually accessible to consciousness. Whereas the *Pcs.* is entirely accessible to the *Cs.*, while remaining non-conscious, 'secondary repression' operates between the *Ucs.* and *Pcs.*, such that communication between them is far less direct. The *Pcs.* is composed of all thoughts that could potentially become conscious, while the *Ucs.* is 'censored', so that it cannot directly communicate with the *Pcs.* (and thus with the *Cs.*).[176]

For Freud, the 'nucleus' of the ucs. consists of 'instinctual representatives which seek to discharge their cathexes'.[177] These representatives are called 'thing-presentations', which are complexes of 'associations made up of the greatest variety of visual, acoustic, tactile, kinaesthetic and other presentations'.[178] As presentations or mental images, they cannot inherently contradict each other or influence one another, and there is 'no negation, no doubt, no degrees of certainty'.[179] As an earlier text puts it, the ucs. 'equate[s] reality of thought with external actuality, and wishes with their fulfilment',[180] or as the 1915 article puts it, there is a '*replacement of external by psychical reality*'.[181] But as 'contents, cathected with greater or lesser strength',[182] all thing-presentations nonetheless participate in a single organising principle which makes them 'coordinate' with one another: the 'pleasure-unpleasure regulation'.[183] We saw earlier that according to the pleasure principle, the pleasure-unpleasure series on the body seeks to maintain a stable pattern for its quantities of intensity or strengths of cathexis.

Very early on, however, the *Ucs.* is almost completely 'overlaid' by the *Pcs.*.[184] The *Pcs.* is composed of 'word-presentations', all of which are capable of becoming conscious. A 'word-presentation' is a 'complex presentation' made up of its own 'visual, acoustic, and kinaesthetic' associations linked to the process of learning a language.[185] However, a word 'acquires its meaning' by being linked to a thing-presentation.[186] Thus a word-presentation includes the presentation of the word and the presentation of the thing corresponding to it.[187] Furthermore, Freud explains that it is thanks to a 'sound-image' that the two components are linked.[188] A sound-image is the image we receive after speaking, it is associated with the sound of one's own speech.[189] We try to learn the words of others by making our sound-image 'as like as possible' to the one which 'gave rise to our speech-innervation',[190] by which Freud means 'the sense of the innervation of a word' or in short its libidinal associations.[191] Freud claims we learn to speak by associating the speech innervation with the 'sound-image', the phoneme or phonemic relation with the intensive quantity or difference in quantity. Yet so long as our speech has not yet developed far and we are still learning a language, we largely associate a sound-image with other sound-images ourselves, according to our own associations,[192] and thus according to the pleasure-unpleasure series. This means that we learn how to associate a word with a thing-presentation according to its sound-image or purely phonemic quality, but that once the word has replaced the sound-image (i.e. once we have learned the meaning of a word), the libidinal associations of the sound-image are overlaid by those of the word-image.

Now, an apparent contradiction emerges because on the one hand Freud claims that the *Ucs.* is censored by the *Pcs.*, yet on the other hand the meaning of the word-presentations composing the *Pcs.* is entirely composed of thing-presentations, which correspond to the *Ucs.* This is resolved by the *Pcs.*'s function of 'hypercathecting' the 'first and true object-cathexis'[193] of the thing-presentation, which is its initial libidinal association with an unconscious complex of presentations as coordinated by an overarching pleasure-unpleasure series. Hypercathecting the thing-presentation means that the original, unconscious, cathexis and its series of associations governed by the pleasure principle (or pleasure-unpleasure regulation) is replaced by a new set of associations governed by the word-presentation corresponding to it. In other words, a particular mental image or presentation loses all its unconscious libidinal associations, which are replaced by a preconscious and potentially conscious set of associations completely determined by the word associated with that mental image, as well as with the other words with which the original one can form relations.

As such, the connections in the unconscious governed by the pleasure principle give way to the 'reality principle', which will determine the associations capable of being formed between words in the *Pcs.* The reality principle requires the individual to submit to the use of

*The Three Syntheses of the Body*

language and to such cultural norms as the incest taboo. Any presentation or psychical act which is not put into words thereby remains unconscious or repressed by the *Pcs.*'s censorship of the pleasure principle.[194] Thus the word-presentation is now to be understood as being composed of a word and a thing-presentation which has lost its unconscious associations or 'memory-images' and is now cathected only to 'remoter memory-traces derived from [the unconscious memory-images]'.[195] The word-presentation is cathected to associations but ones which are determined by a new organising principle. Freud thereby installs what the Lacanian school – most notably Laplanche and Leclaire in their 1960 structural-linguistic re-imagining of Freud's article 'The Unconscious: A Psychoanalytic Study', in which Leclaire first discusses Poord'jeli – view as a structural break located between the unconscious system, on the one hand, and the pre-conscious/conscious system, on the other[196] which, building on Lacan's canonical formulations, they understand at the level of the structural-linguistic distinction between the signifier and the signified.[197]

In his landmark case 'The Wolf Man',[198] which is contemporaneous with 'The Unconscious', Freud explains that the infant knows no distinction between the unconscious and pre/conscious, and following Freud we must view the pre/conscious as literally inscribed on the unconscious (or the infant's body) during the Oedipal or phallic stage. We can understand this at the level of the linguistically communicated or symbolically embedded phantasies shared by the infant and his primary caregivers. In this sense, their pre/conscious comes to impose itself on the infant's 'unconscious', though at this stage there is no real distinction since the infant lives his phantasies at the corporeal level, which we can clearly see in the case of Poord'jeli. We can speak of a *convergence* or conjunction of the (infant's) unconscious and (adults' or caregivers') pre/conscious during the Oedipal stage, followed by a *divergence* or disjunction of the (infant's) unconscious and (infant's) pre/conscious once castrated, between the ages of five and seven, which is followed by the latency stage and the onset of genital sexuality with the arrival of puberty.[199] And at the structural level, as I will show, we can speak of a convergence of phonetic traits and morphemic thresholds, followed by a divergence of esoteric phonemes and semantemes.[200]

Hence, disjunction can be said to produce the quasi-dualism of bodies-language on which Western philosophy's inaugural sensible-intelligible divide can be said to rest. This is a quasi-dualism, for

Deleuze, of esoteric *corporeality* and what we can call semantic *incorporeality* rather than ideality *tout court*, as I will make clear. This framework, while sharing commonalities, can be profitably *opposed* to Leclaire's, who – along with Derrida, to whom he favourably compares this aspect of his work[201] – conceives of letters (phonemes-monemes, as we saw) as *preceding*, and unstably founding, Western philosophy's sensible-intelligible opposition. It is not problematic, for Leclaire, for the symbolic phallus as linguistic construct to inscribe itself on bodies, because letters precede Deleuze's quasi-dualism. In a way Deleuze is therefore perhaps more classically philosophical than Leclaire, since he adopts this distinction all the while attempting to unstably found it in linguistic structure, whereas Leclaire, along with Derrida, calls it into question entirely. In any case, this point helps us explain why Deleuze finds it problematic for Leclaire to view letters as equally phonemic and morphemic, whereas Leclaire does not.[202]

Returning to my argument, in the 'pregenital' (pre-castrated) situation, mother and father for Deleuze are inseparably tied to the physical surface, albeit as distinct images which we have seen are in turn fragmented according to the zones and inscribed there as phonemes. In the 'Oedipal' (castrated) one, we saw they are finally determined as semantemes and inscribed on the (now fully 'genital' or sexuated) genital zone.[203] Now, castration is not the second inscription but the *reaction* of the latter on the former, the disjunction it effectuates at the level of the images' structural or even structural-linguistic distinction. As Leclaire puts it in a provocative formulation, it is the *semanteme* (or conscious 'representation'[204]) which possibly gives the phoneme its singular value *more* than the reverse (which is also true but to a lesser extent).[205] Or put another way, the unconscious phoneme is repressed '*because it is unconscious*',[206] and not because it is inherently transgressive or incestuous.[207] Repression occurs because of the structural-linguistic nature of the element: '*the more structurally unconscious an element is*', the harder it is for it to slide from the level of phoneme to the level of semanteme, or from signifier to sign.[208] The *singularity* of the phoneme – to take on this status – must be reflected in a discourse that is *not singular* (the semanteme). In short, Poord'jeli is repressed first of all because it is non-sensical or lacking semantic value, and only secondarily because it is associated with 'libidinal imperatives'[209] or intentions that jar with genital sexuality, as structured by semantemes and denotable whole objects. Indeed, it is *because* Poord'jeli is non-sensical that its phonemically coded intentions are repressed, building up unresolved

## The Three Syntheses of the Body

or uncathected intensities in the zones incapable of being reduced to zero because of their inability to accord with the reality principle, according to which only semantemes can be invested.

When Deleuze discusses Leclaire's Poord'jeli case, it is precisely to the pages and passages mentioned above that he refers in a footnote, and it is clear that they provide the basis for his understanding of the disjunctive synthesis, as well as its internal 'resonance'. On one of these pages, which Deleuze invokes in the main body of his own text when discussing Poord'jeli, Leclaire writes that the phoneme or 'letter *li* [. . .] takes on signifying value in the conscious order by representing the object *lit* [bed] and, why not, "*le lit de Lili* [Lili's bed]"', the latter functioning as semantemes.[210] The crux of the matter is, of course, that the conscious re-presentation materially depends on the non-sense of the material letter which must also be repressed as letter in order for it to give rise to effects of signification. Here the Freudian notion of what Laplanche and Leclaire call a 'double inscription' comes into play. In 'The Unconscious', Freud offers two possible hypotheses for how the two levels – the *Ucs.* and the *P/cs.* – communicate. In one version, cathexes simply re-cathect the conscious representation (his 'word-presentation'); in the other, cathexes continue to be maintained in both series (with 'thing-' and 'word-presentations'), giving rise to a continued double inscription on both series even after the formation of a structural split, with the onset of post-pubescent or genital sexuality.

Laplanche and Leclaire favour the latter, and using Poord'jeli we can see why this is the case. As the principle of his zones' coordination, genital and post-pubescent sexuality cannot intend or invest semantemes or conscious representations without the repression of the 'secret name' Poord'jeli, since *access to semantemes* depends precisely on this shift or structural inversion. Genital sexuality must *continue to use* the pre-genital phallus of coordination (Poord'jeli), since not only do the zones' coordination and centring on the genital zone continue to rely on it, but *genital sexuality's choice of an external object is determined by its repression of it* or rather structural inability to intend it.[211] We can see this in Philippe's obsessional neurosis. As an adult in his thirties, Philippe has a phobia of little things, of grains of sand rubbing against his (highly irritable, libidinally primed but dammed up) skin, the very causes in infancy of pleasure (the pleasure he took in his feet and in walking barefooted on the sand). The drive's repression or structural inability to intend conscious representations is precisely what motivates its unconscious repetition; if one were to realise the real cause of our attraction to something, we would no longer find it appealing.[212]

Moreover, it is clear that Deleuze also favours this option, most explicitly because he views castration as entailing the emergence of a 'double screen'.[213] While the 'image' refers first to the objects of satisfaction of partial zones, then to the phallus and parental images, it reaches its final form in the 'image of action' or 'action in general'.[214] Deleuze means by this a *different kind of action* from the actions and passions of the erogenous body, which are *singular* not general, esoteric not semantic – though we must specify that this generality cannot as such be separated from, but is articulated with, the singularity of the body, so it is only general at the level of an abstracted form of action, not at the level of content. Properly speaking it is an 'event', which in Deleuze's precise terms is an action capable of *distinguishing itself from its corporeal cause*. This action is 'divide[d] [...] in two' and 'projected' or inscribed on a 'double screen' – a physical and a metaphysical surface (erogenous body and 'cerebral' surface of 'thought', respectively) – and 'determined' on 'each side according to the necessary exigencies of each screen'.[215] The theoretical apparatus of the double screen remains almost impenetrable ('Perhaps we are moving too fast'[216]) if we do not immediately link it back to Laplanche and Leclaire's structural-linguistic reading of double inscription.[217] Moreover, without the double screen as understood in this way, Deleuze's entire theory of castration cannot fully be accounted for, pointing to the centrality of the esoteric word to his reading of the Oedipus complex and structure of the unconscious.

To help us forge this connection between the two projects we should look more closely at Deleuze's theory of the event. What Deleuze calls the 'Freudian theory of the event'[218] – which has close ties to the psychoanalytic phantasm[219] – but which also underlies his theory of the event *tout court*, is that which is 'disengaged' or 'produced' by 'a sort of resonance'[220] of 'two series of independent images', one 'pregenital' (phonemic) and the other 'Oedipal' (semantic).[221] The event disengaged is 'no different from the resonance itself'[222] and so cannot be understood at either the pregenital or Oedipal level when either is taken separately. Deleuze states that it is precisely the pregenital infant's 'good intentions' (of mending the mother and restoring the father) which ultimately divide action in two, which by its internal resonance produces an event.[223] This is what I have been arguing for in the previous section: the infant's self-nomination and as we can now see *unintentional* self-castration.

## The Three Syntheses of the Body

Castration is un-'intentional' because the 'good intentions' bound up with esoteric phonemes find no way of translating themselves into semantemes. The infant is suspended between two worlds neither of which makes sense in terms of the other. At the structural level, phonemes which cannot be subsumed under a semanteme or determined by semantic thresholds – or, more completely, any phoneme which is determined by only a non-semantic morpheme (esoteric word), or which is tied to the body's erogenous organisation – become unconscious. Phonemes which can be lose contact with the body, where they will be initially inscribed because of their sensible basis – their association with phonetic elements as tied to the mouth's morphology,[224] and their indirect impression on the body's erogenous zones with which they retain distant relations at the phonemic level. These phonemes become subsumed under the proposition and the expression of sense, and tied up with what Deleuze calls 'thought' (the *P/cs.*), as distinct from the erogenous body (the *Ucs.*).[225]

Hence, castration is the effect of the structural heterogeneity or disaccord between two distinct orders of language, the non-semantic or esoteric *phoneme* and the *semanteme*, engendering a kind of dualism of body and mind. This dualism is the effect of the sufficiently fluent infant's articulation of propositions composed of Oedipal images. When, from around the age of five – but taking on its full resonance with puberty, when the genital zone reawakens from its latent dormancy – the infant uses semantemes in his speech (such as '*Le lit de Lili*'), he or she will unintentionally castrate himself or herself because well formed propositions automatically distribute and apportion their elements to either the *Ucs.* or the *P/cs.*

Nonetheless, we are dealing with a 'double screen' and not two distinct screens or worlds, so the psycho-physical dualism produced by castration conceals an underlying monism (or monism-effect), that of the event.[226] Both times Deleuze discusses the event disengaged through the resonance of pregenital and Oedipal images, he refers to it as the 'Event',[227] because castration – as a 'castration "effect"'[228] – is the ever-renewed or repeated *event of language*. It is the structural condition for the emergence of any event, or for the semantic re-presentation of any actions and passions (determined as phonemes and phonemic relations) affecting the erogenous body. More precisely, the event is the excess or resistance of the phonemic series (the body) with regard to the semantic series (re-presentational capture), and the evental site is thus precisely located in the disjunction between the esoteric phoneme and the semanteme.

The production of the event is thus coextensive with the emergence and development of esoteric words, and we can also speak of the *body of the event*, just as Leclaire speaks of the 'body of the letter'. The event must be inscribed in the flesh before it can leave the physical surface, even if its *in*-corporeality is precisely its phantasmatic (or ghostly) departure from, or the disjunction it forms with – and continues to maintain (as a haunting) – what birthed it. Indeed, the esoteric word will continue having a crucial function in Deleuze's logic of sense after the 'dynamic genesis' and with his theory of propositional language – discussed in the next chapters – which, together with the event, functions after castration as an unfolding or evolution of the esoteric word.

Now, the double screen is entirely conditioned by the phallus's transformation into the 'phallus of castration', and by the third, disjunctive, esoteric word. I claim it is at this level that the Lacanian symbolic phallus, with its differential sexuated structure (+/−), finally makes an appearance in the dynamic genesis. More precisely, I will demonstrate that despite now having the differential binary *form* of the symbolic phallus, the differential poles do not slip in universal pre-established sexual positions through the back door. Although they are associated with sexual difference and perpetuate the genital overinvestment of the adult infant's own children, since Deleuze's esoteric word does not rely directly on the phallus the difference is primarily *formal* (though also ontological). In other words these two poles refer to the two series: the Oedipal parental images, denoting complete and sexuated individuals (+/−),[229] *on the one hand*, and on the other pregenital parental images on which the drive remains fixated (albeit with the modifications discussed below), and which are at their own level foreign to any notion of binary sexuation. The +/− of the Oedipal series should be viewed more as a *function of semantemes* (he/she) than as the assumption of a symbolic phallic form. Moreover, with regard to Klein we can now see how *whole objects are linguistically generated*.

It is no coincidence that Deleuze's discussion of Lacan's phallus only appears very late on in the dynamic genesis, and specifically at the moment of castration or in the third series of sexuality (disjunction). Returning to his discussion of it in a different context, in an earlier series (on 'serialisation'), Deleuze states that the Lacanian phallus is the paradoxical (ex-centric or self-displacing) unity of the foundational *non-sensical forms* of each of the two heterogeneous base series (pregenital and Oedipal, phonemic and semantic, physical surface and metaphysical surface).²³⁰ These are the (excessive) 'occupant without a place' (replacing the 'mother image' or erogenous body) and the (lacking) 'place without an occupant' (replacing the 'father image' or Voice). These two figures of 'surface nonsense'²³¹ only appear *upon* castration and not prior to it. Rather than being a structuring *cause*, as it is in Lacan, the +/− structure of the phallus of castration, for Deleuze, is a surface- or castration-*effect* (and more completely the subsequent '*quasi-cause*' *of any event that is not non-sensical*).

Using Poord'jeli, we can see how at the 'Oedipal' ('Oedipal image') or semantic level, the phallus (the object of the drive's 'good intentions') is displaced behind all its representations ('*Liliane*', '*Le lit de Lili*', '*Joli corps de Lili*', etc.). It is identifiable with none of them all the while underscoring their unity as what they all commonly diverge from, namely the letter 'li' (and, more completely, 'Poord'jeli' itself). As esoteric phoneme, the phallic 'li' is structurally repressed from or inaccessible to the semantic Oedipal series, but it nonetheless materially conditions that series, since we know that semantemes – or phonemes capable of being semantically determined – take on their structural position and function only through their *difference* from phonemes that are incapable of being semantically determined (esoteric ones).²³² Even though we are dealing with parental images as *semantemes* in the Oedipal series, they *fail to refer to* their singular foundation and principle, being generalities or communally accessible representations. Put otherwise, they all *succeed in referring to an absence*, the *place without an occupant* as that which, *sliding behind* every Oedipal semanteme or re-presentation, signals in the Oedipal semantic series the absence (−) of 'Poord'jeli' from that series. Poord'jeli, as *occupant without a place*, is repressed to the erogenous unconscious where it figures as an excess (+) lacking from the Oedipal/semantic series. Poord'jeli is *conspicuously* absent from the Oedipal semantic series because it is the *condition of that series' unity* – its unity hinging on its shared divergence from what it thereby lacks.

We can see why Deleuze also refers to the two figures of nonsense as the 'word = x' and 'object = x'.²³³ In the Oedipal series is missing a word (= x) (or 'place') that could finally name and designate the object (= x) all semantemes lack (that which each one fails to ever fully designate), namely the phallus. The word = x is missing from the Oedipal series, while the object = x is posited as being that which this word = x could denote (namely the phallus of coordination, hovering over the physical surface).²³⁴ Moreover, we know that Deleuze's innovation with regard to Laplanche and Leclaire's theory is to work into their framework his notion of the event. Thus Deleuze writes that the 'resonance' and 'communication' of the word = x and object = x produces a third figure, that of the 'action = x'.²³⁵ The aforementioned self-displacement of the word = x in relation to the object = x, and vice versa, constitutes this third element.²³⁶

The action = x can be described therefore as the disjunctive esoteric word or phallus in both its aspects (as word = x and object = x), as that which conditions the production of actions (events) detached from the body's corporeal causes or passions. The 'action in general' to which Deleuze refers, in his discussion of the moment of castration in the twenty-ninth series on the Oedipus complex, is indeed this 'action = x', which is the conditioning form of *any* action – or rather of the *event*, which we saw is defined by its being distinguished from corporeal passion. The ultimate structure of castration, for Deleuze, is therefore the action = x, as the resonance of the word = x and object = x of a singular physical surface, further substantiating my claims as to the centrality of structural-linguistic mechanisms to Deleuze's account of ontogenesis.

Here we can see that castration is precisely the castration or loss *of the phallus of coordination* (Poord'jeli as such), which as esoteric word is structurally repressed from the Oedipal and semantic series. Thus the 'phallus of castration' is the *difference* or 'oscillation' between Poord'jeli (the phallus of coordination) and the Oedipal images functioning as semantemes ('*Le lit de Lili*', '*Joli corps de Lili*', etc.), which we have seen repress the former. Deleuze writes that the phallus of castration

> brings about the resonance of the two series that we earlier called pregenital and Oedipal, but which must also receive further qualifications, since we have said that from all (*à travers toutes*) their possible qualifications, one is determined as signified and the other as signifying.²³⁷

In this quotation Deleuze means that upon castration, we are no longer dealing with a pregenital series *and* an Oedipal series, but with a single ('double') screen or mirror that loses its resemblance and identity in its reflection (Alice through the looking-glass).²³⁸

We are dealing with what Deleuze earlier in the book likens to a Möbius strip, a continuity of reverse and obverse sides. The phallus of castration maintains an invisible connection (the point of maximal torsion) between pregenital and Oedipal series, and *purely* at the level of the structural-linguistic distinction between esoteric phoneme and semanteme (signifier and sign). The proliferation of connections between phonemes inscribed on the erogenous body – along with their associated intensive quantities and images (zones' objects of satisfaction) – is lost once the infant is castrated, to the extent that what is determined as 'unconscious' (and was formerly termed the 'physical surface' or erogenous body) now rests solely on the minimalism of the relation between those phonemes which are and those which are not granted access to semantic pre/consciousness.[239] In other words, the 'pregenital series' now takes on a new form as the reverse and resistant side of the semantic ordering of phonemes. It is reduced to having to prosper only in the cracks of the proposition (logical impasses, esoteric pockets), while before it roamed the entire body.

This quoted passage comes amid Deleuze's most sustained discussion of Lacan in the dynamic genesis (of his phallus of castration or symbolic phallus). The above distinction between the esoteric phoneme and the semanteme cuts across all the myriad forces, processes and relations that we have shown in this chapter contribute to forming or qualifying the pregenital and then the Oedipal series, reducing it all to the relation of what is finally a 'signifying' (formerly 'pregenital') series to what is finally a 'signified' (formerly 'Oedipal') series.[240] While it does not inscribe itself directly on bodies – Deleuze's chief confrontation with Lacan – the phallus of castration still comes to determine both the 'corporeal' or signifying series and the 'linguistic' or signified series, through its self-displacement across all libidinally invested semantemes and esoteric phonemes.

We can now see how closely Deleuze's phallus (coordination and castration) is modelled on his reading of Carroll's types of esoteric word. The conjunctive esoteric word – like the Snark, as both nominal regress at the level of bodies or denotation (shark or snake? or Boojum?), and as conjunction of the heterogeneous using the 'it'[241] – conjoins heterogeneous series of bodies and language, phonetic traits and phonemic/morphemic thresholds cut out of the Voice, precisely by being displaced over the physical surface to which it is bound. It is displaced because it is not identifiable with any of the phonemes making it up – as tied to erogenous zones – but this denotational slippage or regress is what synthesises the zones by providing a co-sense to fixate on. This co-sense functions as the morpheme conditioning the phonetic traits as phonemes, even if it is nothing else than their relations, and thus conjoins the ideality of language with the materiality of bodies inside the conjunctive esoteric word itself, as the infant's body as set. Lastly, the esoteric word denotes the set of bodies it forms, *self-referentially* denoting something it creates through its own form.

The disjunctive esoteric word, on the other hand, levers open these previously conjoined phonemes or 'bodies' (the domain of denotation), both from each other and from 'language' (the domain of expression), installing a tension between words and things by allowing phonemes to be distinguished from each other and fixed to a semanteme in a one-to-one correlation. Hence, phonemes such as 'li' can now be distinguished from all erogenous esoteric phonemes, and tied to a single semanteme such as *'Joli corps de Lili'* which, producing what Saussure calls a sign, is now capable of standing in a denotative relation with its referent, a spatio-temporal state of affairs dualistically opposed to the ideality of the signification. This is, hence, why Deleuze associates the phallus of castration with disjunctive esoteric words such as (the both voluble and edible, expressible and denotable) Jabberwock.

While Lacan conceives of the 'Name-of-the-Father' during his seminars of the 1950s as a signifier or paternal 'metaphor', repressing the 'Desire-of-the-Mother' (the body as set of letters as its unconscious signified), in Deleuze's appropriation of the Lacanian phallus, we can see that castration is not imposed by the one on the other through repression (the bar between the signifier and the signified). Instead, it is the *transgression of this bar* which produces castration as an event. It is this transgression, this Möbian torsion between both halves of the double screen, that generates an in-corporeal event as castration-effect, as monism-effect, and as the basis for the construction of a plane of immanence. As we will see further in the following chapters, from disparate elements scattered over the depths, heights, physical and metaphysical surfaces, the dynamic genesis entails the gradual assembly of an element (the event) which will retroactively ground everything that came before it in its univocity.

Lastly, with regard to his engagement with the Lacanian conception of Oedipus, it seems that Deleuze's overall argument is not that castration, as conceived by Lacan, is inevitable due to the structure of language, but rather that once the quasi-dualism inherent to onto-logical being is interpreted and expressed in such a manner by language – in short, as soon as humans begin to extract signifieds from brute noise and to articulate the two series – any infant born into this world will be conditioned indirectly to *repeat it*. This is because castration means that the adults the infant relates to themselves treat

## The Three Syntheses of the Body

each other in a binary manner – as male/female, with both overvaluing the phallus (as a + or excess for the woman and a – or lack for the man) – and thus their field of experience will provide the infant with a tension between a sharply distinguished and frequently oscillating absent/present father image and wounded/unharmed mother image. The infant does not yet, for Deleuze, apprehend the parents as castrated or sexed, but it does notice the sharp distinctions and oppositions of their relation to each other and to the infant. This thereby means that the infant will try precisely to bring them together *within terms that imply they are castrated*, even if the infant is not aware of this.

The infant will attempt to mend the mother's wound and restore the father by using a coordination phallus which serves to bring together height and surface (the conjunctive esoteric word) so as to overcome this parental tension, and so will be fooled into entering a castrated interpretation of the onto-logical quasi-duality made possible by language – whereby ideality and corporeality must be *severed* because they are distinct. This distinction is there in onto-logical being once interpreted by language (through the production of signifieds, as distinct from brute noise), but they do not *need* to be related by means of a *severing* or a binary opposition – which we see later manifests itself as the structural split between the unconscious (or body) and the pre/conscious (or thought). Psycho-physical dualism is a *castrated interpretation* of onto-logical being's quasi-dualism, due to the structural split it locates between bodies (the unconscious) and language or thought (the pre/conscious), a split which it enforces, prohibiting the direct contamination of one side by the other.

Lived in this manner, parents' reality will therefore impose itself on infants who will seek to overcome this split at the level of the construction of a conjunctive esoteric word, fusing father and mother (height and surface) at the level of the phoneme. But since the phoneme is structurally opposed, in the conscious discourse spoken by castrated individuals, to semantemes, the infant has there the basis for his own castration, at the level of the distinction between mother/father and height/surface lived within his own body – insofar as it is a conjunctive esoteric word. In other words, since the production of esoteric phonemes will be completely bound up with the coordination of the infant's genital zones, the ensuing castrative split between esoteric phonemes and semantemes will become a split that is lived by the infant's entire body as the infant's body, as we saw, *is* a conjunctive esoteric word. Language's structural split between esoteric phonemes and semantemes is determined on the infant's body – due to this process of being caught up in a castrated interpretation of the parents – thereby becoming *lived at the heart of the body as the split between corporeality and incorporeality.*

Castration is a split opened up between the infant's singular corporeality and the singular reaction of general semantemes to this corporeality, producing an event as a singular surface-effect, but one which is nonetheless conditioned by an *interpretation* of ontological being's quasi-dualism *passed down to the infant* (rather than a necessary universality of the phallus). Thus the infant's castration is inevitable once this interpretation is in place, but since it occurs at the level of the very disjunction between corporeality and ideality, and thus within the infant's own body, it must occur and be repeated always as a singular event since there can be no split between an erogenous body and de-corporealised semantemes that is not singular. Deleuze therefore does not oppose the necessity of the phallus as viewed in this way; he opposes more the generality of the process as understood by the early Lacan, and the logical form it takes in Lacan as the arbiter of the relation between the universal and the particular.

### 3.6 Conclusion: Good Intentions Are Inevitably Punished

In his very first published work on psychoanalysis, an essay from 1961 titled 'From Sacher-Masoch to Masochism', Deleuze was already criticising the 'inflation of the importance of the father' in Freud,[242] and this is arguably the most enduring feature of Deleuze's eleven-year engagement with psychoanalysis ending with *Anti-Oedipus*.[243] In his longer essay from 1967 *Coldness and Cruelty*, Deleuze reaffirms this perspective and now seems to specifically target Lacan's Name-of-the-Father. As he concisely explains: 'Lacan appears to look upon this as a primary and irreducible operation which is independent of all maternal influence.'[244] My first concluding remark is that, developing his insight from *Coldness and Cruelty*, in his concept of the 'Voice' Deleuze brings together, on the one hand, the linguistic operation of the Name-of-the-Father (Oedipus as structural, psycho-sexual ontogenesis as bound up with language acquisition) and, on the other, Klein's good object (which, contra Lacan, is initially both *mother and father*). As such, and particularly thanks to his philosophically informed innovation of esoteric words, mother and father (now as the ideal heights and physical surface) are more equally knotted in the determination of Oedipus, rather than

## The Three Syntheses of the Body

the one being unilaterally submitted to the other. This is the most direct clinical consequence of Deleuze's attempt to philosophically engage Lacan's thought in *The Logic of Sense*.

If, as I mentioned in section 1.4, Lacan did not himself directly tackle the notion of the 'Names-of-the-Father' until the 1970s, it was therefore primarily interlocutors such as Leclaire and Deleuze who would advance Lacan's work in this area in the 1960s. Moreover, Lacan engages with – and may have been influenced by – Deleuze's critique in Seminar XXI, *Les non-dupes errent* ('The Non-duped Err'/'The Names-of-the-Father'). First of all, in *Coldness and Cruelty*, Deleuze prefigures the theory of self-nomination/self-castration from *The Logic of Sense* (Poord'jeli as the name 'a child creates') when he writes:

> The masochist experiences the symbolic order as an intermaternal order in which the mother represents the law under certain prescribed conditions; *she generates the symbolism through which the masochist expresses himself*. It is not a case of identification with the mother [...] [who] literally expels the father from the masochistic universe. [...] [The father] is deprived of all symbolic function.[245]

Lacan refers to *Coldness and Cruelty* in Seminar XXI, lesson of 12 February 1974, and then goes on to directly allude to this passage, stating approvingly that the masochist 'invents himself'. In this seminar more generally, the imaginary, the symbolic and the real, or the body, language and *jouissance*, are to be seen as 'knotted' together in a 'singular' manner. Instead of being overstructured by the symbolic, as we find in the Lacan of the 1950s, the imaginary, and the mother-infant dyad along with it, is now given a more dynamic role, to the relative detriment of the importance of the symbolic, and with the real figuring as that which is in part produced by this new arrangement. Moreover, throughout the lesson of 18 December 1973, Lacan will speak of this knotting as an 'event', insofar as for him speech speaks the event, which he systematically distinguishes from 'sense' (here, contra Deleuze), and he will tie the latter more to the imaginary and the former more to the real. Indeed, for him it is the event which *does the knotting*, bringing him in close proximity to Deleuze's emphasis on the event's function of disjunctively synthesising language and the body.[246]

Secondly, as well as tempering the unilateralism of the Name-of-the-Father in Lacan, the dynamic genesis also entails a re-reading of Klein's project. The first half of the dynamic genesis up to and including castration (series twenty-nine) can be said to centre on the attempt at realising the Kleinian good object of the depressive position. While the body is fragmented into proto-zones during the schizoid position, and while in the depressive position the Voice as good object promises unity at the level of identification, albeit only as an idealised or mythical unity, the sexual-perverse position is precisely the attempt at making the good object both present (no longer withdrawn into the heights) *and* unified or unharmed (no longer fragmented into proto-zones, later partial surfaces during the depressive position). What then is the expression of nonsense (or 'co-sense') on the physical surface by the conjunctive esoteric word if not *the very* (albeit only momentary) *realisation of the good object in and as this very nonsense?*[247] Deleuze therefore does more than merely provide an account of the linguistic mechanisms underlying her work. He also provides a radical new interpretation of the good object as such in the Oedipal position, conflating it with the co- or nonsense produced on the erogenous body as set of letters.

Hence I would suggest that the title of the twenty-ninth series on the Oedipus complex, 'Good Intentions Are Inevitably Punished', succinctly and literally illustrates the dynamic of Oedipus: 'good intentions' – namely speech (construction of a conjunctive esoteric word by incarnating the Voice, momentary realisation of the 'good' object) – followed by their 'inevitable punishment' – namely the castration-effect. Indeed, Deleuze will later explicitly formulate speech as 'intention-result'[248] – by 'result' he means the event[249] – such that the Oedipus complex can be summarised as ultimately the *failure to reconstitute the good object through speech* or, conversely, as *successfully speaking the event* (of castration). While the event implies its own univocity, this is a univocity fundamentally apart from the ideal myth of dimensional and parental unity which the good object promises.

Furthermore, I would argue that in the formula 'good intentions' the term 'intention' should also be taken literally to mean the drive's intentions or cathexes. Deleuze writes:

> Far from being an agency of the depths, intention is the phenomenon of *the surface as set* (*le phénomène d'ensemble de la surface*), or the phenomenon which adequately corresponds to the coordination of the physical surface.[250]

In other words, rather than stemming from the partial drives (projection and introjection), Oedipal 'good' intentions are coextensive and co-substantial with speech as the construction of the body as esoteric set or as set of letters (coordination of zones). We have seen in section 3.4 how this implies a complex interplay of relations of intensive and phonemic difference. Thus, contra Klein, the Oedipus complex is not to be seen as rooted in the schizoid position ('an agency of the depths') and in the depressive position's reaction to it.[251] Rather, identification with the Voice occurs through its incarnation in speech (as good intention), which is inevitably punished as speech speaks the event (of castration).

# Notes

1. Deleuze, *Logic of Sense*, p. ix.
2. Ibid., p. 263. The wording in the preface could suggest we must understand language in terms of its relation to the unconscious, just as the unconscious is now to be seen as inseparable from language (their 'marriage' has been 'consummated', they have become interpenetrated).
3. Ibid., p. 286.
4. See his 1960 Bergson lecture course and *Expressionism in Philosophy: Spinoza* (1968).
5. Deleuze, *Foucault*, p. 69, emphasis mine.
6. Deleuze and Guattari, *What Is Philosophy?*, pp. 38–9. The original French is '*matière*', whereas the English translation 'substance' fails to fully convey the materiality at issue.
7. As he puts it in the contemporaneous 'Immanence: A Life' (1995): 'Immanence is not related to Some Thing as a unity superior to all things or to a Subject as an act that brings about a synthesis of things: it is only when immanence is no longer immanence to anything other than itself that we can speak of a plane of immanence' (p. 27). Immanence therefore belongs to philosophies of transcendence whenever it is posited as immanent *to* something – be it man's synthetic unity of apperception in Kantian epistemology and Husserlian phenomenology (the priority of thinking over being), or God's analytic unity in pre-Kantian metaphysics as well as, for Deleuze, in Heidegger (the priority of being over thinking). Immanence must be immanent to neither man nor God, neither thinking nor being, and for this requires an impersonal and a-subjective transcendental field populated by non-theological and non-anthropological 'singularities' as fields of force relations. See *What Is Philosophy?*, pp. 44–9, and *Logic of Sense*, pp. 120–3.
8. There are nonetheless obvious and clear distinctions between the plane of immanence of 1991 and the 1969 conception of sense, which I will tackle in Chapter 5.

9. Deleuze speaks of this 'non-relation' as implying a relation of a 'deeper sort' – see *Foucault*, p. 53; on the 'non-relation' see also 'Klossowski or bodies-language', in Appendix II of *The Logic of Sense*. More generally, I consider this 'non-relation' to derive from Deleuze's transformed insubstantial Spinozism, and from the non-causal correspondence or 'parallelism' pertaining in the latter between the attributes of thought and extension, and correlatively the powers of thinking and being.
10. In Montebello's important *Deleuze. La passion de la pensée*, pp. 29–60, he shows that this framework extends from the 1950s and 1960s to the 1990s.
11. The plane's equality is implied throughout *What Is Philosophy?*, and indeed throughout Deleuze's work as a whole, though it is only explicitly acknowledged on a small number of occasions, for instance in the thesis of an absolute equality of powers (of thinking and knowing, and of acting and existing) in the seventh chapter and on the final page of *Expressionism in Philosophy: Spinoza*. Deleuze noted in 1990 that in his 1968 book on Spinoza one 'already' finds a 'plane of immanence' at the level of Deleuze's reworking of Spinozist substance (I would argue, as 'sense') (*Expressionism*, p. 11). The plane's reversibility is stated explicitly in *What Is Philosophy?*, for instance on p. 38: 'this is not a fusion but a reversibility, an immediate, perpetual, instantaneous exchange [...] there is only a fold from one to the other. It is in this sense that thinking and being are said to be one and the same' (as such, Deleuze writes 'the plane of immanence is ceaselessly being woven' on both sides: ibid., p. 38). If we find the thesis of absolute equality in the Spinoza book, the plane's reversibility is arguably only first thought through in *The Logic of Sense*, which I will discuss in detail in Chapters 4–5. On the plane of immanence in Deleuze, see Montebello, *Deleuze*, pp. 29–60, and Cherniavsky, *Concept et méthode*, pp. 110–12.
12. Deleuze, *Logic of Sense*, p. 30.
13. Ibid., p. 105. This quotation comes shortly after a positive reference to 'structuralism'.
14. This should contribute to our understanding of what a plane of immanence is and how it works, since this term remains highly allusive and under-commented on in the secondary literature, despite being arguably the fundamental concept in Deleuze's philosophy.
15. Alliez, 'The BwO Condition or, The Politics of Sensation', pp. 99–100, emphasis in the original. Deleuze himself equates the two in *Negotiations*, writing 'expressionism [is] the counterpart of constructionism' (p. 147).
16. Deleuze, *Logic of* Sense, p. 82. Alliez's work on Deleuze insists on the centrality of the theme of constructivism to his philosophical project (see also Alliez, *The Signature of the World*, pp. 13–14). I would add

## The Three Syntheses of the Body

to this that *The Logic of Sense* is arguably the first fully constructivist Deleuzian text. In the preface to the Italian edition, republished in *Two Regimes of Madness*, Deleuze indeed remarks that *The Logic of Sense* was the 'first time' he 'sought a form that was not in keeping with traditional philosophy' (p. 63).

17. Deleuze, *Expressionism*, p. 335.
18. Ibid., p. 335.
19. In this sense, expressionism points to an insubstantial transformation of Spinozist psycho-physical parallelism, whereby the 'substance' through which radically irreducible attributes and powers (thought/extension and thinking/being) nonetheless articulate, is in fact continually *produced* in this juncture of the heterogeneous (the disjunctive synthesis). This causality is immanent, it is producer-produced with no discernible hyphen.
20. In this case, we are dealing with a linguistic mechanism, but Deleuze will soon replace it in later books with a series of other and at times radically non-linguistic ones. Thus, when Deleuze writes in *The Logic of Sense* that the proposition 'expresses sense', this must be framed by the 1968 Spinoza book, and indeed the Spinoza book should itself be framed by Deleuze's engagement in the late 1960s with propositional logic, though in later works he will sever all ties between expression (in the ontological sense) and the proposition. This is how we must understand Alliez's point that in *The Logic of Sense* expressionism is 'purely linguistic': this is such only because in this book expressionism's constructive counterpart is language or structure.
21. On this see, for instance, Deleuze, *Expressionism*, pp. 169–86.
22. Constructivism functions 'nonphilosophically' for Deleuze. In *What Is Philosophy?* (p. 41) he means by this philosophy's pre-philosophical pre-condition. This puts psychoanalysis in an interesting position with regard to philosophy in *The Logic of Sense*, though I will not directly pursue this question further. In section 5.3 I will more generally tackle the relation of the disciplines in *The Logic of Sense*.
23. The full import of Carroll's work in this regard will be tackled in the final chapter.
24. Deleuze, *Logic of Sense*, p. 29.
25. '[B]ody/language, to eat/to speak' (ibid., p. 30).
26. Ibid., p. 52.
27. Ibid., p. 52.
28. Ibid., p. 52.
29. Ibid., p. 52.
30. Ibid., p. 53.
31. Carroll, *The Hunting of the Snark*, p. 41.
32. See particularly Deleuze, *Logic of Sense*, pp. 4, 30–1, 36–7, 45. Denotation (of bodies or objects), manifestation (of a person or

subject) and signification (of universal or general concepts) are the three 'primary' dimensions of the proposition, while 'expression' is the fourth and most foundational. I will fully tackle Deleuze's theory of the proposition in section 4.2.

33. Deleuze, *Logic of Sense*, pp. 24–5. It is more accurate to say that for Deleuze – insofar as every expressible meaning is at base an 'event' – we should say that the 'becoming-forgetful-of-the-man' is the attribute of the state of affairs, because events are always packaged in verbs stated in the infinitive (see ibid., p. 25). I tackle this further in section 4.3.
34. Ibid., p. 25.
35. I mean in the sense of the infant's ontogenesis and acquisition of language.
36. Ibid., p. 31.
37. Ibid., p. 209. I will explore the connection between speech and expression in detail in Chapter 4.
38. See ibid., pp. 29–33. Deleuze emphasises that Carroll is often preoccupied with the duality of eating and speaking and – I will suggest in Chapter 5 – with its univocal bypassing in the work of art (yet to come). For instance, in *Alice's Adventures in Wonderland*, the Mock Turtle sings about soup (Chapter X), while in *Through the Looking-Glass* Alice recites a poem about fish (Chapter IX), and then elsewhere is told to eat her words. In *Sylvie and Bruno*, Chapter 24, a show about 'Bits of Shakespeare' is presented to frogs, while usually one speaks of 'bits of food' (see also *Logic of Sense*, p. 29). We also see it in the following extract: '"the archbishop of Canterbury found it advisable –," – "Found *what?*" asked the Duck. – "Found *it*", the Mouse replied rather crossly: "of course you know what 'it' means". – "I know what 'it' means well enough, when *I* find a thing", said the Duck: "it's generally a frog or a worm. The question is, what did the archbishop find?"' (quoted in *Logic of Sense*, p. 31), namely that 'it' was advisable to offer the crown to William the Conquerer (see ibid., p. 31).
39. Carroll, quoted in *Logic of Sense*, p. 32.
40. Ibid., p. 32.
41. Ibid., p. 31.
42. Ibid., p. 54.
43. Ibid., p. 54.
44. Ibid., p. 264.
45. On the three syntheses in *The Logic of Sense*, see Faulkner, *Deleuze and the Three Syntheses of Time*, and Hughes, *Deleuze and the Genesis of Representation*. I distinguish my reading from theirs, however, in that I read the three syntheses primarily through psychoanalysis and linguistics, and only secondarily in terms of philosophy, both to be able to appreciate the contribution structuralist psychoanalysis makes to

Deleuze's ontology, and also to be able to better identify the specificity of the syntheses as they appear in *The Logic of Sense* (rather than, for instance, in *Difference and Repetition*).

46. Deleuze, *Logic of Sense*, p. 225. Here Deleuze diverges from at least the early Freud, who does not make this distinction (see Freud, 'Three Essays', pp. 197–9).
47. Deleuze, *Logic of Sense*, p. 226.
48. Ibid., p. 225.
49. Ibid., p. 226.
50. Ibid., p. 226. This is Freud's 'primary repression' as mentioned in Chapter 1, which he views as coextensive with the emergence of the ego.
51. This lays the affective groundwork for the phantasm, in Deleuze, which is modelled on the infinitive verb. See section 4.3.
52. Ibid., p. 228. This emphasis on the zone's 'surface' brings Deleuze close to Lacan's and Leclaire's work on this matter – Leclaire speaks of the body as a 'corporeal surface' (*Psychoanalyzing*, p. 88).
53. Deleuze notes Freud's observations regarding the 'acoustic origin of the superego' (*Logic of Sense*, p. 221), which adds credence to my claim below that the Voice is Deleuze's conception of the Lacanian Name-of-the-Father.
54. Freud, 'Narcissism', p. 68.
55. Ibid., p. 68.
56. Deleuze, *Logic of Sense*, p. 234.
57. Ibid., p. 218.
58. Deleuze writes that rather than introjecting and projecting the Voice as good object (the superego) (ibid., pp. 217–18), the infant identifies with it (p. 219), and as long as the infant identifies with it, it grants the ego 'assistance and love' (p. 218). However, if the infant turns back to the partial objects, and introjects and projects them (the id – pp. 217–18), the good object will manifest 'hatred' towards it (p. 218).
59. This takes us to the next, phallic, stage, and to the problem of conjunction.
60. See Klein, 'Notes on Some Schizoid Mechanisms'.
61. Deleuze, *Logic of Sense*, p. 228.
62. Deleuze offers Lacan's mirror stage as the paradigmatic example of this which, we saw in Chapter 2, Deleuze seeks to rework as an oral-aural synthesis, rather than a scopic-*Gestaltic* one, via the operations of the body without organs.
63. This relates to the notion of threshold which I explore below.
64. I noted the rich manifold and varying fields of experience open to unconscious presentations in Freud's 'The Unconscious' in Chapter 1.
65. Ibid., p. 228, emphasis mine.
66. Ibid., p. 228.

67. Ibid., pp. 228, 234.
68. I will return to this in the next section.
69. Deleuze, *Logic of Sense*, pp. 229, 234. It is not entirely clear whether Deleuze distinguishes between the 'ideal' object and the 'good' object of the depressive position, the former being closer to the combined figure of the parents than the latter, even though Klein does make this distinction clear (see 'Early Stages of the Oedipus Conflict', p. 217). For the sake of clarity, I suggest that we view Deleuze's 'Voice' as having three progressively sexuated incarnations, without nonetheless ever being purely associated with one gender/sex: (1) the Voice as good object, at the start of the depressive position; (2) the Voice as 'good ideal penis', at the beginning of the Oedipal phase, in which the two parents are more discernible; (3) the Voice as tied to the 'father-image'.
70. Deleuze, *Logic of Sense*, p. 234.
71. Klein discusses these issues throughout her early *The Psycho-Analysis of Children* in particular, which Deleuze is drawing on; see also 'A Study of Envy and Gratitude', p. 218. As I will show, it seems that by strongly emphasising the structure of presence/absence (+/−) in parental relations, Deleuze is much closer to a Lacanian reading of the Oedipus complex in which the *separation* of the parents is not an issue.
72. See *The Psycho-Analysis of Children*, Chapters XI–XII. See also 'Early Stages of the Oedipus Conflict', where she links it, firstly, to oral and anal *frustration*, and secondly, to the awareness of the 'anatomical difference between the sexes' (p. 70), thereby bypassing entirely the problem of its cultural construction via the phallus.
73. Whereas Freud understands secondary narcissism as implying a 'desexualisation' ('The Ego and the Id', p. 386) of libido connected with the formation of the ego, Deleuze reverses this by considering secondary narcissism to imply a *sexualisation*, to constitute sexuality as such.
74. We saw this in Chapter 1 with regard to the case of Ernst, who at the age of one and a half would have been around the right age for the Kleinian onset of the properly Oedipal position.
75. Deleuze, *Logic of Sense*, p. 234.
76. Ibid., p. 258.
77. Ibid., p. 103.
78. Ibid., p. 259.
79. Ibid., p. 258.
80. Ibid., p. 226.
81. For example, it has often been noted how infants try to eat or to put in their mouth any object they find once weaned off the breast – and it is no doubt partly on this basis that Deleuze says any denotable object is

## The Three Syntheses of the Body

in principle consumable – since, for Deleuze, the infant is at this stage 'explor[ing] its orifice and field of intensity, from the maximum to the minimum and vice versa' (ibid., p. 259), finding what objects can be used to satisfy its oral drive.

82. In the same way, we saw in section 1.2 that for Leclaire a zone's sensible-intensive difference conditions its object.
83. Ibid., pp. 263–4.
84. Ibid., p. 264. Deleuze explicitly refers here to Leclaire's book *Psychoanalyzing*. This appreciation was indeed mutual – Leclaire considered Deleuze a 'remarkable clinician and excellent reader of Freud', and recognised that in Deleuze the 'surface', as the 'surface of the body', 'assures the distinction between sounds functioning as words, and the sonorous quality of things and of bodily noises' – see *Rompre les charmes*, p. 235, n. 15 (translations mine).
85. Deleuze, *Logic of Sense*, p. 263.
86. Deleuze borrows this observation from the article 'Approche théorique du fantasme', by the Lacanian Robert Pujol (see *Logic of Sense*, p. 268, n. 5).
87. Deleuze, *Logic of Sense*, p. 269, n. 8.
88. Ibid., p. 279.
89. Ibid., p. 221.
90. Ibid., p. 264.
91. In his contemporaneous *Oedipe à Vincennes* seminar, Leclaire also seems to give the oral zone this privilege, based on its having ties to both the organic body and self-preservative drives (such as feeding), and also to the symbolically inscribed erogenous 'surface' which becomes detached from the former. Leclaire posits that the erogenous body is 'centred' or coordinated by one of its zones or 'singularities', particularly by one with a dual status, with one foot in the organic order and the other in the erogenous body, citing the mouth as an example of such a zone (pp. 39–40).
92. On Kleinian reparation and restoration see Riviere's 'On the Genesis of Psychical Conflict in Earliest Infancy', pp. 58, 61; Isaacs' 'The Nature and Function of Phantasy', p. 85; Klein's 'Early Stages of the Oedipus Conflict', p. 79, 'A Contribution to the Psychogenesis of Manic-Depressive States' and *The Psycho-Analysis of Children*. Segal provides a useful introduction to these notions in *Introduction to the Work of Melanie Klein*, Chapters 6 and 8; see also Kristeva's *Melanie Klein*, pp. 78–80.
93. For Deleuze, the Oedipus complex applies equally to boys and girls (as we find in the Lacanian school, and contra Freud and Klein, who also notes differences – see her *The Psycho-Analysis of Children*, Chapters 11 and 12). Whenever the masculine pronoun is used this will be for ease of expression.

94. Deleuze, *Logic of Sense*, p. 240, n. 3.
95. Ibid., p. 235.
96. This is the evolution from the good ideal penis as phantasy of continuous parental copulation. While not completely separate to the extent that this phantasy will still partially subsist (as what Segal (1978, p. 108) calls a 'defensive structur[e]'), in Klein the Oedipus complex is defined by a progressive separation of the parents and weakening of this phantasm.
97. Deleuze, *Logic of Sense*, p. 260.
98. This brings Deleuze closer in line with Lacan, to the extent that the Desire-of-the-Mother is precisely a series of *signifiers* – on this see particularly Chiesa, *Subjectivity and Otherness*, section 3.6. It seems that Deleuze is (1) *delaying*, beyond Klein, the point at which the infant's introjection of partial objects gives way to whole objects (this appears to already start emerging from after the age of three months, for Klein – see 'Contribution to the Psychogenesis of Manic-Depressive States', p. 141, and more generally pp. 141–5), thereby closely associating the unconscious, the drive and *partial* objects (objects (a)), along lines we are familiar with thanks to Chapter 1; (2) proposing that *language* provides the mechanism accounting for how this shift to whole objects occurs, which I will show below is located at the level of sememes and very late on during the Oedipal stage (around age five).
99. During the 1950s (particularly Seminars IV–VI), Lacan repeatedly attacks the priority given to the mother during early infancy in Klein. While he often endorses her positing of the phallus as initially in the mother's body, he views this imaginary scenario as always already overwritten by the symbolic, such that for him Klein fails to account for the *mechanism* explaining *how* the developmental processes she describes effectively take place (on this last point see Seminar IV, pp. 185–6).
100. In *Melanie Klein*, Kristeva goes so far as to call this imaginary triangle a 'dyad' (p. 129), a dyad made of three vertices.
101. Heimann, 'Certain Functions of Introjection and Projection', p. 162, emphasis in the original. Kristeva, in *Melanie Klein*, pp. 129, 172–4, has also strongly emphasised the priority of the Kleinian Oedipal *couple*, and notes that the work of the early Lacan is aimed at filling in the gaps left by the theory of language *lacking* in Klein's work and needed to *support* her theory of the *couple*. Based on Lacan's Seminars IV–VI, it seems rather than Lacan's turn to language *distorted* the very basis of the parental couple rather than providing a linguistic basis for it, and in this regard Deleuze's work is arguably more faithful to this project of linguistically supporting her theory of the Oedipal couple.
102. Though Deleuze is not simply Kleinian. For one, in Klein this imaginary triangle is immersed in the *internal* phantasy life of the infant,

## The Three Syntheses of the Body

and in the projections of oral, anal, urethral and genital drives and incipient 'stirrings' onto the parents and their relations (see Heimann, 'Certain Functions of Introjection and Projection', pp. 163–4). In Lacan, the complex is more plugged into the external world – for instance the parents' symbolic castration, which Deleuze agrees provides the condition of possibility for the traversing of the Oedipus complex. Something like a synthesis of these two positions seems to obtain in Deleuze, though I consider him to lean more on the Lacanian side here.

103. Deleuze, *Logic of Sense*, pp. 260–1.
104. Ibid., pp. 189–90.
105. This is the 'Event' of castration, which I discuss in section 3.5.
106. '[W]hat guarantees [. . .] the first stage in the formation of a language, is the good object of the depressive position up above' (ibid., pp. 220–1).
107. See Seminar XI, pp. 180–9.
108. That is to say equally ontologically and ontogenetically.
109. Deleuze, *Logic of Sense*, p. 261.
110. Ibid., p. 261.
111. We will see this is true even after castration, by attempting to establish a paradoxical connection between its two severed halves (the 'occupant without a place' and 'place without an occupant' – see section 3.5). In short, the Voice as ideality of meaning (the signified) will always be *lacking* from the viewpoint of the signifier (the 'surface'), in line with the structuralist (originally Lévi-Straussian) axiom concerning the signifier's excess over the signified, as ontologised ontogenetically by Deleuze. For a very clear account of this axiom, see Livingston, *Politics of Logic*, Chapter 2. This perceived lack from the viewpoint of the signifier necessitates the employment of a phallus to re-converge the signifier and the signified, always inadequately (again, see section 3.5).
112. As we saw earlier, 'there is no more monism here than dualism' (*Logic of Sense*, p. 30) – dualism is a distortion of onto-logical being's *quasi-dualism* and monism-effect.
113. Deleuze notes that the third, disjunctive, synthesis or series of sexuality 'proves to be the truth and destination of the others [connection and conjunction], to the degree that the disjunction attains its positive and affirmative use' (ibid., p. 262), the latter of which refers to the production of an 'event' as the *basis of language* – see sections 3.5–3.6 and Chapter 4.
114. Ibid., p. 261, emphasis in the original.
115. Ibid., p. 230.
116. Bowden, in *Priority of Events*, pp. 216–17, 242, has also asserted this point of connection with Lacan in his thorough and impressive

reading of the dynamic genesis; however, I develop a partly divergent reading of Deleuze's relation to Lacan, since Bowden locates the entire dynamic genesis within the framework of the Lacan of the mid-1950s, whereas I have proposed that Deleuze's work intends to offer an alternative to the work of the early Lacan. Moreover, Bowden considers the Lacanian phallus to already appear at the level of the 'phallus of coordination', whereas I consider its binary form (+/−) to only appear upon castration, and to still function at that level in a way not entirely reducible to it.

117. There is little in Klein to suggest that, of the disjunctions subsumed under the Voice as good object – absent/present, wounded/unharmed – the absent/unharmed poles must be picked out and worked on in relation to each other. Deleuze simply announces 'We believe now that the cleavage is achieved as follows' (*Logic of Sense*, p. 234).

118. The Voice will always have greater unity, even if only because its transcendence with regard to the physical surface gives it an *ideal* unity lacking at the level of corporeal experience. In short, this unity is imagined, idealised, not real, insofar as the Voice is a projection from the side of the physical surface, and is not how those endowed with language themselves experience existence.

119. Ibid., p. 235.

120. As a rule of thumb, it can be said that Deleuze's dynamic genesis *makes sense* within a Kleinian framework (at least up to the end of the Oedipal stage), but can *only fully* be accounted for if we see reparation as externally pre-conditioned by a kind of Lacanian phallus, and as internally generated by the construction of an esoteric word.

121. It can also be noted here that one of the strongest indications that Deleuze's reading of the Oedipus complex owes more to Lacan than to Klein is the fact that he does not distinguish between the boy's and the girl's confrontation with the initial onset of the complex – following Lacan – whereas Freud (as we saw in Chapter 1) and Klein (as can be seen clearly, for instance, in *Psycho-Analysing Children* and 'Early Stages of the Oedipus Conflict', p. 70) do make such a distinction. Bowden, in *Priority of Events*, has also emphasised this point.

122. Deleuze, *Difference and Repetition*, pp. 130–2.

123. Deleuze, 'How Do We Recognize Structuralism?', p. 188.

124. This can be understood in terms of the Lacanian *Che Vuoi?* – 'What is it that the mother desires beyond me?' – as documented in such cases as Freud's 'Little Hans', where the narrative centres on the infant's continuous line of questioning, partly with regard to whether his mother and sister have a penis (as that which would account for what his mother desires in him).

125. Lacan, 'The Function and Field of Speech and Language', p. 94.

126. Deleuze, *Difference and Repetition*, p. 160, n. 7.

127. Ibid., p. 161, n. 7.
128. Deleuze is referring here to the texts Leclaire wrote during the 1950s, building on Lacan's work on the psychoses, in which he documents the founding unconscious questions lived by the subject, such as 'Am I alive or dead?' (the obsessional neurotic) or 'Am I male or female?' (the hysteric). See 'Jerome, ou La mort dans la vie de l'obsédé', in *Démasquer le réel*, pp. 121–46.
129. See Deleuze, *Logic of Sense*: 'What is the Snark?' (p. 67); in 'How Do We Recognize Structuralism?' Deleuze makes the connection between the snark and the Lacanian phallus even more explicit (p. 187).
130. Deleuze, *Logic of Sense*, p. 67.
131. The incarnation of the 'voice of God' (ibid., p. 221) constitutive of the physical surface represses the body without organs. In the schizophrenic, on the other hand, a violent manic-depressive tension is established between the body without organs and the Voice (as 'infinite judgement of God': see Deleuze, *Essays Critical and Clinical*), which threatens to 'steal' his 'body, thought and speech' (*Logic of Sense*, p. 222) (as we see in the case of Judge Schreber) by determining them morphemically. While still corporeally marked by linguistic elements, the schizophrenic does not morphemically or esoterically structure them as phonemes but allows them to subsist as phonetic blocks. Following Deleuze, we must conclude that, contra the Lacan of Seminar III, the psychotic is not lacking a phallus (the foreclosure of the Name-of-the-Father) but rather a conjunctive esoteric word. However, this does not mean the physical surface simply incarnates the infinite judgement of God, and Deleuze seems to be searching for a way out of Artaud's impasse of either/or. Since we are not dealing with a unilateral inscription of universalities or generalities onto the body, but with a bilateral process, the physical surface is more anti-Christ than Christ, the conjunctive (and later disjunctive) esoteric word founding what Deleuze will call the 'Dionysian sense-producing machine' of the phantasm (ibid., p. 122). Hence Nietzsche is closer to Lewis Carroll than Artaud here.
132. Deleuze, *Logic of Sense*, p. 221, emphasis in the original.
133. Ibid., p. 221. The English translation of this passage is confusing and fails to accurately render the classic Lacanian themes being discussed here (compare *Logic of Sense*, p. 221 with p. 225 of the French). Further evidence for my claim can be found in *Anti-Oedipus*, which refers to the 'eminent unity of the despot' as a 'voice from on high' (p. 224), the despot being associated in the book with Lacan's Name-of-the-Father (the despot 'welds desire to the Law', p. 227), and the term 'eminence' is also used in *The Logic of Sense* to refer to the Voice (see p. 221).
134. Deleuze, *Logic of Sense*, p. 221.

135. See, for instance, Chiesa, in *Subjectivity and Otherness*, pp. 61–2, 78–82, who reminds us that the *infant* must also, in the Lacanian account of the Oedipus complex, actively pass through it rather than being passively subjected to it.
136. This retroactive logic will be explained fully in section 3.5 and in Chapter 4.
137. Deleuze, *Logic of Sense*, p. 265, translation modified. The detail into which I will go below is justified by the in-depth knowledge Deleuze appears to have had of Leclaire's work. In footnotes, Deleuze refers to specific passages from *Psychoanalyzing* and to precise arguments. One of the pages he refers to contains Leclaire's claim that Poord'jeli is the 'secret replica of the proper name' (*Psychoanalyzing*, p. 81).
138. Mengue, in *Proust-Joyce, Deleuze-Lacan*, examines Deleuze's relation to Lacan at the level of their respective uses of literature and nonsense; however, he claims that Joyce is more important in this encounter than Carroll (see pp. 51–2). For an interesting discussion of Deleuze, Lacan and Carroll, see Lecercle, *Philosophy Through the Looking-Glass*, and more recently *Deleuze and Language*.
139. Leclaire, *Psychoanalyzing*, p. 90. This term comes from the linguist Martinet. He does the same when discussing the Wolf Man's 'V', considering it as a letter and all letters as monemes (ibid., p. 62).
140. As Saussure showed, the choice of signifier for a signified is arbitrary ('*arbre*' and 'tree' convey largely the same signified in each language), but once (arbitrarily) selected the relation must remain fixed.
141. This is why Deleuze states that in Leclaire it is the 'image of the phallus' (i.e. phallus of coordination) which 'assures' the 'convergence and continuity' of the 'surface of the entire body', conceived as a 'set or sequence of letters' (*Logic of Sense*, pp. 264–5, translation modified).
142. Leclaire (*Psychoanalyzing*, p. 91) notes that this is what distinguishes the psychotic from the neurotic; lacking a centring phallus, the psychotic is not inscribed by letters but by senseless phonetic elements.
143. In 'Les éléments en jeu', he refers to this phallic signifier as the 'signifier of castration', which he likens to an 'unconscious concept', borrowing Freud's term in his study of the Wolf Man. An unconscious concept, unlike a conscious one, is capable of reuniting under it a number of non-self-identical objects, which in the case of the Wolf Man are 'baby, penis, and faeces', whereas a conscious concept (or signified) must be fixed in relation to one or several self-identical objects.
144. Deleuze, *Logic of Sense*, p. 264, emphasis in the original, translation modified. We can add to this that Leclaire views letters as equally phonemic and/or graphic, while for Deleuze they are solely phonemic. The graphic nature of the letter can be seen particularly clearly in the case of the Wolf Man's 'V' – which Leclaire gives as a prime example of a letter. In his analysis of the Wolf Man case in 'Les éléments en jeu', Leclaire

shows how the letter V takes on its various senses primarily at the graphic or visual/written level, the sense of the 'V' being contaminated by those of its graphic transformations < > M Λ W ^ ^, etc. (kneeling woman and backside (Λ), letter M (Matrona), letter W (Wolf), open wolf ears, open eyes, open mouth, jaws, etc.) which are all graphic or visual manipulations of the original V. However, Deleuze implies the V is in fact closer to the phallus, being too 'general' to be a letter, since it refers to more than one zone (the general movement of 'opening' the eyes, the mouth, etc.), and because it 'connotes several dramatic scenes rather than objects of satisfaction' (*Logic of Sense*, p. 264). Here Deleuze joins a long tradition of twentieth-century French thought in 'denigrating vision', as Martin Jay calls it. *The Logic of Sense* should be seen as an attempt at a *primarily oral*/auditory theory of sense, where vision is subordinated to the mouth/ears, no doubt partly as a corrective to phenomenology's prioritisation of the visual field.

145. Deleuze, *Logic of Sense*, p. 264.
146. Ibid., p. 142, emphasis in the original.
147. See Jakobson, *Fundamentals of Language*; Deleuze refers to this book in 'How Do We Recognize Structuralism?'
148. Deleuze, *Logic of Sense*, p. 264, translation modified.
149. In addition to being associated with movements of libido occurring in all zones (anal, urethral, genital), the distinctive traits supporting the phonemes cut out of the Voice will directly impress themselves on the *ear* as erogenous zone; since this distinctive trait can in turn be parroted by the infant, it will also be transferred to the oral zone.
150. Ibid., p. 264.
151. Ibid., p. 266. I will examine co-sense further in the next section.
152. As Deleuze puts it, the infant literally 'learn[s] to speak on his own body' since the elements of the conjunctive esoteric word 'have not yet a reference other than a sexual one' (ibid., p. 266); and elsewhere, 'phonemes refe[r] to the erogenous zones, morphemes to the phallus of coordination, and semantemes to the phallus of castration' (ibid., p. 266).
153. Whereas in the schizophrenic, for Deleuze, 'the maternal voice must be decomposed [...] into literal phonetic sounds', and 'recomposed [in the depths] into inarticulate blocks [using the body without organs]' (ibid., p. 222), in the non-psychotic these phonetic sounds are hence recomposed on the surface using an esoteric word.
154. Ibid., pp. 265, 280.
155. Ibid., p. 261.
156. In Poord'jeli, we can identify an 'evocative' 'desire to drink', tied initially to '*choif*', and a 'reparative' denial of maternal, and Liliane's, castration, through the construction of the word itself.
157. We can see from Lacan's Seminar XII, lessons of 24 March to 28

April 1965, that the consensus among Lacan's and Leclaire's students and peers was that Poord'jeli was a fundamental fantasy-formation, which Leclaire (along with Lacan) disputes, claiming it to be closer to a proper name (or as Jean Oury calls it in these lessons, a *literal Gestalt*); therefore this immediately connects conceptually to the function of the Name-of-the-Father. In this respect, Deleuze's reading, if my reconstruction is correct, would be accurate and fairly orthodox, if also an ontological interpretation of it (see the 'event' discussed in section 3.5).

158. Thus we can speak of the physical surface as a *phallus-of-coordination-effect* (and castration as a phallus-of-castration-effect), insofar as the phallus (of coordination then of castration) is generated *on and as* the surface itself, through the construction of a conjunctive (then disjunctive) esoteric word, and does not precede it.
159. David-Ménard, *Deleuze et la psychanalyse*, pp. 22–30, 28, translations mine.
160. Ibid., p. 22.
161. Deleuze, *Logic of Sense*, p. 266.
162. On this project see Voss, *Conditions of Thought*.
163. Deleuze, 'How Do We Recognize Structuralism?', p. 176.
164. Ibid., p. 176.
165. Ibid., p. 176.
166. Ibid., p. 176.
167. This invokes the ontological structure or quasi-dualism I outlined in section 3.1. The singularities to which differential relations give rise cannot be considered as existing on the same plane, just as in our discussion above the phonetic traits cannot belong to the same dimension as the morphemic thresholds.
168. Ibid., pp. 176–7, emphasis in the original. This is again repeated in 'Eighth Series of Structure' in *Logic of Sense*, p. 60.
169. Deleuze, 'How Do We Recognize Structuralism?', p. 178. Deleuze refers here to Leclaire's 'Compter avec la psychanalyse (1966–7)', and to the precise pages in which he develops the *binarité/bi-polarité* distinction I mentioned in section 1.3 (see ibid., p. 306, n. 20).
170. Leclaire makes this explicit first in 'L'analyste à sa place', and then in his seminars from the mid–late 1960s (collected as 'Compter avec la psychanalyse', in three parts), particularly in the third part (1966–7), as well as in *Psychoanalyzing*, as we saw in section 1.3 (regarding the 'suture' marked on the forehead). Deleuze would in all likelihood have been aware of this ongoing debate between Leclaire and Miller, which took centre stage in the first issues of the now famous 1960s journal *Cahiers pour l'analyse*, which Deleuze cites repeatedly in *The Logic of Sense*, *Difference and Repetition* and 'How Do We Recognize Structuralism?'

*The Three Syntheses of the Body*

171. See again David-Ménard, *Deleuze et la psychanalyse*, pp. 25–6, who develops similar points and links them to Deleuze's relative demotion of the phallus in relation to the drive.
172. See Deleuze, *Logic of Sense*, pp. 55, 265.
173. Ibid., p. 267, n. 3. In note 2 on the same page, Deleuze brings up this point in the context of Laplanche and Pontalis' 'Fantasy and the Origins of Sexuality', in which, he claims, they understand the pregenital series in terms of images 'fragmented "in the series of moments of the transition to auto-eroticism"', i.e. in the *serial development* of the physical surface's secondary narcissism (auto-eroticism), which Deleuze explains, for them, occurs when the oral drive disengages itself from the partial objects of the depths (ibid., p. 246). Regarding the 'pre-Oedipal parental images', Deleuze writes on page 267, note 3, that they are 'set in motion' by the pregenital series, and 'fabricated in an entirely different manner than they will be later on'. Here, the adults are 'implicate[d] [...] in relation to the child, without the child's being able to "compound" what is in question', as we saw with regard to the Voice as domain of preexistence. On the other hand, the 'Oedipal forms another series, with other and otherwise formed parental images' (p. 262).
174. For Deleuze, the expression of sense depends on denotation as one of the proposition's constituent dimensions (see 'Third Series of the Proposition').
175. We will see in the next section that the phallus of castration in turn steps in again to re-converge this disassociation, to return as phallus of coordination within this disassociation, at the level of the *identity* of the two forms of surface nonsense (occupant without a place and place without an occupant). We have in short a constant tension throughout the dynamic genesis between phallic convergence and the Voice as cause of divergence, or between *castration* and *good intentions*, even after the infant has become castrated.
176. Freud, 'The Unconscious', pp. 195–6.
177. Ibid., p. 190.
178. Ibid., p. 221.
179. Ibid., p. 190.
180. Freud, 'Formulations on the Two Principles of Mental Functioning', p. 42.
181. Freud, 'The Unconscious', p. 191, emphasis in the original. In 'Fantasy and the Origins of Sexuality', Laplanche and Pontalis consider the notion of 'psychical reality' to introduce 'a third category, that of structure' (p. 17), since it is irreducible to the opposition real-imaginary. Deleuze clearly has a Laplanchian conception of the symbolic in 'How Do We Recognize Structuralism?', considering the symbolic to bypass the very same distinction, and indeed in his 'Thirtieth Series

of the Phantasm' in *Logic of Sense* we find the same structural model explicitly being adopted (see p. 241). This is also, as I have shown in section 3.1, Deleuze's conception of immanence. See also Laplanche, *Essays on Otherness*, Chapter 1.
182. Freud, 'The Unconscious', p. 190.
183. Ibid., pp. 190–1.
184. Ibid., p. 192.
185. Ibid., p. 221.
186. Ibid., p. 221.
187. Ibid., p. 207.
188. Ibid., p. 222.
189. Ibid., p. 217.
190. Ibid., p. 218.
191. Ibid., p. 217.
192. Ibid., p. 218.
193. Ibid., p. 207.
194. Ibid., p. 207.
195. Ibid., p. 207.
196. Leclaire will later conceive of this split in terms of the 'primary system' (*Ucs.*) vs. the 'secondary process' (*Pcs./Cs.*), viewing the latter as a 'consciousness effect', to be understood as a relatively superficial if still fundamental aspect of the psyche (*Psychoanalyzing*, pp. 110–11).
197. This is the point I am trying to convey by referring to it as the 'pre/conscious'.
198. Freud, 'From the History of an Infantile Neurosis (The "Wolf Man")'.
199. Deleuze here is strongly influenced by Laplanche and Pontalis' 'Fantasy and the Origins of Sexuality'. Laplanche and Pontalis argue that if in Freud it is fantasy, rather than the drive, which derives from an endogenous evolution of sexuality as phylogenetic inheritance or instinct, it must nonetheless be always contingently activated or transmitted to the infant by the *parents' fantasies*, thereby marrying a priori structure and contingent genesis. They go on to suggest that in Freud, the erogenous zones are 'not only those which most attract the mother's attention, but also those which have an obvious exchange value (orifices or skin covering)', serving not only to 'sustain a local pleasure, but also [functioning as] a meeting place with maternal desire and fantasy' (p. 17). Thus, as we saw regarding Leclaire in Chapter 1, these authors consider parental fantasies as literally inscribed on the infant body's zones.
200. Indeed, in the preamble leading up to Deleuze's analysis of Leclaire's work in the thirty-second series, he states that the infant's 'premonition' of the meaning of words spoken by 'a familial hum of voices which already speak of her', is of 'considerable importance' (*Logic of*

*Sense*, p. 263); the phonemic elements the infant cuts out of the Voice are not completely meaningless to the infant and convey an aspect of the domain of preexistence (its denoted objects, signified concepts, manifested subjects), which founds the third, disjunctive, moment of the genesis.

201. Leclaire, *Psychoanalyzing*, pp. 147–8, n. 18.
202. Éric Laurent has recently suggested, however, that Lacan's usage of topology in his conception of the relation between body and language avoids what Laurent calls the 'flattening' of the two dimensions in Leclaire's work, which suggests that Deleuze's critique could be more applicable to Leclaire than to Lacan himself. See Laurent, 'Parler lalangue du corps.'
203. Deleuze elaborates this further, saying they can be either alternating terms of a single series (mother/father/mother, etc.), or belong to two or more distinct series inscribed on the genital zone (see *Logic of Sense*, pp. 259–60).
204. At the level of the *P/cs*., Leclaire does not speak of semantemes – this is the term Deleuze adopts – but rather of the 'sign' (as opposed to the *Ucs*. letter), which is the Saussurian unity of the signifier and signified, and which refers to an 'objective term' or Saussurian referent (as opposed to the *Ucs*. object). See Leclaire, *Psychoanalyzing*, p. 111.
205. Ibid., p. 85.
206. Ibid., p. 113, emphasis in the original.
207. This further contributes to Leclaire's dismantling of the operative power of the Lacanian Name-of-the-Father. Deleuze makes a similar point, as we saw earlier: the Voice prohibits without us knowing what is prohibited because we will only know it through the sanction of castration.
208. Ibid., p. 113, emphasis in the original.
209. Ibid., p. 113.
210. Ibid., p. 113. As Deleuze puts it, 'as the conjunction [Poord'jeli] forms an entire series, this series enters into a relation of resonance with another divergent and independent series – "*joli corps de Lili*" (Lili's beautiful body) [...] [which] enacts a disjunctive synthesis of the two series (the pregenital and the Oedipal, that of the proper name of the subject [Poord'jeli] and that of Lili), causes the two divergent series to resonate as such and ramifies them. The entire esoteric word, in line with Lacan's thesis, plays now the role of a semanteme' (ibid., p. 265). These examples are taken from p. 85 of *Psychoanalyzing*, where Leclaire first announces his understanding of the relation of the letter and its conscious representation.
211. The symbolic phallus proper, as phallus of castration, is therefore the very *difference* between 'Li' as object of the drive, and Liliane's inscription in the *P/cs*. as a semanteme or as what Leclaire calls a sign. The

drive, post-castration, continues investing 'li', but in doing so it serves to repress this cathexis, or to constitute the very split between the *Ucs.* and *P/cs*. When 'li' is invested, post-castration, 'li' qua letter – along with every letter comprising 'Poord'jeli' – is split off from '*Lit*', '*Le lit de Lili*', etc., repressing 'Poord'jeli' to the *Ucs.*, an *Ucs.* constituted by this very repression of Poord'jeli. For Leclaire, the 'correlative tension of the different incompatibilities', by which he means 'an incompatibility between the conscious representations and the unconscious representatives' of desire, constitutes the 'instinctual force' driving fantasy's very intentionality. Furthermore, this incompatibility stems from the 'intrinsic heterogeneity' of the phallus. See Leclaire, *A Child Is Being Killed*, p. 39.

212. This is why, in *Oedipe à Vincennes*, Leclaire emphasises the fact that the split-subject in Lacan is really a re-split-subject (*refente*), p. 105: while the subject is split once from itself prior to castration, in the subject's relation to the object (0/1), the subject is split from itself a second time at the level of the distinction between unconscious and pre/conscious, or between the subject of the unconscious (the slash in: 0/1) and the subject as 'ego' in the pre/conscious (see *Psychoanalyzing*, p. 111). The object (a) considered most comprehensively, as object of the re-split-subject inscribed within the formula of fantasy as $\$ \lozenge a$, is therefore not the '1' but the difference between the 1 (of 0/1), on the one hand, and on the other the referent of the pre/conscious sign (as unity of signifier and signified); it is the difference *between* partial and denotable empirical objects. Likewise, Deleuze writes that it is at the level of this disjunction ('Oedipal' and 'pregenital', esoteric and semantic) that 'the conditions of a "choice of an external object" are elaborated' (*Logic of Sense*, p. 260).

213. Deleuze, *Logic of Sense*, p. 238. This concept comes in at the end of series twenty-nine, devoted to the purportedly Kleinian account of the Oedipus complex, lending further support to my claim that his dynamic genesis is Leclairian in overall orientation.

214. Ibid., p. 238. Deleuze speaks more specifically of the 'set' (*ensemble*) of 'every possible action' being divided in two and inscribed on two screens. When Deleuze uses the term 'set' (which is mistranslated in the English translation) during the dynamic genesis, it is usually in reference to the physical surface (see pp. 241–2, 269, 289 of the French original), and Deleuze makes clear on p. 289 of the French that by 'set' he means an 'esoteric set' of 'words' identical to the construction of the physical surface during the Oedipal stage. Hence, the 'image of action' is determined on and as the conjunctive esoteric word as 'set' of letters – which is precisely how he defines the body in his discussion of Leclaire (p. 269 of the French). From the conjunctive esoteric word a *delimited sub-set of possible actions* will then be extractable and capable of being

*The Three Syntheses of the Body*

projected onto the metaphysical surface, based on whether or not the phonemes they are associated with can be semantically determined.

215. Ibid., p. 238. These 'exigencies' point to the category of *bodily affection*, actions and passions, as one that is *phonemically-intensively conditioned*, and *retroactively determined* by the disjunction of esoteric phoneme and semanteme. In other words, there can be no bodily affection capable of triggering a thought that is not *linguistically*, and furthermore *semantically*, structured. Conversely, this means that a materiality opposed to language – which is to say of which language speaks – is itself paradoxically internal to language.
216. Deleuze, *Logic of Sense*, p. 238.
217. This connection has been almost completely ignored in the secondary literature, and more generally the double screen has received little in-depth attention. (The latter also applies to his linguistic conception of erogenous zones and psychoanalytic conception of esoteric words.) Deleuze refers to Laplanche and Leclaire's article in series thirty-four, and as I have shown it is implicitly discussed by means of an engagement with Leclaire's work on resonance in Poord'jeli (as found in *Psychoanalyzing*), which builds on the earlier co-authored article. An exception to this is Lacan, who notes in Seminar XVI the 'great pertinence' of Laplanche and Leclaire's article to Deleuze's overall project in *The Logic of Sense*, p. 110.
218. Deleuze, *Logic of Sense*, p. 260.
219. Again this will be fully explored in the next chapter.
220. Notice the *sonorous* terminology used.
221. Ibid., p. 260.
222. Ibid., p. 260.
223. Ibid., p. 238.
224. I discussed this briefly in section 3.4 in relation to Jakobson. In *Organs without Bodies*, Žižek insightfully observes that Lacan's theory of 'symbolic castration', the influence of which he recognises in Deleuze's disjunctive synthesis in *The Logic of Sense*, can be viewed as the gap opened up between corporeality and the incorporeality of the event at the level of the distinction between phonetics and signification (p. 80). Nonetheless, he fails to grasp that this 'symbolic castration' does not open onto the 'universality' of the phallic function in Deleuze, who determines language rather by its being bound to an infinite and univocal, or numerically indivisible, Event which is also itself *singular*. (I discuss this further in section 5.2.)
225. This takes us to the next chapter.
226. This Möbian 'doubling up' produces the (metaphysical) surface as a lining (*doublure*).
227. Deleuze, *Logic of Sense*, pp. 238, 260. He also terms it the '*Eventum tantum*', meaning 'so much of the event', the ultimate event.

228. Ibid., p. 241. The inverted commas around 'effect' is meant to relate this notion back to Deleuze's 'Second Series of Paradoxes of Surface Effects', in which he lays out the general ontological coordinates of the book, distinguishing between corporeal causes and incorporeal 'surface effects' of these causes, which are nonetheless not reducible to them. I will discuss this notion of a double causality in the next two chapters.
229. For instance '*joli corps de Lili*', as sexuated body of a woman, or '*lit*' as site of matrimonial relations between sexuated adults.
230. 'It is the [Lacanian] phallus which is surface nonsense, twice nonsense' (ibid., p. 262).
231. Ibid., p. 262.
232. As Deleuze puts it, 'in line with Lacan's thesis [...] the phallus of Oedipus and of castration is a signifier which does not animate the corresponding [semantic, Oedipal] series without cropping up suddenly in the preceding [phonemic, pregenital] series, in which it also circulates, since it "conditions the effects of the signified by its presence as signifier"' (ibid., p. 265). Although he does not give a reference, this quotation comes from Lacan's 'The Signification of the Phallus', p. 316.
233. Deleuze, *Logic of Sense*, p. 78.
234. In the example of Poord'jeli, we know that the 'li' functions as a kind of object for Leclaire.
235. Ibid., p. 78.
236. Deleuze notes in the 'Eleventh Series of Nonsense' how the object = x always crops up in one series and the word = x in another, such that the two are component halves of a structure. For instance, as Deleuze notes, the disjunctive esoteric word 'Jabberwock' is both a 'fantastic beast' or 'exoteric object' and an 'esoteric word' or 'unheard-of name' (ibid., pp. 78–9). At the same time, Deleuze adds, it must be conceived as 'the object of a formidable *action*' (p. 79, emphasis mine) – the hero's 'great murder' of the Jabberwock (castration or murder of the father as *Eventum tantum*). Likewise, the Snark, Boojum or 'it' cannot function as word = x without the mythical entity (object = x) that – precisely through this nominal regress – cannot be denoted or pinned down, both together constituting the action = x as narrative of the story (the hunting of the Snark).
237. Ibid., p. 262, translation modified. The sense of this passage is lost in the English translation.
238. This topological structure is described by Alliez as follows: 'Immaterial, sense is nothing else than an effect, expressing any *affect* as a surface *effect* – like an optical effect (or *effet de miroir*)' ('The BwO Condition', p. 100, emphasis mine). Sense is the *effect of those affects of the body that are structurally capable of being de-corporealised* as in-corporeal sense, by being tied to a sememe and dis-anchored from the erogenous body.

## The Three Syntheses of the Body

239. Deleuze writes 'There is nothing the sense of which is not *also* sexual, in accordance with the law of the double surface [double screen]' (*Logic of Sense*, p. 266). Language 'doubles' sexuality in the sense that there is no language that is not the transformation of sexuality, even if in this transformation its sexual origin is repressed (and continues to 'insist' in language). The phonemes which are granted access to thought (*P/cs.*) and language 'lose their sexual resonance' by being integrated into the propositional dimensions of denotation, manifestation and signification (ibid., p. 280). While 'sexuality is the surface' that denotation, manifestation and signification 'double', 'phonemes, morphemes and semantemes' are 'themselves the doubling up which builds the surface', such that the 'double screen' that Deleuze is clearly discussing here 'precedes all relations between states of affairs and propositions', even if the latter are founded on the repression or 'neutralisation' of their sexual resonance and origin. Still, Deleuze adds that these repressed sexual elements of language 'continu[e] to jolt [...] like so many extremely disturbing childhood memories' (p. 280), disrupting the psycho-physical dualism installed by castration.
240. This is the closest one gets in the dynamic genesis, I believe, to Lacan's maxim 'the unconscious is structured like a language'.
241. 'They pursued *it* with forks and hope', as edible body and expressible sense.
242. Deleuze, 'From Sacher-Masoch to Masochism', p. 128.
243. In his discussion of the function of the 'despot' in 'barbarian' societies in *Anti-Oedipus*, it is clear that here Deleuze is criticising the Name-of-the-Father, which he claims represses the pleasure principle by phonetically re-'coding' the primarily visual graphic inscription of desire on the body in 'primitive' societies as carved out of 'mother' nature (see pp. 156, 202–3, 227–8). Hence Deleuze traces the 'veritable origin' (ibid., p. 227) of Lacan's Name-of-the-Father, in his own words, back to the emergence of more repressive types of social system. In this way *Anti-Oedipus* can be read in part as a historicisation of the framework of the dynamic genesis.
244. Deleuze, *Coldness and Cruelty*, p. 137.
245. Ibid., pp. 63–4, emphasis mine.
246. This 'event' will later develop into the 'sinthome' in Seminar XXIII, as the 'fourth' ring along with the real, symbolic and imaginary. Verhaeghe and Declercq argue in 'Lacan's Analytic Goal' that in Seminar XXIII, identification with the object (a), rather than with the 'Name-of-the-Father', leads to the 'sinthome' as a 'self-created fiction' (p. 74). We saw a similar process occurring with Philippe in Chapter 1.
247. This theme of a set of voices collected by certain esoteric words to form the body seems at first glance very close to the mechanism of the 'howls-breaths' discussed in Chapter 2, which fuses consonants

('letters-organs') affecting the body using what appears at first sight a connective esoteric word (such as '*rangmbde*'). What they share, however, is little more than Deleuze's predilection for a model of immanent or expressive causality, and he is careful to point out their differences in a footnote to his thirty-second series (*Logic of Sense*, pp. 268–9, n. 7). Deleuze writes that they have 'only a remote correspondence'. While the body without organs prepares for the emergence of the good object (the Voice), the object-relations of the depressive position are foreign to it, and it is these object-relations (informing reparation-evocation) that underlie esoteric words (as good intentions, reparation-evocation of the good object). The key point is that words affecting the body are only letters proper if they enter into their essential differential relations with other series or other letters (which requires the phallus as serial coordinator), which schizophrenic howls/consonants do not (the schizophrenic having foreclosed the phallus in Lacan, or lacking a relation to the 'infinite judgement' of the good object/Voice in Deleuze). Palatalisation in howls-breaths such as '*rangmbde*' cancels differences within phonetic bundles and hence also between conjunctively articulating series or zones, allowing a body without organs (i.e. without zones) to emerge instead.

248. Ibid., p. 283.
249. Ibid., p. 266.
250. Ibid., p. 237, translation modified, emphasis mine.
251. It is in his conception of the phantasm that Deleuze ultimately parts ways with Klein and the Kleinians, since they conceive of the phantasm as only entailing a single level of causality (the drive's intentions). I discuss this in section 4.4.

# 4
# Logic of the Phantasm: From Speech to the Verb

## 4.1 Introduction: The Phantasm between Speech and Language

For Deleuze, speech is a structure summed up by the series title 'Good Intentions Are Inevitably Punished' and by the formulation 'intention-result'[1] – it is a self-dividing intention constitutive of the event (the 'result'). Thus the event is not actually the result of speech but of its *intention*, which in its self-division divides between speech and something else, *in relation* to which alone the event can be seen as a 'result' of speech. This something else is language. As Deleuze writes, 'Speech is never equal to language. It still awaits the result, that is, the event which will make the formation effective.'[2] However, we saw in the previous chapter how the event as castration-effect retroactively constitutes the Voice as a language that *will have* castrated the infant: it is in relation to language – as a 'pre-sense' insisting in the heights – that the infant develops ontogenetically; yet, paradoxically, to accede to language and its sense, the infant must contribute to it *the event* – which is inherent to language if outside it, and essential to language's functioning – as the difference *between* speech and language, or as the limits of sense retroactively imposed on speech (speech is nonsense only in relation to language).[3] Thus, if Deleuze writes soon after his discussion of Poord'jeli as esoteric word that 'Nonetheless, there is still no language; we are still in a prelinguistic domain',[4] this is because speech is literally pre-linguistic – it ontogenetically precedes language. Despite this (or rather *because* of it), speech acts as the crucial mediating structure between language and the bodies from which language must distinguish itself so as to constitute itself *as language*.[5]

Now, while we have established that in ultimately speaking the *event* speech genetically founds language, it is nonetheless ultimately *language* which expresses the event by retroactively framing speech. At the end of the previous chapter I started touching on the articulation between speech and language, but primarily from the side of speech; in order to examine this articulation in more depth and detail, it is necessary to now turn to Deleuze's theory of language (or of the proposition), in relation to which, I will show, speech takes on the function of the *verb*. Furthermore, this articulation is a specifically *phantasmatic* framing of speech by language, and therefore also brings us to an analysis of the functioning of the psychoanalytic phantasm in the dynamic genesis. The phantasm is the culmination of the dynamic genesis or the structure it generates, as well as underpinning *The Logic of Sense*'s theory of the proposition, and finally it also dramatically opens onto the book's ontological and literary themes which I will discuss in the following chapter. Indeed, it is through the phantasm that all these elements combine giving *The Logic of Sense* its topological continuity.

Deleuze circumscribes the phantasm by distilling from it 'three main characteristics'[6] from which he derives 'two fundamental traits'.[7] The characteristics: double causality ('intention-result' or expression); depersonalisation of the ego; quasi-propositional form (that of the verb stated in the infinitive). The traits: 'extreme mobility'[8] (rapid flow between psychic systems); eternal return (perpetual exchange between the beginning and end of the phantasm):[9]

1. The phantasm 'covers the distance between psychic systems with ease, going from consciousness to the unconscious and conversely, as if it belonged to a surface dominating and articulating both the unconscious and the conscious, or to a line connecting and arranging the inner and the outer over two sides.'[10] It is the phantasm which takes the dualism of the physical and metaphysical surfaces and crosses them over each other to form a single surface with two sides, like a Möbius strip. Pre/conscious and unconscious systems thereby become reoriented in relation to each other (and thus to themselves) by the phantasm which 'dominates' their articulation by being the very thing that 'articulates' them. Depth and height, and body and thought, take on a new dimensionality and relation to the other dimensions thanks to the surface (the phantasm) in relation to which everything is now reoriented. Pre/conscious and unconscious become inseparable from their articulation (via the phantasm of the surface), the 'surface' now displacing the distinction between physical and metaphysical surfaces, and now having an essential relation to its internal resonance and redoubling.
2. The phantasm 'returns easily to its own origin'[11] since it is built on the question or problem of its own origin or emergence. The

emergence of the phantasm is not unproblematic for itself, as it cannot fully account for this origin without jeopardising the very thing (object = x) that characterises it, namely: the processing of its own origin, its attempt to make 'sense' of itself. This is also because as incorporeal surface-effect, the phantasm is different in kind from its corporeal cause yet results from it (double causality). It concentrates the paradox of the emergence of incorporeality from corporeality, central to all language and logic, as Deleuze conceives them. Unlike fully formed language, it cannot so easily do away with or repress its founding paradox. Indeed, it circles around and returns eternally to this very problem so that language doesn't have to, so that language can establish itself in a simple relation of duality with bodies (that of denotation).[12] This is why the problem 'where does the phantasm begin [...]?' implies 'another problem [...] where does the phantasm go?',[13] as where it goes is not away from its origin but, in a way, towards it, as an attempt to unfold it and, conversely, where it begins is thereby put in motion *by* this very attempt to understand it. In short, the origin of the phantasm lies neither in the corporeal cause nor in the incorporeal effect, but in the unfinished and unsolvable question of their articulation – a denoting proposition is only ever a partial solution, repressing its paradoxical emergence from what it stands back from (as 'word') in order to logically denote.[14]

All five features converge on the phantasm's position *between words and things* – neither one nor the other yet that which accounts for both and their relations of duality – and as such the phantasm is presupposed by and subtends the proposition, which establishes itself in a duality with states of affairs. To unpack these characteristics and traits, as well as their essential interrelations, I will examine in this order the following issues brought up by Deleuze's theory of the phantasm: (1) the proposition and the phantasmatic 'questions and problems' of language; (2) the verb in its relation to the proposition; (3) depersonalisation of the ego.[15] In this last section I will contrast Deleuze's work to the logic of fantasy developed by the Lacanian school.

## 4.2 Logical Proposition and Ontological Problem

For Deleuze the 'logical proposition' is the conditioning forms any sequence of phonemes, morphemes and semantemes must be submitted to in order to function propositionally, which is to say in order to be able to *denote, manifest* and *signify* – the proposition's three necessary and irreducible 'dimensions' – and ultimately make (or 'express') sense (its underlying and foundational fourth). If the morphemes and sememes of a specific language allow its phonemes to signify and refer outside themselves, the linguistic elements of any language are in turn propositionally conditioned by the workings of the logical proposition.

*Denotation* is the relation of the proposition to an external state of affairs or *datum*.[16] The state of affairs is individuated, and includes bodies, qualities, quantities and relations.[17] Denotation functions by associating the words in a proposition with '*particular* images *which ought* to "represent" the state of affairs'.[18] It has as its criterion the true and the false; if a denotation is 'true' the denotation is 'filled' by the corresponding state of affairs, and by the selection of an appropriate image representing it; if it is false, this is because either the state of affairs is impossible and thus an appropriate image cannot be found (such as a square circle), or because the selection of images is defective and one has not been able to adequately represent a possible state of affairs because of a failure on the behalf of the speaker.[19]

*Manifestation* concerns the relation of the proposition to the person who 'speaks' and 'expresses himself'.[20] A person 'manifests' himself only to the extent that he produces propositions expressing characteristics retrospectively attributed to that person. The 'person' is a linguistic construct, a function of the proposition (it is the result of one of its dimensions). Above all, it is the 'desires and beliefs' of the person speaking that are expressed in a proposition. Desires and beliefs depend on a strict order of causality, implying an underlying structure to the proposition (or rather to series of propositions), and involve 'causal inferences' between propositions, which are deduced from series of propositions rather than being mere 'associations' between images.[21] It is not enough to merely associate, for instance, its being day and its being light on the basis of an impression of connection; rather, one needs to experience its being night (and dark) so as to be able to deduce that day and darkness (and night and light) are mutually exclusive.

Desire relates to the 'internal causality of an image with respect to the existence of the object or the corresponding state of affair'.[22] This means, firstly, that it is the image not the state of affairs which is desired, since the image representing a corresponding state of affairs (by its being filled or unfilled) exists independently of it, and motivates desire by its being unfilled. Secondly, it means that such an image may prompt the existence of its corresponding state of affairs

## Logic of the Phantasm

(if I desire the filled image of a chocolate bar I am motivated to realise the state of affairs corresponding to this image), even if logically a state of affairs precedes its image. Furthermore, drawing on Lacan, Deleuze explains that desire is associated with signification, and not only with manifestation and denotation, because

> desires would not form an order of demands or even of duties, distinct from a simple urgency of needs, [...] if the words in which they were manifested did not refer first to concepts and conceptual implications rendering these desires [...] significative.[23]

As for belief, this is the 'anticipation of this object or state of affairs', insofar as it must be 'produced by an external causality',[24] to which my desire and the production of a denoting image are in turn subjected. Deleuze associates the latter with empirically learned habit.[25] This relates in turn to the causal inferences of manifestation as opposed to mere association.[26]

The logical proposition must signify something beyond the words themselves, namely 'concepts'.[27] *Signification* centres on the relation between the word and 'universal or general concepts', as well as the 'syntactic connections' within or between propositions at the level of the 'implications of the concept'.[28] Implication is concerned with the relation between premises and conclusions whereas assertion corresponds to the affirmation of the conclusion of a premise.[29] The linguistic signifiers 'implies' and 'therefore' are hence particularly useful for determining relations between concepts.[30]

In addition to its three dimensions, the proposition is conditioned by 'good' and 'common' sense. Good sense is associated primarily with denotation, requiring that a state of affairs be individuated (and thus capable of being denoted).[31] Common sense 'finds its source in the person'[32] and thus in manifestation, requiring that the person be identical with itself.

Now, Deleuze accounts for the relations between the three dimensions of the logical proposition as follows. Firstly, insofar as what linguistics calls the 'basic manifester', or 'I', cannot be subsumed under denotation, denotation does not ground manifestation. Deleuze gives an example from Benveniste's work, which shows that:

> We separate 'tomorrow' from yesterday or today, since 'tomorrow' is first of all an expression of belief and has only a secondary indicative value.[33]

Secondly, whereas denotation has as its 'criterion' the true and the false, signification is the '*condition of truth*'.[34] Denotation can be filled or unfilled, true or false, because signification determines in advance the 'set of conditions under which the proposition "would be true"'.[35] If a proposition is false it is because it is unfilled and not because it does not signify anything ('This is a cat' signifies something even if it is unfilled). While denotation depends on signification for its 'set of conditions', and signification would appear to be independent of denotation, Deleuze contends that signification cannot either be considered as the ground of the other dimensions. Signification cannot claim priority over denotation because propositions' significations lay no claim to truth (in the propositional sense) without denotative acts establishing their veracity, either through the impossibility of their being denoted (for instance a square circle), or because they have not yet been empirically verified.

Lastly, Deleuze claims that it is only in the act of speech that the 'I' is primary in relation to concepts,[36] and thus manifestation cannot be said to have priority over signification even if it precedes denotation. Drawing on structuralism's speech/language distinction, Deleuze writes that at the level of language – i.e. considered as a synchronic system and independently from concrete speech acts played out in diachrony – significations are 'valid and developed for themselves',[37] and so would appear to be independent of manifestation. Nevertheless, since the use of such a distinction between speech and language presupposes speech as language's concrete vehicle, signification is granted only *de jure* and not *de facto* priority over manifestation (i.e. only in the order of language considered abstractly as separate from speech).

As such, Deleuze seeks to demonstrate that no single dimension of the proposition has priority over the others, and thus that all three are co-conditioning.[38] This, however, begs the question of what it is that subtends this co-conditioning and makes it possible, if each individual dimension when analysed separately is *conditioned by* one or both of the other dimensions and *conditions* one or both. Seen from the viewpoint of any one dimension, the proposition is not co-conditioning but partly conditioned by it, and partly not. We only arrive at a fully co-conditioning vision of the proposition's workings when we abstract from each of the three dimensions viewed in relation to the other two. Paradoxically, to do so it is necessary, as Deleuze shows, to introduce a fourth, underlying, dimension that, while reducible to none of the other three in their relations to the other two, can nevertheless not itself be pinpointed, insisting essentially *alongside* the relations of *all three* (and not of the other two

## Logic of the Phantasm

considered in relation to any one).[39] This fourth – paradoxically both irreducible and essentially relational – element is 'sense',[40] which is what the fourth dimension of the proposition, 'expression', expresses alongside the relations of all three primary or logical dimensions.

Sense thereby functions as the plane of immanence that these three dimensions construct in their relations of mutual conditioning. Nevertheless, the three logical dimensions themselves *are not* immanent, since while they co-condition one another they are co-conditioning of the *sense* of a proposition and not of their respective elements (concepts, objects and subjects), which we have seen can each be considered as conditioning at least one other dimension (if not all of the dimensions unilaterally). This gives rise to a dualism within the proposition, whereby if sense is immanent, concepts, objects and subjects nonetheless aren't.[41] Still, in this dualism neither sense nor the logical proposition has priority over the other, as they mutually presuppose each other; sense is expressed *by* the proposition, but the proposition needs sense as the plane of immanence in which its three other dimensions operate, *in order* to express it as the 'effect' of their relations and, through sense, in order to denote states of affairs or objects, signify concepts and manifest persons or subjects.[42] Paradoxically, sense appears therefore both as generative matrix of the proposition and as its sterile engendered effect – it is both 'naturing' and 'natured', structuring and structured.[43]

While in 'Third Series of the Proposition' Deleuze arrives at his conception of sense in its relation to the proposition through logical deduction, we already know from previous chapters that, more fundamentally, sense – or, from a related angle, speech – is needed alongside the proposition's three dimensions because language cannot immediately relate to bodies. Since one of the proposition's dimensions (denotation) consists in this relation, sense is needed to mediate them. Sense's role in the proposition is thus as much physical or psychical as it is logical: it attests to the phantasmatic structure of language, the phantasm's insistence in the proposition, and to sense as a 'desexualised energy'[44] reversibly flowing between psychic systems – the physical surface and the de*sexualised* (rather than fully asexual) metaphysical surface or, propositionally, denotation and expression as the proposition's base series.[45]

Now, what connects the proposition to this phantasmatic structure are the 'ontological problems and questions corresponding to language'.[46] This is why Deleuze defines sense as 'the problem to which propositions correspond' as solutions;[47] that is to say that the problem is '*not* propositional, although it does not exist outside the propositions which [...] in their senses [...] express it'.[48] There is a marked difference in kind between propositions and their underlying problems, though the role of the proposition is ultimately to develop or unfold them.[49]

Turning first of all to the 'Ninth Series of the Problematic', Deleuze specifies the relation of problems to questions as follows: 'The question is developed in problems, and the problems are enveloped in a fundamental question.'[50] Like a Möbius strip or eternal return of beginning and end, the question is unfolded or developed in problems which nonetheless remain enveloped in or framed by a question that itself is never resolved (and thus remains open to problematic development). Whereas Deleuze associates questions with the 'empty square' or 'blank word',[51] the place without an occupant or word = x, the problem is situated in 'distributions of singularities corresponding to each series'.[52] Heterogeneous or disjunctive series form 'fields of problems',[53] constituted by series that 'resonate' and 'communicate', and by singularities that are 'displaced, redistributed, transformed',[54] thanks to the question that 'traverses' them[55] (and 'makes them resonate').[56]

Furthermore, in the same series Deleuze writes that 'esoteric words' are 'essentially tied' to questions and problems.[57] He makes this claim more strongly in the 'Twenty-Sixth Series on Language', stating that in the '[secondary] organisation of language' the question or 'decentred point' is 'expressed in language by means of esoteric words of different kinds',[58] and this itself builds on the notion of the 'question' of the phallus developed earlier in Chapter 3. To restate this point, the esoteric word is the precise and sole manner in which the decentred point (question) manifests itself in the domain of language.[59]

For Deleuze, 'portmanteau' or disjunctive esoteric words in particular are 'inseparable from a problem' ('Jabberwock' makes heterogeneous series – eating/speaking – resonate without seeking to overcome this tension); 'on the other hand, blank words [words = x] are inseparable from a question which is displaced along with it: what is the Snark? what is the Phlizz? what is It (*Ça*)'.[60] Indeed, it is because the question (word = x) is eternally displaced in relation to its corresponding object = x that is established between the two heterogeneous series (those of things and words) a relation of resonance and communication: 'Jabberwock' is inseparable from a problem (resonance between jabber/wocer, speaking/eating) because it is first of all

## Logic of the Phantasm

a question ('What is the meaning of the poem "Jabberwocky"'?).[61] In other words, the disjunctive esoteric word has, internally, the structure of a question, giving rise to an ex-centricity of halves, but those halves communicate and resonate as a problem which is gradually unfolded through the life of a structure (on the basis of its underlying question which does not change).

As such, Deleuze's very understanding of the phantasm is rooted in the notion of questions and problems. As he writes, the 'origin of the phantasm' is

> a *question*, the origin of birth, of sexuality, of the differences of the sexes, or of death [...] This is because [the phantasm] is inseparable from *a displacement, an unfolding, and a development within which it carries along its own origin*. Our earlier *problem*, 'where does the phantasm begin, properly speaking?', already implies another *problem*: 'where does the phantasm go, in what direction does it carry its beginning?'[62]

If the 'origin', or 'beginning', of the phantasm is precisely a 'question', the phantasm is also 'inseparable' from a 'displacement, an unfolding, and a development' of this question. I would claim that it is fairly clear and uncontentious to propose that for Deleuze, the question as esoteric word functions as the phantasm's beginning, and is enveloped within the phantasm whose role is to develop or unfold it, in short to establish fields of problems between heterogeneous series and ultimately express sense.

Deleuze states this explicitly in a later series:

> At least in its beginning, the phantasm is nothing else but the internal resonance of two independent sexual series, insofar as this resonance prepares the emergence of the event.[63]

The 'phallus' is what 'cause[s] the series to resonate',[64] and Deleuze later adds to this 'the object = x [...] traverses [the series] and causes them to resonate'.[65] As we saw in section 3.5, the event, at least initially, is nothing else than the resonance of two independent sexual series, as is the phantasm for Deleuze, which 'merges with their resonance',[66] and so the phantasm is in fact no different from the event (hence Deleuze speaks of the 'phantasm-event').[67] Structurally, the question (blank word or word = x) is displaced in relation to itself, incapable of being closed, to the extent that the object = x corresponding to it is constitutively barred from it. This opens up a space of continuous tension or torsion between the series of the phantasm, and it is this problematic tension that drives its unfolding and development.[68] It is, in short, because the question can never be answered, can never fully close up, that the phantasm perpetually twists itself around this unfillable void, accounting for its trait of eternal return between beginning and end (as well as its Möbian structure more generally).

We have now seen what the logical proposition entails, for Deleuze, and introduced the notion that it in turn depends on sense and on extra-propositional questions and problems. We have yet to see, however, how these questions and problems communicate with the proposition and allow it to express sense.

## 4.3 The Third Synthesis of the Body Revisited: Theory of the Verb

If speaking the event (intention-result) must ultimately be framed by language, this requires us to revisit the third synthesis of the body from the viewpoint of language's retroactive disjunction with it. While I analysed the disjunction internal to *speech* in section 3.5, here I need to supplement this with analysis of a further disjunction (that of speech/language) redoubling or framing the first one. As such:

1. The third synthesis of the body (or of speech), as the culmination of all three, must be understood more fully as a *verb*.[69]
2. While being the culmination of speech, the verb is also the means by which speech communicates with language (or the ontological problems and questions of language with the logical conditions of the proposition).
3. Resonance of series and disengagement of an event (as castration-effect) does not belong to speech, but more precisely to the unfolding of speech *within language*.
4. This unfolding is identical to the process of the phantasm.

The verb occupies a special position within Deleuze's logic; it is still within speech – it *is* speech as such, as the end product of the dynamic genesis[70] – but as the third and final moment of speech (disjunction, castration) it already straddles language or the proposition as that which ultimately expresses sense (as 'events' or castration-effects). In other words, the dynamic genesis doesn't end where the 'static genesis' of propositional sense begins. Rather, the dynamic and static geneses of sense occupy co-existent if non-communicating dimensions: the 'secondary organisation' (surface) and 'tertiary ordinance'

## Logic of the Phantasm

(heights) respectively, with the dynamic genesis moving from bodies to the verb (and ultimately to the univocity of sense and nonsense, bodies and language), and the static genesis from the proposition (as made possible by the verb) to denoted objects, signified concepts and manifested subjects.[71] At this point it is necessary to delve further into Deleuze's conception of the 'event' and its relation to sense, before tackling his connected theory of the verb.

Near the beginning of *The Logic of Sense*, in a crucial passage from 'Third Series of the Proposition' which gets to the heart of what, philosophically, is at stake in his understanding of sense, Deleuze writes the following, which is worth quoting extensively because of its clarity and centrality to the work:

> Let us consider the complex status of sense or of that which is expressed. On one hand, it does not exist outside the proposition which expresses it; what is expressed does not exist outside its expression. This is why we cannot say that sense exists, but rather that it inheres or subsists. On the other hand, it cannot at all be conflated with the proposition, for it has an 'objectality' (*objectité*) which is quite distinct. What is expressed has no resemblance whatsoever to the expression. Sense is indeed attributed, but it is not at all the attribute of the proposition – it is rather the attribute of the thing or state of affairs. The attribute of the proposition is the predicate, for example a qualitative predicate like green. It is attributed to the subject of the proposition. But the attribute of the thing is the verb, for example greening, or rather the event expressed by this verb; and it is attributed to the thing denoted by the subject, or to the state of affairs denoted by the proposition in its entirety. Conversely, this logical attribute cannot at all be conflated with the physical state of affairs, nor with a quality or relation of this state. The attribute is not a being and does not qualify a being; it is an extra-being. Green designates a quality, a mixture of things, a mixture of tree and air where chlorophyll coexists with all the parts of the leaf.[72] To green, on the contrary, is not a quality in the thing, but an attribute which is said of the thing, and which does not exist outside of the proposition which expresses it in denoting the thing. And here we return to our point of departure: sense does not exist outside of the proposition ..., etc. But this is not a circle. It is rather the coexistence of two sides without thickness, such that we pass from the one to the other by following their length. *Sense is*, inseparably, *both the expressible or the expressed of the proposition, and the attribute of the state of affairs*. It turns one side toward things and one side toward propositions. But it cannot be conflated any more with the proposition which expresses it than with the state of affairs or the quality which the proposition denotes. It is exactly the boundary between propositions and things [...] It is in this sense that it is an 'event': *on the condition that the event is*

*not conflated with its spatio-temporal actualisation (effectuation) in a state of affairs [...] the event is sense itself. The event belongs essentially to language, it has an essential relationship to language; but language is what is said of things.*[73]

First of all, in this quotation we can identify a second, though connected, paradoxical aspect of sense (the first is its being generating-generated): its irreducibility to either bodies or propositions taken separately, its occupying the precise space of mutual irreducibility bodies and propositions share. Throughout *The Logic of Sense*, Deleuze likens sense to a Möbius strip (here it is the 'coexistence of two sides without thickness, such that we pass from the one to the other by following their length'): it is a reversible fold, a continuous surface that imperceptibly passes from one side of a quasi-dualism to another – not simply 'like' the phantasm, since it is here that we can most clearly identify the very presence of the psychoanalytic phantasm within the proposition as its necessary precondition.

Secondly, Deleuze specifies here sense's relation to the 'event'. While he appears at times to conflate the event and sense, for instance when he uses the term 'sense-event',[74] this is a crucial mistake to avoid as they are not the same. The 'event' is essentially the portion of the fold of sense (Möbius strip, the 'sense-event' as two-sided fold) attributed to and occurring in states of affairs; 'sense' is essentially the portion of the fold of sense expressed by and inhering or subsisting in propositions – Deleuze says this explicitly.[75] They are 'inseparable' yet they cannot be conflated, pointing as they do towards two opposed poles of the linguistic plane of immanence (bodies and language). The event points in a way to the ontological reverse side of the sense expressed in a logical proposition (sense being the epistemological obverse side), though we have seen briefly in the previous chapter that the very aim of Deleuze's ontology (as onto-logic) is to displace or fold the difference between ontology and epistemology.

Sense as a whole (as fold or sense-event) is onto-logically a single entity, according to an onto-logic of the copula or *difference* between ontology and epistemology, bodies and language. As such, it is not the proposition and it is not bodies; it is attributed to bodies, it inheres (or, as he later puts it, 'insists') in the proposition, but it is neither identical to any of the proposition's elements or dimensions, nor to any individuated body, physical quality or real relation.[76] The event is the part of sense *attributed to* bodies (and thus allows sense to be posited as immanent, said of the thing). It is not nonetheless

## Logic of the Phantasm

said of *things*: sense as event is what Deleuze terms the 'attribute' of the thing; it is neither the predicate nor the corporeal quality.[77]

This is why Deleuze writes that it is best expressed by a verb: 'to green' is not a predicate denotatively referred back to a subject (e.g. a green *tree*); rather 'to green' expresses a solely linguistic event (but an event nonetheless) which occurs neither in language itself nor in bodies themselves but in the precise disjoint between the two (their 'non-relation'), as the locus of their mutual failure to comprehend the other's dimension in its irreducibility (and thus the locus of their very *immanence*).[78] The event is said *of* things, while occupying a distinct space away from them, and this space is perfectly equipoised between bodies and propositions because, paradoxically, in order to be said *of things* the event must be *said by* the *proposition*.[79] Again, if it is said by the proposition it does not, however, stay there, being the evental side of sense and thus the side which happens *to* things (by being said *of* them).

Now, it is clear that Deleuze's description of the structure of the sense-event, as a Möbius strip twisting between propositions and states of affairs, is isomorphic to the structure of the disjunctive esoteric word (action = x as ex-centricity of word = x / thing = x). This is because the disjunctive esoteric word, or paradoxical element traversing series and making them resonate, is the mechanism undergirding the fold of the sense-event:

> The line-frontier ['between things and propositions'] brings about the convergence of divergent series; but it neither abolishes nor corrects their divergence. For it makes them converge not in themselves (which would be impossible) but around a paradoxical element, a point [...] circulating throughout the series. [...] It is this point which is expressed in language by means of esoteric words.[80]

This returns us to the role of the phallus as esoteric word: 'the phallus, as object = x and word = x, has the role of nonsense, distributing sense to the two basic sexual series, the pregenital and the Oedipal'.[81] Or, as Deleuze puts it elsewhere:

> It is the phallus which is surface nonsense, twice nonsense [...] and which distributes sense to the two series as something *happening* to the one and as something *insisting* in the other.[82]

Thanks to its structural role of resonating series and different kinds of phoneme (esoteric and semantic), the phallus produces sense as that which, retroactively, will *happen* to the one series (as an *event*) and *insist* in the other series (as *sense*).[83] Deleuze establishes the distinction between insistence and occurrence in the 'Twelfth Series of the Paradox', writing that sense 'insists in one of the series (propositions)' and 'crops up suddenly in the other series (states of affairs)'.[84] Furthermore, he writes:

> What permits therefore the determination of one of those series as signifying and the other as signified are precisely these two aspects of sense [...] and the two verbal aspects (*figures verbales*) of nonsense or of the paradoxical element from which they derive ([...] place without occupant in one series and occupant without a place in the other).[85]

While Deleuze first discusses the relation of propositions to states of affairs, in 'Third Series of the Proposition', independently from structural considerations, it is clear that much of the following series of the first part of the book (up to series thirteen) are designed to root his Möbian fold of sense (the attribute of the thing but expressed by the proposition) in a corresponding theory of structure. Furthermore, it is clear that the final series of the dynamic genesis are designed to account for this structure psychoanalytically.[86]

We have now covered, in this order, the logical proposition (and its phantasmatic questions/problems) and the fold of the sense-event (as isomorphic to structure), but we have yet to see how these questions and problems, or this structure, articulates with the proposition, which is the goal of the present chapter. This brings us to the third point touched on by the long quotation at the start of the section – as evidenced by the example of the infinitive verb 'to green' – namely the propositional role of the *verb*.

It is clear that Deleuze's theory of sense and, correlatively, his entire theory of the phantasm rely heavily on the work of the early twentieth-century French linguist Gustave Guillaume, and particularly Guillaume's theory of the verb as first developed in his 1929 *Temps et verbe*.[87] In *Temps et verbe: théorie des aspects, des modes et des temps*, Guillaume describes how the grammatical systems of aspect, mood and tense operate to produce an image of time, or 'time image', proper to the event expressed by the verb or verbs in a sentence. Mood (*mode* in French) is distinguished from tense (*temps*) in that while tense refers to when an action takes place (past, present, future), mood positions the speaker within tense by reflecting the mode in which the thought is expressed or the action conceived (as opinion, belief or desire).[88] As the main realis mood in most languages, the indicative principally refers to factual statements or questions, i.e.

to the speaker's relation to states of affairs (e.g. 'x is here'; 'x is not here'; 'is x here?'). By contrast, the subjunctive, an irrealis mood, positions the speaker in relation to something that is not necessarily known to be the case nor even capable of being known ('If I were x'; 'I might be x'; 'I wish I were x'). In short, the indicative refers to what can or cannot be ascertained, whereas the subjunctive can also (but does not necessarily) refer to a potentially counterfactual or unrealisable opinion or desire one has regarding it.

Guillaume's starting point in the 1929 work is the French sentence '*Si vous le faites et qu'il s'ensuive un accident, on vous en tiendra rigueur*' ('If you do it and there result an accident, you will be held responsible').[89] For the two moods of the verb in the sentence (indicative and subjunctive) to be coordinate, and thus capable of forming a single representation or image of time, the subjunctive must represent its event as possible ('If you do it and there result an accident') whereas the indicative mood must represent its event as real ('you will be held responsible').[90] Guillaume realised that this implied an *internal temporal relation* between the two moods within the syntax of the sentence, since possibility temporally precedes reality (something can be possible but not real, but not real and not possible). As Hirtle puts it, this meant, for Guillaume, that the speaker must 'think the subjunctive before the indicative in the system of mood'.[91]

Now, Guillaume built on these findings to develop a general theory of language applicable to all sentences, according to which the sentence as a whole functions as a verb expressing a time image. While, according to Binnick, in many respects he was still 'fully a structuralist in the tradition of Saussure',[92] he sought, contra Saussure, to relocate synchrony – that is, the structure of differential relations between linguistic elements – to local, concrete sentences, and to their very unfolding in speech – in short, to *diachrony*.[93] Put a different way, he wished to introduce process *into* synchronic linguistics. For Guillaume, as Hirtle puts it, the Saussurian conception of *langue*, as the totality of possible oppositions between substitutable elements in a language, became seen as 'an abstraction, a purely theoretical construct that has no role to play in actual speaking'.[94] A language's synchronic structure is more than the totality of formally sanctioned relations; its primary frame of reference is the sentence.

As such, synchrony must be reconceived as a *progressive co-conditioning* of the elements based on their positions within the sentence's unfolding, positions and a process of co-conditioning which are ultimately unrepeatable from one sentence to the next. As Hirtle elaborates:

> For Guillaume [...] a grammatical system is the dynamic potential for carrying out a series of operations to produce words in order to construct a sentence expressing one's momentary experience [...] A word is not a ready-made item in an inventory but rather a made-to-order product, reconstructed on each occasion for use in the sentence under construction.[95]

Lastly, this led Guillaume to privilege experience in the construction of a sentence. Hirtle goes so far as to claim that, in Guillaume,

> in every language act the extralinguistic (our experience) conditions the linguistic (meaning), thereby bringing the study of language down to the here and now of an individual act unrolling in the present.[96]

The sentence as verb strongly abstracts from experience, entering these abstractions into a determination of grammatical relations within an ideal space (the time image of a sentence).[97] This space is univocal in that it does not discretely distinguish between or oppose systems of grammar during its construction (either internally or externally).[98] The key point, however, is that it stems from extralinguistic experience which it determines in an unrepeatable manner, outside of an abstracted or universalistic conception of synchrony.[99]

Returning to Deleuze, the first time he refers to Gustave Guillaume's work in *The Logic of Sense* is in a footnote to the following extract from the 'Twenty-Sixth Series on Language':

> It is true that 'phonemes' guarantee every linguistic distinction possible within 'morphemes' and 'semantemes'; but conversely, the signifying and morphological units determine, in the phonematic distinctions, those which are pertinent in a language under examination. The whole cannot be described by a single movement, but by a two-way movement of linguistic action and reaction which represents the circle of the proposition. And if phonic action forms an open space for language, semantic reaction forms an internal time without which this space could not be determined in conformity with a specific language. Independently, therefore, of elements and only from the point of view of movement, nouns and their declension incarnate action, whereas verbs and their conjugation incarnate reaction. The verb is not an image of external action, but a process of reaction internal to language.[100]

Deleuze's understanding of the speech-language relation can be summed up by this 'two-way movement' of action and reaction,

## Logic of the Phantasm

and more precisely of the *action of speech* and the *reaction of language* representing the 'circle of the proposition' and amounting to Deleuze's theory of the verb as such. Furthermore, it seems to allude to Guillaume's work in its conception of the verb as reacting to an open synchronic space ('phonic action'), determining it according to an internal temporality constituted by the grammatical relations of the verb. This is made most evident by the fact that immediately after this quotation, Deleuze inserts a footnote which reads: 'With respect to this process of return or reaction and the internal temporality that it implies, see the work of Gustave Guillaume.'[101]

Now, if we look at the final sentence, it recalls the double screen, discussed in section 3.5, which divides any action in two, inscribing it as phonemic-intensive difference ('phonic action') on the physical surface, as grammatical and semantic linguistic elements on the metaphysical surface, and with the 'event' as their internal resonance. This is a reason why Deleuze couches this discussion in terms of the language of 'action' and 'reaction'. As we saw in that chapter, Deleuze's conception of the event went beyond an 'image of external action', as he puts it above, entailing the internalisation or expression of the cause in accordance with a theory of double causality.

This claim is further supported if we turn to the 'Thirtieth Series of the Phantasm'. Here, Deleuze returns to this precis of Guillaume's theory, strongly implying that it accounts for the very mechanism propelling the psychoanalytic phantasm. He first mentions that the phantasm has an essential relation to the proposition, and that Freud indicated this when he defined the preconscious representation of pregenital material in the phantasm in terms of 'verbal images' (Freud's word-presentations).[102] Reading Freud's term '*verbal* image' literally,[103] Deleuze then writes:

> The phantasm is inseparable from the infinitive mood of the verb and bears witness thereby to the pure event [...] [W]e must conceive of an infinitive which is not yet caught up in the play of grammatical determinations – an infinitive independent not only of all persons but of all tense, of every mood and every voice (active, passive, or reflexive). This would be a neutral infinitive for the pure event, [...] Aion, representing *the extra-propositional aspect of all possible positions, or the set of ontological problems and questions which correspond to language*. From this pure and undetermined infinitive, voices, moods, tenses, and persons will be engendered. Each one of them will be engendered within disjunctions representing in the phantasm a variable combination of singular points,

and constructing around these singularities an instance of solution to the specific problem – the problem of birth, of the difference of the sexes, or the problem of death.[104]

He goes on to write the following, which crystallises his entire theory of the verb:

> The infinitive verb goes from a pure infinitive, opened onto a question as such, to a present indicative closed onto a designation of a state of affairs or a solution case. The former opens and unfolds the ring of the proposition, the latter closes it up, and between the two, all the vocalisations [active/passive/reflexive], modalisations [subjunctive/indicative, etc.], temporalisations [past/present/future], and personalisations [manifested persons] are deployed.[105]

Reading the three quotations together, phonemes, or 'phonic action', provide the physical causal impetus for the phantasm, which itself reacts onto physical causality by determining phonic action morphemically and semantically. From previous chapters, we know it does this by cutting up the presented phonemic-intensive differences according to morphemically and semantically pertinent differences (or 'singularities'), thereby selecting certain phonemes to enter thought and deselecting others. We have also seen how this selection expresses an event (as the event of selection or reaction).[106] Temporally, in the dimension of time Deleuze refers to as 'Aion' – a virtual generative space which I will more fully tackle in the next chapter – pre-linguistic experience, or affections, as transmitted to thought by the erogenous body (phonic action), is grammatically determined by the interplay of the systems of the verb (namely, here, tense and mood),[107] as we have seen in the work of Guillaume. Deleuze specifies that this determination is played out according to a progressive sifting of incompatible disjunctive alternatives (past/future, active/passive, etc.) such that only syntactical compatibilities emerge from this complex space of possibility.[108]

In replacing the duality of series in speech – esoteric and semantic phonemes – the verb reacts onto itself as a single movement, in line with the phantasm's reversible fold or surface (or that of the double screen). In opening onto a question, namely a structure's esoteric word, the verb opens onto the torsion or serial tension constitutive of speech. This firstly opens the verb onto the phonic action the esoteric or erogenous series presents, but it also, more fundamentally, plugs the verb into the tension between the esoteric and semantic series, a tension driving the phantasm as such, and rendering it 'problematic',

*Logic of the Phantasm*

which is to say composed of irresolvable incompatabilities at a structural level, guiding the phantasm's intentionality.[109]

Furthermore, Deleuze conceives of the phantasm, in relation to the verb, as a 'neutral infinitive' prior to any grammatical determination, functioning hence as the plastic affective form of thought (undetermined but determinable). This plastic affective form is itself determined by the conditions of possibility of the logical proposition. However, importantly, insofar as we have seen that the logical proposition itself cannot ground its co-conditioning structure, the verbal schematism conditions that which determines it. Returning to the earlier 'Twenty-Sixth Series on Language', if we read the following passage retrospectively in light of the series on the phantasm we can pinpoint the relation of the verb to the proposition, allowing us to answer this chapter's primary question, the relation of questions and problems to the proposition, or of speech to language:

> It is the verb which constitutes the ring of the proposition, bringing signification to bear upon denotation and the semanteme upon the phoneme. But it is from the verb as well that we infer what the verb conceals or coils up [. . .]: sense or the event as the expressed of the proposition. The verb has two poles: the present, which indicates its relation to a denotable state of affairs in view of a physical time characterised by succession; and the infinitive, which indicates its relation to sense or the event in view of the internal time which it envelops. The entire verb oscillates between the infinitive 'mood', which represents the circle once unwound from the entire proposition, and the present 'tense', which, on the contrary, closes the circle over the denotatum of the proposition. Between the two, the verb curves its conjugation in conformity with the relations of denotation, manifestation, and signification – the set of tenses, persons, and moods.[110]

In the last line of this quotation, Deleuze indicates a connection between the proposition and the verb by pairing the dimensions of the proposition with the grammatical systems of the verb: '. . . relations of denotation, manifestation, and signification – the set of tenses, persons, and moods'.[111] Denotation corresponds to the set of tenses, manifestation to the set of persons, signification to the set of moods. The 'neutral infinitive', by contrast, from the earlier quotation, 'represent[s] the extra-propositional aspect of all possible positions, or the set of ontological problems and questions which correspond to language',[112] partaking of the domain of expression (which is itself not reducible to it, being more completely the grammatical determination *of* this pre-linguistic experience). This extra-propositional or pre-linguistic experience – the 'problems and questions' language poses itself, but which point to the very limits of language, to the pre-linguistic experience informing them (speech) – is therefore determined grammatically in the phantasm by the verb's tenses, persons and moods (as found in a particular language).

The verb oscillates between the expression of a pure event (infinitive mood) and its actualisation in the denotation of a state of affairs as solution case (present tense, or present indicative mood).[113] Signification (mood in general, and its syntax of conceptual implication)[114] and manifestation (the persons corresponding to the opinions, desires and beliefs mobilised in mood, as well as their consistent or self-identical network of relations) lie between the two extremes of expression and denotation, and help to make signification 'bear upon denotation' or in other words generate a denotable state of affairs by sifting the infinitive verb through a grid of exclusive disjunctions (including past *or* future, indicative *or* subjunctive, active *or* passive, etc.). The infinitive mood is prior to the determination of its event as possible/impossible or real (the subjunctive and indicative, respectively),[115] and holds together virtually all the disjunctive alternatives of language (its problems) in a relation of synchrony, whereas the present indicative grammatically requires its propositions to be true *or* false (or stated as a question whose answer is true or false), which are precisely the propositional criteria of denotation (filled and unfilled). Thus the verb opens onto the infinitive mood, as a fertile field of possibility immanent to presented phonic action in given sentences and untrammelled by its later determination by the proposition's conditions of possibility,[116] which enclose it within the denotation a state of affairs as 'solution' to the problems of language and of the phantasm (for instance sexual difference).[117]

Between actualised propositions and states of affairs, and the virtual infinitive verb, the verb is determined in accordance with the three dimensions of the proposition, just as these three dimensions function *by* determining the internal grammatical relations of the verb. In functioning to express sense, the proposition's fourth dimension works on (or indeed *is*) the verb. In doing so, it also allows the other three dimensions to each constitute themselves separately, by providing the internal genetic element on which the proposition depends, as we saw earlier. In short, the proposition's three dimensions condition the verb's grammatical determination within the phantasm – and thus the verb's ability to speak the event – *but in doing so*, they also condition themselves. This is because in using this univocal space of dimensional inter-relationality – where tense,

*Logic of the Phantasm*

person and mood are all involved in a process of progressive co-conditioning – the proposition's own three dimensions (denotation, manifestation, signification) can co-condition one another as *mutually expressive of the same* sense-event they have determined in the phantasm.[118] In working together to express the sense-event, the proposition's three dimensions are thereby afforded an internal generative matrix lacking at their own level when considered separately from the phantasm or verb.

We can summarise the relation between speech and language as follows:

1. The question, or speech, is the fact that before learning to speak a language one must learn to speak, which genetically roots speech in nonsense interwoven with the erogenous body. What this does, most importantly, is prepare for the founding dualism of series on which language is built – which we saw in section 3.1 are denotation and expression. Speech's gift to language is this proto-dualism of series that language fully realises. This proto-dualism of series is rooted in the distinction between esoteric and semantic phonemes, both inscribed on the genital zone of the physical surface, but the latter opening onto or preparing for the emergence of the metaphysical surface.
2. Language is what activates this structure by relaying phonic action to morphemes and semantemes; it is what takes the question of language, namely the latent duality of series, and realises that duality by packaging phonic action in propositional form, sealing the dividing line only latently present in speech by definitively distinguishing between esoteric and semantic phonemes.
3. Lastly, this division continues driving the verb's intentionality, or the phantasm, due to the difference or tension which remains between these two kinds of phoneme or series, which causes the phantasmatic 'question' of speech to never be fully resolved in language. Rather, language is what develops this question, what brings about its latent tension or dualism, without cancelling this difference, such that it continues insisting, implicating itself, in language, as found in the classic Freudian lapsus. Thus, speech continues insisting in language most fundamentally at the level of its ability to communicate with bodily affect and can be defined as follows:
   - As the *affective lining* of language, through which language relates to its corporeal cause (phonemic-intensive difference

on the erogenous body), the sense of which it is the proposition's role to express as an event which occurred on the body's surface, or rather in the phantasm's resonance of series, but which the propositional dimension of denotation refers back to an objective state of affairs posited as the material cause, or at least the physical correlate, of the proposition. We see this in Deleuze's definition of the proposition as a 'circle', which can be uncoiled or unwound to expose a delicate affective membrane (the verbal dimension of expression opened onto an erogenous question), but which is then rewound as the verb is submitted to – and in turn supports the production of – propositional form. This last movement is one of transcendence towards ideality and away from the body's affects, as the proposition closes itself off from its internal genetic core.

– As the *generative matrix* of the proposition, through which its three dimensions co-condition one another. It is because the verb (as conceptualised by Guillaume) entails a single grammatical relational space, which Deleuze maps onto the proposition's three dimensions, and it is because it calls for a processual conception of syntax or synchrony within a sentence or proposition,[119] that it provides the function of generative matrix (or 'circle') of the proposition. Nonetheless, it must not be forgotten that the verb remains at this level, and is extinguished once we reach sense as fully engendered, at which point it gives way to the state of affairs in which is actualised the event it expresses. This is the movement from the pole of expression to that of denotation, within the verb as circle of the proposition, the latter actualising the event generated by the former. Thus the verb is indifferent to the distinction bodies/language (being itself comprised of a two-way movement of action/reaction), but once closed-up (reaction) or propositionally determined, it opposes itself (through denotation) to a state of affairs. The dualism of word/thing is thereby first a dualism of series in *speech* (esoteric/semantic phoneme), then in the *verb* (denotation/expression), then in *language* (proposition/state of affairs), at which point this dualism lies *between* words and things.

Returning to section 4.1, I mentioned that the phantasm had two 'fundamental traits': rapid exchange between psychic systems, and eternal return of beginning and end. The latter relates to the question-problem relation, and will be further unpacked in the following chapter. The former requires us to revise the distribution of psychic registers proposed in section 3.5, in light of speech's envelopment within language. If speech amounts to an opening, from connective series (via conjunction) to disjunction, language is like a closing up of this dispersal, screwing the lid back on. I pointed out in section 4.1 that from a duality of series the first trait gives rise to a single (reversible) surface, which we can understand at the level of the verb's function of *speaking the event* (from speech's duality to the event's univocity). As such, if I claimed in section 3.5 that the physical surface is unconscious and the metaphysical surface pre/conscious, this is in fact only true at the level of speech (or at the level of the pre-linguistic). At the level of language (or at the level of the verb, as speech enveloped in language), it is actually necessary, according to Deleuze, to consider the *surface* as *unconscious*,[120] the dimensions and forms of the proposition as the *preconscious,* and actual engendered propositions as *consciousness*.[121]

The reason for this stems directly from the speech-language relation, as follows: speech provides the internal genetic element of language (affective form and generative matrix); nonetheless, it is determined *by the proposition* (it is the proposition, not speech, that 'expresses sense' as its fourth dimension). The verb is what speaks the event, and it indeed *speaks* the event, but it cannot do so without being propositionally and grammatically determined. This is because even if the event is the disjunctive articulation and resonance of different kinds of phoneme, as discussed in section 3.5, phonemes are spoken in propositions, or rather propositions are what express sense and thus delimit nonsense in relation to sense, on the basis of which speech's disjunctive series (esoteric and semantic) are realised as disjunctive (and thus also as resonant).

Thus I can summarise the speech-language relation as it pertains to the phantasm as follows:

1. Phonemes, morphemes and semantemes are the elements which enter into a process of co-causal self-determination within the virtual or generative space of the phantasm and across divergent series; this generates an event, as nothing else than the resonance of these series; this process is nothing else than the grammatical determination of an infinitive verb opened onto a question.
2. What causes the elements of speech to enter this relation is the proposition. Thus the proposition determines relations between

its dimensions empirically, in consciousness, and at the level of the logical proposition (language as cut off from speech), *at the same time that* transcendentally, in the unconscious, and at the level of the verb (speech enveloped inside language), a sense-event *corresponding* to the relations of the denoted objects, signified concepts and manifested subjects of the logical proposition (fully engendered at their own level) is itself being determined by them, but without attaining the status of object, concept or subject.[122] These latter elements cover over and repress the sense-event they produce, such that sense is the buried fourth dimension of the other three (thus needing to be rediscovered in the modern era of propositional logic through Husserl's phenomenological reduction).[123]

3. Now, this brings us directly to the phantasm. The phantasm moves between psychic systems with ease, being coextensive with the articulation of speech and language, since we know that for the verb to be determined in the unconscious we need the preconscious forms of the logical proposition. However, by becoming empirical and conscious, cut off from the transcendental and unconscious, the logical proposition (language as cut off from speech) is the one part of the system that is transcendent and ungrounded (i.e. not grounded in the plane of immanence of the surface).[124] In repressing speech, the logical proposition transcends≈the surface, holding itself aloft in the transcendent heights of the tertiary ordinance, where absolute 'truth' (as nothing else than filled/unfilled denotative intentions) believes itself to supplant transcendental and immanent sense. In order to function, speech requires the forms of the proposition (which condition the verb grammatically), which are preconscious, but consciousness steps outside the surface by utilising those forms to repress speech (rather than just to condition it on the surface). Nonetheless, the latter *appears* as a necessary prerequisite coextensive with the former: it seems that there is no determination of an event on the surface without the production of transcendent subjects, objects and concepts in the heights. Is this, however, the case? I will leave this question open for now and return to it in section 5.3.

Hence, speech is the internal genetic and transcendental element of the proposition, occurring simultaneously – but on the surface not in the heights – with the proposition's self-determination and

## Logic of the Phantasm

transcendence away from its ground. The sense-event cannot be expressed without the logical proposition (though I will problematise this in the next chapter by bringing in literature), even if speech conditions what determines it. Via sense as desexualised libido, as introduced in section 4.2, the phantasm moves effortlessly between the surface and the heights (and even the depths), or between speech and language, but the empirical proposition of consciousness is what represses its phantasm and its precondition, albeit as a necessary repression without which the phantasm could not provide this very conditioning function – as without empirical propositions we would have no determination of a sense-event on the transcendental or unconscious surface (which again I will problematise using literature in the next chapter).

As we see in an earlier quotation, as *signification* comes to bear upon the *denotation* of a state of affairs, as end product of the proposition's reciprocal self-determination, simultaneously (in the transcendental unconscious) the *semanteme* therefore comes to bear upon the *phoneme*. Thus: (1) the *physical cause* is communicated to the proposition via the phoneme, (2) the proposition *expresses* this cause as a sense-event (in the phantasm) and (3) empirically *refers this cause back* to a denoted state of affairs by actualising it in an image (in the logical proposition),[125] such that (4) signification comes to bear upon denotation (in the logical proposition) at the same time that (5) the semanteme comes to bear upon the phoneme (in the phantasm). This is the verb as 'circle' of the proposition: the verb's movement of action-reaction (in the transcendental unconscious), as the phonemic cause is retroactively expressed or selected by the semanteme, is wound up inside the proposition's movement towards the actualisation of its dimensional relations in the denoting act. The event is thus disengaged within speech at the level of the relations between phonemes, morphemes and semantemes at the same time that sense is expressed by the proposition in its inter-dimensional relations. As such, returning to the fold of the sense-event discussed earlier in this section, we can say that the *verb speaks the event as the reverse side of the proposition's expression of sense* (as its obverse side), both constituting the unconscious transcendental surface but the latter already redoubling itself empirically in the heights.

This almost completes the three primary, or rather psychoanalytic, stages of the dynamic genesis, taking us from noise to the voice, from the voice to speech and from speech to the verb.[126]

## THE PSYCHOANALYSIS OF SENSE

Before engaging a final aspect of Deleuze's theory of the verb in the next section, it would be helpful to reflect back on the dynamic genesis. In the table of contents of the French edition of *The Logic of Sense*, Deleuze structures the dynamic genesis in terms of three stages: paraphrasing the French, they are from noise to the voice; the formation and coordination of partial surfaces; from the physical to the metaphysical surface (the double screen). These correspond to my Chapters 2–4. However, Deleuze then adds 'from the voice to speech' and 'from speech to the verb', as an additional two moments in the dynamic genesis. How are we to reconcile these later additions with the first three stages?

Firstly, we know from the previous chapter that it is precisely *through* the passage from the voice to speech that the partial zones are coordinated. It is also clear that Deleuze introduces Leclaire's work in that series precisely to provide that function – though his work also underscores the transition from the second to the third stage. Just before he begins discussing Leclaire's work, Deleuze writes: 'We ask, therefore, about that which, in language, corresponds to the second stage of the dynamic genesis [coordination of surfaces].'[127] Secondly, I would argue that, again, it is precisely through the passage from speech to the verb that the third stage of the dynamic genesis (the double screen) is fully realised. While the double screen – or intention-result – is the result of speech, it is the result of speech coiled within language (i.e. the verb), and it lays the groundwork for a hidden fourth and final stage of the dynamic genesis, which Deleuze locates in the French table of contents after the passage from speech to the verb, referring to it as the 'end' of the dynamic genesis, and which I will argue in the next chapter is the movement from the verb to univocity.

In short, if there are three stages of sexuality (series twenty-seven to twenty-nine), followed by another two or three stages (covering the rest of the series of the dynamic genesis), this is far from a linear genesis starting in sexuality and ending in language. On the contrary, the movements referred to as 'from the voice to speech' and 'from speech to the verb' are the *linguistic mechanisms undergirding* the second and third stages of the dynamic genesis (coordination of partial surfaces and the double screen, respectively). These series (on the phantasm, thought and on different kinds of series), even though they appear after the first three series of the dynamic genesis (on orality, sexuality and 'Good Intentions Are Inevitably Punished') in which the three stages are supposedly fleshed out, they in fact account

*Logic of the Phantasm*

for them retroactively, as I have explained on a number of occasions in the previous chapter. Thus I would argue that the three primary stages of the dynamic genesis – from noise to the voice, coordination of partial surfaces and the double screen or theory of the phantasm – are accounted for, respectively, by Artaud's schizophrenic literature (which appears earlier in the book's series), Leclaire's Poord'jeli (from the voice to speech) and Guillaume's theory of the verb (from speech to the verb), each partly building on and borrowing features of the previous one.[128]

The general claim I wish to advance here, as well as clarifying Deleuze's schema, is that the entire point of the dynamic genesis – as we will see in particular in the next chapter – is that bodies and language (or each stage of the dynamic genesis and its corresponding linguistic mechanism) are involved in a co-causal genesis which does not prioritise either half of the articulation.[129] We see this especially clearly in the second stage. In 'Thirty-Second Series of Different Kinds of Series', Deleuze writes:

> The organisation of the physical sexual surface has three moments which produce three types of syntheses or series [connective, conjunctive, disjunctive] [...]. Now, these series or moments condition the three formative elements of language – phonemes, morphemes, and semantemes – *as much as they are conditioned by them in a circular reaction*.[130]

Here, Deleuze could not be clearer. Deleuze makes this point again in the thirty-fourth series, writing that phonemes, morphemes and semantemes 'build' the sexual surface,[131] and that the 'sexuality' or 'sexual history' that is 'deployed over the physical surface' during the Oedipal stage is 'strictly coextensive and co-substantial' with the 'esoteric set' (*ensemble*) (translation modified), by which he means the conjunctive esoteric word as set of phonemes.[132] Again, Deleuze is unequivocal: sexuality is 'coextensive' and 'co-substantial' with the construction of the body as set of letters. We have also seen this 'reaction' of language onto the body in his theory of the verb.[133]

## 4.4 Conclusion: The Logic of Perversion – Object-Cause versus Subject-Effect

With his theory of the verb, Deleuze offers an alternative conception of the linguistic unconscious to the one developed by the Lacanian school. He draws on alternative theoretical resources to yield a model of the unconscious amenable to his own ontology, as I will show in detail in the following chapter. In doing so, as I have already shown in my third chapter, he also engages elements of the Lacanian school's own self-critique, as he develops or attempts to develop a fully singular conception of the unconscious – a point again further substantiated by the next chapter. What I would like to home in on here, however, is only one aspect of this alternative linguistic unconscious, though it is one of central importance: the position in it of the subject, and specifically as it relates to the Lacanian school.

For Deleuze, the subject is an *effect* of structure, not one of its components. This is because, I would argue, for Deleuze the subject is nothing more than the events produced within the phantasm, whereas the manifested 'person' is the end product of the grammatical determination of sense in the proposition; it is an effect of grammar. Not only are the opinions, beliefs and desires of the propositional person (he who speaks) constructed by the proposition in the determination of a verb, but the very situation of being an active subject in relation to a passive object, or vice versa, is entirely constituted at the level of the determination of grammatical voice within the verb's genesis.[134] This is part of the reason why Deleuze quietly adds voice and person to the verb's grammatical systems,[135] tethering them to the determination of mood and tense, Guillaume's analyses in *Temps et verbe* only extending to tense, mood and aspect.[136] The aim of doing so is essentially to have the verb entail an engendering of persons and voices, rather than such opinions, beliefs, desires and subject positions (active/passive/reflexive) pre-existing their grammatical construction.[137]

Now, I would argue that Deleuze's evental and asubjective theory of the phantasm can, in part, be understood as a critique of the Lacanian school's 'logic of fantasy', as centred on the object (a).[138] More specifically, I would argue that it aims to develop a hyperperverse conception of the phantasm, aimed at fully depersonalising it. If Lacan writes the 'matheme' for fantasy $\$ \lozenge a$ – the split subject as caught in a conjunctive-disjunctive relation with the object (a), discussed in part in Chapter 1 – his matheme for perversion is written $a \lozenge \$$. The pervert is not subjectively divided by the object (a) he intends; rather his libidinal intentionality lies in being an object (a) for the Other, as we see, for instance, in perverse cases of exhibitionism. For Deleuze, however, it appears to be insufficient to reverse the position of the object (a) in relation to the subject if we are to comprehend the impersonal structure of the phantasm in its essential perversity.

## Logic of the Phantasm

Rather, for him, the structure of the phantasm is perverse – not capable of taking on a perverse structure but fundamentally perverse – because there is no longer a subject, only an object (a) as event which, like the Stoic logical attribute, merges with the propositional subject rather than being predicated of it (the tree *greens*). The Lacanian root of this argument is clear if we look at an earlier essay from 1967, 'Michel Tournier and the World Without Others', republished in Appendix II of *The Logic of Sense*. Here, Deleuze argues that in perversion, the phantasm lacks an opposition between self and other, or a 'structure-Other' as he calls it.[139] In this essay, Deleuze writes approvingly of the Lacanian school's conception of perversion as a 'structure' which 'conditions behaviour',[140] in which one finds: (1) a position 'beyond the Other'; (2) a 'perverse "desubjectivation"', whereby one is neither victim nor accomplice in the interpersonal structure of perverse sexuality, for instance in sadism and masochism, but subjectively bereft;[141] (3) in which the '*Cause* of desire is [...] detached from the *object*',[142] which alludes to Lacan's object (a) as 'object-cause' of desire.[143]

In remaining a logical attribute in the phantasm, and not being predicated of a propositional subject referring to an object in a state of affairs, the event does not react back onto its physical cause (erogenous affect), in order to propositionally denote it in a state of affairs and actualise itself through a denoting image. For Deleuze this characterises instead neurosis (or normality),[144] in which the event is dualised into denoted object and denoting image, as tied to a subject or person, thanks to the presence of a structure-Other which conceives of the cause of desire as an Other (or object). The manifested person is neurotic (or normal) in that it subjectivates or personalises the events or castration-effects of the phantasm, which we can go so far as to term 'subject-effects', and in doing so actualises them as something else. Deleuze therefore topologises or dimensionalises psychopathology, locating psychosis in the depths (the primary order of the body without organs), perversion on the surface (the secondary organisation of the verb) and neurosis and normality in the heights (the tertiary ordinance of the logical proposition).

## Notes

1. Deleuze, *Logic of* Sense, p. 283. This is explicitly stated: 'intention-result (speech)' (ibid., p. 283).

2. Ibid., p. 226.
3. Deleuze also states this programmatically at the very start of 'Twenty-Sixth Series of Language', writing 'Events make language possible. [...] We always begin in the order of speech, but not in the order of language' (ibid., p. 208).
4. Ibid., pp. 265–6.
5. If Saussure inaugurated the speech/language distinction, Deleuze is actually critical of the manner in which Saussure conceives it which, Deleuze believes, puts speech at the service of language subsuming the one under the other and pasting over their difference in kind (see *Difference and Repetition*, pp. 254–6). As such, Deleuze sides with structuralists such as Lacan, whose programmatic 'The Function and Field of Speech and Language in Psychoanalysis' associates speech with the resistance of the unconscious to its total delimitation and erasure by language – to which psychoanalysis, as the 'talking cure', tethers itself to breach the unconscious (as 'full speech').
6. Deleuze, *Logic of Sense*, p. 242.
7. Ibid., p. 250.
8. Ibid., p. 250.
9. The three characteristics make up the whole of 'Thirtieth Series of the Phantasm' and the two traits are discussed in the 'Thirty-First Series of Thought', though they are by no means limited to these two series.
10. Ibid., p. 250.
11. Ibid., p. 250.
12. As Deleuze puts it, the 'beginning' of the phantasm is 'suspended in the void' or difference between the two surfaces, physical and metaphysical (ibid., p. 251) (as is castration (ibid., p. 254)), and thus while being the *effect* of their resonance, the phantasm's origin or *beginning* cannot be reduced to *either* surface since from their resonance it engenders a *single* surface with two sides (extended and realised through the work of art yet to come – see section 5.4). This project to constitute a single surface is therefore the origin of the phantasm, not either surface when taken separately which if they are the causes of the phantasm are not its beginning.
13. Ibid., p. 250.
14. In his translator's introduction to Deleuze's *Foucault*, Hand rightly considers the phantasm in Deleuze to 'topologis[e] thought's materiality' (p. viii). Hand notes that Foucault himself, in his review of *The Logic of Sense*, had characterised Deleuze's ontology in this book as a 'phantasmaphysics', which again is apt as I will show in the next chapter.
15. I have already tackled double causality in sections 3.5–3.6: the phantasm reacts onto or 'expresses' its corporeal cause, giving rise to a double causality whereby corporeal causality is not enough for it to

have effects of sense in language. This other element is the aptly named 'quasi-cause' (the action = x) (Deleuze, *Logic of Sense*, p. 109).
16. Ibid., p. 16.
17. Ibid., p. 16.
18. Ibid., p. 16, emphasis in the original.
19. Ibid., p. 17.
20. Ibid., p. 17.
21. Ibid., p. 17.
22. Ibid., p. 17, my emphasis.
23. Ibid., p. 19.
24. Ibid., p. 17.
25. Ibid., p. 17.
26. Deleuze later adds a third feature of manifestation, the person's 'constitutive projects' which give his or her life meaning (see ibid., p. 137).
27. Ibid., p. 18.
28. Ibid., p. 18.
29. See, for instance, the classic syllogism:
    Major premise: All humans are mortal
    Minor premise: All Greeks are humans
    Conclusion: All Greeks are mortal
30. See ibid., p. 18.
31. Ibid., p. 137.
32. Ibid., p. 137.
33. Ibid., p. 27, n. 1.
34. Ibid., p. 18, emphasis in the original.
35. Ibid., p. 18, translation modified.
36. Ibid., p. 19.
37. Ibid., p. 19.
38. For an analysis of these dimensions, see Bowden, *Priority of Events*, pp. 26–9. See also Hughes, *Deleuze and the Genesis of Representation*.
39. See Deleuze, *Logic of Sense*: 'we can only infer [sense] indirectly' (p. 23) and on the basis of the three other dimensions. We can liken sense to a photographic negative of the logical proposition.
40. Ibid., p. 22.
41. This point will be analysed in section 5.3.
42. This is why the relation of the proposition to sense cannot be aligned with the Deleuzian equation 'expression = construction' (see section 3.1). Since the proposition constructs a plane of immanence (sense) which it *transcends* (at the level of subjects, concepts and objects), the logical proposition itself is not a construct or a constructivism. However, any literature capable of breaking with the proposition's three logical dimensions *is*, and I explore this in Chapter 5.
43. In Deleuze's terminology, the 'secondary organisation' of the

surface (speech) must be distinguished from the 'tertiary ordinance' (*l'ordonnance*) of the logical proposition in the heights (formerly inhabited by the Voice). Both are in turn distinguished from the 'primary order' of schizophrenic depth (see the 'Thirty-Fourth Series of Primary Order and Secondary Organisation').
44. Ibid., p. 251.
45. Deleuze writes that 'castration transform[s] the narcissistic libido into desexualised energy. This neutral or desexualised energy constitutes the second screen, the cerebral or metaphysical surface on which the phantasm is going to develop' (ibid., p. 251). Here Deleuze is referring to Freud, 'The Ego and the Id', who speaks of a 'displaceable energy' of the mind, pp. 384–5, associating it with 'desexualised libido', p. 386.
46. Deleuze, *Logic of Sense*, p. 254.
47. Ibid., p. 139.
48. Ibid., p. 140, emphasis in the original. This is not to say that the problem can only be developed or actualised in propositions, however. The problem is not essentially linguistic but transdisciplinary – as we see in Chapter 4 of *Difference and Repetition* – and must be actualised in a specific disciplinary domain, but its fundamental structure is invariant.
49. Deleuze's conception of the problem is particularly influenced by Albert Lautman – as one can see in the 'Ninth Series of the Problematic' – who emphasised the difference in kind between problems and solutions. On Lautman's work see Barot, *Lautman*, and for his influence on Deleuze see Bowden, *Priority of Events*.
50. Deleuze, *Logic of Sense*, p. 67.
51. Ibid., p. 67.
52. Ibid., p. 66.
53. Ibid., p. 66.
54. Ibid., p. 64.
55. Ibid., p. 64.
56. Ibid., p. 119. This is Deleuze's ontology of univocal repetition – see Chapter 5.
57. Ibid., p. 67.
58. Ibid., p. 210.
59. In this passage, Deleuze views the connective, conjunctive and disjunctive esoteric words as three different kinds of question, each displaced over their respective (connective, conjunctive and disjunctive) series, though it is necessary to stipulate that esoteric words relate to problems proper only in the third kind.
60. Ibid., p. 62. Deleuze repeatedly turns to the French term '*Ça*' – meaning both the pronoun 'it' or 'this'/'that' and the Freudian id – in his writings on structuralism and psychoanalysis, to indicate the strong con-

*Logic of the Phantasm*

nection he identifies between the question and the libidinal phallus. See, for instance, ibid., p. 59.
61. In *Through the Looking-Glass*, 'Jabberwocky' first appears back to front, and must be later deciphered by Humpty Dumpty who reveals the meaning of the portmanteau words in the poem.
62. Deleuze, *Logic of Sense*, pp. 250–1, emphasis mine.
63. Ibid., p. 262.
64. Ibid., p. 262.
65. Ibid., p. 277. Deleuze's association of the phallus with the object = x (rather than the word = x or question) is confusing, but explained by the fact that he sees the object = x as itself displaced in relation to itself, missing its own 'resemblance' and 'identity' (as well as its own 'origin', cf. the phantasm) (ibid., p. 261), and thus seems to use the term object = x as shorthand for the object = x / word = x dis-articulation (see 'the phallus, as object = x and word = x' (p. 279)).
66. Ibid., p. 262.
67. Ibid., p. 242. More precisely, as I argue in section 5.2, the phantasm is ontologically concentrated in the aleatory point in relation to the univocal Event which grounds it, according to Deleuze's formula 'expression = construction'.
68. While the notion of an 'origin' of the phantasm is clearly indebted to Laplanche and Pontalis' article, Deleuze is also dialoguing here with an additional set of issues, namely that of the question-problem complex and thus indirectly esoteric words.
69. Indeed, in the French table of contents, the third stage of the dynamic genesis (after 'from noise to the voice', and 'from the voice to speech') is referred to as 'from speech to the verb' (ibid., p. 390), even if he also claims that the verb *is* speech.
70. 'Secondary organisation (the verb or verbal representation)' (ibid., p. 283); 'The verb is [. . .] "to speak"; it means *to eat/to think* on the metaphysical surface, and causes the event, as that which can be expressed by language, to happen to consumable things, and sense, as the expression of thought, to insist in language' (ibid., p. 278). The verb is clearly given a central role in the production of the fold of the sense-event.
71. See, for instance, ibid., p. 283, which states that the '*dynamic* requirement' (emphasis in the original) requires us to move from the tertiary ordinance of language back down to the primary order of bodies via the secondary organisation of speech, in short relate language back to its emergence from bodies.
72. Here Deleuze is referring to Stoic ontology. In Ancient Stoicism, corporeal bodies were said to be infinitely mixed – a drop of wine mixed with every part of the ocean – to the extent that extended space and time were seen as incorporeal attributes of the thing, not given

in the thing itself, corporeality in Stoicism being composed of forces and relations of force (see Sambursky, *Physics of the Stoics*, pp. 7–8, 18–19). For Stoicism's influence on *The Logic of Sense* see Bowden, *Priority of Events*.
73. Deleuze, *Logic of Sense*, pp. 24–5, translation modified, emphasis in the original.
74. Ibid., p. 25.
75. Ibid., p. 209. See also p. 25: 'the sense-event, or [. . .] the expressible-attribute'.
76. Again, as seen in section 4.2, sense is extremely elusive, reducible to none of its components but drawing them all in, in their relations.
77. Here Deleuze is drawing on Stoic ontology. The Stoics distinguish the corporeal quality, which lies in the domain of bodies understood as fully intermixing forces, from the incorporeal – comprising four further categories: place, time, the void and *expressibles* (*lekta*) (or, as Deleuze calls them, logical attributes) – which occupies a distinct (incorporeal) plane (see Bréhier, *Théorie des incorporels*, pp. 16–18). The latter are senses said *of the thing* (contra Kantian epistemology), and are corporeally caused by forces affecting the body; yet they are said of the thing *by the proposition* (contra naive materialisms and realisms), which acts as what Deleuze calls a 'quasi-cause' expressing something *of* bodies which yet does not belong *to* them. It is also possible to identify what Deleuze sees in the Stoics if we look at the term 'objectality' (*objectité*) which appears in the quoted text above. This term seems to come from Sartre's *The Transcendence of the Ego*, which Deleuze refers to largely positively in a later series (*Logic of Sense*, p. 112), Deleuze finding in Sartre's (1937) text above all the discovery of what he calls on this page an 'impersonal transcendental field'. This field does not have the form of Kant's or Husserl's synthetic unity of apperception – hence it is not subjective, just as sense for Deleuze is not reducible to the proposition even if it is expressed by it – while still being transcendental: it is (transcendentally-empirically) said *of* the thing, not (empirically) said of the *thing*. In both cases, Deleuze appears to be seeking a transcendental theory of sense which is not subjectivistic or anthropocentric, yet which in being necessarily expressed by propositions is not simply materialist or realist.
78. Deleuze also locates here the event's *becoming*, as I will discuss further in the next chapter. 'To green' whisks the bodies to which it is attributed away within a *becoming-incorporeal* (a *becoming-green* of the tree) expressed by language yet not reducible to it.
79. See, for instance, 'sense does not exist outside of the proposition *which expresses it in denoting the thing*' (emphasis mine). Lapoujade, in *Deleuze, les mouvements aberrants*, pp. 116–18, provides a helpful explanation of Deleuze's theory of sense.

## Logic of the Phantasm

80. Deleuze, *Logic of Sense*, pp. 209–10.
81. Ibid., p. 279.
82. Ibid., p. 262, emphasis in the original. As we saw in section 3.5, 'li' (as word = x) *insists* in or is displaced through the statement '*Joli corps de Lili*', and *happens* to another series as an event by repressing it (the event as castration-effect, the occurrence of secondary repression), when the letter subtending 'li' (Poord'jeli as object = x) necessarily diverges from it structurally. The Möbian fold of sense in this way is simply a development of the double screen discussed earlier. As Deleuze puts it, speaking of sexuality's relation to the proposition, '[Sexuality] is a question of a dual surface effect, of reverse and right sides, which precedes all relations between states of affairs and propositions' (ibid., p. 280).
83. In short, this is the double causality of the phantasm, as discussed in section 3.5. The traumatic cause of the phantasm can only *retroactively* be posited as a denotable state of affairs, as the event the state of affairs actualises is coterminous with the sense expressed by the proposition retrospectively attempting to make sense of the trauma.
84. Ibid., p. 92.
85. Ibid., pp. 92–3, translation modified. The perpetual displacement of the word = x throughout structure, thanks to its ex-centricity with the object = x, elongates or preserves language's distinction from bodies: it is because the word = x is displaced throughout language at its own level that the hinge between bodies and language (this very ex-centricity of the word = x / object = x) maintains a minimum of difference between these two orders (thus establishing language *as* language). This structure is in turn reflected in the fold of the sense-event which paradoxically folds the one into the other (*as event* or *as sense*, not as bodies or as language, which preserve their difference), in the manner of a Möbius strip, but whereby the precise location of this switch is again eternally displaced.
86. Deleuze goes so far as to claim that 'paradox is the power (*puissance*) of the unconscious: it occurs always [...] behind the back of consciousness' (ibid., p. 91, translation modified).
87. Deleuze does not mention Guillaume's work at any point in the main text of *The Logic of Sense*, though he dedicates several pages to him in *Difference and Repetition* when discussing the 'linguistic Idea' in Chapter 4. He does, however, mention Guillaume's work, and Ortigues' Kantian reading of it, twice, in footnotes to the 'Twenty-Sixth Series on Language' and 'Thirtieth Series of the Phantasm'.
88. Aspect refers to how in the verb an action, event, or state relates to the flow of time; for instance, there are perfective/imperfective aspects (time as bounded/unbounded), continuous, progressive, habitual

aspects. Deleuze does not engage with this grammatical system, so I will not emphasise it here. This is perhaps because he wishes to introduce Guillaume's theory of the verb into his own ontology of time ('Aion'), rather than abiding by common-sense conceptions of it.
89. Guillaume, *Temps et verbe*, p. 49.
90. This argument presupposes a conception of aspect, tense and mood, as Binnick puts it in *Time and the Verb*, as facets of 'one and the same process of chronogenesis' (p. 198). Binnick notes that Guillaume is unique among linguists in conceiving of these systems together in this manner. As Hirtle puts it, the 'theory of chronogenesis [...] integrat[es] the three systems of aspect, mood, and tense into an operational program that can give rise to the various images of time expressed by the different forms of the French verb [...] Guillaume being, to my knowledge, the only linguist to have integrated grammatical mood as a necessary component of the system of the verb' (*Language in the Mind*, p. 157).
91. Hirtle, *Language in the Mind*, p. 156.
92. Binnick, *Time and the Verb*, p. 198.
93. This led Guillaume to develop the notion of 'operative time'. As Agamben argues in 'The Time that is Left', this refers to the notion in *Temps et verbe* that 'each mental operation, no matter how quick it can be, needs a certain time, which can be extremely short, but is nevertheless real' (p. 4). Guillaume referred to this as a 'microtime', and Hirtle claims that the microtime of 'any mental operation, is so short it escapes perception' (*Language in the Mind*, p. 25). This can be likened to Leibniz's 'little perceptions', which strongly influenced Deleuze's conceptions of the transcendental, of structure and of the unconscious (see *Difference and Repetition*, p. 133). More generally, the notion of an operative time accords with Deleuze's conception of virtual, Aionic, time, as discussed in the next chapter.
94. Hirtle, *Language in the Mind*, p. 19.
95. Ibid., pp. 24–5. Likewise, in *Le discours et le symbole* (1962), p. 125, Ortigues distinguishes between Guillaume and Saussure on the basis that, whereas Saussure's conception of difference is merely 'classificatory' and 'oppositional', understanding *langue* as the totality of oppositions between the substitutable elements of a language, Guillaume views structure as 'positional': elements in a language take on their linguistic value not in relation to the totality of the system (*langue*), but in relation to local processes of determination.
96. Hirtle, *Language in the Mind*, p. 9.
97. See Binnick, *Time and the Verb*, p. 198.
98. Ibid., p. 198.
99. Deleuze will take the notion of a 'time image' from Guillaume, as we

## Logic of the Phantasm

can see from the seminars accompanying his two-volume study of cinema, as well as from *Cinema 2* itself, where Deleuze (1985) writes in the conclusion that cinema is not a '*langue*' but rather constitutes a 'psychomechanics' – Guillaume's term for the mental operations and systems constitutive of a time image (p. 251). Deleuze's larger point on this page is that cinema, like Guillaumian linguistics (and the work of Hjelmslev), is rooted in that which is utterable (or expressible) yet 'of a different nature' from the language of cinema. While 'semiology' tends to 'close the "signifier" in on itself, and cut language off from the images and signs which make up its raw material', 'semiotics' by contrast considers language 'only in relation to this specific content [...] pre-linguistic images and signs' (ibid., pp. 251–2). This notion of a 'pre-linguistic' basis of language is also taken from Guillaume, and we can see therefore that Deleuze's project in *The Logic of Sense* is also already to free up the expressible (the sense-event) from structuralism as semiology, and to conceive of structuralism as a semiotics open to the pre-linguistic (speech, bodies, affect, nonsense). Philosophically, Deleuze is also strongly influenced here not only by Lacan but also Foucault, and his emphasis on the 'non-relation' between seeing and speaking (on this see Deleuze, *Foucault*, pp. 55, 72). On Guillaume's influence on Deleuze, see Dosse, 'Deleuze and Structuralism'.

100. Deleuze, *Logic of Sense*, p. 211.
101. Ibid., p. 213, n. 1. The footnote continues: '[...] and the analysis of this work carried out by E. Ortigues in *Le Discours et le symbole*'. This 1962 work is in large part a philosophically-informed reading of Guillaumian linguistics. In the quoted text above, Deleuze seems to be alluding to p. 149 of *Le discours et le symbole*, where Ortigues compares Guillaume's theory of the verb to Kant's form of interiority. Phonic action thus 'forms an open space for language' (intensive quantities phonemically inscribed on the erogenous zones), and semantic reaction 'an internal time' reacting on the former and temporalising it according to the verb's grammatical determination. This, in short, amounts to a *verbal* schematism of the imagination.
102. See Deleuze, *Logic of Sense*, p. 245.
103. Deleuze even later writes that 'the verb is the "verbal representation" in its entirety' (ibid., p. 278).
104. Ibid., p. 245, emphasis in the original, translation modified. Deleuze partly bases his argument on the article 'Du Fantasme et du verbe' by Luce Irigaray, noting in her work that a 'general infinitive' is 'progressively specified according to the differentiation of formal grammatical relations' (Deleuze, *Logic of Sense*, p. 246). Here Deleuze refers directly to and compares this with Guillaume's work (ibid., p. 249, n. 4).

105. Deleuze, *Logic of Sense*, p. 246.
106. In Kantian terms, thought affects itself in the form of interiority by determining intensive quantity according to a temporal logic. Here the temporal logic is the grammatical determination of the phonic action.
107. I will discuss voice and person in the next section.
108. This will be touched on in the next chapter.
109. As we see in the quotation above, the phantasm's role will be to attempt to provide 'solutions' to these problems, but the question (or founding serial tension constitutive of speech) will remain forever implicated within it. We will have to wait till the next chapter to see in what sense the phantasm can provide solutions.
110. Ibid., p. 211, translation modified.
111. Ibid., p. 211, translation modified.
112. Ibid., p. 245.
113. See ibid., p. 246.
114. We see this particularly in the subjunctive ('If I were x'; 'I might be x'). More generally, signification pertains to the selection of compatible disjunctive alternatives (not past *and* present, not smaller *and* larger) – on which conceptual implication also depends at the level of the subjunctive – and thus has an important role more generally in conditioning the pure event's synchronic space (which is prior to the distinction between the real, the possible and the impossible).
115. This is also Deleuze's definition of univocity, namely the 'minimum of Being common to the real, the possible, and the impossible' (ibid., p. 206), and it is no coincidence that he associates the univocity of being with the infinitive mood of the verb. This is developed further in the next chapter.
116. This is precisely the proposition's problematic basis. In his discussion of the 'linguistic Idea', or problem of language, in *Difference and Repetition*, Deleuze explains that prior to disciplinary distinctions – for instance those of language (phonemes, morphemes and semantemes) – what underlies any problem is a field of pure *difference*, 'the problematic field of a positive multiplicity' (p. 255), which disciplinary domains (or 'Ideas') attempt to determine and actualise. He writes approvingly that, in Guillaume's work, morphology is not simply a continuation of phonology (as in Saussure), but rather it 'introduces properly problematic values which determine the significant selection of phonemes' (ibid., p. 256). Thus phonemes and morphemes cannot be viewed as belonging to the same axis (again contra Saussure), since the one is plugged into a pre-disciplinary and pre-linguistic field of difference, and the other reacts onto these differences within a particular disciplinary domain (language). Deleuze here sides with Guillaume's conception of concrete sentences or propositions, rather

than *langue* as abstract totality, as the locus of morphological determination (p. 256).
117. This is hence only a *propositional* solution, not one which satisfies the phantasm's search to resolve its founding question, which only the work of art yet to come can attempt to answer – see Chapter 5.
118. This partly explains why Deleuze turns specifically to Guillaume's theory of the verb, being unique among linguists in conceiving of mood, tense and aspect as belonging to the *same system* of the verb. Hence, the verb's determination can bring into play all three dimensions of the proposition within this shared medium or single process of determination, dimensions which otherwise are irreducible, each (when viewed separately) with one foot outside the expression of sense, as we saw in section 4.2.
119. We can see that, like Guillaume and contra Saussure, Deleuze locates language at the level of the proposition's dimensional relations and not at the level of an abstract structure. The proposition is determined locally, within each proposition, and not at the level of signification as pre-existing structuring totality.
120. See ibid., p. 118.
121. Ibid., p. 282. This can be reconciled with section 3.5 to the extent that, as I claimed in section 4.1, the phantasm folds into itself the physical and metaphysical surfaces – the *Ucs.* and *P/cs.* when considered statically or at the level of the provisional structural dualism generating the phantasm as event. In short, the verb, as 'the "verbal representation" in its entirety' (ibid., p. 278), subsumes thing- and word-presentations, while maintaining both series and their *double inscription* (the double screen) which, in reacting on itself, it operates.
122. See my summary of the verb as circle of the proposition below.
123. See ibid., pp. 23–4.
124. See my Chapter 5, note 4.
125. Here we see clearly how the surface of the phantasm draws the dividing line between word and thing, *on the basis of which* the proposition is then capable of denoting an 'external' state of affairs pointing 'outside' language.
126. The fourth and final stage, from the verb to univocity, extends beyond psychoanalysis to ontology and literature, as discussed in the next chapter.
127. Ibid., p. 263. Deleuze continues: '[we ask] *about that which founds the different aspects of the sexual position* [its three syntheses or series] – *and which is also founded by them*' (emphasis mine). What 'founds' the three syntheses of sexuality are the three types of esoteric word Deleuze extracts from Leclaire's work, but the point is that they in turn are also *founded by* sexuality.
128. We will see in the next chapter that the final stage – from the verb to

univocity – is accounted for by means of Carroll's literature, as its linguistic mechanism or construct.

129. This framework opposes a tendency in some current Anglophone readings of the dynamic genesis to consider it as functioning as a direct attack on Lacan due to its apparent allegiance to Klein, and more generally to involve a more or less unilateral genesis of sense from the body. By insufficiently emphasising the *equality* of series in the dynamic genesis, these readings are unable to account for large portions of the text and for many of its conceptual intricacies, as well as contradicting what I have shown to be direct textual support for my reading. Furthermore, such readings rely on an interpretation of Deleuze's ontology which cannot be reconciled with the one presented here, which stresses the links between immanence and serial equality. See Widder, 'Negation to Disjunction', and Świątkowski, *Deleuze and Desire*.

130. Deleuze, *Logic of Sense*, p. 265, emphasis mine. The relation between these three 'moments', syntheses or series of the second stage of the dynamic genesis, and the other two stages, is more complex and can be understood as follows: the three moments all belong to the second stage (from the voice to speech), which is, however, more encompassing than the description 'coordination of partial zones', even if it centres on it. 'From the voice to speech' also encompasses the partial zones' independent *connection* and their conjoined *disjunction* with thought; nonetheless, the latter is ultimately subsumed under 'from speech to the verb', and the former is already partly explained by 'from noise to the voice', such that even if the first and third moments of the second stage slightly overlap with the first and third stages, they cannot be conflated. This attests to the continuous movement of the dynamic genesis which cannot ultimately be neatly divided up and builds on what came before it.

131. Ibid., p. 280.

132. Ibid., p. 285.

133. See also the following quote from the thirteenth series: 'Structuralism is right to raise the point that form and matter have a scope only in the original and irreducible structures in which they are organised [. . .] For [. . .] sexuality, lies within the organisation and orientation of these dimensions, before being found in generative matter or engendered form' (ibid., p. 105). Neither the generative matter of the drive nor the engendered forms of language, when considered separately, can explain sexuality.

134. Deleuze approves of Laplanche and Pontalis' critique of Isaacs' conception of the phantasm, which in 'modelling the phantasm on the drive, gives to the subject a determined active place' (ibid., p. 246, n. 2). In conceiving of only a single level of causality in the phantasm,

*Logic of the Phantasm*

this is thus where Deleuze finally parts ways with the Kleinian school in the dynamic genesis. Deleuze sides instead with Laplanche and Pontalis who, in locating the origin of fantasy together with the origin of sexuality – namely in secondary narcissism, which disengages from the partial drives of the depths (orality) and instead auto-erotically invests the surface – argue for a double causality of series (in short, the inscription of linguistically communicated parental fantasies on the erogenous zones and drives). However, he considers that even they do not go far enough in still ultimately anchoring the phantasm to an 'auto-erotic "this-side"' (p. 243), in short in ultimately siding with the physical surface as site of the subject. In the next chapter I will show that for Deleuze the subject of the phantasm is located, rather, in the non-relation or torsion of surfaces.

135. Indeed, person is introduced alongside tense and mood in the series on language, whereas voice is only added in the series on the phantasm.
136. In fact, Deleuze reverses Guillaume, whom Binnick, in *Time and the Verb*, argues was a 'radical idealist' (p. 197) believing chronogenesis to entail a solely internal representation of time. Deleuze uses Guillaume's theory of the verb, instead, to develop a radically impersonal and a-subjective conception of the verb (and of the phantasm). Hirtle's view in *Language in the Mind* is more nuanced, showing that Guillaume himself questioned speech's relation to unconscious thought in a more co-conditioning manner (see p. 235).
137. There is clearly a double causality to this, to the extent that, once generated, the person as consistent network of these opinions, beliefs and desires will come to overstructure the verb's grammatical determination in the phantasm and not simply be its effect. The key point to remember here is that this accreted person is no more substantial once it takes on consistency, and is still just a dimension of the proposition. Deleuze means it literally when he writes that manifestation involves someone who speaks and 'expresses himself' (*Logic of Sense*, p. 17).
138. See, for instance, Lacan's Seminar XIV, *The Logic of Fantasy*, 1966–7.
139. The 'structure-Other' is an early form of Deleuze's function of 'common sense', as it appears in *The Logic of Sense*, which I discuss in the next chapter.
140. These remarks are taken from his reading of the collection *Le désir et la perversion*, published in 1967.
141. As Deleuze explains in *Coldness and Cruelty* (Chapter XI), the sadist lacks an ego, finding the ego in others while embodying the superego, whereas the masochist lacks a superego, locating it in others, but in both cases (sadism and masochism), there is no other, only a psychic apparatus (ego, superego, id) distributed over two or more bodies.
142. Deleuze, *Logic of Sense*, p. 358.

143. On the relation between Deleuze's theory of the event and Lacan's object (a), see Žižek, *Organs without Bodies*.
144. Deleuze, *Logic of Sense*, p. 273.

5

# The Speculative Univocity of Being and Language: From the Verb to Univocity

## 5.1 Introduction: Humour, or the Univocity of Sense

There are a number of ways to view the genesis of sense in *The Logic of Sense*. One way that has been emphasised in the secondary literature is as the emergence of consciousness from the body's affects.[1] There is, however, a more interesting and important genesis at stake beneath this one. If the first genesis takes us from the verb to the logical proposition and empirical consciousness, the second off-piste route goes from the verb to the univocity of being. As Deleuze writes, playing on the literal meaning of the scholastic term univocity[2] – one voice (*voce*) – 'The univocity of Being signifies that Being is Voice, that it is said.'[3]

This second genesis thus remains at the level of – and indeed is the very culmination of – language's secondary organisation (the surface), and is explicitly discussed throughout the final series of the dynamic genesis, the 'Thirty-Fourth Series of Primary Order and Secondary Organisation'. It is for this reason that the book concludes at the level of the *secondary* organisation, and at the level of the relation *between* speech and language, rather than with the tertiary ordinance of language or of the logical proposition. Hence the genesis at stake in Deleuze's logic of sense as a whole moves from noise to the voice, the voice to speech, speech to the verb and from the verb to univocity, without ever moving all the way up to language (as cut off from speech).[4] As such, the current chapter will complete the account of Deleuze's theory of the phantasm given in the previous chapter, which it will do through the addition of the ontological and literary components needed to move from its beginning in sexuality and language to its never fully realised ending beyond sexuality in the univocity of being.

While, as mentioned in section 3.1, immanence is arguably the ultimate object of Deleuze's ontology as onto-logic in *The Logic of Sense* – and indeed in his philosophical project more generally – in the 1960s the term is largely eclipsed by that of univocity, the 'Univocity of being' or, as Deleuze writes on the final page of the thirty-fourth series as the book's concluding formulation, the 'Univocity of sense'.[5] Yet, this latter formulation – in speaking of a univocity of *sense* and not of being, per se – shows a first, *immanent*, sense in which we can understand the notion of univocity, in that it bypasses the equivocity of being and thinking, with sense as the univocity *of* this equivocity or as the univocity of the *difference* of thinking and being, through which they paradoxically communicate and in relation to which they are even reversible.[6]

Deleuze explains a few sentences earlier that univocity emerges from the equivocity of bodies and language as best typified by 'humour', the latter of which *speaks* of bodies and sexuality and through one equivocation 'too many' disengages from it a univocal event.[7] As he writes on the penultimate page in one of the book's culminating passages:

> Beginning with one equivocation too many (*en trop*), humour constructs all univocity; beginning with the properly sexual equivocation which ends all equivocity, humour releases a de-sexualised Univocity – a speculative univocity of Being and language – the entire secondary organisation in one word.

Even if humour – as articulated by the verb ('the entire secondary organisation in one word')[8] – 'ends all equivocity', this 'ending' is only momentary, since Deleuze stipulates a few sentences later that equivocity is forever *implicated within* univocity. Indeed, this is nothing else than the unending implicating-explicating path of the phantasm which problematically circles around its 'question', unable to ever fully answer it.[9] Referring to Carroll, Deleuze writes:

> He makes the energy of sexuality pass into the pure asexual, *without, however, ceasing to ask 'What is a little girl?'* – even if this *question* must be replaced with the *problem* of a work of art yet to come (*à venir*), which alone would give an answer.[10]

If the – it is implied by the context, humorous (and perverse) – work of art 'yet to come' would 'alone' give an answer to this question,[11] it is yet to come (or 'speculative') and thus its answer is never fully actualised or realised in a work. Indeed it would end univocity were it to provide an answer to the phantasm's question, which ties language via the question to sexuality and the body and establishes the equivocal tension on which univocity is based.

A little before these two quotations, Deleuze accounts for this framework psychoanalytically. He writes that the Voice's equivoca-

## The Speculative Univocity of Being and Language

tions (as discussed in section 3.2: neither denoted object nor manifested subject nor signified concept) and equivocal relations with regard to sexuality and the body (its position in the 'heights'), found the body as 'esoteric set' (*ensemble ésotérique*), or as set of phonemes composing the conjunctive esoteric word. While the Voice is radically equivocal in regard to the body, transcendent, it is nonetheless *through* this equivocity that the body becomes something other than brute materiality and drive.[12] Here we return to the framework of my Chapter 3: while Deleuze does not wish to consider language as inscribing itself on bodies, it is precisely in their non-relation, or relation of equivocity, that bodies and language produce something other than bodies and other than language, namely univocity or immanence.[13] Indeed, Deleuze writes here:

> This is what words represent; all the formative elements of language which exist only in relation and in reaction to one another – phonemes, morphemes, and semantemes – form their totality from the point of view of this immanent history with which they are identical [...] [This] sexual history [...] will not be designated, manifested, or signified by these words, but [...] rather will be strictly coextensive and co-substantial with them.[14]

The body becomes an esoteric set thanks to the Voice's equivocal relation to it, just as speech (which is the body as esoteric set) gives way to something else in relation to 'the *other*, desexualised and metaphysical surface'[15] of thought, precisely the univocity of the verb.[16] It is fundamental to Deleuze's ontology, therefore, that the dynamic genesis entail an equal and equivocal articulation of bodies and language (as I have maintained in earlier chapters), supplanted by and grounded in its product (the univocity of the verb). As Deleuze writes, an individual's sexual history is 'strictly coextensive and co-substantial' with the phonemes, morphemes and semantemes used to 'buil[d] the surface',[17] as he puts it earlier in the series.

Nonetheless, even if the univocity of bodies and language can be understood psychoanalytically, and if psychoanalysis provides much of the underlying groundwork needed to tackle this question, the dynamic genesis (and the phantasm in particular) still explicitly culminates in the literary work of art (in the form of humour and nonsense), signalling the ultimate ('critical') limit of Deleuze's 'clinical' project.[18] Moreover, literary nonsense and humour, insofar as it 'constructs *all univocity*',[19] completes the very ontology of Deleuze's logic of sense. It is specifically in relation to humour that Deleuze will speak of a 'speculative univocity of Being and language', the book's crowning ontological thesis by which he means a univocity that while speculative, i.e. only existing in *thought* and taking place only in the construct of the work of art (yet to come), nonetheless entails a univocity of thought *and being* – or from a different but strictly related angle a relation of immanence whereby immanence equates to an *equality* of powers even if it must be constructed by the concept (here the humorous verb). As univocity of being and language, *sense* only exists in thought *yet is irreducible to it*.

## 5.2 IMMANENCE = UNIVOCITY or, the Ideal Game

If the problematic of univocity is inseparable from Deleuze's immanent ontology, as I have suggested above, it is necessary, however, to examine precisely how and why this is the case, rather than lazily conflating the two notions. Distinguishing univocity from immanence, and conversely showing how they co-articulate, will in turn shed light on Deleuze's conception of immanence, as well as allowing us to better understand the relationship between univocity and humour or nonsense in Deleuze's work.[20] This second sense of univocity is discussed throughout the book in the context of what Deleuze calls the 'ideal game' which, returning us to the section above, he writes 'takes place only in art and can only exist in thought and [...] has no other result than the work of art'.[21] The ideal game finalises and never ceases finalising the phantasm, effectuating a perpetual conversion from the psychoanalytic clinic to the literary work.

Now, while the literary use to which Deleuze will put it is inextricable from his theory of the ideal game, Deleuze's primary model for the ideal game is still his reading of Nietzsche's conception of the dice throw. The larger context of this reading is Deleuze's attempt in the 1960s to break with the requirement that ontology choose between either the one or the many as the locus of being,[22] what he will later render as the disjunctive synthesis 'PLURALISM = MONISM'[23] which, like being/thinking, we must also understand as an equivocation giving way to a univocal articulation. In *The Logic of Sense*, Deleuze explicitly locates the dice throw or ideal game in the phantasm, in the thirtieth and thirty-first series (on the phantasm and on thought, respectively) of the dynamic genesis writing 'The phantasm is inseparable [...] from the toss of the dice',[24] and that it is 'the site of the eternal return',[25] the latter of which should be understood ontologically as well as in terms of the model discussed

## The Speculative Univocity of Being and Language

in the previous chapter, both of which reunite in Deleuze's theory as I will show.[26]

Indeed Deleuze privileges the dice throw (and eternal return) in his approach to the thesis of the univocity of being, as we can see from the following extract from the 'Twenty-Fifth Series of Univocity':

> The univocity of Being [...] is the eternal return itself (*en personne*), or – as we have seen in the case of the ideal game – the affirmation of all chance in a single moment, the unique cast for all throws, one Being and only one for all forms and all times, a single insistence (*insistance*) for all that exists, a single phantom for all the living, a single voice for every hum of voices and every drop of water in the sea.[27]

Now, both the dice throw and eternal return, as Deleuze conceives of them, stem from Deleuze's work on Nietzsche from the first half of the 1960s, as most fully elaborated in *Nietzsche and Philosophy* (1962). In the latter, sense is considered as the implication of a force differential or affection that serves as its corporeal cause, experience being according to this framework never merely phenomenal but bathing in forces and relations of force with a potentially cosmic significance and an always potentially ontological power.[28] We can say that for Deleuze's Nietzsche, an affection serves directly as *a being waiting to be ontologised*, and *being* as such (the plane of immanence and of univocity) is the running total of ontologised affections, which means those affections which *return* in the thought that selects them.[29]

Influenced by Nietzsche's late writings on the will to power,[30] Deleuze equates being with selection or return in *Nietzsche and Philosophy* (as well as in later texts including *The Logic of Sense*),[31] writing: 'the eternal return mak[es] something come into being which cannot do so without changing nature. It is no longer a question of selective thought but of selective being; for the eternal return is being and being is selection.'[32] Although the first selection occurs in thought, thought's selection of elements that return constitutes being (= return) and transmutes thought into being (hence the quasi-dualism of being/thinking expresses a monism-effect of return).[33] To summarise Deleuze's argument: only forces that affirm their quantitative difference from one another return; those that do not are disqualified as brute quantity and fall back into the depths of chaos.[34] However, this return needs to be thought in order to be expressed ontologically. I would suggest that according to this ontology, affections or quantitative force differentials impacting the body are beings only capable of taking on being (= return or selection) when thought as such;

affections derive from forces imbued with a pre-ontological power of return in need of ontologisation by thought. Thought expresses the being of beings by selecting only those beings that return, which is to say that, firstly, affirm a force differential or affect the body and, secondly, which return eternally (as being) in the thought that selects them.

This brings us directly to the dice throw and its univocity. Using Nietzsche with but ultimately contra Mallarmé, Deleuze claims: 'To think is to send out a dicethrow.'[35] I would maintain that his reading of the dice throw is essential for understanding how he conceives of this expressive, circular, relation between beings, being and thought.[36]

Using an example taken from statistics, if I throw a six-sided die once it has a one in six chance of landing on a six. The same applies to the second time I throw it, or to the hundredth or thousandth time. But this only applies at the level of each throw and not at the level of throws taken collectively as a series. The probability of throwing five sixes in a row, for instance, is much higher than that of throwing one million sixes in a row. Thus, taken as an individual throw, the probability of landing on a six of the millionth throw in a series of 999,999 prior sixes, is just one in six. But taken as one single throw comprised of a million instances or repetitions, its probability of landing on a six is much slimmer. When approached as a series, each individual throw or repetition of the one Throw reacts back onto and informs the probability of all previous and subsequent throws in the series. For instance, the first throw in a series of a million throws has a one in six chance of landing on a six, but viewed in relation to 999,999 subsequent sixes it retroactively takes on a much smaller probability since it is in fact identical to the millionth throw in the series, there being only one throw and $n$ repetitions when we approach it as a series. Hence, as the first term in a series, the first throw's probability of landing on a six progressively shrinks retroactively, even though it has already happened (qua individual throw but not qua throw in a series), each time we have a subsequent six in the same series. Likewise, each throw proactively informs the probability of each subsequent throw when approached at the level of their place in the series.[37]

Ultimately the point of this example is not to show that the one (Throw) and the many (throws) are the same but for a shift in perspective, but that each throw must be approached *both* as a discrete throw capable of affirming its independent 1/6 chance of landing on a six, and also as a progressively structured element in a series. According to Deleuze's equation 'PLURALISM = MONISM', we need to make the one and the many collide or disjunctively articulate, rather than subsuming the one under the other. While a million sixes is statistically highly unlikely, to affirm chance is to throw each die in the series as if it were probabilistically independent from every other, thus keeping each structure open to its partly unforeseeable outside. To affirm chance is thus to deny the necessity of the existence of the world – as empirically induced and probabilistically modelled on the basis of such induction from experience – but without going as far as requiring that we create a completely new one.[38] The thrower of dice participates in the world's expression by affirming *the necessity of chance*: this means living and acting according to the necessity of the die's outcome once and only once it lands, since when it is thrown it is still capable of virtually informing the structure that will actualise it.[39]

Deleuze seems to suggest in *Nietzsche and Philosophy* that we should take the model of the dice throw as more than a mere analogy for his univocal ontology when he writes:

> The dice which are thrown once are the affirmation of *chance*, the combination which they form on falling is the affirmation of *necessity*. Necessity is affirmed of chance in exactly the sense that being is affirmed of becoming and unity is affirmed of multiplicity.[40]

Being pluralistic and agonistic, forces share with each other nothing else than (1) their quantitative difference from one another, which when affirmed generates a quality or sense as a perspective not only *on* the relating forces but also *as* a new world expressed by it;[41] (2) the *chance* by which they are brought into a relation,[42] these 'encounters of forces of various quantities' being understood precisely as 'the concrete parts of chance'.[43] Chance, as the relation of force with force, is the 'essence' of force[44] – force is quantitative difference affirmed by *chance* (as well as *by* chance). Thought selects forces which in affirming their quantitative difference (chance) express qualities or senses, and it affirms the concatenation of chance across multiple throws; as such, thought conditions the emergence of 'unity' from 'multiplicity' at the same time that 'necessity' is affirmed of 'chance'. Stemming from random and even chaotic bodily affections, throws inject the partly unforeseeable into thought's structuring of experience.

Hence the immanence of body and thought is coordinate with the univocity of chance and necessity (and of the one and the multiple), because thought can never fully contain the body's affections and the outside of forces it communicates to thought. Conversely, without thought one could not induce this very affirmation of chance from affections (such as the one million sixes), since one would have only discrete throws. In short, every affection is itself an affirmation of chance, and in thinking on the basis of the body thought opens itself up to chaos; however, without thought there is no serialisation, or expression of the univocal *necessity*, of the chance of the body's affections.[45]

I would suggest that according to this schema, being is nothing else than the *running total* of throws in a series, and that each throw contributes to this running total, and thus to being, *as much as* being reacts back onto and structures each additional throw, bypassing both pluralism and monism ('multiplicity' and 'unity'). This is what prevents Deleuze's ontology from being transcendent or emanationist: the plane of univocity and immanence is not transcendently concentrated in, cannot be said to emanate from, any point in the system: neither from being nor beings, neither from the one nor the multiple, neither from the image of thought nor the matter of being. This is what Deleuze seems to be getting at in *The Logic of Sense* when he writes that univocity 'wrests Being from beings in order to bring it to all of them at once, and to make it fall back onto (*rabattre sur*) them for all times'.[46]

A throw is *a* being waiting to be ontologised, whereas being as such is expressed by the thought of the eternal recurrence of each throw, a thought which generates univocity in *displacing* the being of each throw such that they can no longer be considered as discrete or equivocal entities. Each throw eternally recurs to the extent that it retroactively and proactively informs each past and subsequent throw in a series. As such, ontologically, there is only one Throw, a univocally single repetition repeated $n$ times. This Throw (or Event)[47] concentrates into the infinitely reduced instant of throwing all future and past throws (or events), and affirms all of chance each throw ('re'-affirming every future and past affirmation), while itself (as instant) being subdivided ad infinitum into the future and past simultaneously, forever displaced in relation to itself.[48] Ultimately, this constitutes a conception of the eternal return, in Deleuze, as the eternal return of *difference*.[49]

As such, being is more fundamentally *becoming*, bringing us to the third part of the earlier quotation. Not only is retroaction constant and ongoing. Since there is never in fact a final term, an $n$th throw, as one can always add another affection or throw to the series, we must ultimately annul probability. If 'necessity is affirmed of chance in exactly the sense that being is affirmed of becoming and unity is affirmed of multiplicity',[50] this means both that being is a running total of throws (their necessity and structural or syntactic 'unity'), *and* that this running total is not a closed totality or Oneness.[51] Affirming the necessity of chance is playing the game according to a potentially infinite number of throws since – particularly in the speculative space of the ideal game and through its practical mode of engaging with the world[52] – one can always add another throw which will counter-actualise the previous one and reopen the univocal space of the Event. In 'Tenth Series of the Ideal Game', Deleuze explains that in ordinary games (of skill or of chance), pre-established rules 'determine hypotheses which divide and apportion chance, that is hypotheses of loss or gain (what happens if . . .) [. . .] Each [throw] brings about a fixed distribution corresponding to one case or another', namely 'victory or defeat'.[53] To the ordinary game, Deleuze opposes the ideal game, in which 'each move invents its own rules',[54] such as the number of throws in a series. Thus there is 'neither winner nor loser'[55] insofar as the 'final' throw will always be deferred if there is no pre-established number. Hence, for both these reasons, chance is 'endlessly ramifie[d] [. . .] with each throw'.[56]

Now, it is the 'aleatory point' which 'always changes the rule',[57] bringing us to Deleuze's theory of subjectivity or lack thereof. The Event is expressed by thought, and exists only in thought's transcendental field or on its phantasmatic surface which, for Deleuze, is *strictly coextensive and co-substantial with the events populating it*.[58] The surface is a work in progress over which the aleatory point is endlessly displaced, preventing it from coalescing around a core or centring point of subjectivity.[59] Still, in the absence of a subject, the aleatory point (which Deleuze also terms a 'counter-self'[60]) is used to account for the functioning of this field. As he writes:

> The set (*l'ensemble*) of throws affirms the whole of chance, and endlessly ramifies it with each throw [. . .] Each throw is itself a series [. . .] Each throw emits singular points, the points on the dice. But the set of throws is included in the aleatory point, a unique cast which endlessly displaces itself throughout all series [. . .] These throws are successive in relation to one another, yet simultaneous in relation to this point which always changes the rule, which coordinates and ramifies the corresponding series, breathing chance over the entire length of each series.[61]

The aleatory point is what 'serialises' (*mise en séries*) the throws or puts them into series, without which univocity cannot be constructed. This is both because it operates the disjunctive synthesis of multiplicity, and because through this it keeps the structure open to its recurrent perversion or counter-actualisation.

Moreover, I would argue that the aleatory point is nothing else than the ontological aspect of the disjunctive esoteric word or phantasmatic question, inducing from the body's affections events spoken by verbs.[62] In other words, the aleatory point is shorthand for the structure of the phantasm (the question-problem relation) in relation to the ideal game played in it. The phantasm provides a shared medium or structure within which a series of irreducible events expressed by the phantasm's verb-form can communicate with one another, precisely by taking place in the 'same' phantasm which, being co-substantial and coextensive with the events produced within it, becomes reduced to the de-centred and ex-centric aleatory point displaced throughout it. In short, the aleatory point figures as the remnants of the constructive element (the verb as culmination of the secondary organisation of language) within the dice throw, which ultimately grounds everything in the dynamic genesis which led up to it, including language itself, in the univocity it expresses (the Event).[63]

To summarise *The Logic of Sense*'s conception of subjectivity:

1. Firstly, we have the subject as body, as conjunctive esoteric word, which is also the ego in the psychoanalytic sense.
2. Next, with castration, the ego 'literally releases [...] like spores' its singularities or castration-effects,[64] which populate the phantasm, 'and bursts as its gets unburdened';[65] likewise, Deleuze writes that 'Aion is populated (*se peuple*) by events at the level of singularities which are subdivided (*réparties*) over its infinitive line'.[66] Singularities occupy an 'impersonal and pre-individual transcendental field, which does not resemble the corresponding empirical fields' and 'cannot be determined as that of consciousness'.[67] This field is irreducible to the singularities' propositional determination which empirically redoubles them; but they are also impersonal in relation to what generated them, namely the sexual ego: singularities lie equipoised between the ego on the one hand, and the proposition and manifested person on the other. At this level the subject is those castration- or subject-effects which the aleatory point extracts from the bodily ego, together with

194

## The Speculative Univocity of Being and Language

their disjunctive synthesis as throws which it operates by being that in relation to which they are thrown – occupying irreducible worlds at the level of the many throws they are unable to directly communicate to each other.[68] This does not constitute a centring point for thought as a priori synthetic unity since the aleatory point is perpetually displaced or 'decentred' in relation to what it (disjunctively) synthesises.[69]

3. The aleatory point or disjunctive esoteric word then gives way to the Event (univocal being, eternal return of difference). While the asexual Event ontologically grounds the process leading up to it in its univocity, in relation to which everything takes on its existence, this is a univocity *of equivocity*, of difference. If Deleuze speaks of univocity in terms of a 'single phantom for all of the living', this is a univocity of the *difference* living/dead. The Event is an *unending* process of de-personalisation and de-sexualisation, as we have seen in regard to the folding/unfolding path of the phantasm encircling its question. If the surface is coextensive and co-substantial with the events populating it, these events must be involved in a perpetually renewed movement of de-personalisation/de-sexualisation, such that univocity is the univocity of the difference sexual/asexual, rather than an asexual and fully de-personalised endpoint. Univocity is hence a ghost haunting the living as a process of incorporeal redoubling, and not a God inhabiting the afterlife.

4. This means that neither the Event (expression) nor the aleatory point as constructive element can take precedence over the other in the genesis of univocity, nor be considered as the subject of the phantasm and ideal game when taken separately. Univocal being does not emanate from either the one or the other, but is the result of their very difference such that we have another equivocal relation giving way to univocity at the level of the equation *expression = construction*.[70]

5. In *Foucault*, Deleuze writes 'All intentionality collapses [. . .] in the "non-relation" between seeing and speaking [. . .] Intentionality is still generated in a Euclidean space that prevents it from understanding itself, and must be surpassed by an other, "topological", space which establishes contact between the Outside and the Inside.'[71] Likewise, between the physical and metaphysical surfaces, or the poles of denotation (of things) and expression (of senses) in the verbal 'circle' of the proposition, all intentionality breaks down because the two series or poles are irreducible

and divergent. Thus the intentional subject is rooted neither in the body nor in the mind, but in the fold of their non-relation (eternal return of beginning/end and inside/outside). The aleatory point functions here as the action = x or intentional pre-cursor, operating a topological folding of the personal/impersonal, and the sexual/asexual. Deleuze seems to derive the term 'intention' (as in 'good intentions') from his essay 'Klossowski or bodies-language': 'Klossowski goes from one sense of the word "*intentio*" to another – corporeal intensity and spoken intentionality',[72] or from 'simulacra (will to power as simulation)' to the 'phantasm of Being (eternal return)'.[73]

6. The person only arrives at the level of constraining the ideal game using the conditions of sense established by the three dimensions of the proposition (including manifestation).

Now, in relation to language which is the ideal game's proper domain, becoming leads to a destabilising of the value of any term in a series, akin to Derrida's *différance*, entailing a generalised excess of pure sense over all significations, manifestations, denotations. Pure sense becomes thereby ontologically privileged because of its openness to constant change and to the effects of retroaction.[74] To express pure sense, however, the ideal game must free itself from the proposition's three primary dimensions.

Early on in the 'Twenty-Fifth Series of Univocity', Deleuze writes 'Incompatibility does not exist between two events, but between an event and the world or the individual which actualises another event as divergent.'[75] Contradictory logical predicates (such as black or white, small or large), are predicated of propositional subjects (a black or white wall, a small or large tree), and give rise to incompatibility within the proposition, necessitating widespread exclusive disjunctions (either/or) throughout its three dimensions, as we also saw in the determination of the verb in section 4.3. Without these systems of exclusive disjunction, incompatibility tears apart syntax or conceptual implication at the level of signification (for instance, in the case of the syllogism discussed in section 4.2);[76] it breaks up the world's unity, what Deleuze calls 'good sense', at the level of denotation – good sense depends on enchained states of affairs whose chronological sequence does not lead to logical contradictions in the world, contradictions which would necessitate positing more than one world (and more than one subject);[77] and at the level of manifestation, it fragments the self-identity of the person, Deleuze's 'common

## The Speculative Univocity of Being and Language

sense', which reduces the difference between being and thinking to the identity of the equation 'Self = Self' within *thought* (giving the option of *either* thinking *or* being),[78] and likewise encloses the self-differing becomings produced by this non-relation (subject-effects) within the form of the individual.

Indeed, good and common sense are coordinate in that self-differing becomings (subject-effects) become in both directions simultaneously (future/past), breaking with good sense, as long as the gap between being and thinking is left open to difference, which breaks with common sense. Self-identity over (chronological) time is coordinate with self-identity across onto-logical difference (being/thinking). Hence Deleuze writes that 'the form of the self ordinarily guarantees the connection of a series; [...] the form of the world guarantees the convergence of continuous series which can be extended':[79] the self or person connects subject-effects displaced over the line of Aion as a single connective series, thereby allowing states of affairs to be conjunctively synthesised (to converge on one another), and over which the subject's continuous series can be 'extended'.[80]

As such, returning to the quotation from 'Twenty-Fifth Series of Univocity', incompatibility only refers, for Deleuze, to relations between events that are actualised in states of affairs or objects, of which their senses are thereby predicated within signifying propositions spoken by subjects. Below the level of denotation, manifestation and signification (objects, subjects and logical concepts) lie unactualised (and indeed unactualisable) events – events expressed by verbs stated in the infinitive, and irreducible to propositional determination.[81] This is why Deleuze distinguishes logical incompatibility (as 'logical contradiction between predicates') from 'alogical incompatibility, an incompatibility of "humour"',[82] which only concerns events and which is played out in the ideal game. Since events are unactualised and unactualisable – or rather since states of affairs are *actualisations of* events which are not themselves exhausted by their actualisation and retain a fine threadlike connection with all events in the eternal return[83] – they are not attributable to identifiable states of affairs, and thus their senses do not share the system of logical incompatibility between subjects and predicates which guarantees the consistency of the proposition's three dimensions.

Thus, still in the series on univocity, Deleuze writes that the 'individual' must

> transcend his form and his syntactical link with a world, in order to attain to the universal communication of events, that is, to the affirmation of a disjunctive synthesis beyond logical contradictions, and even beyond alogical incompatibilities.[84]

The individual must break with his form, the manifested person and its common sense (thus merging with the univocal Event), and with signification and denotation (his syntactical link with a world), in order to arrive at the 'universal communication of events'. We can use the Ur-model of the dice throw to understand this last point. Deleuze writes that 'all events, even contraries, are compatible',[85] since as logical attributes ('the tree greens') they cannot logically contradict one another (contradiction only applies to the relation between *actualised* events, i.e. predicates predicated of subjects in accordance with the proposition's three dimensions). As unactualised, each event (or throw) is radically plural and communicates with other events-throws not by dint of belonging to the same world or self, but because in the affirmation of their irreducibility and difference from all other throws this difference is paradoxically converted, at the level of the Throw, into universal communication (*through* difference, divergence or chance).

However, the question remains, *how* is the individual to break with the proposition's three dimensions, and its good and common sense, to attain this universal communication? On the same page from the 'Twenty-Fifth Series of Univocity', Deleuze explains that it is through the ideal game, and more specifically by constructing disjunctive esoteric words. We can see this for instance with the disjunctive esoteric word 'frumious' – Carroll's invention which combines 'furious-and-fuming' and 'fuming-and-furious', without siding with any valence or weighting of the two, an impossible feat achievable only speculatively, which is to say in the work of art. As Carroll writes, quoted in *The Logic of Sense*:

> 'If your thoughts incline ever so little towards "fuming", you will say "fuming-furious"; if they turn, even by a hair's breadth, towards "furious", you will say "furious-fuming"; but if you have the rarest of gifts, a perfectly balanced mind, you will say "frumious"'.[86]

Deleuze continues:

> Thus, the necessary disjunction is not between fuming and furious, for one may indeed be both at once; rather, it is between fuming-and-furious on the one hand and furious-and-fuming on the other.[87]

## The Speculative Univocity of Being and Language

In the word 'frumious', the site of the disjunction is in the relation between 'fuming-and-furious' and 'furious-and-fuming', as they logically exclude one another – 'furious' and 'fuming' in relation to one another are not disjunctive, nor even opposed. However, it is only as *predicates* that 'fuming-and-furious' and 'furious-and-fuming' mutually exclude one another: in other words, it is when they are conceived in relation to a predicable *subject*, which is *what* cannot (logically) be both more furious than fuming and more fuming than furious, i.e. the subject of the disjunction prohibiting it conceptually (as long as the subject is to remain convergent, identifiable and recognisable). When approached solely as pure events or logical attributes – and outside of good and common sense, a shared world and self – they are no longer logically incompatible. Moreover, through the disjunctive esoteric word 'frumious', they are no longer alogically incompatible either, since their difference is affirmed through this word or disjunctively synthesised.[88]

Deleuze continues, 'the function of the portmanteau [disjunctive] word always consists in the ramification of the series into which it is inserted', hence it 'never exists alone. It beckons to other portmanteau words', showing that any series is 'still further ramifiable'.[89] Deleuze's point is that in selecting both options, a word like frumious causes the series of propositions in which it is embedded to bifurcate (or ramify) at this very point (acting like a 'switch'),[90] since signification (conceptual implication) cannot accept the coexistence of disjunctive alternatives (fuming-and-furious/furious-and-fuming) within the *same* series of propositions.[91] This ramification or multiplication of simultaneously coexisting yet irreducible series pushes syntax or conceptual implication to its breaking point and prohibits the world's convergence of series (denotation), both of which are intensified when portmanteau words combine with others like them (which they 'beckon', by continuing each other's work of spiralling divergence), further ramifying the series in which they are found.[92] Portmanteau words therefore not only affirm divergence (divergent events or alogical incompatibilities) in themselves; more importantly they contribute to a divergent (and resonating) serial and textual fabric at the level of the text (or structure) in which they are located.[93]

While the ideal game is played only in thought and indeed only in the literary work of art, it is not only a game of sense and nonsense; it is also a practical mode of engagement with the world (the affirmation of chance) and directly ontological (the eternal return of being in thought). *Indeed it realises ontology as such*, for Deleuze. We saw in section 4.3 that for every sense expressed by the proposition there is a corresponding event attributed to the thing, and that without this minimal relation to bodies there is no way to conceive of sense as an event. The ideal game is no exception, except that the determination of the verb is resisted, the 'circle' of the proposition goes no further than its opening onto the infinitive mood while issuing from bodies which present the verb with phonic action. In this virtual space (Aion) free from propositional determination, events are free to affirm their irreducibility and divergence from one another. For each affirmed alogical incompatibility in sense ('frumious'), there is a corresponding affirmation of difference in univocal being, which is to say in the Event (Throw) – in Nietzschean terms there is a corresponding affirmation of a difference in force. If the event is the thought of the outside, this is an outside always relative to the sense insisting inside the proposition.[94]

As such, Deleuze considers language – at the level of the ideal game – to 'inherit' the 'communication of events among themselves'.[95] Beyond the forms of good and common sense, language expresses through esoteric words the play of irreducible, ontologically pluralistic and agonistic force differentials underlying being (what Nietzsche called perspectives), which communicate with each other solely *as events*.[96] It is only in the alogical incompatibilies of language that these forces can affirm their differences from one another (and thus their perspectives) within a becoming-indistinguishable of these still respected differences (now as displaced throughout univocal being), and as such univocity is assembled within language, expressed by language.[97] Univocity, for Deleuze, means both the universal communication of events in a single Event – a 'chaosmos', as marriage of nonsense and sense, chance and necessity, chaos and cosmos[98] – and the affirmation of incompatible senses in esoteric words, bypassing the very distinction sense/event by being a universal communication of events 'outside' language possible only within language.[99]

Deleuze's Nietzschean argument here is that affirmed force differentials, 'perspectives', are not equivocal viewpoints nonetheless converging on a shared world (for instance as coordinated by God in Leibniz[100]); rather, in the absence of such a centring point, they create an endless series of new worlds diverging from each other, all the while converging on that from which they diverge, namely the aleatory point displaced throughout. In other words, Deleuze wishes to establish a new conception of univocity and not simply to remain at the level of an irreducible pluralism of worlds. Thus he attempts to

## The Speculative Univocity of Being and Language

show that universal communication between equivocal perspectives – in a chaosmos that is now divergent, ex-centric or decentred, displaced in relation to itself, as well as immanent and non-theological – is possible precisely at the level of their divergence from one another. If each throw of the dice stems from a bodily affection constituted by an irreducibly pluralistic force differential or perspective, then it is thought's role to allow these perspectives to communicate *as* divergent. The dice throw explains how this can take place at the level of causality (chance-necessity), but what we see Deleuze adding to this with his theory of esoteric words and sense-events is that affirmed incompatibility at the level of thought or *sense* (e.g. 'frumious') is always accompanied, on the reverse side of the fold of the sense-event, by divergence at the level of the *event* or of being. The affirmed incompatibility of senses, within the ideal game or literary nonsense, is the mechanism accounting for how irreducible force differentials can universally communicate through their difference.

To do so, forces must 'rise up' to the surface[101] and become events corresponding to senses (as their reverse sides), such that in becoming the outside *of language*, they carve a shared space inside it. In this rising up we can discern a movement from corporeal pluralism to incorporeal monism, as seen in the distinction Deleuze draws between the becomings of the partial objects (as 'simulacra'), which imply their own kind of becoming and of communication, and the unlimited becoming of the surface where all events are located and which alone constitutes the universal communication of all events in one.[102] Hence, Nietzsche's pluralism of forces – inscribed on the body first as partial objects, then as erogenous images and finally as events[103] – is filtered through a linguistic and psychosexual model of adequacy (in the Spinozist sense), whereby affections are only capable of taking on being by being determined as events on the surface (i.e. by being castrated). Affections that cannot be linguistically determined on the surface as events fail to participate in the universal communication of events and thus are not selected by the eternal return.[104] As Deleuze writes:

> *Everything now rises back up (remonte) to the surface* [...] the unlimited returns. Becoming-mad, becoming unlimited is no longer a ground which rumbles. It rises (*monte*) to the surface of things and becomes impassive.[105]

Forces rise up to the surface in order to recur there eternally as the Event, and hence univocity is linguistically constructed over the course of the dynamic genesis, even if it is irreducible to language as such.

Now, returning to a quotation introduced earlier in this section – and turning to this section's title – Deleuze writes that the univocity of being, as dice throw in the ideal game, means 'a single insistence (*insistance*) for all that exists'.[106] Here we see the problematic of the one and the many folded into the problematic of the relation of thinking and being. A *single insistence*, namely sense (that which 'insists', as we saw in the previous chapter), for all that exists (namely events, which happen to things as 'extra-being'),[107] or, in a formulation I have used throughout this book taken from Deleuze's essay 'Klossowski or *bodies-language*', it is specifically a case of the *singleness* of language and the *plurality* of bodies,[108] which together express the *univocity* of sense. It is through the singleness of sense, or its syntactical openness, that both the many events bypass their pluralism to express a single univocal Event (frumious), *and* that the corporeal forces underlying these events merge with sense, or are at least grounded in it through selection. If Deleuze uses the dice throw to explain how univocity 'merges with the [...] disjunctive synthesis',[109] he therefore also tacitly uses it to explain how *thinking and being* (bodies and language) can, through another kind of disjunctive synthesis, sidestep their own equivocity or non-relation to construct a plane of immanence as monism-effect. Conversely, he shows how the relation of (the singleness of) *sense* and (the plurality of) *events*, or of thinking and being taken in their fully univocal dimension, can be used to disjunctively synthesise *a plurality of throws* (or events).

Hence for Deleuze 'univocity brings in contact the inner surface of language (insistence)', namely the sense said, 'and the outer surface of Being (extra-Being)',[110] namely the event occurring 'outside' language, as a Möbius strip twisting inner and outer into one another. The univocity of the sense-event folds the dualistic poles of the image of thought and the matter of being into itself, rendering being as 'extra-being' or as an *in-corporeal*, and not ideal, event expressed as the reverse side of sense. I introduced the notion at the start of this chapter that the first sense of univocity is the univocity of being and thinking (immanence), which we clearly see in the quotation above as well as when Deleuze writes 'univocal being is the [...] form of exteriority which relates things and propositions'.[111] Even if Deleuze does not explicitly emphasise the theme of immanence in *The Logic of Sense*, we can see that his conception of univocity is partly designed to engage this very notion, and it can be argued that

## The Speculative Univocity of Being and Language

the manner in which he conceives of univocity in *The Logic of Sense*, which he illustrates with frequent allusion to the reversibility of the two sides of the Möbius strip, makes a convincing case for its being a prototype of the plane of immanence's paradoxical reversibility of absolutely equal – which is to say parallel or a non-relation of – powers.

Furthermore, as I have shown, Deleuze accounts for immanence within an overarching conception of univocity which moves diagonally or zigzags *between* two disjunctive syntheses or non-equations: the one and the many (pluralism = monism, or difference = repetition), and thinking and being (being = thinking), both of which meet in the formula *bodies = language* as the univocity of two distinct conceptions of univocity (the one horizontal, the other vertical),[112] or as the synthesis of two disjunctive syntheses. Indeed, Deleuze will at the end of his career write this 'IMMANENCE = UNIVOCITY',[113] once he has properly disengaged the notion of immanence from that of univocity.[114] Nonetheless, I have shown that in *The Logic of Sense* both are already present even if they are terminologically subsumed under the notion of univocity, and that both conceptions of univocity – the one 'immanent', the other later termed 'univocal' (i.e. the dice throw) – ontologically and genetically require one another: without thought's selection of material affections the dice throw could not express an Event (immanence within univocity), and without the dice throw thought could not bypass its non-relation with materiality by expressing being as an incorporeal event (univocity within immanence).

If I showed in section 4.3 that insistence (sense) and existence (event or extra-being) constitute two sides of a single and even reversible fold (the sense-event), despite pointing to heterogeneous dimensions, it is thus precisely through a *single* insistence for all that exists, a single sense (the Event) for all events. Sense and the event are reversible only because the singleness of sense is a function of the disjunctive synthesis of events in relation to one another in the eternal return. The non-relation of thinking and being or bodies/language is sidestepped, and indeed made a reversible fold (sense-event), thanks to the ideal game which articulates sense with the events it disjunctively synthesises to constitute itself as single. In short:

1. The ideal game transmutes a provisional pluralism of equivocal throws or events into a univocal Event which, as univocal, is no longer the reverse side of the sense the ideal game expresses, but ontologically subsumes sense into it.

2. The plane of immanence (or sense-event) thereby constructed ontologically *bypasses* the equivocity of thinking/being and the equivocity of throws simultaneously, but does not *overcome* or sublate the equivocity of either as the event 'has an essential relation to language'[115] or to sense even if it is both *irreducible to* and *ontologically grounds* sense.
3. The Event is paradoxically the effect of what it ontologically (univocally) grounds (equivocity).

Lastly, we can now specify the relation of the verb to univocity. Deleuze writes that 'The Verb is the univocity of language, in the form of an undetermined infinitive [...] It connects the interiority of language to the exteriority of being'.[116] The verb opens onto a field of force relations (phonic action) which it folds into itself at the level of expression (the infinitive verb), and at this purely virtual level (in Aion), infinitive verbs as dice throws allow the verb to 'inheri[t] therefore the communication of events among themselves'.[117] In this way we can also understand what connects verbs to becoming, in that the infinitive mood shares becoming's temporality ('Aion') and ontology. Deleuze writes of Aion that it is 'the pure infinitive [...] the straight line', as opposed to the coiled up circle of the present indicative (denoting proposition), and that, as we have seen in the case of the dice throw, 'it permits no distinction of moments, but goes on being divided formally in the double and simultaneous direction of the past and the future'.[118]

## 5.3 Three Planes of Sense? Philosophy and Language

Deleuze's onto-logic of sense posits an essential relation between language and univocity, and thus between language and (the univocity of) being.[119] If the famous line from the 'Twenty-Fifth Series of Univocity' which reads 'Philosophy merges with ontology'[120] has been used in the secondary literature on a number of occasions to justify ontological readings of both Deleuze in general and *The Logic of Sense* in particular, this assumption is immediately, and amply, problematised by the rejoinder '*but* ontology merges with the univocity of being'.[121] This requires a 'but' because, for Deleuze, 'Univocity means that it is the same thing which occurs and is said: the attributable to all bodies or states of affairs and the expressible of every proposition',[122] in short 'being cannot be said without also occurring'.[123] If it cannot be said without also occurring, ontology

## The Speculative Univocity of Being and Language

ceases to be a discourse on what there is, since the very act of describing what there 'is' in fact produces it.[124]

Yet there is still more to it than that, since, at the risk of oversimplification, we can say that language is marked, ontologically, by its *failure* to describe what there is:[125] when language speaks of what there is, it speaks of what *happens to* things (events), and never of things themselves. When it tries to speak of things themselves it can only do so by denoting states of affairs (the matter of being) corresponding to *images* (the image of thought), and thus remains *within thinking*.[126] To reach being, which for Deleuze is univocal and thus not reducible to either materiality or thought when taken separately, the proposition's ontological dimension must *express* itself beyond – or rather as the impasse of – its logical dimension (not only of denotation, but also of signification and manifestation), namely through the ideal game. Nonetheless, the key point here, which tempers the unilateral critique of the logical proposition in the previous section, is that the production of being rests on the failure *of the logical proposition*, which does not simply fail to delimit being but which *conditions its very production* through its failure to denote, signify and manifest it. This is why (ontological) expression is the fourth, underlying, dimension of the *logical proposition*, even if it is not reducible to the logical proposition as such (since it is not reducible to any of its dimensions).

Language thus speaks of what *happens* to things, never of things themselves, and furthermore since it *speaks* of what happens to things, it must speak *inside language* of what happens to things *outside language* ('the event is not the same as the proposition',[127] it is irreducible to it). Ontology becomes the study of what language manages to say about its relative outside which, in this very process, converts itself into what there is absolutely (univocity, the plane of immanence). Instead of describing what there is, ontology must now *produce* what there is by *failing* to contain it within language – producing it as strictly *relative to each failure* of containment, not positing it as an independent outside which language simply fails to reach. On the one hand, this does not equate to a reduction of ontology to language, since what in language happens to things strictly exceeds (or 'perverts') the forms of the proposition, to the extent that what in language happens to things (the purview of univocal ontology) is *becoming*, the becoming of the sense-event in relation to any individuated state of affairs and corresponding proposition. Becoming is form's reverse side (the event is the outside *of language*).

On the other hand, this does not equate to a reduction of language to ontology which, for Deleuze, must complete itself in literary nonsense and humour.[128]

We could say that the univocity of being relegates ontology to the reverse side of the sense-event (the study of extra-being), while literature must occupy the obverse side (the production of sense), and indeed philosophy becomes literary analysis insofar as it must now study the extra-being produced by literature. Shortly after the lengthy passage on the fold of the sense-event discussed in section 4.3 – which forms the propositional basis of Deleuze's univocal ontology in *The Logic of Sense* – Deleuze notes that 'in Carroll's work, everything that takes place occurs in and by means of language'.[129] The becomings in *Alice's Adventures in Wonderland* with which the very first series of *The Logic of Sense* opens, such as Alice's becoming both larger and smaller simultaneously ('Alice does not grow without shrinking, and vice versa'),[130] are becomings *expressed by language*, by the literary work of nonsense and humour:[131] Carroll, for Deleuze, is not describing the extra-linguistic reality of Alice's becoming, but rather in the very act of describing this becoming – or indeed in failing to, or better still by pushing linguistic form to its breaking point – *produces it within language as its relative outside*: Alice becomes at the very limits *of language* and nowhere else – in short 'becoming is coextensive with language'.[132]

If in this book Deleuze privileges literary nonsense and humour and above all, it seems, the work of Carroll, it is furthermore because of the 'exemplary logical and linguistic formalism'[133] Deleuze finds in the latter, inextricably coupled with the 'profound psychoanalytic content'[134] of Carroll's work. This is a paradoxical formalism built on what pushes form to its limit such that, firstly, Carroll's literary innovation is strictly correlative to his logical formalism, and secondly, his literature in turn sheds light on the nature of language – both its formal structure (paradox) and its bodily genesis (both of which are coordinate). As Deleuze writes, 'We cannot get rid of paradoxes by saying that they are more worthy of Carroll's work than they are of the *Principia Mathematica*. What is good for Carroll is good for logic.'[135] He adds:

> The force of paradoxes is that they are not contradictory; they rather allow us to be present at the genesis of the contradiction. The principle of contradiction is applicable to the real and the possible, but not to the impossible from which it derives, that is, to paradoxes or rather to what paradoxes represent.[136]

## The Speculative Univocity of Being and Language

'What paradoxes represent' is immanence: the profound psychoanalytic 'content' Deleuze finds in Carroll corresponds immanently to Carroll's articulation of the paradoxical 'form' of language. In short, language is paradoxical because of its uneasy disjunctive relation to bodies at the point of its own genesis. As the limit of language, paradox indicates its opening onto bodies (the 'genesis of the contradiction').

Unsurprisingly, Deleuze directly equates paradox and becoming: 'They [the "paradoxes of sense"] always have the characteristic of going in both directions at once'[137] which, as we saw with the retroaction of the dice throw and with Alice's becoming smaller-larger, underlies becoming. This is because paradox and becoming are both immanent, occurring at the point at which language fails to reduce bodies to form – specifically as the point at which bodies transgress *language* (implying an equal articulation on *both* sides) – and indeed we have seen in the previous chapter that the paradoxical element in structure is founded on language's disjunction with the body. Along with literature and psychoanalysis, it is paradox (as the 'power of the unconscious') which allows Deleuze to develop a univocal ontology which is not dogmatic in the critical sense, yet which authorises him to speak of positive ontological entities at the limits of thought (while simultaneously claiming that being lies in a radical non-relation with thinking).[138] Rather than being epistemological limits, paradox (and nonsense) function here as the indices of beings, or rather becomings, swarming at the edges of the crack opening thought onto immanence.[139]

Now, if *What Is Philosophy?* largely *differentiates* between philosophy, logic and art – each one corresponding to an irreducible disciplinary plane (of 'immanence', 'reference' and 'composition', respectively) – and only one of which maintains a close relation with language (logic),[140] *The Logic of* Sense would thereby appear to propose an irreconcilable conception of transdisciplinarity, converging on sense and language.[141] According to this model, philosophy needs psychoanalysis, art and even logic to think immanence – which according to *What Is Philosophy?* is the disciplinary object proper to *philosophy* alone.[142] Nonetheless, to what extent can we still maintain that in *The Logic of Sense* there appear three irreducible *planes of sense* corresponding to these three disciplines?

In the previous chapter I mentioned two paradoxes of sense: both generating-generated and twisting between bodies-language. Above I have extensively discussed the ontological implications of the second of these, but the first has yet to be positioned within the framework of the current chapter. This is because this first paradox can entail two distinct trajectories: one towards the logical proposition and the other towards the ideal game. According to the second of these, the plane of immanence of sense appears as both generating (at the level of its double causality) and generated (at the level of the monism-effect), or as plane of univocity it appears as generating at the level of each throw and generated at the level of the Event – and in both cases (which are really one and the same) it is generated *as a self-causing* plane, namely as a 'transcendental field' or 'unconscious surface'.[143]

By contrast, in ordinary conditions, when language is unable to break free from the three dimensions of the proposition and their good and common sense, what is generated is sense as *sterile* (*Denatured nature*) – sense as reduced to the relations between a particular empirical proposition's dimensions and elements which *transcend* it such that it becomes, in relation to them, a plane of reference.[144] If sense is the plane of immanence and univocity of the proposition, therefore, once generated the proposition transcends the very plane from which it emerged (sense as generative matrix), and sense is reduced to the spent trace or faded reflection of this process. If, however, language realises its immanent power (the ideal game), it is caught in a becoming and thus never fixes as sterile (denoting image), even if it is still understandable as effect (running total, or Event, at whatever point in the open series one has reached). In other words, only with the logical proposition does engendered sense differ from the plane of immanence of sense (with the ideal game, engendered sense is part of this plane), since denotation in particular actualises, or in terms of *What Is Philosophy?* slows down, events in states of affairs (sense as plane of reference).[145]

This is why Deleuze defines the ideal game – as well as 'humour', or 'esoteric language', at its most comprehensive level – as 'the coextensiveness of sense with nonsense'.[146] The plane articulates nonsense elements (alogical incompatibilities, events spoken by infinitive verbs) to express pure sense (the Event), but this pure sense is a becoming-unlimited which cannot be fixed by any concept, object or subject, and whose perpetual becoming makes it indistinguishable, from the viewpoint of the logical proposition, from nonsense (hence 'coextensive'). We have a kind of generating-generated causality at play, at the level of the opposition nonsense/sense, but the generated sense is in fact a becoming coextensive with nonsense. By contrast, in the logical proposition, the plane of immanence of sense articulates events spoken by infinitive verbs, but as empirically redoubled by the elements of the propositional determination of these events, as the sense expressed by a proposition (grammatical determination of the verb). The elements it articulates are nonsense from the viewpoint of fully generated sense and empirical propositions (the transcendental field does not resemble the empirical one),[147] but their effect is sense (rather than a coextensiveness of sense with nonsense). In other words, the logical proposition dualises sense and nonsense vertically – as transcendent, conscious, sense, versus immanent, unconscious, nonsense (the generative matrix of the phantasm from which sense emerges through grammatical determination of a verb) – whereas the ideal game allows sense and nonsense to overlap each other horizontally.

Can we add a third plane? If sense as plane of immanence, breaks off into the (unconscious) plane of immanence of a (conscious) plane of reference, in the case of the logical proposition, with art we finally have a means of returning to the plane of immanence but only in and through the work of art. The ideal game is the literary-textual means by which the plane of immanence can be 'rediscovered' (though now as a kind of plane of composition); no longer as the unconscious, in the perverse artist the plane of immanence rises to a kind of consciousness,[148] but not as the consciousness of the empirical proposition (plane of reference).

To answer my question – are there three planes in *The Logic of Sense*? – it is actually necessary to answer in the negative, since the plane of immanence of sense (immanent causality of generating-generated) is only achievable as such, which is to say as a plane that is both cause and effect of itself, in the work of art. Without the ideal game's ability to disjunctively synthesise events via esoteric words and other means, the plane of immanence remains the ideal horizon of immanent uses of language, rather than realisable as such (and indeed, a fully immanent plane of immanence is only art's ideal, *yet to come*, not its achievable result). There is not a plane of immanence of the unconscious, a plane of reference of consciousness and a plane of composition of art; rather, it is necessary to conceive of the unconscious as only the generative matrix and the proposition and work of art as its two generated avenues. To put it another way, the plane of immanence realises itself (as immanent self-cause, as both generating *and generated*) only in art (where it is no longer unconscious) and indeed only fully in the work of art yet to come.

The plane of immanence fails to realise itself as both generating *and generated* in one and the same movement, in the logical proposition, because once generated (as monism-effect), this monism-effect is immediately doubled and made transcendent (and hence separated from its immanent half). The genesis of a logical proposition always entails both, at the unconscious transcendental level, a sense-event (fold of bodies-language) and, at the conscious empirical level, the event's actualisation in a state of affairs corresponding to a denotational image. There can be no denotational and empirical use of the proposition without the simultaneous subsistence of a corresponding transcendental sense-event. The very (empirical) distinction between word and thing, proposition and state of affairs, presupposes (at the transcendental level) the fold of the sense-event, which while siding with neither word nor thing both draws the dividing line between them and allows them to articulate:[149] denotation, after all, refers to something other than itself, presupposing the possibility of a relation, as well as a relation that is necessarily one of opposition. In sum, the sense-event seals the distinction or border ('surface') between word and thing, but does not yet attain the frame (denotation) through which to consider this distinction as a dualism.

However, this fold is not a pre-existing structure generated once which then gives way to the empirical proposition but, as a fold no more substantial than the sense-*events* composing it and giving it its inner consistency, is an ongoing process contingent upon particular propositions, such that it must be produced and re-produced each time as the transcendental half of an empirical proposition. In short, in relation to the empirical or logical proposition, the plane of immanence of sense must fork its generated pole into two halves, an empirical double which attempts to subsume, constrain and ultimately do away with the immanence of its transcendental half. A sense-event mediates the relation between a denotational image and a state of affairs, as the transcendental basis of the distinction between an image and the thing it re-presents. The image thereby fixes the event at its own level, curtailing or enclosing within thought the event's inherent perversity or becoming-unlimited which remains at the surface, in the same way that in *What Is Philosophy?* the 'image' of thought slows down the infinite speed of the event of being-thinking, and uses it to oppose itself to the 'matter' of being. The point is that the image is the curtailing of the event at the level of thought, without which it cannot take on the empirical function of reference, but that the sense-event nonetheless continues to subsist at its own level and can be more fully realised in art.

Hence, we can speak of the plane of immanence coiled inside the plane of reference, on the one hand, just as we saw in the last chapter that the problem is coiled inside the proposition (and the question nested within the problem), and on the other we can speak of the plane of immanence freed from reference and completed as immanent, but *only in the ideal game of art*. The plane of immanence, in itself and for itself, thus does not seem to exist in *The Logic of Sense*, we only have the plane of immanence in relation to the plane of reference or in relation to the ideal game as a kind of plane of composition.

## 5.4 Conclusion: Symptoms and the Work of Art Yet to Come – On Alice's Adventures

While I have shown that *The Logic of Sense* both entails a serious engagement with the psychoanalytic clinic and uses this framework partly as the basis for the ontology the book develops, the *literary* (or 'critical') condition of the phantasm's completion ultimately amounts to an anti-Oedipal stance predicating 'health' on the dispersal of Oedipus and sexuality.[150] For Deleuze, the death drive is the condition of the psychoanalytic cure as reconfiguration and dispersal of the body's symptoms. This is precisely insofar as the phantasm's completion in the work of art leaves the body and sexuality behind altogether; it is a *phantom* de-personalising affect as impersonal Event. The crux of the matter is, of course, that this is an unreachable horizon of health insofar as the phantasm's completion depends on the work of art *yet to come* (*à venir*) – the speculative univocity of being and language is a mirage oriented towards the future (*l'avenir*). This is, however, its point insofar as, as *becoming* (*devenir*), it could never be, or as the univocity *of* the equivocity of being and language it cannot overcome this *difference*. As such, the situation gives rise to what Deleuze terms a pendulum swing in the phantasm,[151] an eternal return of beginning and end which never ultimately does away with Oedipus and sexuality as its founding equivocity (the difference eating/speaking)[152] conditions univocity, even if this univocity functions paradoxically to ground Oedipus in an anti-Oedipal 'beyond'.[153]

In the 'Thirty-Third Series of Alice's Adventures', Deleuze opposes the 'neurotic's novel' to the 'artist's novel as a work of art'.[154] Deleuze writes: 'The neurotic can only actualise the terms and the story of his novel: the symptoms are this actualisation, and the novel has no other meaning (*sens*)'.[155] The neurotic is only capable of relating to his symptoms by means of the tertiary ordinance of language, and thus denotatively. Symptoms' physical causes act on the work which reacts by actualising them in denotations. Here the literary critic *can* function diagnostically as a 'doctor' in relation to the neurotic as 'patient' ('It is not by chance that the neurotic creates a "familial romance"').[156] By contrast, what distinguishes the 'work of art' from the neurotic novel is that it attempts to 'go from the cause of the symptoms to the quasi-cause of the *oeuvre*',[157] in short from the actualisation of bodily affect in states of affairs to its counter-actualisation by the aleatory point in the ideal game.[158] As such, 'authors, if they are great, are more like doctors than patients',[159] since by counter-actualising their symptoms they can work towards de-personalising the affect.

Alice is so central to Carroll's writings because she appears both as symptomatic question ('what is a little girl?')[160] or as 'little girl-phallus',[161] and as the aleatory point assembling the work's univocity.[162] Dodgson *becomes* – and never ceases becoming – Carroll through Alice.[163] As Deleuze writes, 'An entire *oeuvre* is needed, not in order to answer this question ['what is a little girl?'] but in order to evoke and to compose the unique event which makes it into a question'.[164] The question (and the phantasm as such) is retroactively given its ultimate function by the work of art yet to come in relation to which alone the question serves as univocity's quasi-cause, a quasi-cause univocity eternally attempts to subsume into itself. This partly accounts for the basis and method of Carroll's *humour*: his inability to fully let go of the sexual surface – and through this his ability to construct its univocity.

For instance, we can find this assembling of univocity in the Cheshire Cat's transformation or reversal from ideality (image of thought, Voice) in *Alice's Adventures in Wonderland* to denotable state of affairs (Alice's pet cat Dinah as matter of being) in *Through the Looking-Glass* by means of a series of intermediaries in *Through the Looking-Glass*: the Jabberwock, the crow, the Red King and White Queen, the Sheep, Humpty Dumpty, the White Knight, and the Red Queen (as the Event of their univocity). These intermediaries do not resemble one another, and relate to different dimensional levels of the surface (physical surface, metaphysical surface, height's transcendence of the surface, depth's transcendence of the surface, etc.). What allows them to express a single becoming is precisely Alice (as aleatory point), who links them in the narrative as she moves through the book's chapters (series).

What is particularly interesting about this narrative, in the context of this section, is that it simultaneously narrates the (psychoanalytic) genesis of sense from bodies and the (ontological) expression of univocity from difference, which I have suggested are inseparable components of the pendulum swing of the phantasm (or the equivocations of humour). The narrative never entirely breaks free from psychoanalytic coordinates – and indeed provides remarkable parallels with some of the features of the dynamic genesis – while not being reducible to them either. It provides a not quite familiar Oedipal landscape, a psychosexual genesis but from the perspective of its forces, events and impersonal singularities.

Looking at the two texts more closely, Deleuze's central claim is that in *Alice's Adventures in Wonderland* Alice gradually rises up to the surface after first falling through the rabbit hole into the shafts and tunnels of the depths, with *Through the Looking-Glass* extending this further into an exploration of how she builds the surface itself once positioned there. Deleuze understands this ascent in *Alice's Adventures in Wonderland* in terms of a manic-depressive polarity of ideal heights and corporeal depths. The key chapter in this regard is Chapter VI ('Pig and Pepper'), which shows how if Carroll consigns animals to the depths, to the shafts and tunnels in which Alice first finds herself after falling through the rabbit hole, then it is the Cheshire Cat which orients her climb back up to the surface, by introducing the distinction between depth, height and surface.

Alice chooses the heights thanks to the Cheshire Cat, which appears to be Deleuze's primary model for the superegoic 'Voice'. It is a specifically *ideal* good object, contra Klein's positing of the good object as initially belonging to the same plane as the bad partial objects.[165] As Deleuze points out, the Cheshire Cat is clearly ideal, hovering as an image, as well as manifesting the characteristics of Klein's good object – namely disjunctions of unharmed/wounded and absent/present, sometimes being present as a head or disembodied smile (indeed a 'Voice'), sometimes as a whole object.[166] Nonetheless, despite being ideal, the Cat is also an animal and thus originates from the depths, just as we saw in Chapter 2 that the Voice is a surface projection of the depths.

If we turn now to *Through the Looking-Glass*, Deleuze's central interpretative claim can be understood as follows: rather than falling through the rabbit hole into the depths and then climbing back up to the surface, Alice's second adventure takes place between the physical and metaphysical surfaces. After entering the looking glass (metaphysical surface, incorporeal double) she first encounters the physical surface as a chessboard – her erogenous zones-squares as coordinated by the phallus-Queen – and then as a grid of contiguous fields which she must cross to 'become a Queen', which is to say to first re-constitute her erogenous body through coordination of squares-fields, and then return to the metaphysical surface (become castrated).[167] The chessboard is also a 'logical diagram'[168] of this process (Alice's 'becoming Queen' as she moves from D2 to D8), a surface *plan/e*.[169] The poem 'Jabberwocky', which Alice finds near the board, is also a meta-reflection on this process. The poem is apparently non-sensical and it is Alice's task to produce sense from it, which she does only later in the story. The poem is written back-to-front and must be read in a mirror, but even then it cannot be understood, being written in esoteric words which Alice will need help deciphering.

Furthermore, Alice explores the surface primarily through logico-linguistic means, rather than reaching the surface by passing through corporeal becomings and encounters with an ideal image, as we find in Alice's first adventure. As Deleuze points out, the question of coordinating the body's zones now has a corresponding problem different from Alice's ascent to the surface from the depths as oriented by the 'unique and withdrawn voice' of the Cheshire Cat.[170] If in *Alice's Adventures in Wonderland* the Cheshire Cat leads Alice to the surface and to the phallus of castration (Queen of Hearts), in *Through the Looking-Glass* it is the Red Queen (echoing the Queen of Hearts) who accompanies Alice through much of her adventure, initially showing her the path she must follow to herself become a Queen, and reappearing at the end of the book when Alice herself becomes one. Similarly, we saw in Chapter 3 how the phallic investment of the genital zone is the precondition for the infant's construction of an erogenous body: the phallus precedes the body's coordination even if this coordination produces the phallus as such (as the phallus of coordination morphs into the phallus of castration as castration-effect).

For Deleuze, in *Through the Looking-Glass* it is no longer a question of a 'unique' Voice speaking to the manic-depressive infant, but rather an Oedipal child who can now speak and who is engaging with multiple parental voices. Now the problem has become one of 'multiple discourses'[171] – a confrontation not between height and depth but between different kinds of series: connective, conjunctive, disjunctive.[172] Moreover, this process is bound up with the construction of a new proper name.

After entering the fields in Chapter II, Alice forgets her proper name in Chapter III, remembering only 'L' – a point Deleuze gives a programmatic status in *The Logic of Sense* by including this point at the end of the book's first series.[173] While Deleuze considers this as an example of a connective series, 'the proper name so contracted

## The Speculative Univocity of Being and Language

that it is no longer remembered',[174] this definition is better reserved for 'y'reince' as found in another text, and it could be seen rather as a case of the nonsensical *letter*.

In Chapters (squares/fields, or indeed series) IV and VI, Deleuze claims that we encounter a conjunctive followed by a disjunctive series. Having lost her proper name, or rather returned to the nonsensical letter, Alice must reconstitute it. Here we find two key arguments underlying Deleuze's account of the dynamic genesis: firstly, the failure of the Voice (as Name-of-the-Father) to actively name the infant (Alice forgets her name); secondly, the coextensiveness of the construction of a new proper name with the coordination of erogenous zones. Having lost her name in Chapter III, in Chapter IV Alice encounters the proper names 'Tweedledum' and 'Tweedledee' – as Deleuze puts it, 'so similar they are almost indistinguishable',[175] with Alice joining hands with them both soon after the beginning of the chapter. As we read in the song Alice recites, although initially opposed, Tweedledum and Tweedledee forget their differences when faced with a 'monstrous crow' which flies down. Here the heights – reminiscent of the Cat's fearsome claws – lead the partial zones to 'forget their quarrel' and enter into a convergence of series (coordination of zones).[176]

In Chapter IV we find the Red King asleep, and in Chapter V, Alice meets the White Queen, which Deleuze understands as the father and mother image.[177] The father image – far from the castrating Queen of Hearts in *Alice's Adventures in Wonderland* – is ineffectual and silent, the mother wounded and plaintive. Indeed, she morphs into a sheep later on – animals being associated by Carroll with the depths, as we see in the first chapters of *Alice's Adventures in Wonderland*, and thus she is associated with the wounded body. Later in Chapter V, she will give way to the Sheep's shop where the egg Alice has bought recedes whenever she approaches it. The shop is made up of shelves – or places without occupants[178] – which are always empty when one approaches them even if they at first look full.

The egg Alice wishes to buy – the occupant without a place – is then encountered in the following chapter, when Alice finds Humpty Dumpty sat on a wall. Humpty Dumpty is the *identity* of the place without an occupant (shelf, wall) and the occupant without a place (egg), and Deleuze considers Humpty Dumpty to function as a disjunctive series or semanteme. If the poem 'Jabberwocky' – and the fearsome Jabberwock along with it – incarnates castration and *disjunction*, Humpty Dumpty embodies the internal *resonance* of disjunctive series.[179]

Whereas the Cheshire Cat is comprised of disjunctive alternatives (presence/absence, wounded/unharmed) and only anticipates castration, the Jabberwock occupies the wound of castration; the Jabberwock is the castrative transformation of the Cheshire Cat, hovering less high (less idealised) but still with the Cat's many teeth and long claws. As we saw in section 3.1, the disjunctive esoteric word Jabberwock is a *portmanteau word*, opening up a space between denotation and expression – bodies and language, physical and metaphysical surfaces, the very locus of castration.

It is no coincidence therefore that in Chapter VI, Alice asks Humpty Dumpty to explain the poem 'Jabberwocky' to her, unpacking the portmanteau words (like 'lithe' and 'slimy' for 'slithy') and recombining them within denotative statements. Indeed, it is in this chapter that Carroll coins the term 'portmanteau word'. Humpty Dumpty translates 'Jabberwocky' as set of esoteric words into a semantic scene – if not empirically denoted state of affairs – portrayed by Carroll's illustrator. Thus we move from disjunctive esoteric word (Jabberwock) to semanteme (Humpty Dumpty), and from (esoteric) word to image or thing. By resonating the occupant without a place (egg) and place without an occupant (shelf, wall), Humpty Dumpty allows disjunctive series – like the expression *jabber* (speaking volubly) and the edible body *wocer* (a fruit) – to express sense from nonsense (the erogenous *letter* of the poem written backwards, understandable only in the mirror or metaphysical surface). Humpty Dumpty is like the mirror in which 'Jabberwocky' needs to be reflected in order to express its sense – Humpty Dumpty is a *redoubling*, pasting over the crack of thought represented by the Jabberwock. At the same time that the poem's sense is expressed, the Jabberwock (the denotable monster) morphs into Humpty Dumpty himself. If the Jabberwock descends upon the poem's protagonist, threatening to wound (castrate) him, it is ultimately the protagonist who (self-)castrates the Jabberwock by removing his head – and this occurs simultaneously with Humpty Dumpty's decipherment of the poem (production of semantemes).

Indeed, this poem foretells what Alice herself will do in relation to the Red Queen at the end of *Through the Looking-Glass* as a reversal of the castrating Queen of Hearts in *Alice's Adventures in Wonderland*: 'Jabberwocky' is about the monster's castration by the child, it is about a 'great murder'[180] (murder of the father and castration of the mother), which Alice herself will carry out at the end of the tale when she self-castrates. Along with the chessboard and then

## The Speculative Univocity of Being and Language

the square fields, 'Jabberwocky' functions as a meta-reflection on the story as a whole: traversal of the surface and self-castration.

What results is Humpty Dumpty now sitting on a wall above Alice, and no longer hovering in the air like the Jabberwock. Humpty Dumpty brings together the physical and metaphysical surfaces rather than merely threatening the physical surface as does the Jabberwock. Humpty Dumpty is a cohesive egg – he is not distributed across two different bodies-zones, as are Tweedledum/Tweedledee – but he risks falling and his unity risks disintegrating at any moment (fragmentation of the physical surface). While no longer fearing castration from above (the crow, the Jabberwock), having passed through castration, Humpty Dumpty is nonetheless only delicately poised on the surface of the wall, like the White Knight in Chapter VIII who keeps falling off his horse, despite preparing for every eventuality, be it attacks from the depths (sharks) or from the surface of the horse (mice). As with language, the White Knight exists in a world of *possibility* as distinct from the necessity of corporeal causes, but cannot account for the possibility of the fall itself (genesis of language and its roots in bodies, and its subsequent return to them).

Finally, Alice becomes a Queen by Chapter IX, where the dinner table (metaphysical surface) replaces the chessboard (physical surface), and the univocity and reversible immanence of the dinner cloth replaces the segmented board.[181] Alice blames the Red Queen for the commotion, pulling away the dinner cloth or surface and shaking (or 'taking', as in chess) the Red Queen till she becomes a kitten as denotable state of affairs once Alice has returned to the heights (the passage from 'shaking' to 'waking'). Like the masochist who has expelled the father and draws on maternal symbolism to self-castrate, as we find in Deleuze's reading of masochism, Deleuze notes that in Carroll the ontogenetic process is 'finished off voluntarily by Alice herself'.[182]

As was suggested in section 3.1, *The Logic of Sense* consists in both a philosophical reading of structuralism, particularly the work of the Lacanian school, and an investigation of the conditions in which structure is adequate to the body's affects, i.e. capable of constructively undergirding expressionism. We have seen in the last three chapters how affects, for Deleuze, are events produced by the proposition's – or more specifically structure's – reaction onto, or expression of, its corporeal cause; the chaos of bodily mixtures, interacting forces, is expressed as the event of language through the progressive construction of the phantasm (structure as such) during the dynamic genesis. This is also why affects are becomings. Structure is adequate to the body's affects as long as it can express – rather than represent and cancel – their becoming, which it does by expressing the becoming of bodies *as something other than bodies* yet still as immanent to them (this is the double causality at stake).[183] Hence, forces rise to the surface in order to eternally recur there as the in-corporeal (and not ideal) Event of univocity and of immanence. Structure is adequate to – which is to say expressive of – becoming as specifically the *becoming-incorporeal* (and becoming-univocal or becoming-immanent) of the body's affects, only on condition that such an expression take place in the ideal game and work of art yet to come. Carroll thus provides Deleuze with the means to 'critique' the psychoanalytic clinic of the 1960s: if read in terms of Deleuze's ontology of univocity and becoming, structure is only adequate to the body if mobilised in literature.

## Notes

1. See as an example of this Hughes, *Deleuze and the Genesis of Representation*, Chapter 2.
2. Deleuze describes Duns Scotus' *Opus Oxoniense* as 'the greatest book of pure ontology', in which 'univocal being is understood as neutral [...] indifferent to the distinction between the finite and the infinite, the singular and the universal, the created and the uncreated' (*Difference and Repetition*, pp. 48–9). Scotus nonetheless only '*thought*' a pre-established univocal ontology (p. 49) in his work of 'pure' ontology; completing Scotus' project, Deleuze considers that in Spinoza, univocity 'becomes a truly expressive and affirmative proposition' (i.e. both speculatively and practically constructed) and that in Nietzsche it is 'effectively realised' (in the eternal return) through a 'practical selection' (see ibid., pp. 49–51). *The Logic of Sense* arguably attempts to realise this non-linear history of the concept of univocity; in this chapter we will see how the dice throw, as articulated in an expressive proposition, gives rise to sense as 'indifferent' to the distinction singular/universal (as well as created/uncreated or profane/Divine). On univocity in Deleuze during the late 1960s, see Smith, 'The Doctrine of Univocity'; for a broader take on the notion of univocity as it functions in Deleuze's *oeuvre*, see Montebello, *Deleuze*, pp. 61–96.
3. Deleuze, *Logic of Sense*, p. 205.
4. See ibid., p. 283, which states that the 'deployment of series' in the 'preliminary, *founding*, or poetic [secondary] organisation [...] precede the elaborate products of the *static* genesis' (first emphasis

## The Speculative Univocity of Being and Language

mine), namely denoted object, signified concept, manifested subject. Unlike the dynamic genesis (the genesis of the verb and its univocity), the static genesis does not found what causes it. Univocity founds everything in the dynamic genesis leading up to it; the static genesis, while also being the result of the dynamic genesis, does not found what caused it, being founded on '"object representation"' rather than '"verbal representation"' (p. 283), namely concepts, objects and subjects of the tertiary ordinance of language.

5. Ibid., p. 286. This is arguably because of the relation between immanence and philosophy. Deleuze does not wish to explicitly tackle the theme of immanence because he is not yet ready to tackle the question 'what is philosophy?', even though we find this question, in this form, on p. 153 of *The Logic of Sense*, in the 'Nineteenth Series of Humour'. Indeed, one can say that humour, being that which 'constructs all univocity' (ibid., p. 285), plays the role philosophy (as 'constructivism') does in *What Is Philosophy?* As Deleuze writes, 'to the person who asks "what is philosophy?", Diogenes responds by carrying about a cod at the end of a string. The fish is indeed the most oral of animals; it poses the problem of muteness, of consumability, and of the consonant in the wet/palatalised element – in short, the problem of language' (pp. 153–4) – namely the duality of eating/speaking together with the verb's muteness as their univocity (Deleuze writes on p. 278 that the verb is 'silent' insofar as it is oriented towards a becoming-incorporeal (and silent) of Eros' 'sonorous' affects). Moreover, this is a reason why Deleuze privileges not only Carroll but also the Stoics (and Cynics), in *The Logic of Sense* (p. ix), namely their practice of philosophy which emphasises the paradox and nonsense of the surface, the reversibility of thinking and eating ('If you pose abstract and difficult questions, [Diogenes] will respond by designating some bit of food' (p. 147)).

6. This is to be understood in terms closely parallel to the ones developed in section 3.1: univocity is not a dogmatic substance, a mind-independent substrate grounding being and thinking, but rather the (retroactively grounding) effect of their non-relation.

7. Humour in Deleuze is closely allied with his conception of perversion. We see this most clearly in his 1965 essay 'Klossowski or bodies-language' from Appendix 2 of *The Logic of Sense*: 'There is no obscene in itself, says Klossowski; that is, the obscene is not the intrusion of bodies into language, but rather their mutual reflection and the act of language which fabricates a body for the mind' (p. 322).

8. We saw in the previous chapter that for Deleuze the secondary organisation comes to fruition in the verb; see also *Logic of Sense*, p. 283: 'Secondary organisation (the verb or verbal representation) it itself the result of this long itinerary [the dynamic genesis].'

9. In this quotation we see that Deleuze's use of the term 'begins' is

technical. As we saw in section 4.1, Deleuze speaks of the phantasm's ('intrinsic') 'beginning' as the dualism of series it implicates (pre-genital and Oedipal, the physical and metaphysical surface respectively, in short bodies and language). Deleuze privileges the phantasm (as well as Laplanche and Pontalis' reading of it) because of the way it internalises equivocity in this way.

10. Ibid., p. 285, emphasis mine.
11. The question *What is a little girl?* can be understood more generally in terms of the phantasm's founding questions, as discussed in section 4.1, such as the origin of sexuality, of sexual difference, and so on, which all centre on the relation of bodies to language, of the physical to the metaphysical surface, as shown in section 3.5.
12. In a footnote, Deleuze explains that the Voice's equivocity in relation to the body or 'sexuality' is precisely what 'totalises' the body (determining it as 'esoteric set', as shown in section 3.4) and imposes a 'limit' on it (the metaphysical surface generated from the body's esoteric word), which Deleuze states 'render[s] the univocal possible' (ibid., p. 288, n. 5). In short, it is precisely the Voice's equivocal relation with the body (physical surface) during the Oedipal stage that later makes univocity possible at the level of the structure of the verb, with which the dynamic genesis concludes. Furthermore, in establishing the body's 'limit', the Voice provides the basis for humour, namely the body's *transgression of this limit* (cf. its becoming), which we also see when bodies continue *insisting in language at the level of nonsense* (or of the paradoxical element). The Voice's equivocity is thus prohibitive and also productive of univocity through its failure to fully distance itself from or contain bodies.
13. It is not coincidental that immediately after discussing the 'speculative univocity of Being and language' Deleuze writes in a footnote 'We cannot here follow Lacan's thesis, *at least insofar as we understand it as related by Laplanche and Leclaire in "L'Inconscient"*' (ibid., p. 287, n. 5, emphasis mine), criticising their *equivocal* conception of sense (as built on a double inscription yet without onto-logically bypassing it). However, what Deleuze misses is that in his 'Position of the Unconscious', Lacan had already developed a similar critique of Laplanche and (the early) Leclaire, claiming that they posit the unconscious and pre/conscious as a structure, whereas for Lacan it is the object (a)'s re-splitting of the subject (as we saw in section 3.5) that *retroactively* structures structure (see especially p. 708) – as such the object (a) is *the event of structure*. As Éric Laurent has pointed out in 'Parler lalangue du corps', in Lacan's 1970 preface to Anika Lemaire's *Jacques Lacan* (the same year as 'Radiophonie'), he hints at Deleuze's misreading of him in that footnote, writing 'Where is this object "a", the major incorporeal of the Stoics, to be situated. In the unconscious

or elsewhere?' (p. 10). Nonetheless, even if, for instance, in Seminar XIV, Lacan clearly shows that the object (a) problematises the neat distinction between thinking and being, and in Seminar XX develops the notion of a '*substance jouissante*' (p. 23) that cannot be reduced to either body or mind taken separately, this does not necessarily cancel Lacan's Cartesian inheritance even if it disrupts it. Deleuze's theory of the event (as hyper-perverse object (a)) thus arguably belongs to a unique attempt at articulating a *fully univocal* conception of structure. To conclude this part of the book, Deleuze's critique of psychoanalysis' insufficient engagement with the problems posed by psycho-physical dualism is arguably (and unknowingly) more targeted at Leclaire than Lacan; Leclaire examines the articulation of the real body (of the drive and object (a)) and the symbolic, but not according to a psycho-physical dualism, whereas it is only the *early* Lacan who does not sufficiently question the articulation of bodies-language. Lacan moved from an imaginary conception of the body (on which the symbolic Name can phallically write itself but only insofar as this body is an *image*) to a progressively more real one from around the same time that he first introduced his theory of Names (the early–mid 1960s), problematising the symbolic's ability to overwrite the body in its full materiality and singularity. Nonetheless, what the late Lacan still lacks, from Deleuze's vantage point, is a fully univocal articulation of bodies-language.

14. Deleuze, *Logic of Sense*, p. 285, translation modified. The notion of 'totality' here is to be understood in terms of the limit equivocity places on the body in relation to language, conditioning the emergence of univocity or the totality of what there (univocally) is.
15. Ibid., p. 285, emphasis in the original.
16. Ibid., p. 285.
17. Ibid., p. 280.
18. In his uneasy stance regarding the status of univocity – a difference that never ceases *becoming* univocally sutured (although isn't actually) – Deleuze arguably remains, from a psychoanalytic perspective, philosophical. Freud, and Lacan after him, characterised philosophers as being preoccupied with patching up the universe (suturing sexual difference). Yet, in the 'Twenty-Second Series – Porcelain and Volcano', which speaks, negatively, of the 'ridiculousness' of the 'abstract thinker' (ibid., pp. 178–9), and not, positively, of their speculative humour, Deleuze seems to acknowledge this. The series begins with the line from Fitzgerald 'Of course all life is a process of breaking down' (quoted in ibid., p. 176), including, above all, the sexual couple (p. 176); what 'breaks down' is precisely univocity, the equivocal 'crack' of thought widening not narrowing. This series, in fact, calls into question, or at least counterbalances, the ('philosophical') thesis of the majority of

19. Ibid., p. 285, emphasis mine. I would argue that the usage of the term 'constructs' in this quotation is also technical in the sense discussed in section 3.1. The French is *'construit'*, whereas Deleuze will use *'bâtit'* (builds) elsewhere to refer to construction or building more generally, outside its technical sense (see p. 282 of the French edition).
20. I discuss this further in sections 5.3–5.4.
21. Ibid., p. 71. We should not understand this in the least to mean a merely ideal existence. Indeed, immediately after this quotation, Deleuze adds, it is also by means of the ideal game, nonetheless, that 'thought and art are real and disturbing reality, morality, and the economy of the world' (ibid., p. 71), which I will touch on below regarding the ethics of the dice throw.
22. This is Parmenides' exclusive disjunctive alternative. As Badiou puts it: 'What *presents* itself is essentially multiple; *what* presents itself is essentially one. The reciprocity of the one and being is certainly the inaugural axiom of philosophy [...] "What is not *a* being is not a *being*" [...] yet it is also its impasse [...] [I]f being is one, then one must posit that what is not one, the multiple, *is not*' (*Being and Event*, p. 23). In actually *rejecting* this 'inaugural axiom' as false alternative, Deleuze arguably sidesteps the full brunt of Badiou's critique of the One. To Badiou's pluralist ontology of non-being (the void), we must oppose Deleuze's univocal ontology of the void of equivocity filled by its own monism-*effects* of divergence and non-relationality.
23. Deleuze and Guattari, *A Thousand Plateaus*, p. 23.
24. Deleuze, *Logic of Sense*, p. 244.
25. Ibid., p. 253.
26. Nietzsche first mentions the eternal return in aphorism 341 of *The Gay Science*, writing: 'This life as you now live it and have lived it you will have to live once again and innumerable times again' (p. 194), adding that it is an 'ultimate eternal confirmation and seal' (p. 195). In *Thus Spake Zarathustra* (e.g. pp. 179, 244–7) he discusses it together with the dice throw, distinguishing between the 'table of the gods' and the earth: the die is thrown on the former and lands on the latter (pp. 244–5). It is thrown by man who affirms chance in throwing it, even if it affirms a result (the number it lands on) determined by the gods (*necessity* of chance). He further develops the eternal return in the texts collected as *The Will to Power* (pp. 544–50).
27. Deleuze, *Logic of Sense*, p. 205, translation modified.
28. See *Nietzsche and Philosophy*, pp. 1–6, and all of Chapter 2.
29. Affections do not return in the tertiary ordinance where the affection feeding a verb is fully determined and its event actualised in a state of affairs, closed off from the play of difference and repetition, unending

## *The Speculative Univocity of Being and Language*

becoming, to which verbs open up as long as we remain at the level of the secondary organisation (the phantasm), accessible only to the artist (and analyst).

30. In *The Will to Power*, Nietzsche writes 'Not every action *can* be returned' (p. 489) and 'Everything becomes and recurs eternally [...] The idea of recurrence as a *selective* principle, in the service of strength' (p. 545, emphasis in the original), which Deleuze understands as the selection of only forces that affirm their quantitative difference from one another.

31. For instance, Deleuze writes 'Humour is inseparable from a selective force: in that which occurs (an accident) [state of affairs], it selects the pure event' (*Logic of Sense*, p. 171), and 'The eternal return has a sense of selection' (ibid., p. 204).

32. Deleuze, *Nietzsche and Philosophy*, p. 66.

33. Deleuze is keenly aware that this extends beyond what Nietzsche himself had intended at the level of the specific ontological coordinates of this framework: 'Nietzsche was able to rediscover depth only after conquering the surfaces. But he did not remain at the surface, for the surface struck him as that which had to be assessed from the renewed perspective of an eye peering out from the depths' (*Logic of Sense*, p. 147). By conceiving of sense as the implication of a force differential, he arrives at a new conception of sense and force, but grounds this new surface in the depths. Interestingly, this self-distancing from Nietzsche occurs around the time of his dalliance with structuralism. In his short 1965 monograph 'Nietzsche', Deleuze writes (in a quasi-Heideggerian manner): 'The philosopher of the future is the explorer of ancient worlds, of peaks and caves, who creates only inasmuch as he recalls something that has been essentially forgotten. [...] the unity of life and thought. It is a complex unity: one step for life, one step for thought. Modes of life inspire ways of thinking; modes of thinking create ways of living. Life *activates* thought, and thought in turn *affirms* life. Of this pre-Socratic unity we no longer have even the slightest idea' (p. 66, emphasis in the original). While Deleuze discusses 'peaks' of thought and 'caves' of life, there is no reference here to the immanent surface, although otherwise it is a plane of immanence (as I have analysed it) that Deleuze is sketching here. By the time we reach the later structuralism-influenced *The Logic of Sense*, any schema which views sense (as complex unity of thought and life or being) as 'fundamentally forgotten and veiled' is in error (*Logic of Sense*, p. 83). Rather, what Deleuze considers to be the 'importance of structuralism in philosophy' is 'the news that sense is never a principle or an origin, but that it is produced' as 'a surface effect' (p. 83), whereby 'the origin is a sort of nonsense' (p. 85, n. 4) and 'sense is produced always as a function of nonsense' (p. 84). This is why in this book, although

## THE PSYCHOANALYSIS OF SENSE

Nietzsche's thought is still heavily relied on, 'The staff-blow philosophy of the Cynics and the Stoics' – the staff designating bits of food when asked abstract or difficult questions (see above) – 'replaces the hammer-blow philosophy' (p. 150).

34. See Deleuze, *Nietzsche and Philosophy*, pp. 39–41, 46–7.
35. Ibid., p. 30.
36. On Deleuze's reading of the dice throw, see Chapter 1 of *Nietzsche and Philosophy*, sections 11–16 (especially pp. 24–7). On the relation between the body, chance and the will to power, see also Klossowski, *Nietzsche and the Vicious Circle*, p. 21.
37. Deleuze will sometimes use the statistical model of the Markov chain to explain what he means by the dice throw (see Deleuze and Guattari, *Anti-Oedipus*, p. 42, and Deleuze, *Foucault*, p. 71). That is, 'at random but under extrinsic conditions laid down by the previous draw [...] a mixture of the aleatory and the dependent' (*Foucault*, p. 71). Necessity is the previous throws in the series, whereas chance is each additional throw; as such, all previous throws are themselves mixtures of chance and the necessity of the previous, $n-1$, throw. Deleuze notes that, although Nietzsche is ultimately against statistical models of the dice throw, 'In two texts of *The Will to Power* Nietzsche presents the eternal return in a probabilistic perspective and as being deduced from a large number of throws' (Deleuze, *Nietzsche and Philosophy*, p. 190, n. 23). On Deleuze, the Markov chain and language, see Lecercle, *Deleuze and Language*, pp. 96–8.
38. In the translator's introduction to Deleuze's *Pure Immanence*, John Rajchman makes the convincing claim that Deleuze's work on the dice throw grew directly out of his earlier work on probabilism in Hume (pp. 12–18). As Deleuze writes in the essay 'Hume': 'fusion in the imagination constitutes habit (I expect), while the distinction in the understanding calculates belief in proportion to those cases that have been observed (probability as a calculation of the degrees of belief)' (p. 164). Being indifferent to the distinction between throws, the dice throw goes beyond empiricism as calculation of probabilities towards what Deleuze calls a 'superior empiricism' (*Nietzsche and Philosophy*, p. 46) based on the affirmation of chance.
39. Deleuze stipulates 'It should not be thought that, according to Nietzsche, chance is *denied* by necessity' (*Nietzsche and Philosophy*, p. 190, n. 22).
40. Ibid., p. 24, emphasis in the original.
41. On this point see Zourabichvili, *Deleuze: Une philosophie de l'événement*, pp. 37–43.
42. Deleuze, *Nietzsche and Philosophy*, p. 49.
43. Ibid., p. 41. See also 'Nietzsche identifies chance with multiplicity, with fragments, with parts [...] What Nietzsche calls *necessity* (destiny) is

*The Speculative Univocity of Being and Language*

thus never the abolition but rather the combination of chance itself' (ibid., pp. 24–5, emphasis in the original). Conversely, if chance brings forces together, what conditions their relations once encountered is the will to power, which Deleuze understands as a 'plastic' undetermined but determinable affective form coextensive and co-substantial with the ongoing relations of force affecting the body (see ibid., pp. 39, 46–51, 57–9). The verb-form of the phantasm provides this precise function in *The Logic of Sense* (both entail tacit engagements with Kant's schematism of the imagination).

44. Deleuze, *Nietzsche and Philosophy*, p. 37.
45. In this regard, the *plane* of immanence (*plan d'immanence*) is equally a transcendental *plan* orienting the construction of immanence on the basis of previous throws or series in the structure. Here the transcendental is a posteriori in relation to the previous throws and a priori in relation to subsequent ones. This is why Deleuze sometimes conflates the plane of immanence with the image of thought in *What Is Philosophy?*, despite their obvious differences, since the plan orients the construction of that which will overcome its opposition to matter.
46. Deleuze, *Logic of Sense*, p. 206, translation modified. Along with Nietzsche, we can recognise in this quotation the influence of Alfred Jarry's pataphysics. In *Exploits & Opinions of Dr. Faustroll, Pataphysician*, Jarry writes that 'Pataphysics is the science of that which is superinduced upon metaphysics, whether within or beyond the latter's limitations, extending as far beyond metaphysics as the latter extends beyond physics. [. . .] Pataphysics will be, above all, the science of the particular, despite the common opinion that the only science is that of the general' (p. 21). For Deleuze, this constitutes a theory of 'the Being of the phenomenon' (*Foucault*, p. 91), according to which 'Being is the epiphenomenon of all *beings*' (see 'How Jarry's Pataphysics Opened the Way for Phenomenology', p. 75) – in *The Logic of Sense*, Deleuze will call this 'extra-Being' (see below) – specifically mobilising Jarry here as 'the realisation of Heidegger's philosophy' (*Foucault*, p. 91). In *Difference and Repetition*, Deleuze criticises Heidegger for failing to reach a conception of pure difference – as the difference or 'Fold' (p. 78) of the ontic and the ontological – by prioritising the latter: 'Heidegger [. . .] follows Duns Scotus and gives renewed splendour to the univocity of Being. But does he effectuate the conversion after which univocal Being belongs only to difference and, in this sense, revolves around being? [. . .] It would seem not, given his critique of the Nietzschean eternal return' (p. 79). In the quotation in the main text above, we see on the contrary that univocity for Deleuze wrests 'Being from beings' – Being as the epiphenomenon of all beings, as revolving around and displaced throughout them. As Deleuze writes later in *Foucault*: 'We must not refuse to take

Heidegger seriously, but we must rediscover the imperturbably serious side to Roussel (or Jarry). The serious ontological aspect needs a [...] sense of humour' (p. 91). Jarry's humour is literally levity, wresting Being from the pre-Socratic depths in which it remains buried and forgotten in Heidegger (and Nietzsche), as only ever partially recoverable in the ontic. On Deleuze's relation to Heidegger, see Montebello, *Deleuze*, pp. 49–50.

47. Deleuze distinguishes in *The Logic of Sense* between 'events' and the Event or '*Eventum tantum*' ('so much of the event'), as events' univocity (see *Logic of Sense*, p. 238).

48. This is Deleuze's definition of the temporality of 'Aion' in *The Logic of Sense*, which temporalises the dice throw – see particularly the 'Twenty-Third Series of the Aion' and the 'Tenth Series of the Ideal Game'. In the virtual temporality of Aion, events are subdivided ad infinitum in both directions of time simultaneously (past and future), such that they 'become' (pp. 74–6, 188–92). They are infinitely subdivided by the 'instant' (aleatory point), which is what makes the throws pro- and retro-act on one another by being the temporal point they all share, even if as something they all lack. As aleatory point (disjunctive esoteric word plugged into an erogenous body), the instant is displaced throughout all events in Aion, communicating to thought the bodily affect it siphons from the corporeal present of actions and passions (Chronos). As radically opposed to corporeality, events in Aion thus displace themselves in relation to the instant (the instant is what infinitely subdivides them into future and past in relation to it). Nonetheless, the instant is also that through which events communicate with each other across their divisions. This account of Aion ontologically underscores the functioning of the verb-form in the phantasm ('a neutral infinitive for the pure event, [...] Aion' (ibid., p. 245)).

49. Deleuze speaks of it as 'a thought of the absolutely different' (*Nietzsche and Philosophy*, p. 43). In *Difference and Repetition*, he writes: 'The throws are formally distinct, but with regard to an ontologically unique throw, *while the outcomes implicate, displace and recover their combinations in one another throughout the unique and open space of the univocal* [...] being is said "in all manners" in a single same sense [...] but is said thereby of [...] a difference which is itself *always mobile and displaced within being*' (p. 377, my emphasis). In terms of the ontology of *Difference and Repetition*, repetition paradoxically makes difference *different* (pure, in itself, perpetually different and not fixed by its relata), by displacing difference in relation to itself in the eternal return. Repetition thus replaces *the One*, since although it is univocally single, it is precisely the repetition of *difference*, which in turn replaces *the many*, since difference is only different within its univocally single repetition. While Nietzsche speaks initially

## The Speculative Univocity of Being and Language

of the eternal return as the eternal return of the same, there are passages in *The Will to Power* implying differentiation, as we saw above.
50. Deleuze, *Nietzsche and Philosophy*, p. 24.
51. This is why 'Eternal return [...] affirms the being of becoming', but as the 'self-affirming' of becoming (ibid., p. 67). Becoming has being insofar as it is a structure (a series of throws), but precisely insofar as it is serial it is open (it becomes). We can also understand this formulation in terms of the need to break with being as such, insofar as being and thought 'become' a plane of immanence when equally articulated.
52. Like the dice throw, even if the ideal game 'can only exist in thought and [...] has no other result than the work of art, [it] is also that by which thought and art are real and disturbing reality, morality, and the economy of the world' (*Logic of Sense*, p. 71).
53. Ibid., p. 69.
54. Ibid., p. 70.
55. Ibid., p. 69.
56. Ibid., p. 70. If the dice throw ontologically underlies the ideal game, Deleuze nonetheless seems to primarily extract the latter from Carroll's work, citing numerous examples where such games are found in his writings, such as the game of croquet in *Alice's Adventures in Wonderland* where 'the loops [are] soldiers who endlessly displace themselves from one end of the game to the other' (ibid., p. 69).
57. Ibid., p. 70.
58. See ibid., p. 119.
59. See ibid., pp. 120–3. Deleuze's anti-humanist agenda is identifiable in *Nietzsche and Philosophy* (see Chapter 5) and earlier.
60. Deleuze, *Logic of Sense*, p. 201.
61. Ibid., p. 70, emphasis in the original, translation modified.
62. On the relation between the aleatory point and disjunctive esoteric word, see ibid., p. 75: 'the aleatory point endlessly displaced, appearing as an empty square on one side and as a supernumerary object on the other'.
63. 'As it expresses in language all events in one, the infinitive verb expresses the event of language – language being a unique event which merges now with that which renders it possible' (ibid., p. 212).
64. These singularities are 'liberated from the ego through the narcissistic wound' (ibid., p. 244), i.e. through the genital zone on which is inscribed the difference between esoteric and semantic phonemes.
65. Ibid., p. 244.
66. Ibid., p. 246, translation modified.
67. Ibid., p. 118.
68. Deleuze writes that 'the individuality of the ego merges with the event of the phantasm itself, even if that which the event represents in the phantasm is [...] a series of other individuals through which the

dissolved ego passes. The phantasm is inseparable therefore from the toss of the dice' (ibid., p. 244). This should be understood as a specifically *perverse desubjectivation*, and not a psychotic one (which belongs to the depths).
69. Ibid., p. 199. Deleuze uses the aleatory point to explain how events can be synthesised in the absence of a transcendental subject. Crucially, this argument should not be taken too far in the opposite direction, as evidence that for Deleuze being spontaneously syntheses itself. The aleatory point is the mediating constructive element guiding the 'auto-unification' (ibid., p. 118) of events through linguistic structure (as *impersonal* if anchored to the erogenous body of a dissolved ego).
70. Deleuze, Negotiations, p. 147.
71. Deleuze, *Foucault*, pp. 90–1. I would argue that the theory of 'subjectivation' found in Deleuze's later *Foucault* is largely isomorphic to this theory of the subject-effect. In both, the subject is located in the void of the non-relation of bodies and language (or in the later work seeing and speaking), i.e. the disjunctive esoteric word (or in the later work the 'fold'), a void made full or populated by its own effects of non-relationality or divergence (events as castration- or subject-effects) (see ibid., pp. 86, 99).
72. Deleuze, Logic of Sense, p. 338.
73. Ibid., p. 340. In *Spinoza Contra Phenomenology*, Knox Peden is right to insist that Deleuze's philosophy is a conjuncture of Heideggerian phenomenology and postwar French rationalism (of which structuralism is an example): Heidegger's ontic-ontological fold of intentionality (beyond Husserlian phenomenology) is now articulated within a structuralist conception of language (and according to a fold of non-relationality between words and things). Structural 'production' on the surface replaces hermeneutical interpretation as the unveiling of a 'forgotten and veiled [. . .] Origin' of sense anchored to the pre-Socratic depths (*Logic of Sense*, p. 83; see also p. 85, n. 4).
74. During the late 1960s one can identify a 'post-structuralist' language of displacement, decentring, ex-centricity, in Deleuze.
75. Deleuze, Logic of Sense, p. 203.
76. Deleuze has in mind here Kant's three Ideas of reason (World, Self, God, as denotation, manifestation, signification – see ibid., p. 200) as well as their Nietzschean critique which holds that they are functions of language: 'Nietzsche's predication about the link between God and grammar has been realised' (ibid., p. 322). As Deleuze puts it, 'the form of God, as Kant had clearly seen, guarantees disjunction in its exclusive or limitative sense' (p. 200). Much of this was prepared for by 'Klossowski or bodies-language', particularly pp. 334–6; indeed this essay can be seen as a condensed first draft of *The Logic of Sense*,

## The Speculative Univocity of Being and Language

bringing together a Nietzschean framework and proto-structuralist themes. On these points see Smith, 'From the Surface to the Depths', p. 137, and Lecercle, *Deleuze and Language*, pp. 119–23.

77. 'This order of time, from the past to the future, is [...] established in relation to the present, that is, in relation to a determined phase of time. Good sense [...] is essentially to foresee' (*Logic of Sense*, p. 87); 'Good sense could not fix any beginning, end, or direction (*sens*) [...] if it did not transcend itself toward an instance capable of relating the diverse to the form of a subject's identity, or to the form of an object's or a world's permanence, which one assumes to be present from beginning to end' (ibid., p. 90). Good sense is a little like the structuring influence of the previous throws on later ones, *without* its being open to subsequent throws' retroactive effects.

78. On the equation 'Self = Self', used to characterise Kant's Idea of Self, see *What Is Philosophy?*, p. 57; it is helpful to compare the transcendence of the three dimensions of the proposition (in relation to the immanence of the secondary organisation) with the location of Kant's three Ideas in the 'machinic portrait of Kant' on p. 56. In *Difference and Repetition*, p. 183, Deleuze conflates common sense with Kant's Idea of Self. The latter unilaterally submits the manifold of sensation given in experience (or being) to the conditions of possibility laid down by the a priori requirement of the subject's synthetic unity of apperception, as *recognition* of the subject's unity in the concept of the object, and thanks to the 'object = x'. Hence conceptual identity (A = A) is made to fully overlap with recognition of the subject in the object. Thus when Deleuze writes in *The Logic of Sense*, 'Common sense identifies and recognises, no less than good sense foresees' (*Logic of Sense*, p. 89), we can identify its principle reference point. See 'Of the *A Priori* Grounds for the Possibility of Experience', in the first edition of Kant's *Critique of Pure Reason*, pp. 121–71.

79. Deleuze, *Logic of Sense*, p. 200.

80. We will see these two coordinate axes again below in regard to the relation between immanence and univocity, both of which this time break with Kant's Ideas. Good sense pastes over ontological difference at the level of the throws' irreducibility, common sense pastes over ontological difference at the level of being and thought's irreducibility.

81. See ibid., p. 200: 'at the surface [...] only infinitive events are deployed'.

82. Ibid., p. 203.

83. The reason for this is that events, as seen in the Ur-model of the dice throws/dice Throw, are ontologically a single Event, even if epistemologically they can be viewed as actualised in distinct states of affairs.

84. Ibid., p. 203.

85. Ibid., p. 203.
86. Ibid., p. 55.
87. Ibid., p. 55.
88. In the 'Thirtieth Series of the Phantasm', Deleuze gives as a further example of this the 'grammatical transformations' found in sadism or voyeurism (ibid., p. 244). As he writes in his essay on Tournier, in perverse desubjectivation the pervert, for instance the sadist, cannot be conflated with either the aggressor or the victim or accomplice (or in voyeurism, with the viewer or the viewed): 'It is striking to see in Sade's work to what extent victims and accomplices, with their necessary reversibility, are not at all grasped as Others [...] The world of the pervert is a world without Others' (pp. 358–9). The grammatical transformations in question here – namely the active/passive/reflexive voice of the verb – can be seen as involved in a play of contraries (active/passive, self/other) which affirm their difference or irreducibility. The phantasm (as we know, essentially perverse) immanently surveys the phantasmatic scene occupying every position in the field at once, or rather being the univocity of these divergent positions (aggressor/aggressed, etc.). In Freud's analysis of grammatical voice in the phantasm 'A Child Is Being Beaten', mentioned in the series on the phantasm, for Deleuze it is not a question of processing a trauma inflicted on a subject (the child) – which is only a function of the proposition (manifestation and common sense) – by disowning the experience and viewing it as if on a screen happening to someone else; rather it is a question of immanently surveying irreducible events or perspectives in an intersubjective scene expressed by their grammatical relations or senses.
89. Ibid., p. 55.
90. Ibid., p. 55.
91. Hence one can follow the syntactical path (relations between signifieds, conceptual implication) opened by selecting *one* of the alternatives, *or* one can follow the path opened by selecting the other alternative, but one cannot keep both alternatives in mind simultaneously when establishing the signified of a series (the product of that series' syntax or chain of conceptual implications). Disjunctive esoteric words are like portals in that they not only cause series to diverge around them, but can also allow these divergent series to resonate and coexist through them (beyond signification, denotation and manifestation).
92. Here Deleuze also has in mind Borges' 'The Garden of Forking Paths', which he quotes: 'Fang can kill the intruder, the intruder can kill Fang, both can be saved, both can die and so on and so on. In Ts'ui Pen's work, all possible solutions occur, each one being the point of departure for other bifurcations' (quoted in ibid., p. 131).

## The Speculative Univocity of Being and Language

93. As Deleuze puts it in *Essays Critical and Clinical*, 'when another language is created within language, it is language in its entirety that tends toward an "asyntactic", "agrammatical" limit, or that communicates with its own outside' (p. lv).
94. As Deleuze puts it: 'The limit is not outside language, it is the outside *of* language. It is made up of visions and auditions that are not of language, but which language alone makes possible' (ibid., p. lv, emphasis in the original).
95. Deleuze, *Logic of Sense*, p. 211.
96. In *Nietzsche and Philosophy*, Deleuze writes: 'By affirming chance we affirm the relation of *all* forces. And, of course, we affirm all of chance all at once in the thought of the eternal return. But all forces do not enter into relations all at once on their own account. Their respective power is, in fact, fulfilled by relating to a small number of forces' (p. 41, emphasis in the original). Thought puts forces into series and, through the aleatory point and ideal game, the thinker can affirm 'everything in a single moment' (p. 67) by counter-actualising a throw and thereby expressing the Event.
97. This is how Deleuze can speak of the phantasm as entailing a 'generalised grammatical "perspectivism"' (*Logic of Sense*, p. 246).
98. Ibid., p. ix.
99. On this point see Zourabichvili, *Deleuze*, p. 45.
100. Deleuze's ontology here is a perversion of Leibniz's. According to Deleuze, Leibniz saw that alogical compatibility and incompatibility (in Leibniz's terms, compossibility and noncompossibility of monads) precedes and founds both the order of bodies, on the one hand, and the order of concepts, on the other: 'Physical causality inscribes the incompatibility only secondarily in the depth of the body, and the logical contradiction translates it only in the content of the concept' (*Logic of Sense*, p. 196). To the extent, however, that Leibniz privileges alogical compatibility (or as Deleuze terms it 'convergence'), in conceiving of God as calculating in advance the best of all possible worlds (according to the ordinary rather than the ideal game), he conflates sense with signification, subordinating the affirmation of alogical incompatibilities to the domain of signification and its exclusive disjunctions (hence the pertinence of Nietzsche's conflation of God with grammar).
101. Ibid., p. 10.
102. In the depths, 'it is through infinite identity that contraries communicate' (ibid., p. 200): partial objects are at once 'the subject, the copula, and the predicate', mouth, breast, and suction (p. 200). At the surface, 'only infinitive events are deployed; each one communicates with the other through the positive characters of its difference [i.e. divergence] and by the affirmative character of the disjunction' (p. 200).

THE PSYCHOANALYSIS OF SENSE

103. Ibid., p. 247.
104. See also Alliez, 'The BwO Condition': 'The main question for [...] *The Logic of Sense* is to invest [...] the propositional articulation of sense and language in the actions and passions of bodies able to climb up to the surface of language' (p. 100).
105. Deleuze, *Logic of Sense*, p. 10, emphasis in the original, translation modified.
106. Ibid., p. 208, translation modified.
107. It is in this context that we should understand the notion that the ideal game only 'exist[s]' in thought (ibid., p. 71).
108. We saw this earlier in the associated formulation 'a single phantom' (the asexual Event) 'for all the living' (sexual and egoic bodies perpetually about to be re-castrated in accordance with the dynamic of the double screen).
109. Ibid., p. 205.
110. Ibid., p. 206.
111. Ibid., p. 206. Paraphrasing Montebello, *Deleuze*, p. 23, we can say that univocal being in Deleuze is solely thinkable (hence an 'ideal' game, 'speculative') yet, paradoxically, entirely real and not merely ideal.
112. The eternal return, in Deleuze, can be visualised as a Möbius strip placed on its side, as an infinity symbol, passing from left (past) to right (future) and back again (the retroaction of the dice throw), while *simultaneously* passing from thought (the obverse side of the strip) down to being (the reverse side) and back up again (thought affirmatively selecting the body's affections as throws), in a figure of eight which twists both these dualisms into one another. This is also a useful way to visualise his conception of psycho-physical parallelism.
113. In 'Of Life as a Name of Being, or, Deleuze's Vitalist Ontology', Badiou, p. 193, recalls that Deleuze wrote this, in capital letters, in a letter sent to him (during the 1990s).
114. Montebello, in *Deleuze*, p. 70, argues that Deleuze's conception of univocity in the late 1960s entails the knotting of *sense and being*, which thereby distinguishes it from immanence (the knotting of thinking/being), and which seems to render univocity inherently linguistic and even propositional. This would partially explain Deleuze's later conflation of philosophy with immanence and not univocity (philosophy in *What Is Philosophy?* is specifically 'not propositional', p. 22). However, this neat division is made problematic by Montebello's claim that univocity in Deleuze's work persists beyond *The Logic of Sense* (*Deleuze*, p. 19). Furthermore, while Montebello proposes that reversibility is the operation specific to immanence, and the disjunctive synthesis the operation specific to univocity (ibid., pp. 16–18), I have suggested that the disjunctive synthesis operates along these two

## The Speculative Univocity of Being and Language

axes simultaneously. On univocity and immanence in Deleuze, see also Cherniavsky, *Concept et méthode*, pp. 47–8, and Zourabichvili, *Deleuze*, pp. 54–66, 81–4.
115. Deleuze, *Logic of Sense*, p. 25, translation modified.
116. Ibid., p. 211.
117. Ibid., p. 211.
118. Ibid., p. 211.
119. This is with the proviso, as stated in section 3.1, that as *construct*, language is essential to being, but this construct need not essentially be *linguistic*, which it is in *The Logic of Sense* as a case study of one construct.
120. Ibid., p. 205.
121. Ibid., p. 205, emphasis mine. Badiou's entire text *Deleuze. The Clamor of Being*, sets itself the task of understanding Deleuze's conception of univocity (p. 24). He writes 'Deleuze purely and simply identifies philosophy with ontology. One misses everything if one disregards such explicit declarations as "Philosophy merges with ontology"' (p. 19). What Badiou entirely misses, however, is thought's absolutely equal constructive power in regard to being. On Badiou's failure to acknowledge being's necessary construction in Deleuze, see Alliez, 'Badiou: The Grace of the Universal'. A much better reading of Deleuzian univocity is found in Zourabichvili, *Deleuze*. As Aarons puts it, 'The general problematic of Deleuze's thought, Zourabichvili argues, is not Being but *experience*. [...] [H]owever [...] this opposition between ontological and transcendental problems is not static, but is rather the consequence of a kind of self-immolation immanently affecting ontology itself, a logical undertow that draws us *through* ontology toward a thought of experience that outstrips it', leading to a '"pure logic of sense"' (pp. 1–2, emphasis in the original). Still, we should be careful not to *overemphasise* this move away from ontology when reading Deleuze, not that Zourabichvili is necessarily guilty of it, as we are dealing with an equality of being/thinking, as Montebello clearly shows in his *Deleuze*.
122. Deleuze, *Logic of Sense*, p. 206. As we can see this is the fold of the sense-event discussed in section 4.3.
123. Ibid., p. 205.
124. Likewise, in *Difference and Repetition*, Deleuze writes 'There has only ever been one ontological proposition: Being is univocal' (p. 44), spending the next eight pages sketching out this ontological 'proposition' in terms of the 'circular' (p. 45) relation between 'expressed sense' and 'designated being' (pp. 44–5), as found in Scotus, Spinoza and Nietzsche (pp. 44–52). Yet again, in *A Thousand Plateaus*, while now adopting a distinct conception of language, we find the following passage concluding the book's introduction: 'American literature, and

already English literature [...] know how to move between things, establish a logic of the AND, overthrow ontology' (p. 28). An Anglo-American literary 'logic' of the AND (*et*) overthrows ontology as the study of what is (*est*) through an excess (*n* + 1) of addable statements (what is said) over the things they refer to (what there is). In *Dialogues*, Deleuze likens the AND (contra the verb 'to be') to 'extra-being' (from *The Logic of Sense*) or 'inter-being' (p. 57). See also *Foucault*, which states that the 'hallucinatory theme of Doubles and doubling', of the visible in relation to the sayable and vice versa, 'transforms any ontology' (p. 92).

125. We see this particularly when considering the psychoanalytic framework developed in my previous chapters, which shows how for Deleuze thought reacts to its cause through either neurotic or perverse forms of repression, being wholly incapable of directly confronting materiality except through psychosis. The event (castration-effect), which feeds the verb and in turn the proposition, is built on this very failure to confront materiality; yet this failed contact with materiality is what also conditions the logical proposition by providing it with a corporeal cause to react to (through denotation), and by providing it with its internal genetic element (the event or castration-effect spoken by the verb, as 'ring' of the proposition).

126. Any relation of dualism of this kind is, for Deleuze, 'logical' or 'scientific', as opposed to 'philosophical', as he puts it in *What Is Philosophy?*, since being is univocal (or immanent) and thus not reducible to matter.

127. Deleuze, *Logic of Sense*, p. 208.

128. As Deleuze seems to suggest in the book's final series (ibid., pp. 278–80), there are ultimately four series or two series redoubled: the sense-event itself is the redoubling of the physical and metaphysical surfaces as articulated in speech, on which are inscribed esoteric phonemes and semantemes, together expressing events (as a 'double screen'). Thus events are the effect of the resonance of two series (of speech or of sexuality), and events themselves are the reverse side of another plane or series (the surface proper, i.e. considered in relation to language), giving us four series: esoteric phonemes and semantemes (speech), events and sense (language). If the event is a two-sided entity, it is itself one side of another two-sided entity, the sense-event. Thus language and its outside are complexly layered.

129. Ibid., p. 25.

130. Ibid., p. 3.

131. Deleuze writes in the 'First Series of Paradoxes of Pure Becoming' that 'It is language which fixes the limits (the moment, for example, at which the excess begins), but it is language as well which transcends the limits and restores them to the infinite equivalence of an unlimited

becoming [...] Hence the reversals which constitute Alice's adventures' (ibid., p. 4). Becoming is the transgression of (linguistic) form, but this transgression itself occurs *through* language (literary nonsense and humour).

132. Ibid., p. 11. We also saw this in the dice throw: becoming is assembled by the putting-into-series of each throw, it is assembled by a certain formalism, but the reverse side of this formal assembly is precisely what the putting-into-series allows, which is the unforeseeable being induced through this assembly and exceeding the very forms (the discrete throws and their serialisation) which made it possible. In other words, becoming is greater than the sum of its formal parts.
133. Ibid., p. ix.
134. Ibid., p. ix.
135. Ibid., p. 86.
136. Ibid., p. 86.
137. Ibid., p. 87.
138. Deleuze's univocal ontology is not dogmatic as it does not posit being independently of thought's construction of it, though (through his univocal ontology of sense) this construction becomes ontological and not merely epistemological.
139. In the above discussion I would concur with Paul Livingston that Deleuze's ontology shares key features, in this specific regard, of Lacan's work during this period, to the extent that for the latter, as seen in his seminars of the late 1960s and early 1970s, the real is presented at the level of the impasse of formalisation (in short paradox or logical inconsistency), and furthermore is strictly coextensive with (failed) attempts to formalise it or present it in language (rather than pre-existing such failures). Furthermore, for both, this paradoxical ontology subtends functioning language, 'insisting' in it (see Livingston, 'How do we recognize strong critique?', pp. 101–2). Livingston calls this in both cases a form of 'strong' critique, because paradox signals the limits of anthropocentric finitude, and both positions contribute to his own 'metaformal realism', according to which paradox opens up thought to the absolute as the objective limits of thought imposed by the necessity that any formalism be either complete and inconsistent (the 'paradoxico-criticism' of Deleuze, Lacan and others), or consistent and incomplete (as in Badiou's non-critical set-theoretical ontology), as demonstrated by Gödel's incompleteness theorems (see also Livingston, *The Politics of Logic*).
140. Deleuze writes that the philosophical concept is decidedly 'not propositional' (*What Is Philosophy?*, p. 22) in this late work, even if this is somewhat compromised by the claim that the philosophical concept 'speaks the event' (ibid., p. 21), and by the paradoxical reversibility of the plane of immanence which *The Logic of Sense* accounts

for linguistically. As Alliez points out in 'The BwO Condition', from *Francis Bacon: The Logic of Sensation* onwards Deleuze will also privilege the image in art, and indeed in *What Is Philosophy?* painting and the plastic arts are prioritised in the chapter on art.
141. On the relation between *The Logic of Sense* and *What Is Philosophy?*, see Dumoncel, *Deleuze face à face*, pp. 175–80, concerning transdisciplinarity, and Zourabichvili, *Le vocabulaire de Deleuze*, pp. 34–5, in regard to ontology.
142. See Chapter 2 of *What Is Philosophy?*.
143. Deleuze, *Logic of Sense*, p. 118.
144. As Deleuze will put it later in 'Immanence: A Life': 'Were it not for consciousness, the transcendental field would be defined as a pure plane of immanence, because it eludes all transcendence of the subject and of the object' (p. 26). Deleuze writes that 'as long as consciousness traverses the transcendental field at an infinite speed everywhere diffused, nothing is able to reveal it. It is expressed, in fact, only when it is reflected on a subject that refers it to objects. That is why the transcendental field cannot be defined by the consciousness that is coextensive with it, but removed from any revelation' (p. 26). In short, if the plane of immanence is necessarily located in the transcendental – for otherwise it would be immanent *to* 'Some Thing as a unity superior to all things' (p. 27) and thus transcending the plane of immanence, as we find, for instance, in pre-critical metaphysics – this transcendental field is only that of a subject when the event infinitely and univocally dispersed throughout it is actualised in an object (through a denotative image) and referred back to a subject (manifested person). When this happens, the transcendental field becomes immanent *to* the subject that transcends it (as in Kant and Husserl), and that relates to it as a plane of reference. See also *What Is Philosophy?*, pp. 44–9 ('Example 3'). Thus the transcendental field as plane of immanence becomes plane of reference through subjects and objects.
145. *The Logic of Sense*'s theory of the verb is clearly a prototype of both the 'time image' in *Cinema 2* and the philosophical concept in *What Is Philosophy?*. On the former, see Deleuze's 1980s seminars on the cinematic image, which discuss the work of Gustave Guillaume (available at <http://www2.univ-paris8.fr/deleuze/> (last accessed 25 August 2015)). In the latter, Deleuze writes that philosophical concepts travel at 'infinite speed' (*What Is Philosophy?*, p. 75), which we know is also the temporality of the infinitive verb in Aion.
146. Deleuze, *Logic of Sense*, p. 159.
147. Ibid., p. 118.
148. This aligns with the clinic of perversion which finds that in perversion, as opposed, for instance, to hysteria, the individual is capable of becoming conscious of their fundamental fantasy. This appears

*The Speculative Univocity of Being and Language*

to be what Deleuze is referring to when he speaks of the perverse 'knowledge' (*savoir*) (ibid., pp. 5, 287, n. 2) or 'esoteric knowledge' (p. 281) of the perverse artist. Building on points made in my Chapter 3, we can say that the pervert (contra the psychotic) is castrated, yet disavows their (nonetheless real) castration by psychically investing the phallus of coordination (see p. 281) – and Deleuze adds, with castrated, desexualised libido (sense), i.e. with 'speculative' investment; in this way, the perverse artist arrives at a (philosophical, univocal) position beyond a castrated interpretation of being's quasi-dualism as a real psycho-physical dualism, yet from the side of castration not of psychosis, using the desexualised energy of castration (sense) to re-invest what came before it (phallus of coordination). In short, in line with the thesis of this chapter, the perverse artist builds univocity from equivocity (i.e. from castration), and indeed from a failure to fully disavow it, and so their 'esoteric knowledge' is also ontological or univocal: if dualism is a castrated interpretation of being, it is *also being's necessary prerequisite*.

149. Ibid., p. 142.
150. On Deleuze's literary clinic, see Tynan, *Deleuze's Literary Clinic*, and Daniel W. Smith's translator's preface to Deleuze's *Essays Critical and Clinical* (pp. xi–liii).
151. Deleuze, *Logic of Sense*, p. 277.
152. 'Sexuality is in between eating and speaking' (ibid., p. 279).
153. On this point I disagree with Widder, 'Negation to Disjunction', who claims that in *The Logic of Sense* the eternal return 'go[es] beyond its sexual origins, [...] makes way for a creative break' thanks to the 'destruction of the Oedipal Law' (p. 226), since Oedipus and sexuality remain implicated in what explicates them.
154. Deleuze, *Logic of Sense*, p. 273.
155. Ibid., p. 273.
156. Ibid., p. 273.
157. Ibid., p. 273.
158. 'Quasi-cause' is another term for the paradoxical element or disjunctive esoteric word, emphasising its relation to causality, or more specifically to the double-causality of the phantasm as discussed in sections 3.5–3.6 (just as the aleatory point is the exact same entity, but stresses its relation to the dice throw). See ibid., pp. 108–10.
159. Ibid., p. 273.
160. Ibid., p. 274.
161. Ibid., p. 281. Alice functions, perversely, as phallus of coordination.
162. Thus Deleuze finds it insufficient to say that Carroll's work attests to the perverse disavowal (*Verleungung*) of castration ('the impossibility of confronting the Oedipal situation' (ibid., p. 272)), since this marks only the work's starting point.

163. In this respect, she functions as his 'conceptual persona', to use a term from *What Is Philosophy?*: 'The conceptual persona and the plane of immanence presuppose each other [...] On the one hand, [the conceptual persona] plunges into the chaos from which it extracts the determinations with which it produces the [...] features of a plane of immanence: it is as if it seizes a handful of dice from chance-chaos so as to throw them on a table. On the other hand, the persona establishes a correspondence between each throw of the dice and the intensive features of a concept that will occupy this or that region of the table' (p. 75). This description of the conceptual persona is very close to the functioning of the aleatory point in *The Logic of Sense*, plunging into the chaos of bodily affect to extract throws which it then coordinates on a plane. *What Is Philosophy?* also mentions that the conceptual persona 'counter-effectuates the event' (p. 160).
164. Deleuze, *Logic of Sense*, p. 274.
165. This is reversed at the start of *Through the Looking-Glass* where it is now Alice who is a scalding or loving voice to her cats, and when Alice enters the looking-glass she is again manifested to the chess pieces first as a disembodied voice from above.
166. See Deleuze, *Logic of Sense*, p. 271.
167. Lacan also makes a strong connection between Alice's adventures and the function of the phallus – see Seminar VI, lesson of 4 March 1959.
168. See Deleuze, *Logic of Sense*, p. 274.
169. Ibid., p. 12.
170. Ibid., p. 272.
171. Ibid., p. 272.
172. Deleuze's analysis of *Through the Looking-Glass* in the thirty-third series retrospectively substantiates the claim that the surface, in the dynamic genesis, is serially constructed, and it is no coincidence that immediately after his discussion of Leclaire in the thirty-second series, Deleuze returns at the beginning of the thirty-third to the three types of esoteric word and their associated series in Carroll (see ibid., p. 270).
173. In the same paragraph, Deleuze links this to the loss of the Ideas of Self, World and God (as the proposition's three dimensions).
174. Ibid., p. 272.
175. Ibid., p. 272.
176. Carroll, *Through the Looking-Glass*, p. 157.
177. Deleuze, *Logic of Sense*, p. 272.
178. See ibid., p. 49.
179. 'Humpty Dumpty is [...] the Master of words, the Giver of sense' (ibid., p. 91).
180. Ibid., p. 79.
181. Hence, in their univocity and reversibility, the *dinner* table is now the

site of *thinking* (metaphysical surface), and correlatively the *chessboard* as 'logical diagram' is the site of *eating*.
182. Ibid., p. 272. This is an improvement on the end of *Alice's Adventures in Wonderland*, where the Queen of Hearts is the one who threatens castration ('Off with their heads!'), and where castration leads the physical surface to burst (release its singularities, or playing cards, onto the metaphysical surface, as the process of the phantasm emerging from the wound of castration) of its own accord. In *Through the Looking-Glass*, Alice therefore takes on more agency in regard to her self-nomination/self-castration.
183. Clearly, Deleuze will soon abandon this model of adequacy after his encounter with Guattari, no longer believing structure to be adequate to the body's affects, flush with the real. On this see Alliez, 'Rhizome (With No Return)'.

# Bibliography

Aarons, K., 'The Involuntarist Image of Thought', in G. Lambert and D. W. Smith (eds), François Zourabichvili, *Deleuze: A Philosophy of the Event: Together with The Vocabulary of Deleuze* (Edinburgh: Edinburgh University Press, 2012), pp. 1–18.

Agamben, G., 'The Time That Is Left', *Epoché,* vol. 7, no. 1, Fall 2002, pp. 1–14.

Alliez, É., 'The BwO Condition or, The Politics of Sensation', in J. de Bloois et al. (eds), *Discernements: Deleuzian Aesthetics / Esthetiques deleuziennes* (Amsterdam: Editions Rodopi, 2004), pp. 93–112.

Alliez, É., *The Signature of the World: What Is Deleuze and Guattari's Philosophy?* (London: Continuum, 2004).

Alliez, É., 'Badiou: The Grace of the Universal', *Polygraph*, 17, 2005, pp. 267–73.

Alliez, É., 'Rhizome (With No Return)', *Radical Philosophy*, 167, May/June 2011, pp. 36–42.

Artaud, A., *To Have Done with the Judgement of God*, 1948, <http://www.surrealism-plays.com/Artaud.html> (last accessed 12 February 2014).

Aulagnier-Spairani, P. et al. (eds), *Le désir et la perversion* (Paris: Seuil, 1967).

Badiou, A., *Deleuze: The Clamor of Being* (London: University of Minnesota Press, [1997] 1999).

Badiou, A., *Being and Event* (London: Continuum, [1988] 2007).

Badiou, A., 'Of Life as a Name of Being, or, Deleuze's Vitalist Ontology', *Pli*, 10, 2000, pp. 191–9.

Barot, E., *Lautman* (Paris: Les Belles Lettres, 2009).

Binnick, R., *Time and the Verb: A Guide to Tense and Aspect* (Oxford: Oxford University Press, 1990).

Bowden, S., *The Priority of Events. Deleuze's Logic of Sense* (Edinburgh: Edinburgh University Press, 2011).

Bréhier, É., *La théorie des incorporels dans l'ancien Stoïcisme* (Paris: Vrin, 1928).

Butler, J., *Subjects of Desire. Hegelian Reflections in Twentieth-Century France* (New York: Columbia University Press, 1999).

Carroll, L., 'Alice's Adventures in Wonderland', in *Alice's Adventures in*

# Bibliography

Wonderland and Through the Looking-Glass (London: Penguin Books, [1865] 1998), pp. 1–110.

Carroll, L., 'Through the Looking-Glass and What Alice Found There', in *Alice's Adventures in Wonderland and Through the Looking-Glass* (London: Penguin Books, [1871] 1998), pp. 111–246.

Carroll, L., *The Hunting of the Snark: An Agony, in Eight Fits* (Oxford: Oxford University Press, [1876] 2007).

Carroll, L., *Sylvie & Bruno* (Stroud: Nonsuch Publishing, [1889] 2007).

Cherniavski, A., *Concept et méthode: La conception de la philosophie de Gilles Deleuze* (Paris: Publications de la Sorbonne, 2012).

Chiesa, L., 'Lacan with Artaud: *j'ouïs-sens, jouis-sans, jouis-sens'*, in S. Žižek (ed.), *Lacan: The Silent Partners* (London: Verso, 2006), pp. 336–64.

Chiesa, L., *Subjectivity and Otherness: A Philosophical Reading of Lacan* (Cambridge, MA: MIT Press, 2007).

David-Ménard, M., *Deleuze et la psychanalyse. L'altercation* (Paris: Presses Universitaires de France, 2005).

Deleuze, G., 'Lecture Course on Chapter Three of Bergson's *Creative Evolution*', *SubStance* #114, 36 (3), [1960] 2007, pp. 72–90.

Deleuze, G., 'From Sacher-Masoch to Masochism', *Angelaki*, 9 (1), [1961] 2004, pp. 125–33.

Deleuze, G., *Nietzsche and Philosophy* (London: Continuum, [1962] 2006).

Deleuze, G., 'Nietzsche', in *Pure Immanence: Essays on a Life* (New York: Zone Books, [1965] 2005), pp. 53–102.

Deleuze, G., *Coldness and Cruelty* (New York: Zone Books, [1967] 2006).

Deleuze, G., *Difference and Repetition* (London: Continuum, [1968] 2008).

Deleuze, G., *Expressionism in Philosophy: Spinoza* (New York: Zone Books, [1968] 2005).

Deleuze, G., *The Logic of Sense* (London: Continuum, [1969] 2004).

Deleuze, G., *Logique du sens* (Paris: Les Éditions de Minuit, 1969).

Deleuze, G., 'How Jarry's Pataphysics Opened the Way for Phenomenology', in D. Lapoujade (ed.) *Desert Islands and Other Texts, 1953–1974* (London: Semiotext(e), 2004), pp. 74–6.

Deleuze, G., 'Hume', in D. Lapoujade (ed.), *Desert Islands and Other Texts, 1953–1974* (London: Semiotext(e), 2004), pp. 162–9.

Deleuze, G., 'How Do We Recognize Structuralism?', in D. Lapoujade (ed.), *Desert Islands and Other Texts, 1953–1974* (London: Semiotext(e), 2004), pp. 170–92.

Deleuze, G., *Francis Bacon: The Logic of Sensation* (London: Continuum, [1981] 2005).

Deleuze, G., *Cinema 2: The Time-Image* (London: Continuum, [1985] 2005).

Deleuze, G., *Foucault* (London: Continuum, [1986] 2006).

Deleuze, G., *Negotiations, 1972–1990* (London: Columbia University Press, [1990] 1997).

Deleuze, G., *Essays Critical and Clinical* (London: Verso, [1993] 1998).

Deleuze, G., 'Immanence: A Life', in *Pure Immanence: Essays on a Life* (New York: Zone Books, [1995] 2005), pp. 25–33.

Deleuze, G., *Two Regimes of Madness: Texts and Interviews, 1975–1995* (New York: Semiotext(e), 2007).

Deleuze, G. and Guattari, F., *Anti-Oedipus: Capitalism and Schizophrenia* (London: Continuum, [1972] 2004).

Deleuze, G. and Guattari, F., *A Thousand Plateaus: Capitalism and Schizophrenia* (London: Continuum, [1980] 2004).

Deleuze, G. and Guattari, F., *What Is Philosophy?* (London: Verso, [1991] 1999).

Deleuze, G. and Parnet, C., *Dialogues* (London: Columbia University Press, [1977] 1987).

Dosse, F., 'Deleuze and Structuralism', in H. Somers-Hall and D. W. Smith (eds), *The Cambridge Companion to Deleuze* (Cambridge: Cambridge University Press, 2012), pp. 126–50.

Dumoncel, J.-C., *Deleuze face à face* (Paris: M-EDITER, 2009).

Duns Scotus, J., '*Opus Oxoniense*', in L. Wadding (ed.), *Opera Omnia* (Paris: Vivès, 1891–5).

Faulkner, K., *Deleuze and the Three Syntheses of Time* (London: Peter Lang, 2005).

Eyers, T., *Post-Rationalism: Psychoanalysis, Epistemology, and Marxism in Post-War France* (London: Bloomsbury Academic, 2013).

Fink, B., *The Lacanian Subject. Between Language and Jouissance* (Princeton, NJ: Princeton University Press, 1996).

Freud, S., 'Project for a Scientific Psychology', *Standard Edition of the Complete Psychological Works of Sigmund Freud*, Vol. I (London: Vintage, [1895] 2001), pp. 283–397.

Freud, S., *Interpreting Dreams* (London: Penguin Books, [1899] 2006).

Freud, S., 'Three Essays on the Theory of Sexuality', *Standard Edition of the Complete Psychological Works of Sigmund Freud*, Vol. VII (London: Vintage, [1905] 2001), pp. 125–245.

Freud, S., 'Analysis of a Phobia in a Five-year-old Body ["Little Hans"]', in *Sigmund Freud The Wolfman and Other Cases* (London: Penguin Books, [1909] 2002), pp. 3–122.

Freud, S., 'Formulations on the Two Principles of Mental Functioning', in *The Pelican Freud Library Vol. 11, On Metapsychology: The Theory of Psychoanalysis* (London: Pelican Books, [1911] 1987), pp. 35–44.

Freud, S., 'On Narcissism: An Introduction', in *The Pelican Freud Library Vol. 11, On Metapsychology: The Theory of Psychoanalysis* (London: Pelican Books, [1914] 1987), pp. 65–97.

Freud, S., 'Instincts and Their Vicissitudes', in *The Pelican Freud Library*

*Bibliography*

Vol. 11, *On Metapsychology: The Theory of Psychoanalysis* (London: Pelican Books, [1915] 1987), pp. 113–38.

Freud, S., 'Repression', in *The Pelican Freud Library Vol. 11, On Metapsychology: The Theory of Psychoanalysis* (London: Pelican Books, [1915] 1987), pp. 145–58.

Freud, S., 'The Unconscious', in *The Pelican Freud Library Vol. 11, On Metapsychology: The Theory of Psychoanalysis* (London: Pelican Books, [1915] 1987), pp. 167–222.

Freud, S., 'From the History of an Infantile Neurosis [The "Wolfman"]', in *Sigmund Freud The Wolfman and Other Cases* (London: Penguin Books, [1918] 2002), pp. 205–320.

Freud, S., 'Beyond the Pleasure Principle', in *The Pelican Freud Library Vol. 11, On Metapsychology: The Theory of Psychoanalysis* (London: Pelican Books, [1920] 1987), pp. 275–338.

Freud, S., 'The Ego and the Id', in *The Pelican Freud Library Vol. 11, On Metapsychology: The Theory of Psychoanalysis* (London: Pelican Books, [1923] 1987), pp. 351–407.

Grigg, R., *Lacan, Language, and Philosophy* (Albany, NY: State University of New York Press, 2008).

Guillaume, G., *Temps et verbe* (Paris: Honoré Champion, [1929] 2000).

Heimann, P., 'Certain Functions of Introjection and Projection in Early Infancy', in J. Riviere (ed.), *Developments in Psycho-Analysis* (London: Hogarth Press, 1952), pp. 122–68.

Hirtle, W., *Language in the Mind: An Introduction to Guillaume's Theory* (London: McGill-Queen's University Press, 2007).

Hughes, J., *Deleuze and the Genesis of Representation* (London: Continuum, 2008).

Irigaray, L., 'Du fantasme et du verbe', *L'Arc*, 34, 1968, pp. 97–106.

Isaacs, S., 'The Nature and Function of Phantasy', in J. Riviere (ed.), *Developments in Psycho-Analysis* (London: Hogarth Press, 1952), pp. 67–121.

Jakobson, R., *Fundamentals of Language* (The Hague: Mouton, 1956).

Jarry, A., *Exploits & Opinions of Dr. Faustroll, Pataphysician* (Boston: Exact Change, [1898] 1997).

Jay, M., *Downcast Eyes: The Denigration of Vision in Twentieth-Century French Thought* (London: University of California Press, 1993).

Johnston, A., *Time Driven: Metapsychology and the Splitting of the Drive* (Evanston, IL: Northwestern University Press, 2005).

Kant, I., *Critique of Pure Reason* (London: Penguin Classics, [1781/1787] 2007).

Klein, M., 'Early Stages of the Oedipus Conflict', in J. Mitchell (ed.), *The Selected Melanie Klein* (London: Penguin Books, [1928] 1991), pp. 69–83.

Klein, M., *The Psycho-Analysis of Children* (London: Virago Press, [1932] 1989).

Klein, M., 'A Contribution to the Psychogenesis of Manic-Depressive States', in J. Mitchell (ed.), *The Selected Melanie Klein* (London: Penguin Books, [1935] 1991), pp. 115–45.

Klein, M., 'Notes on Some Schizoid Mechanisms', in J. Riviere (ed.), *Developments in Psycho-Analysis* (London: Hogarth Press, 1952), pp. 292–320.

Klein, M., 'Some Theoretical Conclusions Regarding the Emotional Life of the Infant', in J. Riviere (ed.), *Developments in Psycho-Analysis* (London: Hogarth Press, 1952), pp. 198–236.

Klein, M., 'A Study of Envy and Gratitude', in J. Mitchell (ed.), *The Selected Melanie Klein* (London: Penguin Books, [1956] 1991), pp. 211–29.

Klossowski, P., *Nietzsche and the Vicious Circle* (London: Continuum, [1969] 2008).

Kristeva, J., *Melanie Klein* (New York: Columbia University Press, 2001).

Lacan, J., *The Seminar Book I: Freud's Papers on Technique (1953–1954)* (London: W. W. Norton, 1991).

Lacan, J., *The Seminar Book II: The Ego in Freud's Theory and in the Technique of Psychoanalysis (1954–1955)* (London: W. W. Norton, 1991).

Lacan, J., *The Seminar Book III: The Psychoses (1955–1956)* (London: W. W. Norton, 1997).

Lacan, J., *Le Séminaire Livre IV: La relation d'objet (1956-7)* (Paris: Seuil, 1998).

Lacan, J., 'The Seminar Book V: The Formations of the Unconscious (1957–8)', trans. C. Gallagher, unpublished.

Lacan, J., 'The Seminar Book VI: Desire and its Interpretation (1958–9)', trans. C. Gallagher, unpublished.

Lacan, J., *The Seminar Book X: Anxiety (1962–3)* (London: Polity Press, 2014).

Lacan, J., *The Seminar Book XI: The Four Fundamental Concepts of Psychoanalysis (1964)* (London: W. W. Norton, 1998).

Lacan, J., 'The Seminar Book XII: Crucial Problems for Psychoanalysis (1964–5)', trans. C. Gallagher, unpublished.

Lacan, J., 'The Seminar Book XIV: The Logic of Fantasy (1966–7)', trans. C. Gallagher, unpublished.

Lacan, J., *Le Séminaire Livre XVI: D'un Autre à l'autre (1968–9)* <http://staferla.free.fr/S16/S16.htm> (last accessed 28 August 2015).

Lacan, J., *The Seminar Book XX: Encore (1972–3)* (London: W. W. Norton, 1999).

Lacan, J., *Le Séminaire Livre XXI: Les non-dupes errent (1973–4)* <http://staferla.free.fr/S21/S21.htm> (last accessed 28 August 2015).

Lacan, J., *Le Séminaire Livre XXIII: Le Sinthome (1975–6)* <http://staferla.free.fr/S23/S23.htm> (last accessed 26 August 2015).

# Bibliography

Lacan, J., 'The Mirror Stage as Formative of the Function of the *I* as Revealed in Psychoanalytic Experience', in *Écrits: A Selection* (London: Routledge, [1966] 2006), pp. 1–8.

Lacan, J., 'The Function and Field of Speech and Language in Psychoanalysis', in *Écrits: A Selection* (London: Routledge, [1966] 2006), pp. 33–125.

Lacan, J., 'The Agency of the Letter in the Unconscious or Reason Since Freud', in *Écrits: A Selection* (London: Routledge, [1966] 2006), pp. 161–97.

Lacan, J., 'On a Question Preliminary to any Possible Treatment of Psychosis', in *Écrits: A Selection* (London: Routledge, [1966] 2006), pp. 198–249.

Lacan, J., 'The Direction of the Treatment and the Principles of Its Power', in *Écrits: A Selection* (London: Routledge, [1966] 2006), pp. 250–310.

Lacan, J., 'The Signification of the Phallus', in *Écrits: A Selection* (London: Routledge, [1966] 2006), pp. 311–22.

Lacan, J., 'The Subversion of the Subject and the Dialectic of Desire in the Freudian Unconscious', in *Écrits: A Selection* (London: Routledge, [1966] 2006), pp. 323–60.

Lacan, J., 'Position of the Unconscious', in *Écrits: The First Complete Edition in English* (London: W. W. Norton, [1966] 2006), pp. 703–21.

Lacan, J., 'Radiophonie', *Scilicet*, 2/3, 1970, pp. 55–99.

Laplanche, J., *Essays on Otherness* (London: Routledge, 1999).

Laplanche, J. and Leclaire, S., 'The Unconscious: A Psychoanalytic Study', *Yale French Studies*, 48, [1960] 1972, pp. 118–75.

Laplanche, J. and Pontalis, J.-B., 'Fantasy and the Origins of Sexuality', *International Journal of Psychoanalysis*, 49 (1), 1968, pp. 1–18.

Lapoujade, D., *Deleuze, les mouvements aberrants* (Paris: Les Éditions de Minuit, 2014).

Laurent, É., 'Parler lalangue du corps' <http://www.radiolacan.com/en/topic/583> (last accessed 12 August 2015).

Lecercle, J.-J., *Philosophy Through the Looking-Glass: Language, Nonsense, Desire* (Chicago: Open Court, 1986).

Lecercle, J.-J., *Deleuze and Language* (London: Palgrave Macmillan, 2002).

Leclaire, S., 'L'analyste à sa place?', *Cahiers pour l'analyse*, 1, February 1966, pp. 50–2. Available at <http://cahiers.kingston.ac.uk/pdf/cpa1.4.leclaire.pdf> (last accessed 18 July 2014).

Leclaire, S., 'Les éléments en jeu dans une psychanalyse (à propos de l'Homme aux loups)', *Cahiers pour l'analyse*, 5, November/December 1966, pp. 6–40. Available at <http://cahiers.kingston.ac.uk/pdf/cpa5.1.leclaire.pdf> (last accessed 4 September 2014).

Leclaire, S., 'Compter avec la psychanalyse (Séminaire de l'ENS, 1966–67)', *Cahiers pour l'analyse*, 8, October 1967, pp. 91–119. Available at <http://cahiers.kingston.ac.uk/pdf/cpa8.6.leclaire.pdf> (last accessed 2 September 2014).

Leclaire, S., *Psychoanalyzing: On the Order of the Unconscious and the Practice of the Letter* (Stanford, CA: Stanford University Press, [1968] 1998).
Leclaire, S., *Démasquer le réel. Un essai sur l'objet en psychanalyse* (Paris: Seuil, 1971).
Leclaire, S., *A Child is Being Killed. On Primary Narcissism and the Death Drive* (Stanford, CA: Stanford University Press, [1975] 1998).
Leclaire, S., *Écrits pour la psychanalyse: Demeures de l'ailleurs (1954–1993)* (Paris: Arcanes, 1996).
Leclaire, S., *Oedipe à Vincennes. Séminaire 69* (Paris: Fayard, 1999).
Leclaire, S., *Rompre les charmes: Recueil pour des enchantés de la psychanalyse* (Paris: Seuil, 1999).
Lemaire, A., *Jacques Lacan* (London: Routledge, [1970] 1996).
Lévi-Strauss, C., *The Elementary Structures of Kinship* (New York: Beacon Press, [1949] 1970).
Lévi-Strauss, C., *Structural Anthropology, Vol. 1* (London: Basic Books, [1958] 1974).
Livingston, P., *The Politics of Logic: Badiou, Wittgenstein, and the Consequences of Formalism* (London: Routledge, 2012).
Livingston, P., 'How do we recognize strong critique?', *Crisis and Critique*, 3, 2014, pp. 85–115.
Mackay, R., 'Editorial Introduction', *Collapse*, 3, November 2007, pp. 5–38.
McNulty, T., 'Desuturing Desire: The Role of the Letter in the Miller-Leclaire Debate', in P. Hallward and K. Peden (eds), *Concept and Form: Selections from Cahiers Pour L'analyse Part 1* (London: Verso Books, 2012).
Mengue, P., *Proust-Joyce, Deleuze-Lacan: lectures croisées* (Paris: L'Harmattan, 2010).
Miller, J.-A., 'Suture (elements of the logic of the signifier)', *Screen*, 18 (4), [1966] 1973, pp. 24–34.
Montebello, P., *Deleuze. La passion de la pensée* (Paris: Vrin, 2008).
Nietzsche, F., *The Gay Science* (Cambridge: Cambridge University Press, [1882] 2001).
Nietzsche, F., *Thus Spake Zarathustra. A Book For Everyone and No One* (London: Penguin, [1883] 2003).
Nietzsche, F., *The Will to Power* (London: Penguin Books, 1968).
Ortigues, E., *Le discours et le symbole* (Paris: Beauchesne, [1962] 2007).
Peden, K., *Spinoza Contra Phenomenology: French Rationalism from Cavaillès to Deleuze* (Stanford, CA: Stanford University Press, 2014).
Riviere, J., 'On the Genesis of Psychical Conflict in Earliest Infancy', in J. Riviere (ed.), *Developments in Psycho-Analysis* (London: Hogarth Press, 1952), pp. 37–66.

# Bibliography

Sambursky, S., *Physics of the Stoics* (London: Routledge, 1959).
Sartre, J.-P., *The Transcendence of the Ego* (London: Routledge, [1937] 2004).
Saussure, F. de, *Course in General Linguistics* (New York: Columbia University Press, [1916] 1995).
Sauvagnargues, A., *Deleuze and Art* (London: Bloomsbury Academic, 2013).
Segal, H., *Introduction to the Work of Melanie Klein* (London: Hogarth Press, 1978).
Smith, D. W., 'The Doctrine of Univocity: Deleuze's Ontology of Immanence', in M. Bryden (ed.) *Deleuze and Religion* (London: Routledge, 2001), pp. 167–83.
Smith, D. W., 'From the Surface to the Depths: On the Transition from *Logic of Sense* to *Anti-Oedipus*', *Symposium*, 10 (1), Spring 2006, pp. 135–53.
Sontag, S., 'Artaud. An Essay', in S. Sontag (ed.), *Antonin Artaud: Selected Writings* (Berkeley, CA: University of California Press, 1988), pp. xvii–lix.
Świątkowski, P., *Deleuze and Desire: Analysis of The Logic of Sense* (Leuven: Leuven University Press, 2015).
Tynan, A., *Deleuze's Literary Clinic: Criticism and the Politics of Symptoms* (Edinburgh: Edinburgh University Press, 2012).
Van Haute, P., *Against Adaptation: Lacan's Subversion of the Subject* (New York: Other Press, 2002).
Verhaeghe, P., 'Subject and Body. Lacan's Struggle with the Real', in P. Verhaeghe (ed.), *Beyond Gender. From Subject to Drive* (New York: Other Press, 2001), pp. 65–97.
Verhaeghe, P. and F. Declercq, 'Lacan's Analytic Goal: *Le sinthome* or the Feminine Way', in L. Thurston (ed.), *Re-inventing the Symptom. Essays on the Final Lacan* (New York: Other Press, 2002), pp. 59–82.
Voss, D., *Conditions of Thought: Deleuze and Transcendental Ideas* (Edinburgh: Edinburgh University Press, 2013).
Widder, N., 'From Negation to Disjunction in a World of Simulacra: Deleuze and Melanie Klein', *Deleuze Studies*, 3 (2), December 2009, pp. 207–30.
Wolfson, L., *Le Schizo et les langues* (Paris: Gallimard, 1970).
Žižek, S., *Organs without Bodies. On Deleuze and Consequences* (London: Routledge, 2003).
Zourabichvili, F., *Deleuze: Une philosophie de l'événement* (Paris: Presses Universitaires de France, 1994).
Zourabichvili, F., *Le vocabulaire de Deleuze* (Paris: Ellipses, 2003).

# Index

Aarons, K., 233n
absence/presence, 10, 12–14, 29, 32, 36, 38, 53, 73, 75–6, 79, 86–8, 113, 126n, 216
action
  action = x, 114, 140, 155, 163, 173; see also aleatory point; cause (or causality): quasi-cause; paradox: paradoxical element (place without an occupant and occupant without a place); phallus: of castration
  actions and passions, 51–2, 56, 61n, 110–11, 114, 137n–9n, 140n, 156, 158–60, 164, 167, 177n, 179n–80n, 223n, 226n, 232n; see also affections
  action-words and passion-words, 51, 61n
  image of action in general, 110, 138n; see also action: = x
  phonic, 158–60, 162–3, 179n–80n, 200, 204; see also phoneme: esoteric, pregenital
affect (or affective), 21, 41n, 51, 55–6, 61n, 67, 125n, 140n, 160, 163–5, 171, 179n, 180n, 185, 190, 211–12, 217–18, 219n, 225n–6n, 238n–9n; see also becoming; events; univocity
affections, 62n, 139n, 160, 189–94, 201, 203, 222n, 232n; see also action
affirmation, 129n, 189–91, 193, 199–200, 218n, 223n, 227n, 230n–2n
  of chance, 189–93, 198–9, 222n, 224n, 231n; see also dice throw; game: ideal
  of difference, 198–200, 230n–1n
Agamben, G., 178n
Aion, 159–60, 178n, 180n, 194, 197, 199, 204, 226n, 236n; see also becoming; instant; verb
aleatory point, 193–6, 200, 212, 226n–8n, 231n, 237n–8n; see also action: = x; instant; paradox: paradoxical element (place without an occupant and occupant without a place); phallus: of castration; cause (or causality): quasi-cause
Alice (Carroll), 114, 206–7, 211–17, 234n, 238n–9n
Alliez, É., 67, 122n–3n, 140n, 232n–3n, 236n, 239n
art, 4, 55, 59, 124n, 172n, 181n, 186–8, 198–9, 207, 209, 211–12, 218n, 222n–3n, 227n, 235n, 237n
  plane of composition, 209, 211
  in relation to perversion, 237n
Artaud, A., 4, 50–2, 54–8, 58, 59n, 61n, 131n, 169

Badiou, A., 6, 222n, 232n–3n, 235n
Barot, E., 174n
becoming, 40, 65–6, 124n, 176n, 191–3, 196–7, 200–1, 204–8, 210–14, 217–18, 219n–20n, 221n, 223n, 226n–7n, 234n–6n
  becoming-unlimited, 201, 208; see also univocity
  corporeal becomings ('simulacra'), 53, 62n, 214, 201; see also partial objects
  in relation to paradox, 206–7
  in relation to the verb, 204, 208, 223n, 226n, 236n
  see also events
being, 5, 64–8, 84–5, 97, 116–18, 121n–3n, 129n, 153, 188, 190–3, 196–7, 199, 201–7, 210–12, 220n, 222n–3n, 225n, 227n–9n, 232n–3n, 235n, 237n
  extra-being, 153, 202–3, 206, 225n, 234n; see also events

248

# Index

belief and opinion, 146–7, 156–7, 162, 170, 183n, 224n
Binnick, R., 157, 178n, 183n
body
  erogenous, 4–5, 50, 56, 58, 60n, 64, 66, 71–4, 77, 80–1, 85–6, 88–90, 93–6, 98, 100–5, 107, 109–21, 125n, 127n–8n, 131n–3n, 136n–42n, 144, 152, 154, 160, 163–4, 169, 176n, 182n, 185–7, 189–92, 194, 196, 201, 207, 211, 214–18, 219n–21n, 224n–6n, 228n, 231n–2n, 239n; see also esoteric: set
  fragmented, 51, 53, 55–6, 58
  in Klein, 53, 57
  in Klossowski, 219n, 224n
  in the Lacanian school, 2, 15–17, 21–5, 27–8, 30–3, 35–6, 39n–40n, 42n, 44n–9n, 58, 221n
  in Nietzsche, 189–92, 194, 225n, 232n
  without organs, 50–8, 61n–2n, 72, 79, 131n, 142n, 171
Bowden, S., 58, 60n, 63n, 129n–30n, 173n–4n, 176n
Butler, J., 37n

Carroll, L. (C. L. Dodgson), 4, 51, 59n, 64, 68–70, 79, 82, 92, 115, 123n–4n, 131n–2n, 182n, 186n, 198, 206–7, 212–13, 215–18, 219n, 222n, 227n, 237n–8n
  *Alice's Adventures in Wonderland*, 124n, 206, 212–16, 227n, 239n
  *Through the Looking-Glass*, 70, 124n, 175n, 212–14, 216, 238n–9n
castration, 12–13, 15–16, 22, 28–31, 35, 38n, 43n, 45n–8n, 71, 74, 83, 85–8, 89–91, 97–9, 101–4, 107–8, 110–18, 120–1, 129n–30n, 132n–3n, 135n, 137n–41n, 143, 152, 172n, 174n, 194, 201, 214–17, 232n, 237n–9n
  desire for castration, 24, 26, 29–31, 48n, 93
  -effect, 91, 104, 111, 113, 116, 120, 134n, 143, 152, 171, 177n, 194, 214, 228n, 234n; see also events; monism (-effect); subject: -effect
  self-castration (or self-nomination), 90–1, 98–9, 110–11, 119, 216–17, 239n; see also Name-of-the-Father

(paternal metaphor): *Re-père* (paternal function or names-of-the-father); sinthome
cause (or causality), 11–12, 66, 94, 109–10, 135n, 219n
  corporeal, 110, 114, 140n, 145, 163, 167, 171, 172n, 176n–7n, 189, 211–12, 217, 234n; see also actions and passions; affections
  double causality, 140n, 144–5, 159, 167, 172n, 177n, 183n, 208, 218, 237n; see also expression
  immanent, 142n, 149, 207–9, 211
  object-cause, 169, 171; see also cause (or causality): quasi-cause; object (a) (or *objet petit a*)
  quasi-cause, 113, 173n, 175n–6n, 212, 230n, 237n; see also aleatory point; instant; paradox: paradoxical element (place without an occupant and occupant without a place); phallus: of castration
  structural, 113, 135n, 137n, 149, 151, 163, 166–7, 172n, 199, 207–9, 211, 230n
chaos, 189, 192, 217, 237n
  chance-chaos, 238n
  chaosmos (chaos-cosmos), 64, 200–1
  in relation to the body, 191–2, 238n
Cherniavsky, A., 122n, 233n
Cheshire Cat, 212–14, 216
Chiesa, L., vi, 37n–40n, 59n, 128n, 132n
Chronos, 226n
communication
  between word = x and object = x, 114, 150–2, 163, 167, 186, 192, 231n; see also non-relation
  of bodies in depth, 53, 62n, 201, 231n
  of events, 150, 194–5, 198, 200–1, 204, 226n; see also events: event (*Eventum tantum*); univocity
compatibility and incompatibility (logical and alogical), 160, 180n, 196–200, 231n
conceptual persona, 238n
construction, 12, 14, 23, 26, 28–30, 44n, 50, 56–7, 61n, 73, 77, 84, 89–92, 95, 97–9, 101, 103–5, 108, 117, 120–1, 126n, 130n, 133n–4n, 138n, 146, 149, 157–9, 169–70, 198, 214–15, 218, 222n, 238

249

# Index

constructivism (philosophical or ontological), 1, 5n, 61n, 65–8, 116, 123n, 173n, 182n, 186–8, 194–5, 201–2, 204, 212, 217, 218n–19n, 222n, 225n, 228n, 233n, 235n
   in relation to expression, 67, 122n–3n, 173n, 175n, 195
convergence, 27–8, 33, 66, 70, 76, 79, 84–5, 97, 107, 129n, 132n, 135n, 145, 155, 197, 199, 215
   in Leibniz, 231n
counter-actualisation, 193–4

David-Ménard, M., vi, 98, 134n
demand, 9–10, 12–13, 17, 24–6, 28, 35, 37n, 44n, 48n, 88–90, 96–7, 147
'Che Vuoi?', 11, 26, 130n
denotation, 65, 68–70, 92, 95, 104, 115–16, 123n, 126n 135n, 137n, 141, 145–9, 161–4, 167, 187, 195–9, 205, 208, 210–11, 216, 228n, 230n, 234n
   denotative image, 146–7, 171, 208, 236n
   plane of reference, 208–11, 236n
depth(s), 5n, 52–4, 56–9, 59n, 61n–3n, 71–3, 77, 81–2, 85, 87, 116, 120–1, 133n, 135n, 144, 167, 171, 174n, 183n, 189, 212–15, 217, 223n, 226n, 228n, 231n
desexualisation, 126n, 195
desire, 7, 9–15, 17, 19–20, 22, 24–31, 34–5, 37n–9n, 41n, 43n–5n, 47n–8n, 60n, 89, 93, 130n–1n, 133n, 136n, 138n, 141n, 146–7, 156–7, 162, 170–1, 182n–3n
'Desire-of-the-Mother', 14–15, 34, 39n, 86, 116, 128n
   representative, 21, 26, 41n, 44n, 105, 137n
dice throw, 188–91, 193–4, 198, 201–4, 207, 218n, 222n, 224n, 226n–9n, 232n, 234n, 237n–8n; see also affirmation of chance; game: ideal; serialisation
difference (ontological), 65–6, 70, 84–6, 92, 94, 99, 145, 154, 174n, 180n, 186, 195, 197, 211, 213, 221n, 225n, 229n
   in relation to repetition (return/recurrence), 192, 195, 203, 223n, 226n–7n

divergence, 85, 107, 113, 135n, 155, 165, 198–201, 222n, 228n, 231n
domain of preexistence (the symbolic), 78, 90, 95, 104, 135n–6n; see also sense: pre-sense; symbolic (Lacan)
double inscription, 109–10, 181n, 220n
double screen, 110–12, 114, 116, 139n–41n, 159–60, 168–9, 177n, 181n, 232n, 234n
drive, 9, 14–22, 26–7, 29–30, 32, 34–5, 40n–2n, 44n–5n, 48n–9n, 52–3, 68, 72, 74–5, 77, 80, 82, 90, 95–8, 101–3, 109, 112–13, 120, 127n–9n, 135n–7n, 142n, 182n–3n, 187, 221n
   death, 29, 48n, 211; see also phantasm (and phantasy/fantasy): as phantom
   syncope (Leclaire), 20, 30, 33, 42n, 46n–8n
   see also libido
dualism/duality, 65–70, 84–5, 97, 111, 117, 129n, 141n, 144–5, 149, 160, 163–5, 171, 181n, 220n–1n, 232n, 234n, 237n
   quasi-dualism (or quasi-duality), 66, 68–9, 79, 84–5, 87, 97, 107–8, 111, 116–18, 129n, 134n, 154, 189, 202, 209–10, 237n
   see also equality of powers; equivocity
Dumoncel, J-C., 236n
Duns Scotus, J., 218n, 225n

ego, 57–8, 72–3, 75–6, 125n–6n, 138n, 144–5, 183n, 194, 227n–8n, 232n
emanation, 68, 192; see also transcendence
empirical, 138n, 147–8, 166–7, 176n, 185, 191, 194, 208–10, 216
empiricism, 224n
   transcendental empiricism, 176n, 224n
equality of powers, 65–6, 122n, 182n, 188, 233n; see also dualism/duality; equivocity
equivocity, 186–8, 195, 202, 204, 211, 213, 220n–2n, 237n; see also dualism/duality; equality of powers; non-relation
erogenous zones (partial surfaces), 2, 7, 9, 12, 15–28, 32–5, 38n–43n,

250

45n–8n, 53–4, 69, 71–81, 84–5, 87, 89–90, 92–8, 101–3, 108–10, 115, 120, 125n, 127n, 133n, 136n, 139n, 168, 179, 183n, 215, 217
coordination of zones, 9, 23, 32–3, 73–4, 76, 81–2, 87, 89–94, 96–8, 101–2, 104, 109, 115, 117, 120–1, 127n, 142n, 168–9, 182n, 213–15; *see also* phallus: of coordination
genital zone, 7, 9, 16, 74–5, 79–82, 86–8, 96–8, 104, 108, 111, 137n, 163, 214, 227n

esoteric
knowledge, 237n; *see also* perversion
language, 208; *see also* humour
set, 121, 138n, 169, 187, 220n; *see also* body: erogenous; surface: physical
esoteric words, 4, 68, 71, 88, 90, 92, 94–9, 101–4, 110–12, 114–18, 130n, 133n–4n, 137n, 139n, 141n, 143, 150–1, 155, 163, 174n–5n, 181n, 200–1, 209, 214, 216, 220n, 226, 237n–8n
connective, 44n, 68, 77, 79–80, 95, 103, 142n
conjunctive, 68–70, 89, 91–2, 95–7, 117, 120, 131n, 133n, 138n, 142n, 169, 187, 194, 198–9
disjunctive (or portmanteau), 70, 89, 91, 98, 112, 114, 140n, 151, 155, 194–5, 216, 227n–8n, 230n
eternal return (Nietzsche), 188–90, 192, 195–7, 199, 201, 203, 212, 218n, 222n–7n, 231n–2n, 237n; *see also* events: event (*Eventum tantum*); univocity
events, 69, 83, 90–1, 110–14, 116, 118–21, 129n, 134n, 139n, 141n, 143, 151–5, 159–61, 164–7, 170–1, 171n–2n, 176n–7n, 181n, 184n, 192–205, 208–10, 213, 217, 220n–3n, 226n–30n, 234n–5n, 238n
event (*Eventum tantum*), 111, 129n, 139n–40n, 175n, 192–5, 198, 200–4, 208, 211–12, 217, 226n–7n, 229n, 231n–2n, 236n; *see also* becoming: becoming-unlimited; univocity: of being or sense
as logical attributes, 124n, 153–5

as spoken by verbs, 124n, 156, 161–2, 165, 170, 175n, 180n, 227n, 231n, 235n
as thought of the outside, 200
*see also* castration: -effect; monism (-effect); subject: -effect
expression, 52, 62, 65, 67–70, 83–4, 92, 96–7, 102–3, 111, 116, 119–20, 122n–4n, 128n, 135n, 140n–1n, 143–4, 146, 149–56, 158–65, 167, 173n, 175n–9n, 181n, 183n, 189–97, 200, 202–6, 208–9, 212, 216–18, 218n, 227n, 230n–1n, 233n–4n, 236n
in relation to constructivism, 67–8, 122n–3n, 173n, 175n, 195, 217
*see also* cause (or causality): double causality; immanence; monism (-effect)
Eyers, T., 39n

Faulkner, K., 124n
fixation, 20–2, 26, 31–3, 41n–2n, 47n, 78, 80, 94, 96, 102, 112, 115
force, 51, 61n–2n, 115, 121n, 176n, 189–92, 200–2, 204, 206, 213, 217–18, 223n, 225n, 231n
as quantitative difference, 62n, 189–91, 200–1, 223n
'Fort! Da!', 13–14, 80, 88
*Francis Bacon: The Logic of Sensation* (Deleuze), 61n–2n, 236n
Freud, S., 7, 9–10, 13–14, 16–21, 36n, 38n–44n, 48n, 52–3, 58, 60n, 71–3, 75–7, 80, 88–9, 98, 105–7, 109–10, 118, 125n–7n, 130n, 132n, 136n, 159, 163, 174n, 221n, 230n
'Frumious', 198–201
frustration, 11–12, 14, 37n, 52–4, 60n, 73, 75, 126n
symbol, 13, 38n, 88

game
ideal, 188–9, 193–203, 205, 208–9, 211–12, 218, 222n, 227, 231n–2n; *see also* affirmation: of chance; art; humour
ordinary, 193, 231n
*Gestalt*, 37n, 58, 63n, 125n, 134n
God, 50, 121n, 131n, 195, 200, 222n, 228n, 231n, 238n

## Index

Good object, 53–8, 60n, 62n, 73, 75–6, 78–9, 81, 83–4, 87, 94, 96, 102, 118, 120, 125n–6n, 129n–30n, 142n, 213; *see also* superego; voice
good ideal penis, 74–5, 81–2, 86–8, 126n, 128n
Grigg, R., 48n
Guillaume, G., 156–60, 164, 169–70, 177n–81n, 183n, 236

height(s), 5n, 52, 57–8, 62n–3n, 72–6, 82–7, 89–90, 94–5, 103–4, 116–18, 120, 143–4, 153, 166–7, 171, 171n, 174n, 187, 212–15, 217
Hirtle, W., 157–8, 178n, 183n
howls-breaths (Artaud), 51, 54–8, 61n, 79, 141n–2n
Hughes, J., 60n, 124n, 173n, 218n
humour, 186–8, 197, 206, 208, 212–13, 219n–21n, 223n, 226n, 235n; *see also* esoteric: language
Humpty Dumpty, 175n, 212, 215–17, 238n

identification, 10–13, 15, 26, 29, 38n, 44n–5n, 57, 60n, 63n, 74–5, 82, 87, 94, 96, 113, 115, 119–21, 125n, 141n
imaginary (Lacan), 9–13, 24, 27–31, 34–5, 37n–8n, 44n–5n, 48n, 63n, 82, 91, 119, 128n–9n, 135n, 141n, 221n
immanence (plane of), 5, 65–6, 68, 84, 116, 121n–2n, 135n, 149, 154–5, 166, 173, 182, 185, 187–9, 191–2, 202–5, 207–10, 217–18, 219n, 223n, 225n, 227n, 229n, 232n, 235n–8n; *see also* expression; monism (-effect); surface: metaphysical (or cerebral)
instant, 192, 226n
instinct, 7, 10, 13, 17, 21
intensity, 14, 18–23, 25, 31–2, 42n, 47n, 76–80, 93–4, 102, 105–6, 109, 115, 121, 127n, 138n, 159–60, 163–4, 179–80, 196, 238n
intensive difference, 18–21, 25, 36n, 40n–1n, 75, 105, 136n–7n
intention, 15, 17, 19–20, 22, 26, 34, 97, 101, 108–9, 111, 120, 138n, 143, 160, 163, 166, 170
'good intentions', 76, 97, 104, 110–11, 113, 120–1, 135n, 142, 168, 170, 195–6, 228n; *see also* Good object
'intention-result', 120, 143–4, 152, 168, 171n; *see also* castration: -effect; cause (and causality): double causality
*see also* drive
introjection and projection (Klein), 53–8, 60n, 62n, 65, 72–4, 78–83, 86–7, 94, 110, 120, 125n, 128n–30n, 213
Irigaray, L., 179n
Isaacs, S., 127n, 182n

'Jabberwocky', 51, 70, 116, 140n, 150n–1n, 175n, 212, 214–17
Jakobson, R., 93, 133n, 139n
Jarry, A., 225n–6n
Jay, M., 133n
Johnston, A., 41n
*jouissance*, 19, 22, 33, 42n, 47n–8n, 119; *see also* intensity; libido (id)

Kant, I., 99, 121n, 176n–7n, 179n–80n, 225n, 228n–9n, 236n
Klein, M., 4, 36n, 50, 52–4, 56–8, 60n, 62n, 71–2, 74–7, 79–82, 84, 88, 91, 104, 112, 118–21, 126n–30n, 138n, 142n, 182n–3n, 213
Klossowski, P., 196, 219n
'Klossowski or bodies-language' (Deleuze), 122n, 196, 202, 219n, 228n
Kristeva, J., 128n

Lacan (and Lacanian school), J., 2–4, 6–19, 23–6, 31, 34–6, 37n–48n, 52, 58, 62n–3n, 64, 66, 68, 71, 74–7, 80–6, 88–92, 94, 98, 101, 107, 112–13, 115–16, 118–19, 125n–34n, 137n–42n, 145, 147, 169–71, 172n, 179n, 182n–4n, 217, 220n–1n, 235n, 238n
lack, 11–12, 15, 22, 24, 32, 37n, 40n, 44n–5n, 55–6, 69, 74–5, 80–1, 86–9, 93, 95, 98, 100, 103, 108, 113, 117, 129n–32n, 142n
*langue* (Saussure), 157, 178n–9n, 181n
Laplanche, J., 135n
Laplanche, J., and S. Leclaire, 34, 42n, 44n, 107, 109–10, 114, 139n, 220n

252

# Index

Laplanche, J., and J.-B. Pontalis, 40n, 42n, 62n, 135n–6n, 175n, 182n–3n, 220n
Lapoujade, D., 176n
Laurent, É., 45n, 137n, 220n
Lautman, A., 174n
Lecercle, J.-J., 132n, 224n
Leclaire, S., 2, 4, 15–26, 28–36, 39n–48n, 50, 76, 78, 89, 91–4, 98, 100–1, 104, 107–10, 112, 114, 119, 125n, 127n, 131n–4n, 136n–40n, 168n–9n, 181n, 220n–1n, 238n
    Letter, 15, 18, 20–4, 26–8, 31–6, 39n, 41n–3n, 45n, 47n–9n, 78, 92–5, 98, 100, 102, 108–9, 112–13, 116, 120–1, 132n–4n, 137n–8n, 141n–2n, 169, 177n, 215–16
    in relation to phonemic-intensive difference, 17–18, 25, 27, 31–2, 34, 40n, 46n, 77–8, 93, 95–6, 100–1, 106, 142n, 159–60, 163
    in relation to sensible-intensive difference, 18–23, 25, 31–3, 41n–2n, 47n, 78, 93–4, 102, 106, 127n
Lévi-Strauss, C., 8–11, 36n, 129n
libido (id), 16, 18, 20, 72–3, 76, 126n, 133n, 167, 174n, 237n; *see also* intensity; *jouissance*
Livingston, P., 6n, 129n, 235n

McNulty, T., 43n
manic-depressive position, 56–7, 63, 71–4, 75–6, 78–81, 83–4, 87, 94–7, 102, 120–1, 126n, 129n, 142n
manifestation (proposition), 78–9, 83, 94, 102, 123, 125n, 137n, 141n, 146–50, 153, 160–2, 166, 170–1, 173n, 183n, 187, 194, 196–8, 205, 213, 219n, 228n, 230n, 236n, 238n
maternal function, 15, 35
Mengue, P., 132n
mental apparatus (topographical model)
    difference between *Ucs.* and *P/cs.*, 112–14, 137n–8n, 163, 172n, 177n; *see also* phantasm (and phantasy/fantasy): rapid exchange (*Ucs./P/cs.*)
    pre/conscious systems (*P/cs.*), 105–7, 109, 111, 136n–8n, 141n, 159, 165–6, 181n
    unconscious system (*Ucs.*), 105–11, 113, 115–17, 136n–8n, 144, 165–7, 208–10, 181n, 220n
'Michel Tournier and the World Without Others' (Deleuze), 171, 230n
Miller, J.-A., 34, 41n, 101, 134n
monism (-effect), 65–7, 69, 111, 116, 129n, 188–9, 191–2, 201–3, 208–9, 210, 222n; *see also* expression; immanence
Montebello, P., 122n, 226n, 232n–3n
morpheme, 71, 78, 90–3, 95–6, 98, 100–3, 107–8, 111, 115, 131n, 133n–4n, 141n, 145–6, 158, 160, 163, 165, 167, 169, 180n, 187
    as phallus, 91–2, 133n

Name-of-the-Father (paternal metaphor), 15–16, 29–30, 34–5, 39n, 86, 90, 116, 118, 125n, 131n, 134n, 137n, 141n, 215
    *Re-père* (paternal function or names-of-the-father), 29, 34–5, 92, 119
    *see also* castration: self-castration (or self-nomination); sinthome
narcissism, 72–3, 75–6, 96, 126n, 135n, 183n
need, 9, 21, 35–6, 37n, 43n–4n, 48n, 52–3, 72, 147
neurosis, 16, 40n–1n, 132n, 171, 211–12, 234n
    hysteria, 16, 41n, 48n–9n, 131n, 236n
    obsessional, 23–4, 41n, 45n, 48n–9n, 109, 131n
Nietzsche, F., 61n–2n, 131n, 188–91, 200–1, 218n, 222n–8n, 231n, 233n
noise, 54–9, 62n, 83–4, 116–17, 127n, 167–9, 175n, 182n, 185
non-relation, 65, 122n, 155, 179n, 183n, 187, 195–7, 202–3, 207, 219n, 222n, 228n

object (a) (or *objet petit a*), 15–18, 20–3, 25, 27–8, 31–6, 39n, 41n–2n, 45n, 47n–9n, 128n, 137n–8n, 140n–1n, 184n, 220n–1n
    in perversion, 170–1
    in relation to events, 170–1, 184n, 220n

253

## Index

object (a) (or *objet petit a*) (*cont.*)
  *see also* cause (or causality): object-cause; cause (or causality): quasi-cause; partial objects
Oedipus complex, 3–4, 7, 9–12, 23–6, 36, 38, 44n, 46n, 48n, 71, 75–6, 79–82, 84–92, 95–7, 99, 102–4, 107–8, 110, 114, 120–1, 126n–30n, 132n, 138n, 169, 211, 213–14, 220n, 237n
Ortigues, E., 177n–9n
otherness, 9–11, 17, 22, 30, 37n, 40n, 42n, 44n, 48n, 53, 58, 63n, 89, 106, 170–1, 183n, 227n, 230n
  structure-Other, 171, 183n; *see also* self: idea (Kant)

paradox, 17, 42n, 64–6, 70, 103, 112, 129n, 139n, 143, 145, 148–9, 154–6, 171n, 177n, 186, 198, 203–4, 206–8, 211, 219n–20n, 226n, 232n, 235n
  paradoxical element (place without an occupant and occupant without a place), 113, 129n, 135n, 150, 155–6, 207, 215–16, 220n, 237n; *see also* action: = x; aleatory point; cause (or causality): quasi-cause; phallus: of castration
  paradoxical formalism, 206, 235n
parallelism (Spinoza), 122n–3n, 203, 232n; *see also* equality of powers; equivocity; non-relation
paranoid-schizoid position, 52–8, 63n, 71–3, 79–80, 83–5, 120–1
parental couple (Klein), 74–5, 82, 128n
parental image (mother image, father image), 75–6, 81–4, 86–8, 90, 103–4, 110, 113, 117, 215
  Oedipal series (Oedipal parental images), 81, 83, 104, 108, 110–15, 135n, 137n–8n, 140n, 155, 220n
  pregenital series (pre-Oedipal parental images), 81, 103–4, 108, 110–15, 135n, 137n–8n, 140n, 155, 220n
partial objects, 7, 9–10, 53–7, 61n, 72, 231n
  bad object (breast), 54–5, 57–8, 72–3, 75, 78, 80–1, 125n, 128n, 134n, 213
  as internal penises, 80

objects of auto-erotic satisfaction (erogenous images), 72, 77–9, 81, 94, 96, 115, 127n–8n, 133n, 137n–8n, 142n
  *see also* object (a) (or *objet petit a*)
Peden, K., 228n
penis/vagina, 10–11, 37n–8n, 86, 130n
person (manifestation), 146–7, 149, 159–62, 170–1, 183n, 194–8, 219n, 236n
perspectivism, 191, 200–1, 212, 223n–4n, 230n–1n
perversion, 59, 73, 103, 120, 170–1, 186, 209–10, 219n, 221n, 228n, 230n, 234n, 236n–7n; *see also* esoteric: knowledge
phallus
  of castration, 71, 78, 84–5, 88, 91, 95, 99, 104, 112–16, 133n–5n, 137n, 214; *see also* action: = x; aleatory point; cause (or causality): quasi-cause; paradox: paradoxical element (place without an occupant and occupant without a place)
  of coordination, 71, 76, 78, 80–1, 84–7, 89, 90–2, 95–6, 98, 104, 109, 112–17, 130n, 132n–5n, 142n, 213–14, 237n–8n; *see also* phallus: as image
  as effect, 134n
  having and being, 12–13, 38n
  as image, 74–5, 81, 110, 132n; *see also* phallus: of coordination
  imaginary, 12–13, 15, 25, 28–9, 37n–8n, 40n, 43n, 85–6, 128
  symbolic, 9, 11–15, 16, 22–5, 27–36, 37n–8n, 40n, 43n–5n, 47n–8n, 81, 84–94, 96, 98, 101, 103, 108, 112–14, 115–18, 126n, 129n–31n, 133n, 135n, 137n–8n, 140n, 142n, 150–1, 155, 175n, 212, 238n
phantasm (and phantasy/fantasy), 5, 110, 112, 128n, 131n, 142n, 169, 173n–4n, 177n, 185, 194, 218, 223n, 237n, 239n
  beginning (or origin) and end, 144–5, 151–2, 160, 164, 172n, 175n, 183n, 186, 195–6, 211, 213, 220n
  in Klein (and the Kleinians), 60n, 62n, 75, 128n–9n, 182n
  in Lacan (fantasy), 47n, 134n, 138n, 145, 170–1

254

## Index

in Laplanche and Pontalis (fantasy), 40n, 136n, 182n–3n, 220n
in Leclaire (fantasy), 24, 35–6, 43n, 47n, 98, 134n, 137n–8n
as phantom, 112
questions and problems, 149, 151, 156, 159–60, 162–3, 180n–1n, 186, 195, 212, 220n
rapid exchange (*Ucs./P/cs.*), 144, 164, 166–7, 181n; *see also* mental apparatus (topographical model): difference between *Ucs.* and *P/cs.*
in relation to the ideal game, 175n, 181n, 187n–8n, 194–6, 211–12, 227n–8n, 231n
in relation to perversion, 170–1, 230n, 236n
in relation to the proposition, 149, 154, 164, 167, 171, 181n, 209
in relation to the verb, 125n, 152, 156, 159–63, 165, 167, 179n, 183n, 194, 209, 225n–6n
phoneme, 8, 22–33, 43n, 46n–7n, 71, 76–81, 83, 90–7, 100–4, 106–13, 115–18, 121, 131n–3n, 138n, 141n, 145–6, 155, 157–61, 163–5, 167, 169, 178n–80n, 187, 234n
esoteric, pregenital, 95, 104, 107, 110–11, 113, 115–18, 139n, 155, 160, 163–5, 227n, 234n; *see also* action: phonic
phonemic/phonetic/graphic difference, 8, 22–3, 25–33, 42n–3n, 46n–7n, 51, 76, 78–9, 93–4, 106, 121, 142n, 157, 178n, 180n
phonetic traits, 31, 51, 54–6, 101–3, 111, 115, 131n–4n, 136n, 141n–2n
semantic, 104, 110–15, 139n–40n, 155n, 158–60, 163–5, 179n, 227n; *see also* semantemes
pleasure, 7, 14, 17, 19–22, 32–3, 39n, 41n–3n, 48n, 50, 61n, 76n, 97, 105–7, 109, 136n
principle, 14, 17, 22, 42n, 61n, 76, 97, 105–7, 141n
pluralism, 192, 200–3
'PLURALISM = MONISM', 188, 191–2, 203
Poord'jeli ('the dream with the unicorn'), 4, 23, 28–30, 34, 36, 46n–8n, 90–3, 101, 107–9, 111–14, 119, 132n–4n, 137n, 137n–40n, 143, 169, 177n

'Joli corps de Lili', 104, 113–14, 116, 137n, 139n, 177n
predicate (logic), 153, 155, 171, 196–9
presentation (Freud), 13, 20–2, 32, 58, 62n–3n, 67
mnemic image, 20–2, 32–3; *see also* presentation: thing-
thing-, 41n, 105–7, 125n; *see also* presentation: mnemic-image
word- (conscious or verbal representation), 105–7, 107, 109, 159, 175n, 179n, 181n, 219n
primary order, 171, 174n–5n, 185
privation, 11–12, 37n–8n, 86
probability, 43n, 190–1, 193, 224n
problem, 89, 99–101, 108, 144–5, 149–52, 156, 159–62, 165, 174n–5n, 180n, 186, 194, 211, 233n
proper name, 15, 30, 39n, 46n, 90, 132n, 134n, 137, 214–15
proposition, 5, 47n, 65–6, 68–9, 80, 91, 103, 111–12, 115, 123n–4n, 135, 141, 144–50, 152–6, 159–67, 170–1, 173n–4n, 176n–7n, 180n–1n, 183n, 185, 195–200, 202, 204–6, 208–10, 217, 218n, 229n–30n, 232n–5n, 238n
psychosis, 40n, 61n, 131n–3n, 171, 228n, 234n, 237n
schizophrenia, 51–2, 54–5, 59, 61n, 131n, 133n, 142n, 169, 174n

question, 9, 11, 15, 75, 89, 96, 108, 130–1, 144–5, 149–52, 156, 159–62, 163–6, 174n–5n, 180n–1n, 186, 194–5, 211–12, 219n–20n, 224n

Rajchman, J., 224n
reaction (and retroaction or falling back), 158–60, 164, 167, 169, 179, 187, 192, 196, 217, 232
real (Lacan), 19, 37n–8n, 42n, 47n, 63n, 119, 135n, 141n, 221n, 235n
real father (Lacan), 15, 90
reality principle, 106, 109
Red Queen, 212, 214, 216–17
reparation (and evocation), 76, 80–2, 88–9, 91, 96–8, 101–4, 127n, 130n, 133n, 142n
repetition (unconscious), 14, 20, 22, 42n, 110–11, 116, 118

# Index

repression, 15, 21, 32–4, 38n–9n, 41n–2n, 44n, 47n–8n, 85, 88, 90, 105, 107–9, 113–14, 116, 125n, 131n, 138n, 141n, 145, 166–7, 177n, 234n

resonance, 33, 109–11, 114, 137n, 139n, 141n, 144, 150–2, 155, 159, 164–5, 172n, 199, 215–16, 230n, 234n

Sartre, J.-P., 176n

Saussure, F. de, 42n, 116, 132n, 157, 172n, 178n, 180n–1n

secondary organisation, 150, 152, 171, 173n–5n, 185–6, 194, 218n–19n, 223n, 229n

selection, 43n, 96, 101–2, 160, 167, 180n
  ontological (eternal return), 189–91, 201–3, 218n, 223n, 232n

self, 10–11, 14, 22–3, 26, 30, 32, 43n, 47n–8n, 53, 58, 72, 76–7, 90–2, 95–6, 98–9, 110, 116, 119, 127n, 141n, 143, 171, 216–17, 230n, 239n
  'counter-self', 193; *see also* aleatory point
  idea (Kant), 197–9, 228n–9n, 238n; *see also* otherness: structure-other

semantemes, 47n, 71, 78, 81, 90, 95–6, 104, 107–9, 111–18, 128n, 133n, 137n–8n, 140n–1n, 145–6, 158, 161, 163, 165, 167, 169, 180n, 187, 215–16, 234n

sense, 1, 8, 11, 33, 47n, 51, 53–4, 64–5, 67, 69, 80, 83, 93, 95, 104, 106, 111–12, 119, 131n, 133n, 140n, 143, 145, 148–9, 152, 155–6, 164, 166, 171n–3n, 176n–7n, 187–8, 191, 196, 207–12, 214, 216, 220n, 222n–3n, 226n, 228n, 230n–3n, 238n
  co-sense, 95–6, 102, 115, 120, 133n
  as desexualised libido or energy, 149, 167, 237n
  as generative matrix, 148–9, 163–5, 208–9
  good and common sense, 147, 178n, 183n, 196–200, 208, 229n–30n; *see also* self: idea (Kant); world (idea)
  as insistence in the proposition, 155–6, 200, 202–3; *see also*

paradox: paradoxical element (place without an occupant and occupant without a place) nonsense, 1, 64, 95, 109, 112–13, 120, 132n, 135n, 140n, 143, 153, 155–6, 163, 165, 172n, 179n, 182n, 185, 187–8, 199–201, 206–9, 214–16, 219n–20n, 223n–4n, 235n
  onto-logic of, 1, 2, 5, 50, 154, 204
  pre-sense, 143, 171n; *see also* domain of preexistence; symbolic (Lacan)

psychoanalysis of sense, 1, 66
  in relation to expression, 67, 69–70, 111, 123n, 135n, 141n, 146, 149–52, 154, 161–2, 165–7, 173n, 175n–6n, 181n, 195, 200, 209, 212, 216, 233n
  in relation to immanence, 65–6, 68, 121n–2n, 149, 166, 173n, 186, 208–9
  in relation to paradox, 207
  in relation to univocity, 4–5, 64, 71, 153, 186, 191, 193, 202–3, 218n, 225n–6n, 232n–3n, 235n
  as reversible fold (sense-event), 65–6, 122n, 153–5, 160, 162, 165–7, 176n–7n, 179n, 186, 200–6, 210, 217, 219n, 230n, 232n–5n, 238n
  as sterile effect, 148–9, 164, 208–9

serial syntheses, 71
  connective, 68, 77–8, 229n
  conjunctive, 66, 77–8, 98, 102, 115, 197, 229n
  disjunctive, 65, 109, 119, 123n, 129n, 137n, 139n, 152, 188, 194–5, 198–9, 202–3, 209, 232n

serialisation, 192, 194, 235n

sexual difference, 7–9, 11–14, 16, 18, 21–4, 35, 38n, 45, 63n, 81, 97–8, 112, 126, 151, 159, 162, 220n–1n

signification, 61n, 95, 99–100, 109, 116, 124n, 137n, 139n, 141n, 147–8, 153, 156, 161–2, 166–7, 180n–1n, 187, 196–9, 205, 219n, 228n, 230n–1n

singularity, 4, 16, 18–21, 31, 34–6, 40n–1n, 46n–7n, 70, 77, 89–91, 93, 95, 98–103, 108, 110, 113–14, 118–19, 121n, 127n, 134n, 139n, 150, 159–60, 170, 193–4, 213, 218n, 221n, 227n–8n, 239n

256

## Index

sinthome, 34, 141n; *see also* castration: self-castration (or self-nomination); Name-of-the-Father (paternal metaphor): *Re-père* (paternal function or names-of-the-father)
Smith, D. W., 218n, 229n, 237n
'Snark', 69–70, 131n, 140n, 150
Sontag, S., 50, 59n
speech, 5, 9, 15, 18, 31, 37n, 68, 71, 78–9, 86, 89–90, 106, 111, 119–21, 124n, 131n, 143–4, 148–9, 152, 157, 159–62, 163–9, 171n–2n, 174n–5n, 179n–80n, 182n–3n, 185, 187, 234n
  difference from language, 143, 150, 172n
  in relation to eating, 68–71, 79, 123n–4n, 126n–7n, 150, 175n, 211, 219n, 237n
splitting (Klein), 52–7, 72, 75, 80–1, 83, 220n
stage (developmental), 7, 52, 71, 84, 167–9, 182n
  mirror, 10, 38n–9n, 58, 63n, 125n
  oral and anal, 4, 9–11, 26, 37, 40n, 52–5, 57, 60n, 62n, 71, 73, 79–80, 84, 129n
  phallic or Oedipal, 26, 71, 73, 75–6, 79–80, 82, 85–6, 88–9, 95–7, 102–4, 107, 125n, 128n, 130n, 138n, 169, 220n
Stoicism and Cynicism, 45n, 171, 175n–6n, 219n–20n, 224n
structuralism (and 'post-structuralism'), 3–5, 6n, 18, 41n, 45n, 67, 99–100, 122n, 124n, 129n, 148, 157, 172n, 174n, 179n, 182n, 217, 223n, 228n
subject, 30–3, 36, 37n, 39n, 41n, 44n, 46n–8n, 53, 89, 121n, 124n, 131n, 137n–8n, 149, 153, 155, 166, 170–1, 173n, 176n, 182n–3n, 187, 193–9, 208, 219n–20n, 228n–31n, 236n
  desubjectivation (or depersonalisation), 144–5, 170–1, 228n, 230n
  -effect, 169-70, 194, 197, 228n; *see also* castration: -effect
superego, 72–3, 75, 125n, 183n, 213; *see also* Name-of-the-Father; Voice
surface, 5n, 16–17, 22, 24–5, 35, 48n, 52, 59n, 61n, 71–3, 75, 77, 81–5, 87, 89–90, 97, 102–5, 113, 117, 125n, 127n, 129n, 132n–5n, 140n–1n, 144, 152, 154–5, 160, 164–7, 171, 172n, 174n, 183n, 185, 187, 201–2, 208, 210, 212–14, 217–18, 219n, 223n, 228n–9n, 231n–2n, 238n
  -effect, 83, 113, 118, 177n, 140n, 145, 177n, 223n; *see also* castration: -effect; events; monism: -effect; subject: -effect
metaphysical (or cerebral), 110, 113, 116, 138n, 144, 149, 159, 163, 165, 168, 174n–5n, 181n, 187, 193, 195, 212–14, 216–17, 220n, 234n, 238n–9n; *see also* immanence (plane of); transcendental: as impersonal and pre-individual field
physical, 76, 80, 82–5, 87, 96–7, 105, 108, 110, 112–13, 114–15, 118, 120, 130n–1n, 134n–5n, 138n, 144, 149, 159, 163–5, 169, 183n, 187, 212–14, 216–17, 220n, 234n, 239n; *see also* body: erogenous; esoteric: set
Świątkowski, P., 182n
symbolic (Lacan), 8–15, 17, 26–7, 29–30, 33–4, 37n–40n, 45n, 47n, 63n, 82, 90–1, 99–100, 107, 119, 127n–8n, 135n, 141n, 221n; *see also* domain of preexistence; sense: pre-sense
symbolisation, 15, 19, 21, 32, 75, 88
symptoms, 211–12

tertiary ordinance, 152, 166, 171, 174n–5n, 185, 211, 219n, 222n
theatre of cruelty, 52, 55
thought
  crack of, 207, 216, 221n
  image of, 65, 192, 202, 205, 210, 212, 225n
  in relation to eating, 219n, 238n–9n
  power or attribute of, 66, 85, 105, 110–11, 117, 122n–3n, 131n, 138n, 140n, 144, 160n, 172n, 175n, 180n, 182n, 187–93, 195, 197, 199–201, 203, 207, 216, 221n–3n, 226n–7n, 229n, 231n–5n
time image, 156, 158, 178–9n, 236n

257

## Index

transcendence, 58, 87, 97, 121n, 130n, 164, 167, 212, 229n, 236n
transcendental, 166–7, 176n, 178n, 193, 208–10, 225n, 228n, 233n, 236n
  as impersonal and pre-individual field, 121n, 176n, 194; *see also* immanence (plane of); surface: metaphysical (or cerebral)
truth, 129n, 147–8, 166

universality (of the symbolic), 16, 18, 34–6, 91–2, 98, 101, 112, 118, 131n, 139n, 158
univocity
  of being or sense, 4–5n, 52, 54, 64, 71, 139n, 153, 174n, 180n, 185–9, 195, 200, 202–6, 210–12, 218n–20n, 222n, 225n–6n, 230n, 232n–4n; *see also* becoming: becoming-unlimited; events: event (*Eventum tantum*)
  of the event, 116, 120, 165, 175n, 186, 193–4, 195, 198, 200–5, 208, 212, 218n, 226n
  as phantom, 189, 195, 232n
  in relation to Heidegger, 225n

Van Haute, P., 39n
verb, 5, 70, 124n–5n, 144–5, 152–3, 155–71, 175n, 177n–83n, 185–8, 194–7, 200, 204, 208–9, 219n–20n, 222n–3n, 225n–7n, 230n, 234n, 236n
Verhaeghe, P., 45n
Verhaeghe, P., and F. Declercq, 141n
voice
  of God, 131n
  grammatical, 159, 161–2, 170, 180n, 183n, 230n
  in Lacan, 9, 17, 21, 63n
  a single voice (univocity), 185, 189
  the voice (Deleuze), 4, 55, 57–9, 62n–3n, 71–4, 76, 78–9, 81–5, 87, 89–91, 93–7, 101–5, 113, 115, 118, 120–1, 125n–6n, 129n–31n, 133n, 135n–7n, 141n–2n, 143, 167–9, 174n–5n, 182n, 186–7, 212–15, 220n, 238n; *see also* good object; Name-of-the-Father (paternal metaphor); superego

Widder, N., 60n, 182n, 237n
will to power, 61n–2n, 189, 196, 224n–5n
'Wolf Man' (Freud), 43n, 107, 132n, 136n
Wolfson, L., 61n
world (idea), 196–200, 228n–9n, 238n

Žižek, S., 6, 139n, 184n
Zourabichvili, F., 224n, 231n, 233n, 236n

Printed in Great Britain
by Amazon